Maximal Planar Graph Theory and the Four-Color Conjecture

Jin Xu

Maximal Planar Graph Theory and the Four-Color Conjecture

 Springer

Jin Xu
School of Computer Science
Peking University
Beijing, China

ISBN 978-981-96-4744-6   ISBN 978-981-96-4745-3 (eBook)
https://doi.org/10.1007/978-981-96-4745-3

This work was supported by Jin Xu.

© The Editor(s) (if applicable) and The Author(s) 2025. This book is an open access publication.

Open Access This book is licensed under the terms of the Creative Commons Attribution 4.0 International License (http://creativecommons.org/licenses/by/4.0/), which permits use, sharing, adaptation, distribution and reproduction in any medium or format, as long as you give appropriate credit to the original author(s) and the source, provide a link to the Creative Commons license and indicate if changes were made.
The images or other third party material in this book are included in the book's Creative Commons license, unless indicated otherwise in a credit line to the material. If material is not included in the book's Creative Commons license and your intended use is not permitted by statutory regulation or exceeds the permitted use, you will need to obtain permission directly from the copyright holder.
The use of general descriptive names, registered names, trademarks, service marks, etc. in this publication does not imply, even in the absence of a specific statement, that such names are exempt from the relevant protective laws and regulations and therefore free for general use.
The publisher, the authors and the editors are safe to assume that the advice and information in this book are believed to be true and accurate at the date of publication. Neither the publisher nor the authors or the editors give a warranty, expressed or implied, with respect to the material contained herein or for any errors or omissions that may have been made. The publisher remains neutral with regard to jurisdictional claims in published maps and institutional affiliations.

This Springer imprint is published by the registered company Springer Nature Singapore Pte Ltd.
The registered company address is: 152 Beach Road, #21-01/04 Gateway East, Singapore 189721, Singapore

If disposing of this product, please recycle the paper.

Preface

During a lunch break in July 1985, when I was about to take a nap, a "proof approach" to the Four Color Conjecture (FCC) popped up in my head. At that time, I was only a postgraduate student, and for me, this "sudden fabulous gift" was so exciting that my palms were sweating, and I could not fall asleep. So, in the afternoon, I told these to my supervisor, Professor Wang Ziguo. Professor Wang said that FCC was a difficult math problem for which no mathematical proof had been found over 100 years. He also emphasized that "it is not so easy as you think" and "you should think it over." His words slowly calmed me down. That evening I found the idea was false. However, this "heart-pounding experience" did arouse my enthusiasm for graph theory. Also, the nature of "they who know nothing fear nothing" of a 20-year-old who attempted to seek the mathematical proof of FCC.

After completing my master's degree, I returned to my Alma Mate, Shanxi Normal University, and worked as a teacher in the Department of Mathematics. I set up a seminar on graph theory, where we had a discussion once a week. Five teachers in our department were involved. In a workshop in 1991, I jokingly proved FCC on the blackboard using the chromatic polynomial method. In the derivation process, I unexpectedly obtained a surprising result. This result proves FCC can boil down to the study of the characteristics of 4-colorable coordinated graphs; meanwhile, it suggests a construction method of maximal planar graphs—extending and contracting operations system of maximal planar graphs, which combines the coloring with construction organically. These works will be described in detail in Chaps. 6 and 7, respectively.

At that time, I thought that there were two classes of 4-colorable coordinated graphs, i.e., uniquely 4-colorable maximal planar graphs and quasi-uniquely 4-colorable maximal planar graphs. It is trivial that the latter is separable, which would not be considered. As for the uniquely 4-colorable maximal planar graphs, I proposed a conjecture soon that every uniquely 4-colorable maximal planar graph is a recursive maximal planar graph. So, I optimistically thought that FCC would be proved mathematically. But this was not the case: first, 4-colorable coordinated graphs contain another class of graphs that were not discovered then, and we named them pseudo-uniquely 4-colorable maximal planar graphs afterward. The structures of this class of graphs are more complicated than that of uniquely 4-colorable maximal planar graphs, so it is more difficult to figure out their characteristics. Second, I was not the first to discover the conjecture that uniquely 4-colorable maximal planar graphs are recursive maximal planar graphs, which is still open until now.

For 18 years, from 1991 to 2009, I taught in many colleges and universities, including (in sequential order) Shaanxi Normal University, Xidian University, Huazhong University of Science and Technology, and Peking University. During this time, I worked on the proof of the uniquely 4-colorable planar graph conjecture. Unfortunately, I obtained nothing and almost gave it up. However, I still hoped that a miracle could happen someday.

On the morning of May 4, 2009, when I was pondering the proof of uniquely 4-colorable maximal planar graph conjecture at home (Yanbeiyuan), my mentor, Professor Yu Daoheng, suddenly came to my house. I confessed the secret of studying FCC and showed him the 43-page manuscript I wrote in 1991. He was very surprised at the manuscript and hoped I could continue studying it. Professor Yu's encouragement inspired me to explore the proof of FCC.

I spent the next several months organizing my thoughts systematically. I realized that there was no shortcut to solving a math problem with a history of more than 100 years, and it was necessary to figure out the characteristics of its research objects. Why have not the Goldbach conjecture and Twin Prime Conjecture been solved so far? The reason is very simple, i.e., the mathematicians have not figured out the properties of the family of prime numbers. Similarly, FCC has not been proved mathematically because the structure of maximal planar graphs is not recognized clearly. So, if we want to give a short mathematical proof of FCC, we must study the structures of maximal planar graphs deeply and figure out their "viscera."

Since 2009, I have studied the maximal planar graphs from three aspects: structures and constructions, coloring operations, and chromatic coordinate systems. The purpose of constructions is to know from different angles where each maximal planar graph comes from, who its "ancestors" is, and how many "children" it can produce. It should be especially closely related to coloring; coloring operations intend to derive all the colorings of a graph from a given coloring; the theory of chromatic coordinate system intends to encode the basic characteristics of the 4-colorable coordinate system graphs. In other words, this means to solve the unique 4-colorable maximal planar graph conjecture and give the features of pseudo-unique 4-colorable maximal planar graphs.

The two volumes of this book revolve around these three aspects, among which the specific chapters of the first volume are summarized as follows: Chap. 1 mainly introduces some of the most basic definitions, notations, and theories used in the book, especially some basic theories related to the planar graphs, such as the well-known Kuratowski theorem, plane test algorithms, etc. Chapter 2 uses the "discharge" as a tool to study the structural features of planar graphs. Chapter 3 presents the principle of proving FCC through a computer, mainly involving the work by Heesch, Haken, Simon, etc. Chapter 4 investigates a construction method of the maximal planar graphs in the same order, viz., edge-flipping. It is proved that two arbitrary maximal planar graphs with the same order can be transformed by a finite number of edge-flipping operations, and the bound of the required times of edge-flipping is given. Chapter 5 proposes a construction method of maximal planar graphs with different order-recursive generation operations, which constructs the required maximal planar graph based on the ones with small order. Chapter 6 is devoted to a construction method called generating system, which combines structure and coloring and contributes to the mathematical proof of FCC. Chapter 7 presents a recursive formula for solving the chromatic polynomial of maximal planar graphs, based on which two ideas for proving FCC are obtained. Chapter 8 studies intensively the structure and characteristics of the dumbbell maximal planar graphs and the recursive maximal planar graphs and shows an idea of proving the unique 4-colorable maximal planar graph conjecture by combining with the extending and contracting operations in Chap. 6. Chapter 9 focuses on the Kempe transformation, a σ-characteristic graph that describes the relationship between all colorings, three types of non-Kempe graphs, etc. The Kempe change is the essence of Kempe's proof of FCC. It derives another 4-coloring from one 4-coloring of a maximal planar graph. The fundamental reason for Kempe's failure in proving FCC by this transformation is that there are many maximal planar graphs for which it is impossible to derive all the 4-colorings from a 4-coloring. Whereas, since the coloring problem is **NP**-complete, the Kempe change has been a basic tool in studying the coloring theory of planar graphs and non-planar graphs, algorithms, and applications for more than 130 years from 1879 to the present.

In the process of completing this book, many helpful discussions are conducted with Professor Yu Daoheng at Peking University and Wang Jianfang at the Chinese Academy of Sciences, Professor Yao Bing and Chen Xiangen from Northwest Normal University, and Professor Wu Jianliang from Shandong University. In addition, several of my students have worked hard to make the book delivered on time. They are Zhu Enqiang and Li Zepeng, Liu Xiaoqing, Wang Hongyu, Zhou Yangyang, Zhao Dongyang, Ma Mingyuan, Su Jing, etc. I gratefully acknowledge the contributions of every one of them.

During the completion of this book, many leaders, experts, and colleagues in the School of Information Science and Technology of Peking University gave me strong encouragement and support, including Academician Yang Fuqing, Academician Wang Yangyuan, Academician He Xingui, Academician Mei Hong, Academician Huang Ru, Professor Qu Wanling, Professor Wang Hanpin, Professor Cao Yongzhi, Associate Professor Liu Tian, and Associate Professor Bian Kaigui. I would like to express my sincere gratitude to all of them.

Sincere thanks to several respected teachers for their years of training. They are Academician Bao Zheng, Academician Wang Yingluo, Professor Bian Kaiguo, Professor Wang Guojun, Professor Wang Ziguo, Professor Wei Xiansun, Professor Wang Chaorui, Professor Wang Jianfang, Professor Zhang Fuji, Professor Zhang Zhongfu, and so on.

This book was supported by the National Major Scientific Instruments and Equipment Development Project of National Natural Science Foundation of China (No. 62427811) and Key Project of National Natural Science Foundation of China (No. 62332006).

Due to the limitation of time, the book inevitably contains shortcomings and even mistakes. The readers are respectfully invited to share their valuable comments and criticisms.

Beijing, China   Jin Xu

Declarations

Competing Interests The authors have no competing interests to declare that are relevant to the content of this manuscript.

Contents

1 Graph Theory Fundamentals 1
   1.1 Definitions and Types of Graphs 1
   1.2 Degree-Sequence 7
      1.2.1 Definitions and Properties 7
      1.2.2 Graphic Sequence 8
      1.2.3 Enumeration and Construction of Graphic Sequence 9
   1.3 Graph-Operations 10
      1.3.1 Subgraphs and Unary Graph-Operations 10
      1.3.2 Binary Graph-Operations 12
      1.3.3 The Sequel to Unary Graph-Operations 14
   1.4 Isomorphisms 17
      1.4.1 Definition and Terminology 17
      1.4.2 Isomorphism Algorithms 18
      1.4.3 Application of Graph Isomorphism 19
   1.5 Graph Matrix 19
   1.6 Planar Graph 22
      1.6.1 Definitions 22
      1.6.2 Euler's Formula and Applications 23
      1.6.3 Kuratowski's Theorem 25
      1.6.4 Planar Embedding Algorithms 25
   1.7 Graph Coloring 26
      1.7.1 Definition and Classification 26
      1.7.2 Chromatic Number 28
      1.7.3 Graph Coloring Algorithms 29
      1.7.4 Applications of Graph Coloring 32
   References 33

2 Discharging and Structure of Maximal Planar Graphs 37
   2.1 Discharging 37
   2.2 Structure of Path 38
      2.2.1 Edges 39

		2.2.2 3-Path	42
	2.3	Faces	53
	2.4	Cycle and Star	64
		2.4.1 The Weight of Cycle and the Restriction on the Degree	64
		2.4.2 Stars	65
	References		67
3	**Computer-Based Proofs of Four Color Conjecture**		**71**
	3.1	Four Color Conjecture	71
	3.2	Kempe's Proof and Heawood's Counterexample	72
	3.3	Reducible Unavoidable Set	76
		3.3.1 Basic Definition	76
		3.3.2 Unavoidable Set	77
		3.3.3 Reducibility	78
	3.4	Proof by Computer	81
	3.5	Discussion and Conclusion	93
	References		116
4	**Construction of Maximal Planar Graphs with the Same Order**		**117**
	4.1	Definitions and Notation	117
	4.2	Transformation Between Two Maximal Planar Graphs with the Same Order	119
	4.3	Upper Bounds of the Number of Diagonal Flips	121
	4.4	Lower Bounds of the Number of Diagonal Flips	126
	References		128
5	**Construction of Maximal Planar Graphs with the Different Order**		**131**
	5.1	Pure Chord-Cycle Construction	131
	5.2	Generating 5-Connected Maximal Planar Graphs	133
	5.3	Generating 3-, 4-Connected Maximal Planar Graphs of Minimum Degree 5	137
	5.4	Generating Maximal Planar Graphs of Minimum Degree at Least 4	140
	5.5	Generating Maximal Planar Graphs of Even Number Order	141
	5.6	Maximal Planar Graphs of Minimum Degree 5 and of Orders 12 ~ 19	144
	References		146
6	**Generating System of Maximal Planar Graphs**		**149**
	6.1	Basic Extending-Contracting Operations System of Maximal Planar Graphs	149
	6.2	Domino Extending-Contracting Operational System	152
		6.2.1 Consecutive Extending-Contracting Operation and Domino Extending-Contracting Operation	152
		6.2.2 Domino Extending-Contracting Operations with Inner Vertices ≤ 3 and Domino Configuration	153
		6.2.3 Set of Objects of Domino Extending Wheel Operations	156

		6.2.4 General Definition of Domino Configurations	157
		6.2.5 Properties of Domino Configurations	160
	6.3	Ancestor-Graphs and Descendent-Graphs	163
		6.3.1 Descendent-Graphs	164
		6.3.2 Ancestor-Graphs	167
	6.4	Construction of Maximal Planar Graphs	169
		6.4.1 General Theory on Constructing Graphs	169
		6.4.2 Construction of Separating Maximal Planar Graphs	170
		6.4.3 Basic Theorem on Non-separating Maximal Planar Graphs Construction	173
		6.4.4 A Recursive Method of Generating Non-separating Maximal Planar Graphs	175
	6.5	Conclusion	177
	References		178
7	**Recursion Formulae of Chromatic Polynomial and Four-Color Conjecture**		**179**
	7.1	Recursion Formulae of Chromatic Polynomial by Contracting Wheels	179
	7.2	Two Mathematical Ideas for Attacking Four-Color Conjecture Based on Theorem 7.2	184
	References		187
8	**Purely Tree-Colorable and Uniquely 4-Colorable Maximal Planar Graph Conjectures**		**189**
	8.1	Introduction	189
	8.2	Tree-Colorings and Cycle-Colorings	191
	8.3	Purely Tree-Colorable Maximal Planar	193
		8.3.1 Purely Tree-Colorable Maximal Planar Graph Conjecture with Minimum Degree 5	193
		8.3.2 Dumbbell-Maximal Planar Graphs	194
	8.4	Recursive Maximal Planar Graphs	197
		8.4.1 Basic Properties	198
		8.4.2 (2,2)-Recursive Maximal Planar Graphs	199
		8.4.3 The Colorings of Extending 4-Wheel Operation Graphs	203
	8.5	An Idea to Prove the Uniquely 4-Colorable Maximal Planar Graph Conjecture	204
	8.6	Conclusion and Prospection	205
	References		206
9	**Kempe Change**		**209**
	9.1	Definitions and Fundamental Properties	209
	9.2	Kempe Classes	212
		9.2.1 **K**-Classes with Respect to Vertex Coloring	212
		9.2.2 **K**-Classes with Respect to Edge Coloring	213
		9.2.3 Reconfiguration Graph of the k-Colorings	214

9.3	σ-Operation		216
	9.3.1	2-Chromatic Ears	216
	9.3.2	The σ-Operation	220
9.4	σ-Characteristic Graphs		222
	9.4.1	Definition	222
	9.4.2	Basic Properties	223
9.5	Kempe Classes of Maximal Planar Graphs		226
	9.5.1	Tree-Type **K**-Class	226
	9.5.2	Cycle-Type **K**-Class	227
	9.5.3	Circular-Cycle-Type **K**-Classes	229
References			231

Chapter 1
Graph Theory Fundamentals

Abstract In this section, we will discuss some of the basic terminologies and concepts of graph theory, which will be assumed throughout the rest of this book, together with a few fundamental properties that characterize planar graphs, e.g., the well-known Kuratowski Theorem and planarity testing algorithm, etc.

1.1 Definitions and Types of Graphs

We use $X^{(k)}$, $k \geq 2$ to denote the set of all k-subsets of a nonempty set X, where a k-subset of X is a subset of X of size k. We then define a **graph** (**undirected graph**) as an ordered pair (V, E), where V is a nonempty set of elements called **vertices**, and E is a subset of $V^{(2)}$ called **edges**. We call V and E the **vertex-set** and **edge-set**, respectively. Throughout the book, we use the letter G to denote a graph, and $V(G)$ and $E(G)$ are the vertex-set and edge-set of G, respectively. Furthermore, when a given graph G is clear in the context, we omit the letter G from graph-theoretic symbols and write, for example, V and E instead of $V(G)$ and $E(G)$.

For an edge $\{u, v\} \in E$ of a graph G, we in general write $\{u, v\}$ as uv simply, in which u and v are vertices of G. If $e = uv$ is an edge of G, then u, v are **ends** of e, u is said to be **adjacent** to v, and e is **incident** with u and v.

Let v be a vertex of a graph G. We use $N_G(v)$ (or $N(v)$) to denote the set of vertices adjacent to v in G, which is called the **neighborhood** of v in G. Two edges e_1 and e_2 are said to be *adjacent* if they are incident with a common vertex of G. Let $V' \subseteq V$ and $E' \in E$. We call V' an **independent set** (or **stable set**) of G if any pair of vertices of V' are not adjacent in G and E' an **matching** (or **independent set of edges**) of G if E' contains no adjacent edges in G.

Remark 1.1 For a graph $G = (V, E)$, since V and E are sets, there contain no duplicate elements. Observe that $V^{(2)}$ are the set of unordered pairs of distinct elements of V; we see that E has no duplicate edges, every edge of E is incident with two distinct vertices and $uv = vu$ if $uv \in E$. Therefore, the graph defined in the above is also called **simple undirected graph**.

© The Author(s) 2025
J. Xu, *Maximal Planar Graph Theory and the Four-Color Conjecture*,
https://doi.org/10.1007/978-981-96-4745-3_1

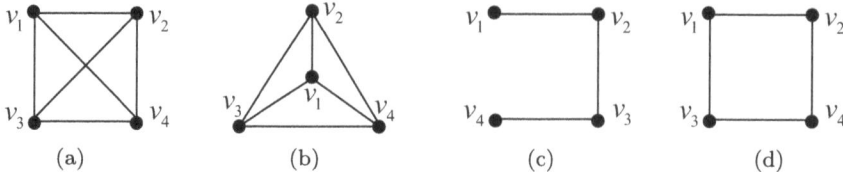

Fig. 1.1 Diagrams of K_4, P_4 and C_4

A graph G is **finite** if both V and E are finite; otherwise, G is **infinite**. In this book, we study only finite graphs, and so the term 'graph' always means a 'finite graph'. The values of $n = |V|$ and $m = |E|$ are called the **order** and **size** of G, respectively, and we refer to a graph of order n and size m as a (n, m)-**graph**.

For a given graph G, we usually draw it on the plane such that each vertex is indicated by a point (small circle) and each edge uv by a line jointing u and v. Such a drawing is called a **diagram** of G. This graphical representation of graphs can help us to understand the structures of graphs more clearly and intuitively and further evolve many of their properties, which shows the charm of graph theory. We often view a diagram of a graph as the graph itself, so we call its points 'vertices' and its lines 'edges'.

Let $G = (V, E)$ be a n-order graph where $V = \{v_1, v_2, \ldots, v_n\}$. If $E = V^{(2)}$, we call G a **complete** n-**graph**, written as K_n; Fig. 1.1a, b give two distinct diagrams of K_4. The characteristic of complete graphs is that every pair of vertices are adjacent. On the contrary, if $E = \emptyset$, then G is called an **empty** n-**graph** (or **null** n-**graph**), written as N_n. Complete n-graphs and empty n-graphs are called **complete graph** and **empty graph** (or **null graph**) when we discard the order n. Moreover, if V can be arranged in a linear sequence, say $v_1 v_2 \ldots v_n$, such that $E = \{v_1 v_2, v_2 v_3, \ldots, v_{n-1} v_n\}$, then G is called a **path of length** $n - 1$ or an n-**path**, denoted by P_n (see Fig. 1.1c, a diagram of P_4); likewise, if V can be arranged in a linear cyclic sequence, say $v_1 v_2 \ldots v_n v_1$, such that $E = \{v_1 v_2, v_2 v_3, \ldots, v_{n-1} v_n, v_n v_1\}$, then we call G a **cycle of length** n or an n-**cycle**, denoted by C_n (see Fig. 1.1d, a diagram of C_4). A **chord** of a cycle C in a graph G is an edge in $E(G) \setminus E(C)$ both of whose ends lie on C. A graph is **bipartite** if its vertex-set can be partitioned into two subsets X and Y so that every edge has one end in X and one end in Y; such a partition (X, Y) is called a **bipartition** of the graph, and X and Y its parts. We denote a bipartite graph G with bipartition (X, Y) by $G[X, Y]$.

Remark 1.2 When draw a diagram on the plane, we always hope that there are as many disjoint edges (that is, edges intersect only at their ends) as possible; meanwhile, the shapes of points (large or small, round or flat, empty or solid, etc.) and lines (long or short, thick or thin, curved or straight, etc.) usually have no significance.

1.1 Definitions and Types of Graphs

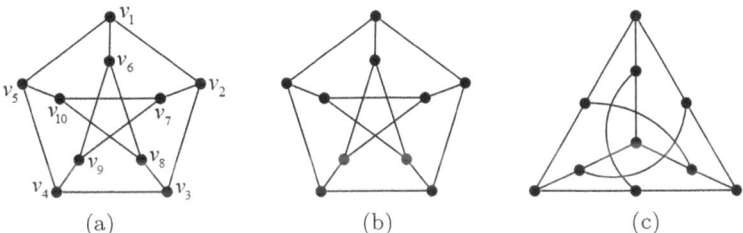

Fig. 1.2 Petersen graph

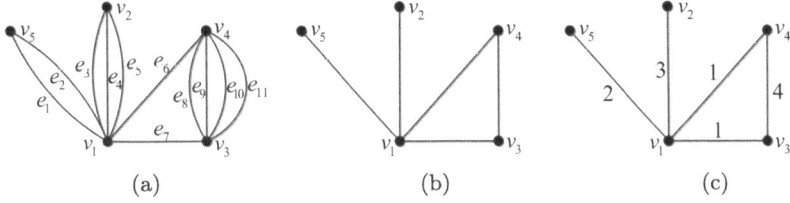

Fig. 1.3 A multigraph $G_=$, its underlying graph and weighted graph

Example 1.1 Let $G = (V, E)$ be a graph such that $V = \{v_1, v_2, \ldots, v_{10}\}$, $E = \{v_1v_2, v_2v_3, v_3v_4, v_4v_5, v_5v_1, v_6v_8, v_8v_{10}, v_{10}v_7, v_7v_9, v_9v_6, v_1v_6, v_2v_7, v_3v_8, v_4v_9, v_5v_{10}\}$. This is the well known **Petersen graph** (see Fig. 1.2a). Figure 1.2b, c shows its two distinct diagrams.

For a graph $G = (V, E)$, if we assign an identification for each vertex in V, then G is called a **labeled graph**; otherwise a **non-labeled graph**. For example, the graph shown in Fig. 1.2a is a labeled graph while the graphs shown in Fig. 1.2b, c are non-labeled graphs. Since a labeled graph presents the graph itself, we also call a labeled graph as a graph.

Observe that a simple graph $G = (V, E)$ implies that any two elements of E are distinct (that is, $e \neq e'$ for any $e, e' \in E$). If we remove the restriction that the edges must be distinct, then it may happen that there are two or more edges joining the same pair of vertices of V which called **multiple edges**. We then call G a **multigraph** if G has multiple edges. The following give a detailed explanation:

Let $V_=^{(2)}$ be an extension of $V^{(2)}$, in which duplicate elements are permitted. Then, a multigraph, denoted by $G_=$ can be defined as an ordered pair $(V, E_=)$, where $E_= \subseteq V_=^{(2)}$ and the duplicate elements in $E_=$ are **multiple edges**.

Example 1.2 Let $G_= = (V, E_=)$ be a multigraph, where $V = \{v_1, v_2, v_3, v_4, v_5\}$ and $E_= = \{e_1, e_2, e_3, e_4, e_5, e_6, e_7, e_8, e_9, e_{10}, e_{11}\}$ such that $e_1 = e_2 = v_1v_5$, $e_3 = e_4 = e_5 = v_1v_2$, $e_6 = v_1v_4$, $e_7 = v_1v_3$, $e_8 = e_9 = e_{10} = e_{11} = v_3v_4$. Figure 1.3a exhibits a diagram of $G_=$.

Fig. 1.4 A pseudograph

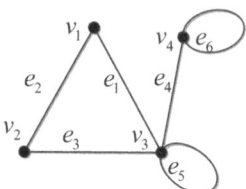

The **underlying graph**, denoted by $M(G)$ of a multigraph $G_=$ is a simple graph based on $G_=$ such that $V(M(G)) = V(G_=)$ and each pair of vertices are adjacent in $M(G)$ if and only if there is at least one edge between them in $G_=$; for example, the underlying graph $M(G)$ of the multigraph $G_=$ shown in Fig. 1.3a has vertex-set $V(M(G)) = \{v_1, v_2, v_3, v_4, v_5\}$ and edge-set $E(M(G)) = \{v_1v_5, v_1v_2, v_1v_3, v_1v_4, v_3v_4\}$ (see Fig. 1.3b).

In the definition of simple graphs and multigraphs, every edge must join distinct vertices (that is, if $e = uv$ be an edge, then $u \neq v$). If we also remove this restriction, then the edge incident with one vertex is called a **loop**. We call a graph **pseudograph** if it contains loops. More specifically, in the definition of simple graphs and multigraphs, we extend $V^{(2)}$ or $V_=^{(2)}$ to a new set $V_o^{(2)}$ of 2-subsets of $V = \{v_1, v_2, \ldots, v_n\}$, which allows the existence of $\{\{v_j, v_j\}\}$ for some $j \in \{1, 2, \ldots, n\}$. Then, a **pseudograph**, denoted by G_o can be defined as an order pair (V, E_o) where $E_o \subseteq V_o^{(2)}$ and the elements $\{v_j, v_j\}$, $1 \leq j \leq n$ are **loops**.

Example 1.3 The graph $G_o = (V, E_o)$ shown in Fig. 1.4 is a pseudograph, in which $V = \{v_1, v_2, v_3, v_4\}$, $E_o = \{e_1, e_2, 3_3, e_4, e_5, e_6\}$ and $e_5 = v_3v_3$ and $e_6 = v_4v_4$ are loops.

Remark 1.3 Observe that multigraphs must contain multiple edges and pseudographs must contains loops.

Let $G_= = (V, E_=)$ be a multigraph. If in the underlying graph $M(G)$ of $G_=$ each edge $uv \in E(M(G))$ is labeled with a value, (e.g., the number of multiple edges between u and v in $G_=$), then edges of $M(G)$ are weighted. For example, Fig. 1.3c is the underlying graph of the multigraph shown in Fig. 1.3a, in which each edge is weighted by the number of multiple edges between its two ends in the multigraph.

If we use $w(e)$ to denote the weight associated with each edge e of a graph G, then an **edge-weighted graph** can be defined as an ordered triple $(V, E, w(E))$ consisting of a nonempty set V of vertices, a set $E \subseteq V^{(2)}$ of edges, and an **edge-weighted vector** $w(E) = (w(e_1), w(e_2), \ldots, w(e_m))$ where $E = \{e_1, e_2, \ldots, e_m\}$. Thus, the graph shown in Fig. 1.3c is $(V, E, w(E))$ where $V = \{v_1, v_2, v_3, v_4, v_5\}$, $E = \{e_1 = v_1v_2, e_2 = v_1v_3, e_3 = v_1v_4, e_4 = v_1v_5, e_5 = v_3v_4\}$ and $w(E) = (3, 1, 1, 2, 4)$.

Edge-weighted graphs are natural models for many complicated networks. As an example, consider the following traffic network $(V, E, w(E))$: V denotes the set of cities; each edge $e = uv \in E$ means that the two cities corresponding to vertices u and v, respectively, are connected (that is, there exists a rode, a railway, an air line or

1.1 Definitions and Types of Graphs

a waterway, etc. between u and v); for each edge $e \in E$, $w(e)$ denotes the distance between u and v (including the distance of the rode, railway, air line or waterway, etc.).

The biological neural network can also be modeled as an edge-weighted graph, denoted by $N_B = (V, E, w(E))$: V is the set of all neurons of an organism (e.g. human); E is the set of synapses among neurons; for each $e = uv \in E$, $w(e)$ denotes the thickness (the connection intensity) between the neurons u and v. There are about 10^{12} neurons and $10^{15} \sim 10^{16}$ synapses in human brain, but there are few studies on the thickness of synapses (i.e., less research has been conducted on $W(E)$). Such research is absolutely necessary and very significant to the development of brain science.

Edge-weighted graphs have also many other applications in the real world, including plant metabolic network, gene network, electric network, software vulnerability, etc.

We now, analogously to edge-weighted graphs, define a **vertex-weighted graph** as an order triple $(V, E, w(V))$ consisting of a simple graph $G = (V, E)$ and an **vertex-weighted vector** $w(V) = (w(v_1, w(v_2), \ldots, w(v_n)))$, where $V = \{v_1, v_2, \ldots, v_n\}$ and $w(v_i)$ is the weight of v_i for $i = 1, 2, \ldots, n$.

Figure 1.5 is a vertex-weighted graph $(V, E, w(V))$ for which $V = \{v_1, v_2, \ldots, v_{12}\}$ and $w(V) = (1, 2, 3, 4, 1, 3, 2, 4, 1, 4, 3, 2$. Observe that $w(v_i) \in \{1, 2, 3, 4\}$ for $i \in \{1, 2, \ldots, 12\}$ and the two ends of every edge has distinct weights. Therefore, we can view this way of weighting as a **vertex coloring** of the graph, where the weights on vertices represent colors assigning to vertices. In this example, the color set is $\{1, 2, 3, 4\}$

Vertex-weighted graphs also have a wide range of applications in the real world, such as traffic signals designing, scheduling problem, route planning, etc.

To explore more applications, one needs to take into account weights on both vertices and edges. As a result, the **mixed weighted graph** (or **weighted graph** simply) is introduced, which is an ordered quadruple $(V, E, w(E), w(V))$ such that (V, E) is a simple graph and $w(E)$ and $w(V)$ are the edge-weighted vector and vertex-weighted vector (as was defined above), respectively.

Fig. 1.5 A vertex-weighted graph

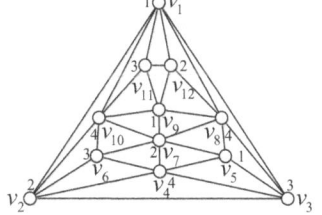

According to the above discussions, undirected graphs can be classified into the following categories.

$$\text{undirected graphs} \begin{cases} simple\ graphs \\ multigraphs \\ pseudographs \\ weighted\ graphs \begin{cases} edge\ weighted\ graphs \\ vertex\ weighted\ graphs \\ mixed\ weighted\ graphs \end{cases} \end{cases}$$

Remark 1.4 If there is no specific explanations, graph in this book always means 'finite simple graphs'.

In the definition of a graph, if we change elements of $V^{(2)}$ from 'unordered' to 'ordered', then the resulting object is called a **digraph**.

Let $V = \{v_1, v_2, \ldots, v_n\}$ and $V^{[2]}$ the set of all ordered pairs of elements in V. For $i, j \in \{1, 2, \ldots, n\}, i \neq j$, we use (v_i, v_j) (or $v_i v_j$ simply) to denote the ordered pair from v_i to v_j. For example, when $n = 3$, $V^{[2]} = \{(v_1, v_2), (v_1, v_3), (v_2, v_3), (v_2, v_1), (v_3, v_1), (v_3, v_2)\}$.

Based on $V^{[2]}$, we can define a **simple digraph** D, similar to the definition of an undirected graph, as an ordered pair (V, A) for which $V \neq \emptyset$ is the **vertex-set** of D and $A \subseteq V^{[2]}$ the **arc-set** of D. We call elements in V and A **vertices** and **arcs** of D, respectively. If $a = uv \in A$, then a is said to join u to v, where u, v are the two **ends** of a, u is the **tail** of a, and v is the **head** of a; we also say that a is **incident from** u and **incident to** v, and u **dominates** v. If $uv \in A$ and $vu \in A$, then we call them a pair of **symmetric arcs**.

The **inverse** of a digraph $D = (V, A)$, denoted by D', is a digraph with $V(D') = V$ and $A(D') = \{uv : uv \in V^{[2]}, uv \notin A\}$. The **underlying graph** of D, denoted by $M(D)$, is an undirected graph on the same vertex-set simply by replacing each arc by an (undirected) edge with the same ends. Figure 1.6 shows a digraph D and its inverse and underlying graph.

A **complete symmetric digraph** is a digraph in which every two vertices are joined by exactly a pair of symmetric arcs (see Fig. 1.7a). A **tournament** is a digraph in which every two vertices are joined by exactly one arc. That is, a tournament is a diagraph whose underlying graph is a complete graph (see Fig. 1.7b). Tournaments are a class of digraphs with wide applications.

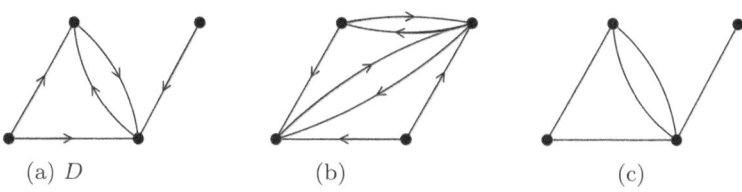

Fig. 1.6 A digraph, its inverse and underlying graph. (**a**) D. (**b**) D'. (**c**) $M(D)$

1.2 Degree-Sequence

Fig. 1.7 A complete symmetric digraph of order 5 and a tournament of order 5

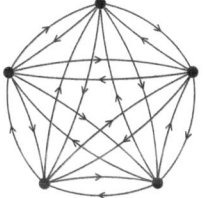
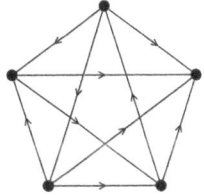

The digraphs defined in the above simple digraphs. Analogously, we can also define the multidigraphs, pseudodigraphs and weighted digraphs. Also, digraphs can be classified into the following categories.

$$\text{digraphs} \begin{cases} simple\ digraphs \\ multigraphs \\ pseudodigraphs \\ weighted\ digraphs \begin{cases} arc\ weighted\ digraphs \\ vertex\ weighted\ digraphs \\ mixed\ weighted\ digraphs \end{cases} \end{cases}$$

In this book, we mainly consider undirected graphs. So, this section only provides a brief introduction to the basic definitions and classifications of digraphs. More systematic theories on digraphs can be found in literature [67], and for more information about the definitions, terminologies and basic theories of undirected graphs one can refer to literature [4, 64].

1.2 Degree-Sequence

1.2.1 Definitions and Properties

Let $G = (V, E)$ be a simple graph. For each vertex $v \in V$, the number of edges incident with v is called the **degree** of v in G, denoted by $d_G(v)$ (or by $d(v)$, if there is no possibility of confusion). Clearly,

$$d_G(v) = |N_G(v)|, \ \ or \ \ d(v) = |N(v)| \tag{1.1}$$

The maximum and minimum degrees of G are denoted by $\Delta(G)$ and $\delta(G)$, respectively, which are defined as follows: $\Delta(G) = \max\{d_G(v_1), d_G(v_2), \ldots, d_G(v_n)\}$, $\delta(G) = \min\{d_G(v_1), d_G(v_2), \ldots, d_G(v_n)\}$, where $V = \{v_1, v_2, \ldots, v_n\}$. A vertex of degree k in G is called a k-vertex. A 0-vertex is called an **isolated vertex**, and a 1-vertex is called an **end-vertex**.

The **degree-sequence** of G, denoted by $\pi(G)$, is the sequence of degrees of the vertices of G, usually arranged in non-increasing order or non-decreasing order. If

$$d_G(v_1) \geq d_G(v_2) \geq \ldots \geq d_G(v_n) \tag{1.2}$$

then $\pi(G) = (d_G(v_1), d_G(v_2), \ldots, d_G(v_n))$ is the non-increasing degree-sequence of G. If

$$d_G(v_1) \leq d_G(v_2) \leq \ldots \leq d_G(v_n) \tag{1.3}$$

then $\pi(G) = (d_G(v_1), d_G(v_2), \ldots, d_G(v_n))$ is the non-decreasing degree-sequence of G. For example, the non-increasing and non-decreasing degree-sequences of the graph shown in Fig. 1.3b are $\pi(G) = (4, 2, 2, 1, 1)$ and $\pi(G) = (1, 1, 2, 2, 4)$.

A trivial conclusion on degree-sequence is presented as follows.

Theorem 1.1 *Let $G = (V, E)$ be a simple (n, m)-graph with $V = \{v_1, v_2, \ldots, v_n\}$ and $d_i = d_G(v_i)$ for $i = 1, 2, \ldots, n$. Then,*

(1) $0 \leq d_i \leq n - 1$;
(2) *there exist $i, j \in \{1, 2, \ldots, n\}, i \neq j$ such that $d_i = d_j$;*
(3) $\sum_{i=1}^{n} d_i = 2m$.

Proof Since G is a simple graph of order n, it follows that every vertex is adjacent to at most $n - 1$ vertices and at least zero vertex (when G has isolated vertices) in G. This verifies the statement (1). By the pigeonhole principle, we derive the conclusion (2) from (1). For (3), since each edge has two ends, the sum of the degrees is exactly twice the number of edges. ∎

1.2.2 Graphic Sequence

Let $\pi = (d_1, d_2, \ldots, d_n)$ be a sequence of nonnegative integers. π is **graphic** or a **graphic sequence** if there is a simple graph G with degree-sequence π; we also call G a **realization** of π. There is a natural question: what is the necessary and sufficient conditions of π being graphic? The following two theorems answer this question perfectly.

Theorem 1.2 *Let $\pi = (d_1, d_2, \ldots, d_n)$ be a sequence of nonnegative integers, where $n - 1 \geq d_1 \geq d_2 \geq \ldots \geq d_n$ and $\sum_{i=1}^{n} d_i$ is even. Then, π is a graphic if and only if*

$$\pi' = (d_2 - 1, d_3 - 1, \ldots, d_{d_1+1} - 1, d_{d_1+2}, \ldots, d_n) \tag{1.4}$$

is graphic.

1.2 Degree-Sequence

Theorem 1.3 *Let $\pi = (d_1, d_2, \ldots, d_n)$ be a sequence of nonnegative integers, where $n - 1 \geq d_1 \geq d_2 \geq \ldots \geq d_n$ and $\sum_{i=1}^{n} d_i$ is even. Then, π is a graphic if and only if*

$$\sum_{i=1}^{r} d_i \leq r(r-1) + \sum_{i=r+1}^{n} \min\{r, d_i\}, \ 1 \leq r \leq n - 1 \tag{1.5}$$

The detailed proofs of Theorems 1.2 and 1.3 can be found in literature [64] (Sect. 1.3.1). From these two theorems, we have addressed the characteristics of graphic sequences in terms of general simple graphs. As for graphic sequences corresponding to special classes of graphs, there have been a large number of works that have been done (see literature reviews [39, 65]).

1.2.3 Enumeration and Construction of Graphic Sequence

Let $\pi = (d_1, d_2, \ldots, d_n)$ be a graphic sequence. Then, π has at least one realization. We use $G(\pi)$ to denote the set of all realizations of π. How to compute the exact value of $|G(\pi)|$ is the **realizable enumeration problem** of graphic sequence and how to construct all graphs in $G(\pi)$ is the **construction problem** of graphic sequence.

Suppose that $\pi = (d_1, d_2, \ldots, d_n)$ is a graphic sequence. Let $G_1 \in G(\pi)$, $ab, cd \in E(G_1)$ and $ac, bd \notin E(G_1)$. The **switching operation** is to delete edges ab, cd and then add edges ac, bd. Based on this operation, Eggleton [13] posed a method of constructing $G(\pi)$; see Theorem 1.4.

Theorem 1.4 *Suppose that $\pi = (d_1, d_2, \ldots, d_n)$ is a graphic sequence. Let G_1 be a realization of π. Then, each graph in $G(\pi) \setminus \{G_1\}$ can be obtained from G_1 by conducting a sequence of switching operations.*

At the end of this section, we discuss an interesting class of graphic sequences: **unique graphic sequence** which is a graphic sequence with exactly one realization. This problem begun in the 1960s. Since then, several scholars have studied this problem, such as Hakimi [19, 20], Johnson[25–27], Koren [31–33], etc. As an instances, let us see the sequence $\pi = (4, 4, 3, 3, 2)$ which is a unique graphic sequence (Fig. 1.8 presents a diagram of its unique realization). In addition, one can readily check that $\pi = (6, 5, 4, 3, 2, 2, 2,)$ is also a unique graphic sequence.

The following theorem characterizes a special class of unique graphic sequences.

Fig. 1.8 A diagram of the unique realization of the graphic sequence $\pi = (4, 4, 3, 3, 2)$

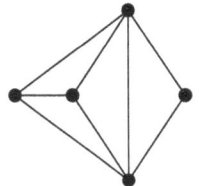

Theorem 1.5 ([64]) *Let* $\pi = (d_1, d_2, \ldots, d_p)$ *be a graphic sequence such that* $d_2 = d_{p-1}$. *Then, π is unique if and only if one of the following condition holds:*

(1) $d_1 = d_p, d_p \in \{1, p-1, p-2\}$;
(2) $d_1 = d_p = 2, p = 5$;
(3) $d_1 > d_2 = d_p = 1$;
(4) $d_1 > d_2 = d_p = 2, d_1 \in \{p-1, p-2\}$;
(5) $p - 2 = d_1 = d_{p-1} > d_p$;
(6) $p - 3 = d_1 = d_{p-1} > d_p = 1$;
(7) $p - 1 = d_1 > d_2 = d_p = 3, p = 6$;
(8) $p - 1 = d_1 > d_2 = d_p = p - 2$.

1.3 Graph-Operations

There are in total four basic mathematical operations of numbers, including addition, subtraction, multiplication and division, each of which possesses an exclusive function. Based on these basic operation, a number of distinct operations are deduced: such as pow, radication, trigonometric operation, etc. Also, these deduced operations have their own functions. Apart from operations of numbers, there are many operations based on vectors and matrices.

To construct new graphs from old graphs (one or more), many operations on graphs have been introduced, each of which has its own function. With the development of graph theory, more and more graph-operations will be created. This section is devoted to the introduction of some basic graph operations and some operations related to maximal planar graphs.

1.3.1 Subgraphs and Unary Graph-Operations

A **subgraph** of a graph $G = (V, E)$ is a graph H such that $V(H) \subseteq V(G)$ and $E(H) \subseteq E(G)$. There are two important classes of subgraphs: spanning subgraphs and induced subgraphs which are defined as follows.

Let H be a subgraph of a graph G. If $V(H) = V(G)$, then H is called a **spanning subgraph** of G. Let $V' \subseteq V(G)$. The **subgraph of G induced by** V', denoted by $G[V']$, is a subgraph of G such that $V(G[V']) = V'$ and $E(G[V']) = \{uv | u, v \in V', uv \in E(G)\}$. A **(vertex) induced subgraph of** G is a subgraph of G induced by some subset of $V(G)$. Analogously, a **subgraph induced by a** $E' \subseteq E(G)$, denoted by $G[E']$ is a subgraph of G with edge-set E' and vertex-set consisting of the ends of all edges of E'. An **edge induced subgraph of** G is a subgraph of G induced by some subset of $E(G)$.

To obtain a smaller graphs from a given graph G, there are two natural ways: operations of vertex deletion and edge deletion.

1.3 Graph-Operations

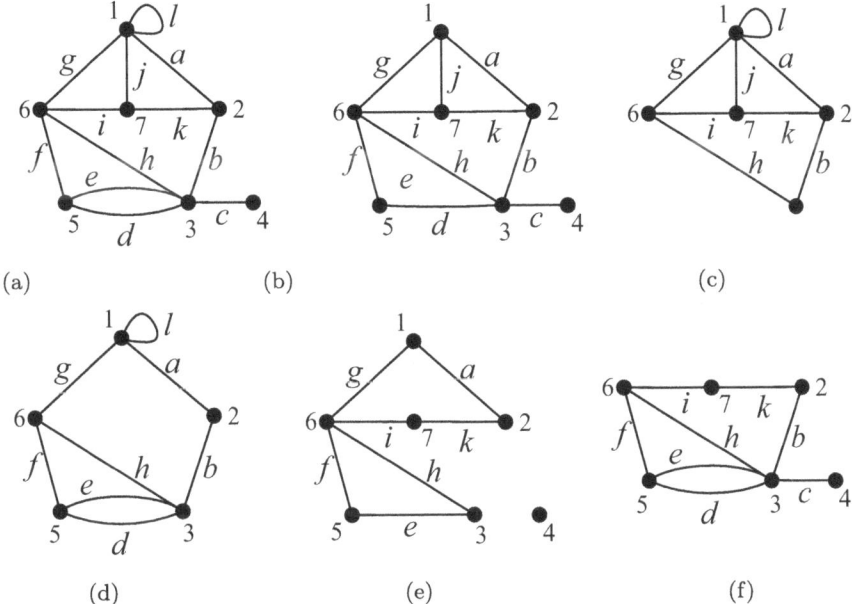

Fig. 1.9 Illustrations of various of subgraphs. (a) A graph G. (b) A spanning subgraph of G. (c) $G - \{4, 5\}$. (d) $G[\{1, 2, 3, 5, 6\}]$. (e) $G - \{b, c, d, j, \ell\}$. (f) $G[\{b, c, d, e, f, h, i, k\}]$

(1) Vertex deletion: for any $V' \subseteq V(G)$, we use the notation $G - V'$ to denote the resulting graph from G by deleting vertices of V' and their incident edges. Clearly, $G[V \setminus V'] = G - V'$. When V' contains only one vertex, say $V' = \{v\}$, we replace $G - \{v\}$ with $G - v$ simply and call it a **vertex-deleted subgraph**.

(2) Edge deletion: for any $E' \subseteq E(G)$, we use the notation $G - E'$ to denote the resulting graph from G by deleting edges of E'. When E' contains only one edge, say $E' = \{e\}$, we replace $G - \{e\}$ with $G - e$ simply and call it an **edge-deleted subgraph**. Various kinds of subgraphs are illustrated in Fig. 1.9.

The operations of vertex deletion and edge deletion are called **unary graph operations**, since they involve only one graph.

Based on subgraphs we now introduce connected graphs and trees. Let G be a graph of order n. If for every pair of vertices $u, v \in V(G)$, there exists a path from u to v, then G is **connected**; otherwise, **disconnected**. We call a connected G **k-connected** if the removal of at most $k - 1$ vertices can not disconnect G. If G contains a subgraph isomorphic to a cycle, then G is said to be a **cycle-unfree graph**; otherwise a **forest**. A connected forest is called a **tree**, i.e., a connected graph which contains no cycles.

Let G be a connected graph. We call a **spanning subgraph** T of G if T is a tree. Theories on trees and connected graphs can be found in literature [24, 48, 63] and [4, 62], respectively.

1.3.2 Binary Graph-Operations

In this section, we consider graph-operations involving two graphs, which called **binary graph-operations**, including union, intersection, subtraction, oplus, join, product, strong product, composition.

Two graphs are said to be **vertex-disjoint** if they share no common vertex, and **edge-disjoint** if they have no edge in common. Let G_1 and G_2 be two graphs.

(3) The **union** of G_1 and G_2, denoted by $G_1 \cup G_2$, is the graph with vertex-set $V(G_1) \cup V(G_2)$ and edge-set $E(G_1) \cup E(G_2)$. Moreover, if G_1 and G_2 are edge-disjoint, then $G_1 \cup G_2$ is called the **disjoint-union** of G_1 and G_2. In what follows, we always assume that the two graphs involved in disjoint-union are edge-disjoint.

(4) The **intersection** of G_1 and G_2, denoted by $G_1 \cap G_2$, is the graph with vertex-set $V(G_1) \cap V(G_2)$ and edge-set $E(G_1) \cap E(G_2)$. Notice that when G_1 and G_2 are vertex-disjoint, their intersection is the empty graph.

(5) The **subtraction** of G_1 and G_2, or G_1 **subtracting** G_2, which is denoted by $G_1 - G_2$, is the graph obtained from G_1 by deleting vertices in $V(G_1) \cap V(G_2)$ and edges in $E(G_1) \cap E(G_2)$.

(6) The **oplus** of G_1 and G_2, denoted by $G_1 \oplus G_2$, is the subtraction of the union of G_1 and G_2 and the intersection of G_1 and G_2. That is, $G_1 \oplus G_2 = (G_1 \cup G_2) - (G_1 \cap G_2) = (G_1 - G_2) \cup (G_2 - G_1)$.

Figure 1.10 illustrates these concepts.

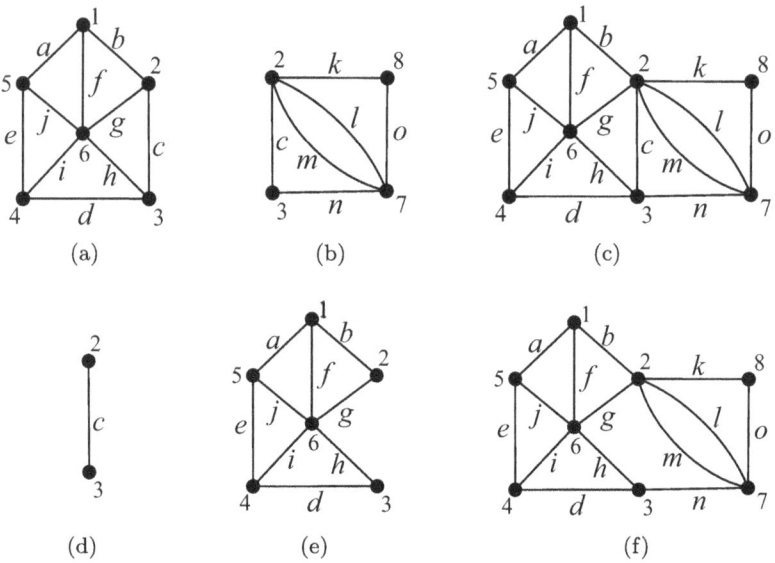

Fig. 1.10 The union, intersection, subtraction, and oplus of two graphs. (a) A graph G_1. (b) A graph G_2. (c) $G_1 \cup G_2$. (d) $G_1 \cap G_2$. (e) $G_1 - G_2$. (f) $G_1 \oplus G_2$

1.3 Graph-Operations

Fig. 1.11 The join of two graphs. (a) G_1. (b) G_2. (c) $G_1 + G_2$

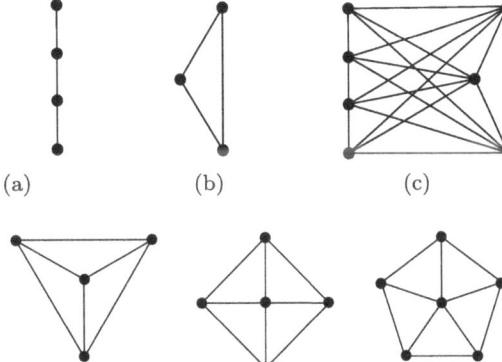

Fig. 1.12 Wheels W_3, W_4, W_5

(7) The **join** of G_1 and G_2 where G_1 and G_2 are vertex-disjoint, denoted by G_1+G_2, is the graph with vertex-set $V(G_1)\cup V(V_2)$ and edge-set $E(G_1)\cup E(G_2)\cup \{u_1u_2|u_1 \in V(G_1), u_2 \in V(G_2)\}$. Figure 1.11 illustrates the join of two graphs.

Based on the operation of join and empty graphs, we now define a special family of graphs: **complete n-partite graphs**, denoted by $K_{p_1,p_2,...,p_n}$, is the join of n empty graphs $N_{p_1}, N_{p_2}, \ldots, N_{p_n}$. That is,

$$K_{p_1,p_2,...,p_n} = N_{p_1} + N_{p_2} + \ldots + N_{p_n} \qquad (1.6)$$

Clearly, the order and size of $K_{p_1,p_2,...,p_n}$ are $\sum_{i=1}^{n} p_i$ and $\sum_{1\leq i<j\leq n} p_i p_j$. When $n = 2$, $K_{p_1,p_2,...,p_n}$ is called a **complete bipartite graph**.

Let G be a graph. If $|V(G)| = 1$, then G is said to be **trivial**. The join of a trivial graph K_1 and a n-cycle C_n is referred to as a **wheel with n spokes** and denoted W_n, where C_n is called the **wheel-cycle** and the vertex of K_1 is called the **wheel-center** of W_n. For convenience, we sometimes use C^x to denote the wheel-cycle of a wheel. The graphs of Fig. 1.12 are W_3, W_4 and W_5.

(8) The **product or cartesian product** of G_1 and G_2, denoted by $G_1 \times G_2$, is the graph with vertex-set $V(G_1) \times V(G_2)$ and edge-set consisting of all pairs $(u_1, u_2)(v_1, v_2)$ satisfying either $u_1 = v_1$ and $u_2v_2 \in E(G_2)$, or $u_2 = v_2$ and $u_1v_1 \in E(G_2)$. As an example, Fig. 1.13c depicts the cartesian product of two paths P_2 and P_5 which are shown in Fig. 1.13a, b, respectively.

Based on cartesian product, we now introduce an important family of graphs, called n-**hypercube** (or n-**cube** simply) and denoted Q_n, which can be recursively defined as follow: $Q_1 = K_2$ and $Q_n = K_2 \times Q_{n-1}$ for $n \geq 2$. The **Hamming distance** of two n-tuples X and Y, denoted $d_H(X, Y)$, is the number of coordinates at which the corresponding symbols are distinct. Given an n-cube Q_n, it is easy to see that $|V(Q_n)| = 2^n$. Thus, Q_n can also be defined as the graph whose vertex-set

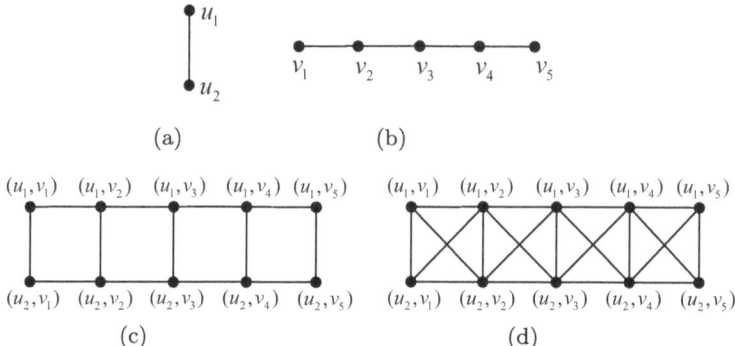

Fig. 1.13 The cartesian product and strong product of two pathes P_2 and P_5. (**a**) P_2. (**b**) P_5. (**c**) $[P_2 \times P_5$. (**d**) $P_2 * P_5$

is the set of all n-tuples of 0s and 1s, where two n-tuples X and Y are adjacent if and only if

$$d_H(X, Y) = 1 \qquad (1.7)$$

Due to the distinctive structure, the n-cube plays a very significant role in science studies, which is widely used as an essential technical tool for the research not only in computer science, but also in intelligent science [52, 58, 69], e.g., neural networks, genetic network.

(9) The **strong product** of G_1 and G_2, denoted $G_1 * G_2$, is the graph with vertex-set $V(G_1) \times V(G_2)$ and edge-set $\{(u_1, u_2)(v_1, v_2) | u_1 = v_1$ and $u_2v_2 \in E(G_2)$, or $u_2 = v_2$ and $u_1v_1 \in E(G_2)$, or $u_1v_1 \in E(G_1)$ and $u_2v_2 \in E(G_2)\}$. The operation of strong product has an important application in computing Shannon capacity of graphs [41, 49]. Figure 1.13d illustrates the strong product of two paths P_2 and P_5.

(10) The **composition of** G_1 **on** G_2, denoted $G_1[G_2]$, is the graph with vertex-set $V(G_1) \times V(G_2)$ in which two vertices $\{(u_1, u_2)$ and (v_1, v_2) are adjacent if and only if $u_1v_1 \in E(G_1)$ or $u_1 = v_1, u_2v_2 \in E(G_2)$. Figure 1.14 illustrates the compositions of P_2 on P_5 and P_5 on P_2.

1.3.3 The Sequel to Unary Graph-Operations

In addition to the unary graph-operations of vertex deletion and edge deletion, there are several other operations which can be used to gain a new graph from one graph. In this section, we introduce the following four operations: complement, contraction, identification, subdivision.

(11) The **complement** of a simple graph G, denoted by $\overline{G}$, is the graph with the same vertex-set as G and edge-set $\{uv | u \in V(\overline{G}), v \in V(\overline{G})$ and $uv \in E(G)\}$.

1.3 Graph-Operations

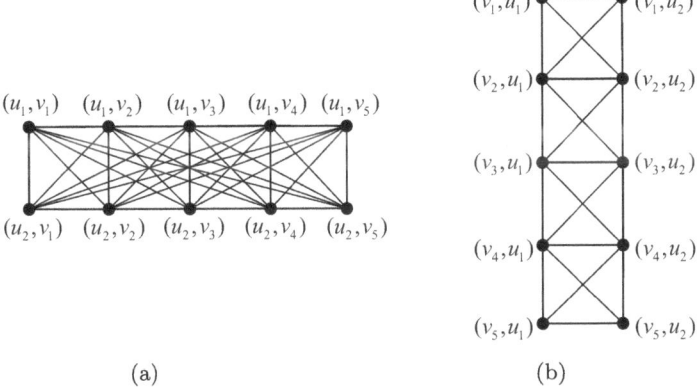

Fig. 1.14 The compositions of P_2 on P_5 and P_5 on P_2. (a) $P_2[P_5]$. (b) $P_5[P_2]$

Fig. 1.15 A graph and its complement. (a) G. (b) $\overline{G}$

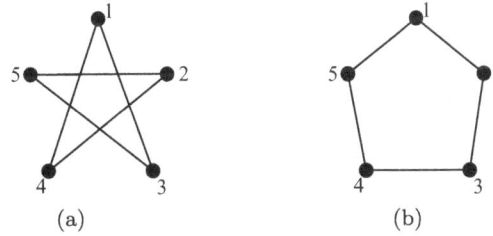

Figure 1.15 illustrates a graph and its complete. Clearly, the union of a n-order graph G and its complement is the n-order complete graph K_n. So,

$$|E(G)| + |E(\overline{G})| = \binom{n}{2} = \frac{1}{2}n(n-1)$$

Remark 1.5 A graph is complete graph if and only if its complement is a null graph.

In the study of network analysis or system analysis, when the structure of a network is complex, we can characterize its properties by analyzing its complement.

The following theorem is straightforward.

Theorem 1.6 *Let G be a simple graph. If G is disconnected, then $\overline{G}$ is connected.*

(12) The **contraction**: for a simple graph G, let $V' \subseteq V(G)$. We can obtain a new graph from G by deleting vertices of V' and adding a new vertex v' in such a way that v' is incident with all those edges which were originally incident with a vertex of V'; this is called **contracting** V' or the **contraction on** V', and the resulting graph is denoted by $G \circ V'$ and called the **contracted graph on** V'. In particular, when $e = uv$, we refer to the operation of contracting $\{u, v\}$ as **contracting the**

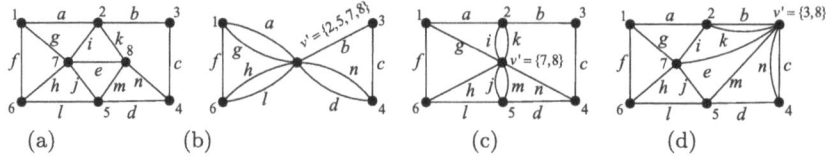

Fig. 1.16 A graph and its contracted graphs. (a) G. (b) $G \circ \{2, 5, 7, 8\}$. (c) $G \circ e$. (d) $G \circ \{3, 8\}$

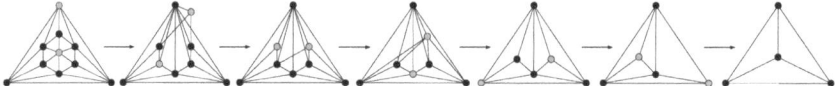

Fig. 1.17 An illustration for Conjecture 1.1

Fig. 1.18 Illustrations of subdivision

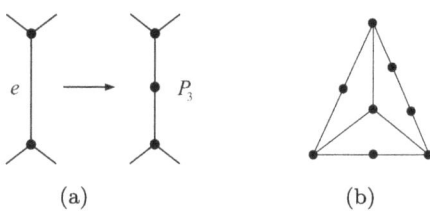

edge e or **edge contraction** and the resulting graph is denoted by $G \circ e$. Figure 1.16 give an example of a graph G, $G \circ \{2, 5, 7, 8\}$, $G \circ e = 78$, and $G \circ \{3, 8\}$.

(13) The **identification**: let G be a graph and u, v its two nonadjacent vertices. The operation of contracting $\{u, v\}$ is called **identifying** u and v (see the last graph of Fig. 1.16).

Identification is a special contraction, which can be used as an approach to study the well-known Four Color Conjecture; see the following conjecture.

Conjecture 1.1 Every maximal planar graph can be contracted to K_4 by a sequence of identifications.

Conjecture 1.1 has been determined for all the graphs in appendix I. Figure 1.17 gives an illustration of the process that the graph 10-2 in appendix I is contracted to K_4, in which we identify the two gray vertices in every stage.

(14) The **subdivision**: let e be an edge of a graph G. To **subdivide** edge e is to replace e by a 3-path, as in Fig. 1.18a. A **subdivision of** G or a G-**subdivision** is the graph derived from G by a sequence of subdivisions. A subdivision of K_4 is shown in Fig. 1.18b. The subdivision is a basic operation in graph theory, which is often used to characterize special graphs, e.g., the Kuratowski's theory to planar graphs.

In general, the graph-operation is the way to obtain our desired graphs, starting from one or more graphs. In the following chapters, we will propose several graph-operations in terms of the construction of maximal planar graphs.

1.4 Isomorphisms

1.4.1 Definition and Terminology

From the definition of graphs, we see that graphs are just a way to describe the relation between every pair of vertices in a vertex-set. The relative position of vertices of a graph and the shapes of edges have no significance. For that reason, two graphs with distinct diagrams may be the same one. For example, the graphs G and G' in Fig. 1.19 are represented by distinct diagrams, but they do have identical structure, and are said to be isomorphic; see the following formal definition.

Two simple graphs G_1 and G_2 are **isomorphic**, written $G_1 \cong G_2$, if there is a bijection σ from $V(G_1)$ to $V(G_2)$ such that for any pair of vertices $u \in V(G_1)$ and $v \in V(G_1)$, $uv \in E(G_1)$ if and only if $\sigma(u)\sigma(v) \in E(G_2)$; such a mapping σ is called an **isomorphism** between G_1 and G_2.

To show that two graphs are isomorphic, we must find an isomorphism between them. The mapping σ defined as: $\sigma(v_i) = i$ for $i = 1, 2, 3, 4, 5, 6$ is an isomorphism between the graphs G and G' in Fig. 1.19, where $V(G) = \{v_1, v_2, v_3, v_4, v_5, v_6\}$ and $V(G') = \{1, 2, 3, 4, 5, 6\}$.

The isomorphisms between two multigraphs, weighted graphs and digraphs can be defined similarly. As a representation, the following definition define the isomorphism between two vertex-weighted graph weighted graph.

Let $(G_1, w(V_1))$ and $(G_2, w(V_2))$ be two vertex-weighted graphs, where $V(G_i) = V_i = \{v_1^i, v_2^i, \ldots, v_n^i\}$ for $i = 1, 2$. Then, $(G_1, w(V_1))$ and $(G_2, w(V_2))$ are **vertex-weighted isomorphic**, written $(G_1, w(V_1)) \cong (G_2, w(V_2))$, if there is a bijection σ from V_1 to V_2 such that for any pair of vertices $u \in V_1$ and $v \in V_2$, $uv \in E(G_1)$ if and only if $\sigma(u)\sigma(v) \in E(G_2)$ and $w(u) = w(\sigma(u))$, $w(v) = w(\sigma(v))$.

As an example, consider the two vertex-weighted graphs $(G, w(V))$ and $(G', w(V'))$ shown in Fig. 1.20, where $V = V(G) = \{v_1, v_2, v_3, v_4, v_5, v_6, x, y, z\}$,

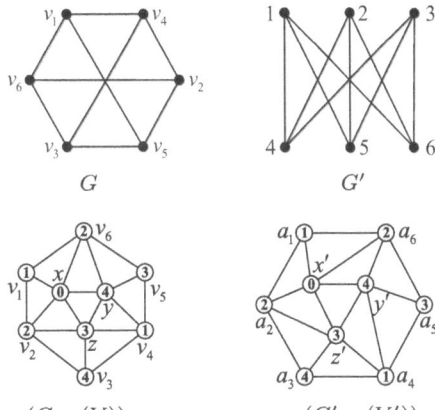

Fig. 1.19 Two classic isomorphic graphs. (**a**) G. (**b**) G'

Fig. 1.20 Vertex-weighted isomorphic graphs. (**a**) $(G, w(V))$. (**b**) $(G', w(V'))$

$V' = V(G') = \{a_1, a_2, a_3, a_4, a_5, a_6, x', y', z'\}$, $w(V) = \{1, 2, 4, 1, 3, 2, 0, 4, 3\}$ and $w(V') = \{1, 2, 4, 1, 3, 2, 0, 4, 3\}$. One can readily check that the mapping σ defined as:

$$\sigma(v_i) = a_i, i = 1, 2, 3, 4, 5, 6; \sigma(x) = x', \sigma(y) = y', \sigma(z) = z'.$$

is an vertex-weighted isomorphic between $(G, w(V))$ and $(G', w(V'))$.

1.4.2 Isomorphism Algorithms

The **graph isomorphism problem** is the computational problem of determining whether two given graphs are isomorphic or not. There is so far no efficient polynomial-time algorithms known to solve this problem and also no proof to show it to be NP-complete. But academics generally believe that it is NP-complete.

In the following, we depict three straightforward methods to determine graph isomorphism.

Approaches 1 Decision by the numbers of vertices and edges.

Theorem 1.7 *Let G_1 and G_2 be two graphs. If $G_1 \cong G_2$, then $|V(G_1)| = |V(G_2)|$, $|E(G_1)| = |E(G_2)|$; the reverse is not true.*

Theorem 1.7 is obvious, by which we can derive two graphs G_1 and G_2 are not isomorphic if $|V(G_1)| \neq |V(G_2)|$ or $|E(G_1)| \neq |E(G_2)|$. Since there are numerous of nonisomorphic graphs with the same number of vertices or edges, this method is insufficient to determine whether two graphs are isomorphic. Figure 1.21 presents three nonisomorphic (4,3)-graphs.

The following obvious result gives another way to determine two nonisomorphic graphs.

Approaches 2 Decision by degree-sequence.

Theorem 1.8 *Let G_1 and G_2 be two graphs. If $G_1 \cong G_2$, then $\pi(G_1) = \pi(G_2)$; the reverse is not true.*

Theorem 1.8 can be used to determine whether two graph are nonisomorphic. If two graphs have distinct degree-sequences, then they must be nonisomorphic. Observe that there are a number of nonisomorphic graphs with the identical degree-sequence, e.g., the degree-sequence (2,2,2,2,2,2) corresponds to two distinct 6-order

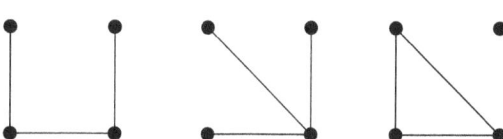

Fig. 1.21 Three nonisomorphic (4,3)-graphs

graphs: one is the 6-cycle C_6 and the other consists of two 3-cycles. Therefore, this method is also not enough to determine two graphs to be isomorphic.

Approaches 3 Decision by its complement.

Theorem 1.9 *Let G_1 and G_2 be two graphs. $G_1 \cong G_2$ if and only if $\overline{G_1} \cong \overline{G_2}$.*

Theorem 1.9 follows directly from the definition of complement. When two graphs G_1 and G_2 have more edges, we can determine whether G_1 and G_2 are isomorphic by considering their complements.

In general, it is a tough work to determine whether two graphs are isomorphic. Many algorithms have been proposed to solve this problem. These algorithms include conventional algorithms [45], neural network algorithms [28], genetic algorithms [57], to name a few.

1.4.3 Application of Graph Isomorphism

Graph isomorphisms are used in a variety of real applications. In this sections, we simply introduce two direct applications. One is applied in the field of system engineering, where determining successfully that two systems are isomorphic or approximate isomorphic has highly practical values in system modeling. The other one is to construct graphs through computer programming. In order to generate graphs efficiently, we must eliminate a large amount of isomorphic graphs in the process by using an efficient graph isomorphic algorithm. In this situation, by designing good graph isomorphic algorithms, Australian professor McKay obtained the Ramsey number $r(3, 8) = 28$ [42], $r(4, 5) = 25$ [44] and $r(5, 5) \leq 48$ [43].

1.5 Graph Matrix

An **graphical invariant** (or **invariant** simply) is a function (a **number** or **vector**) on the class of all graphs, which takes the same value on isomorphic graphs. The order and size of graphs are examples of graphical invariants, as are the chromatic, maximum independent set and degree-sequence. In general, graphical invariants can not be used to characterize the structures and properties of graphs.

This section introduces three graphic invariants, which are suitable for storing graphs in computers and applying mathematical methods to study structures and properties of graphs. These three invariants are three matrices associated with a graph, the incidence matrix, adjacency matrix and Laplacian matrix.

Let G be a (n, m)-graph with $V(G) = \{v_1, v_2, \ldots, v_n\}$ and $E(G) = \{e_1, e_2, \ldots, e_m\}$. The **incidence matrix** of G is the $n \times m$ matrix $M(G) = (m_{ij})_{n \times m}$, where m_{ij} is the number of times (0, 1, or 2) that vertex v_i and edge e_j are incident

Fig. 1.22 A graph and its incidence matrix. (a) G. (b) $M(G)$

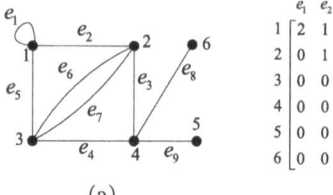

(a)

for $i = 1, 2, \ldots, n$ and $j = 1, 2, \ldots, m$. Incidence matrices of the graph G of Fig. 1.22a is shown in Fig. 1.22b.

Remark 1.6 If a graph G contains no loop, then $M(G)$ is a 0-1 matrix.

The incidence matrix of a graph specifies structures of the graph by depicting the relation between its vertices and edges. When graphs have more edges than vertices, we can specify the graph by their adjacency matrices.

Let G be an n-order graph with $V(G) = \{v_1, v_2, \ldots, v_n\}$. The **adjacency matrix** of G is the $n \times n$ matrix $A(G)=(a_{ij})_{n \times n}$, where a_{ij} is the number of edges joining vertices v_i and v_j for $i, j = 1, 2, \ldots, n$. The adjacency matrix of the graph G of Fig. 1.22a is shown in the following.

$$A(G) = \begin{array}{c} \\ 1 \\ 2 \\ 3 \\ 4 \\ 5 \\ 6 \end{array} \begin{array}{c} 1\ 2\ 3\ 4\ 5\ 6 \\ \begin{bmatrix} 1 & 1 & 1 & 0 & 0 & 0 \\ 1 & 0 & 2 & 1 & 0 & 0 \\ 1 & 2 & 0 & 1 & 0 & 0 \\ 0 & 1 & 1 & 0 & 1 & 1 \\ 0 & 0 & 0 & 1 & 0 & 0 \\ 0 & 0 & 0 & 1 & 0 & 0 \end{bmatrix} \end{array}$$

As for the adjacency matrix of a graph G, the following properties are clear for its definition.

(1) $A(G)$ is a symmetric matrix, and the diagonal elements of $A(G)$ are zero if and only if G contains no loop.
(2) $A(G)$ is a 0-1 matrix whose diagonal elements are zero if and only if G is a simple graph.

Remark 1.7 Since we can uniquely construct a graph according to one 0-1 symmetric matrix whose diagonal elements are zero and every graph uniquely corresponds to one 0-1 symmetric matrix whose diagonal elements are zero, there is a one-to-one correspondence between the set of all simple graphs and the set of 0-1 symmetric matrices whose diagonal elements are zero. By this observation, many properties of graphs can be characterized by their adjacency matrices; see the following theorem.

1.5 Graph Matrix

An $u - v$ walk of length ℓ of a simple graph G is a sequence $v_0 e_1 v_1 \ldots v_{\ell-1} e_\ell v_\ell$, whose terms are alternately vertices and edges of G (not necessarily distinct) for which $u = v_0$, $v_\ell = v$ and v_{i-1} and v_i are the ends of e_i, $1 \le i \le \ell$.

Theorem 1.10 *Let $A(G) = (a_{ij})_{n \times n}$ be the adjacency matrix of a simple graph G of order n. Then,*

(1) *the value of the (i, j) element of A^ℓ, the ℓ-power of $A(G)$, is the number of $v_i - v_j$ walks of length ℓ in G;*

(2) $a_{ii}^{(2)} = \sum_{j=1}^{n} a_{ij} a_{ji} = d(v_i);$

(3) $a_{ii}^{(3)}$ *is two times the number of triangles with v_i as one vertex in G.*

Proof

(1) By induction on the power ℓ. When $\ell = 0$, $A^0(G)$ is the n-order identity matrix I_n. The conclusion follows from the observation that the diagonal elements of I_n are 1 and other elements are zero, and for every vertex $v_i \in V(G)$, there is a $v_i - v_i$ walk of length 0 and there is no $v_i - v_j$ walk of length 0 for any $v_j \in V(G)$ and $v_j \ne v_i$.

Suppose that the conclusion holds for $\ell = p \ge 0$, and consider the case $\ell = p + 1$. Since $A^{p+1}(G) = A(G)A^p(G)$, it follows that $a_{ij}^{p+1} = \sum_{k=1}^{n} a_{ik} a_{kj}^{(p)}$. Observe that a_{ik} is the number of $v_i - v_k$ walks of length 1 and $a_{kj}^{(p)}$ the number of $v_k - v_j$ walks of length p; in addition, any distinct pair of a $v_i - v_k$ walk of length 1 and a $v_k - v_j$ walk of length p form a unique $v_i - v_j$ walk of length $p + 1$. We have that $a_{ij}^{(p+1)}$ is the number of $v_k - v_j$ walk of length $p + 1$ in G.

(2) Observe that every $v_i - v_i$ walk of length 2 of G has the form $v_i e' v_j e' v_i$ where e' is incident with v_i and v_j in G. Therefore, by (1) the conclusion (2) holds.

(3) Analogously, every $v_i - v_i$ walk of length 3 of G has the form $v_i e_1 v_j e_2 v_k e_3 v_i$, where $e_1 = v_i v_j$, $e_2 = v_j v_k$, $e_3 = v_k v_i$. Observe that $v_i e_3 v_k e_2 v_j e_1 v_i$ is also a $v_i - v_i$ walk (different from $v_i e_1 v_j e_2 v_k e_3 v_i$). Therefore, the conclusion (3) holds. ∎

A graph is k-**regular** if every vertex of the graph has degree k. The following theorem depicts the relation between the incidence matrix and adjacency matrix of a regular graph. We here leave the proof of Theorem 1.11 to readers.

Theorem 1.11 *Let G be a k-regular graph, and $M = M(G)$, $A = A(G)$. Then,*

$$MM^T = A + kI_n \tag{1.8}$$

Where M^T is the transpose of M.

Given a graph G of order n with $V(G) = \{v_1, v_2, \ldots, v_n\}$, the **Laplacian matrix** of G is the $n \times n$ matrix $L(G) = D(G) - A(G)$, where

$$D(G) = \begin{pmatrix} d_1 & 0 & \cdots & 0 \\ 0 & d_2 & \cdots & 0 \\ \vdots & \vdots & \ddots & \vdots \\ 0 & 0 & \cdots & d_n \end{pmatrix}$$

is the degree matrix which is a diagonal matrix whose diagonal element d_i is the degree of v_i in G, $i = 1, 2, \ldots, n$, and $A(G)$ is the adjacency matrix of G. The Laplacian matrix of a graph G possesses the following characteristics.

(1) $L(G)$ is a symmetric positive semidefinite matrix.
(2) the rank of $L(G)$ is equal to $n - k$ where $n = |V(G)|$ and k is the number of components of G.
(3) for any n-vector X, we have $X^T L(G) X = \sum_{i \sim j} (x_i - x_j)^2$.
(4) the sum of entries in each row (and each column) is zero.
(5) the algebraic cofactors of every pair of elements of $L(G)$ are identical.

1.6 Planar Graph

Observe that the objects of Four-Color Conjecture, Uniquely Four Chromatic planar graphs conjecture and the Nine-Color Conjecture are maximal planar graphs, which is an important class of planar graphs. Thus, this section gives a comprehensive introduction to maximal planar graphs.

1.6.1 Definitions

An undirected graph G is said to be **embeddable in the plane**, if it can be drawn in the plane so that its edges intersect only at their ends. Such a drawing of G is called a **planar embedding** of G. If G is embeddable in the plane, then we call G a **planar** graph; otherwise a **nonplanar graph**. A planar embedding of a planar graph is called a **plane graph**. From the definition, a planar embedding of a planar graph G is a geometric realization which can be regarded as a graph isomorphic to G. Figure 1.23b depicts a planar embedding of the planar graph shown in Fig. 1.23a, but the graphs in Fig. 1.23c, d are nonplanar graphs. By the definition, a plane graph G partitions the rest of the plane into a number of arcwise-connected open sets, which are called the **faces** of G. Thus, each plane graph has exactly one unbounded face, called the **outer face**; other faces are called **inner faces**. The **boundary** of a face of a plane graph is the boundary of the open set in the usual topological sense. If a vertex (and an edge) lies on the boundary of a face, then we say that it is **incident**

1.6 Planar Graph

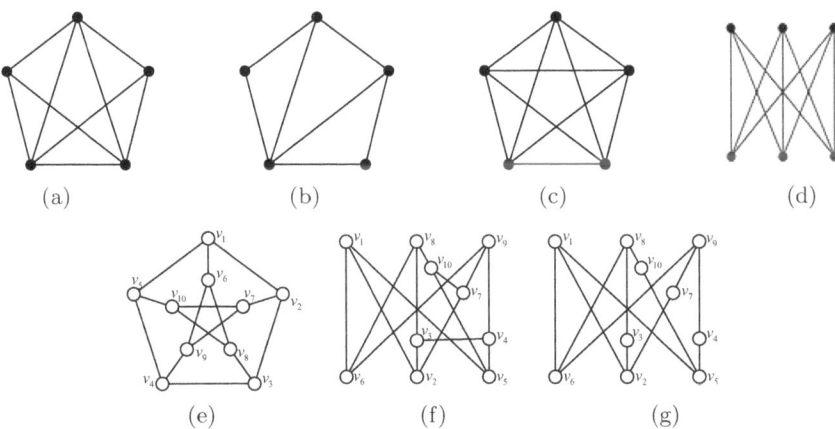

Fig. 1.23 Planar graph, plane graph, nonplanar graph, Peterson graph and the subdivision of $K_{3,3}$

with the face or simply that it is a vertex (and an edge) of the face. Two faces are **adjacent** if their boundaries share an edge. The **degree**, $d(P)$, of a face P is the number of edges in its boundary, cut edges being counted twice. A k-**face** is a face of degree k.

A simple plane graph is called a **maximal planar graph** if the addition of any edge results in a nonplanar graph. Since all faces of a maximal planar graph have degree three, maximal planar graphs are also known as **plane triangulations**, or a **triangulations** for short. Let G be a plane graph. If G has exactly one face (the outer face of G) whose boundary is a cycle C of length at least four and all other faces (inner faces of G) have degree three, then we call G a **semi-maximal planar graph on** C or, for short, **semi-maximal planar graph**, denoted by G^C, where the cycle C is called the **outer cycle** of G^C. A semi-maximal planar graph is also called a **configuration**. A cycle of a maximal planar graph is called **separating cycle** if it contains no chord and there are vertices inside as well as outside the cycle. A maximal planar graph G is called **separating** if G has a **separating triangle** (separating 3-cycle). In what follows, we use the notation $\triangle xyz$ to denote a 3-face incident with vertices x, y, z; in particular, for maximal planar graphs, we simply denote by xyz the 3-face incident with x, y, z.

1.6.2 Euler's Formula and Applications

For a connected planar graph, there exists a simple formula relating the numbers of vertices, edges and faces. This is the well known **Euler's Formula**, which was first established by Euler. There are many ways to prove Euler's Formula, for example, by induction on r (see the book [2]) which is presented as follows.

Theorem 1.12 (Euler's Formula) *For a connected planar (n, m)-graph G, let r be the number of faces of G. Then,*

$$n - m + r = 2 \tag{1.9}$$

Proof By induction on r. If $r = 1$, each edge of G is a cut edge and so G is a tree, since G is connected. Hence, $m = n - 1$ and the conclusion holds. Suppose that the result holds for all connected plane graphs with $r'(< r)$ faces, $r \geq 2$, and let G be a connected plane graph with r faces. Let $e \in E(G)$ be an edge that is not a cut edge. Then, e belongs to two faces and the two faces of G separated by e coalesce to form one face of $G - e$, i.e., $G - e$ is a connected planar graph with $r - 1$ faces. By the induction hypothesis, we have $n - m + r = n - (m - 1) + (r - 1) = 2$ and the theorem holds. ∎

By Euler's Formula, one gets the following theorem.

Theorem 1.13 *Let G be a planar (n, m)-graph such that the minimum degree ℓ of faces of G is at least 3. Let r be the number of faces of G. Then,*

$$m \leq \frac{\ell}{\ell - 2}(n - 2) \tag{1.10}$$

In particular, when G is a maximal planar graph, the upper bound is achieved, i.e.,

$$m = 3(n - 2) \tag{1.11}$$

Proof Since the sum of degrees of all faces of G is twice the number of edges of G, that is, $2m \geq \ell r$, it follows by Euler's Formula that $2m \geq \ell r = \ell(2 - n + m)$, which implies that $m \leq \frac{\ell}{\ell-2}(n - 2)$. Moreover, when G is maximal planar graph, we have $2m = 3r = 3(2 - n + m)$ and hence $m = 3(n - 2)$. ∎

Theorem 1.14 *K_5, $K_{3,3}$ and the subdivisions of them are nonplanar.*

Proof By contradiction. Suppose that K_5 or $K_{3,3}$ are planar graphs. Observe that the minimum degrees of K_5 and $K_{3,3}$ are 3 and 4, respectively. Then, by the Formula (1.10) in Theorem 1.13, it has that $|E(K_5)| \leq 9$ and $|E(K_{3,3})| \leq 8$. This contradicts the fact that $|E(K_5)| = 10$ and $|E(K_{3,3})| = 9$.

In addition, for any planar graph G and its subdivision G' by subdividing one edge, we have $|V(G)| = |V(G')| - 1$, $|E(G)| = |E(G')| - 1$ and the minimum degrees of faces of G and G' are equal. Therefore, by the Formula (1.10) we can also obtain a contradiction if we assume that some subdivision of K_5 or $K_{3,3}$ is planar. ∎

Graphs shown in Fig. 1.23e $\sim$ g are subdivisions of $K_{3,3}$ and hence are nonplanar by Theorem 1.14, where the graph of Fig. 1.23e is the well known Petersen graph.

Theorem 1.15 *Let G be a planar graph of order $n \geq 4$. Then, $\delta(G) \leq 5$; in particular, when G is a maximal planar graph, $3 \leq \delta(G) \leq 5$.*

Proof Let $|E(G)| = m$ and r the number of faces of G. Since every face of G has degree at least 3, it follows, by Formula (1.10), that $m \leq 3(n-2)$. Observe that $\sum_{i=1}^{n} d_G(v_i) = 2m$ where $v_i \in V(G)$ for $i = 1, 2, \ldots, n$. Therefore,

$$\delta(G)n \leq 2m = \sum_{i=1}^{n} d_G(v_i) \leq 2(3n-6).$$

This implies that $\delta(G) \leq 5$. Moreover, if G is a maximal planar graph, it is obvious that $\delta(G) \geq 3$. ∎

1.6.3 Kuratowski's Theorem

The problem of deciding whether a given graph is planar is a fundamental problem in the theory of planar graphs. Theorem 1.14 provides a sufficient condition to this problem. In 1930, the mathematician Kuratowski proved that this condition is also necessary and gave an excellent characterization for planar graphs [37].

Theorem 1.16 *A graph is planar if and only if it contains no subdivision of either K_5 or $K_{3,3}$.*

The proof of Theorem 1.16 can be found in many books of graph theory; see book [4].

1.6.4 Planar Embedding Algorithms

Although Theorem 1.16 characterizes planar graph beautifully, it is hard to present a polynomial-time algorithm to deciding whether a graph is planar or not [15]. Due to the computational intractability and good applications of planar embedding, many scholars have done different research on planar embedding in several points of view.

Planarity testing and embedding a planar graph in the plane have several applications. For example, the design of printed circuit board, the routing of large scale integrated circuit, visualization problem (such as gene regulation), and computer science [38]. In these applications, the layout of printed circuit boards is the most immediate use, in which the circuit diagram is modeled as a simple connected graph whose vertices represent electronic components and edges the wires. Then, the problem requires testing whether a given circuit diagram can be printed in the plane without short-circuits can be transformed into the problem of deciding whether a graph is planar, i.e., the planarity testing problem. Hence, studying planar embedding algorithms have practical significance, which have provided with single and multi-layer routing schemes for printed circuit boards.

Planarity testing algorithms were first studied in 1964 by Demucron, Malgranye and Pertuiset [9], who started with a cycle, searched for all of the bridges on the cycle and determined whether each bridge is embeddable in the plane. In 1974,

Hopcroft and Tarjan [21] first established a linear-time algorithm based on "path addition approach", but the algorithm is quite involved since the partial planar subgraph constructed at each iteration needs to be continually modified to obtain a final planar embedding. Afterwards in 1993, Shih and Hsu [50] established a simple linear-time testing algorithm based only on a depth-first search tree, in which a graph-reduction technique is applied so that the embeddings for the planar biconnected components constructed at each iteration never have to be changed.

In the nineteen-seventies, Wu and Liu [40, 61] studied planarity testing problem by using topological methods and translated it to the problem of solving algebraic equations. This approach is known as the Wu-Liu method [46].

In recent thirty years, planar embedding algorithms based on bionic computation, such as genetic algorithm, ant colony algorithm and neural network algorithm, etc., have been established [2, 14, 23]. The basic idea of bionic computation is to translate the planar embedding problem into the corresponding computing model and then give a solution to it. Yoshiyasu [51] in 1989 studied the planar embedding problem using Hopfield neural network, which corresponds the planar embedding to the minimum energy point of network. On the basis of this work, literature [16] proposed a novel algorithm by defining a new cross function and an improved energy function, which improves the convergence speed and can obtain the optimal solution simply.

1.7 Graph Coloring

Graph coloring is the starting point and one of the most important branches of graph theory, which has a profound influence on the development of graph theory. Graph coloring enjoys many practical applications, such as scheduling problem, protein structure prediction problem, code breaking problem, etc.

1.7.1 Definition and Classification

A k-**vertex-coloring** of a graph G, or simply a k-**coloring**, is a mapping f from $V(G)$ to a k-**color-set** $C(k) = \{1, 2, \ldots, k\}$, such that $f(x) \neq f(y)$ for any $xy \in E(G)$. A graph is k-**colorable** if it permits a k-coloring. The **chromatic number** of G, denoted $\chi(G)$, is the minimum integer k for which G has a k-coloring. If $\chi(G) = k$, then G is said to be a k-**chromatic graph**.

A k-coloring f of a graph G can be viewed as a partition $\{V_1, V_2, \ldots, V_k\}$ of $V(G)$, where $V(G) = V_1 \cup V_2 \cup \ldots \cup V_k$ and V_i (possibly empty) is the set of vertices assigned color i under f. We call the sets V_i the **color classes** of f and the partition $\{V_1, V_2, \ldots, V_k\}$ a k-**partition of color classes**. Two k-partitions of color classes $\{V_1, V_2, \ldots, V_k\}$ and $\{V_1', V_2', \ldots, V_k'\}$ are **equivalent** if $\{V_1, V_2, \ldots, V_k\} = \{V_1', V_2', \ldots, V_k'\}$, with the permission that $V_i \neq V_i'$ for $i =$

1.7 Graph Coloring

Fig. 1.24 A uniquely 3-colorable graph

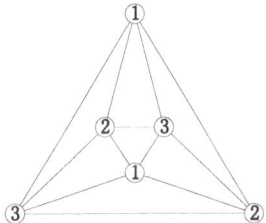

$1, 2, \ldots, k$. All of the k-colorings of G such that any pair of them are equivalent form a equivalent class, which is called a k-**coloring equivalent class** of G. Clearly, each k-coloring of G uniquely belongs to a k-coloring equivalent class containing $k!$ k-colorings. Denote by $C_k^0(G)$ the set of all k-colorings of G, each of which is a representative of a k-coloring equivalent class of G. Let $f \in C_k^0(G)$, we use the notation G_{ij}^f to denote the subgraph of G induced by vertices assigned colors i and j, named **bichromatic induced subgraph**, where $i, j \in C(k), i \neq j$. When there is no scope for confusion, we replace G_{ij}^f with G_{ij}. The components of G_{ij}^f are called ij-**components** (or **bichromatic components**) **with respect to** f.

A graph G is said to be **uniquely k-colorable** if $|C_k^0| = 1$. Figure 1.24 illustrates a uniquely 3-colorable graph.

A k-**edge-coloring** of a graph G is a mapping $f \colon E(G) \to \{1, 2, \ldots, k\}$, such that for any $e, e' \in E(G)$ $f(e) \neq f(e')$ if e and e' are adjacent. If G has a k-edge-coloring, then G is said to be k-**edge-colorable**. The **edge-chromatic number** of G, denoted $\chi'(G)$, is the minimum integer k such that G admits a k-edge-coloring. If $\chi'(G) = k$, then G is called a k-**edge-chromatic graph**.

Every k-edge-coloring can be viewed a partition $\{E_1, E_2, \ldots, E_k\}$ of $E(G)$, where E_i denotes the (possible empty) set of edges assigned color i, $i = 1, 2, \ldots, k$, i.e.,

$$E(G) = \bigcup_{i=1}^{k} E_i; \; E_i \cap E_j = \emptyset, i \neq j, i = 1, 2, \ldots, k$$

The sets E_i are called the edge color classes of f.

A k-**total coloring** of a graph G is a coloring f from $V(G) \cup E(G)$ to the k-color set $\{1, 2, \ldots, k\}$ such that any pair of incident or adjacent elements receive different colors. If G has a k-total-coloring, then G is said to be k-**total-colorable**. The **total-chromatic number** of G, denoted $\chi_t(G)$, is the minimum integer k such that G permits a k-total-coloring.

In addition to the above vertex-coloring, edge-coloring and total-coloring, there are also some other colorings. For example, to planar graphs, there are face-coloring, vertex-face-total-coloring, edge-face-total-coloring [22], vertex-edge-face-total-coloring [36], to name a few.

1.7.2 Chromatic Number

In Sect. 1.7.1, we introduced three basic classes of colorings of graphs and the corresponding chromatic numbers. There are two natural questions in terms of these three kinds of chromatic numbers. One is how to determine these chromatic numbers? The other is whether the chromatic numbers have relation to other invariants of graphs?

Theorem 1.17 ([7]) *For every graph G, it has that $\chi(G) \leq \Delta(G) + 1$.*

Theorem 1.17 gives the upper bound on the chromatic number, which are attained by odd cycles and complete graphs. The following conclusion, known as Brooks' Theorem, shows that when a graph is not odd cycle or complete graph, the upper bound in Theorem 1.17 can be improved.

Theorem 1.18 ([7]) *If G is a connected graph, and is neither an odd cycle nor a complete graph, then $\chi(G) \leq \Delta(G)$.*

The following result presents a better upper bound than Brooks' Theorem.

Theorem 1.19 ([11]) *Let G be an arbitrary graph. Then,*

$$\chi(G) \leq \max\{\delta(H)|H \subseteq G\} + 1 \tag{1.12}$$

Observe that when $\chi(G) = 2$ every 2-coloring corresponds to a 2-partition of color classes $\{V_1, V_2\}$, that is, $V(G)$ can be partitioned into two independent sets. Therefore, any edge incident with a vertex of V_1 (or V_2) it must be incident with a vertex of V_2 (or V_1). This implies that G is a bipartite.

Theorem 1.20 *Let G be a graph. Then, $\chi(G) = 2$ if and only if G is bipartite.*

In 1961, Hajos [11] proposed a conjecture on chromatic number from the perspective of structure of graphs.

Hajós' Conjecture [18] Every k-chromatic graph contains a subdivision of the complete k-graph K_k.

Hajós' Conjecture has been proved for the case of $k \leq 4$ [12], while was disproved by Catlin [8], who found the 8-chromatic graph which contains no subdivision of K_8. When $k = 5$, Hajós' Conjecture is equivalent to The Four-Color Conjecture [56].

In the definition of edge-chromatic number, we see that $\chi'(G) \geq \Delta(G)$ for every graph G. The following result gives the exact value of edge-chromatic number of bipartite graphs.

Theorem 1.21 ([30]) *Let G be a bipartite graph. Then, $\chi'(G) = \Delta(G)$.*

Observe that if G is not bipartite one cannot necessarily conclude that $\chi'(G) = \Delta(G)$. An important theorem due to Vizing and independently Gupta asserts that any simple graph G has edge-chromatic number either $\Delta(G)$ or $\Delta(G) + 1$.

1.7 Graph Coloring

Theorem 1.22 (Vizing's Theorem [17, 54]) *For any simple graph G, we have* $\Delta(G) \leq \chi'(G) \leq \Delta(G) + 1$.

Vizing's Theorem is a strong conclusion, since there exist both graphs G with $\chi'(G) = \Delta(G)$ and graphs G with $\chi'(G) = \Delta(G) + 1$. However, how to determine graphs G with $\chi'(G) = \Delta(G)$ is an open problem to be solved.

As for the total-coloring, there is an famous conjecture posed by Behzad and Vizing, independently.

Total Coloring Conjecture (TCC) [3, 55] For any graph G, it has that

$$\Delta(G) + 1 \leq \chi_t(G) \leq \Delta(G) + 2 \tag{1.13}$$

So far, TCC has been confirmed for graphs with maximum degree Δ at most 5 [34, 35, 53], and for planar graphs with $\Delta \geq 9$ by Borodin [6], for planar graphs with $\Delta = 8$ by Yap [68] and Andersen [1], and for planar graphs with $\Delta = 7$ by Zhao [47]. Therefore, the only open case for planar graphs is $\Delta = 6$.

1.7.3 Graph Coloring Algorithms

It is well-known that the problem of deciding whether a given graph is k-colorable is NP-complete and the problem of finding the chromatic number of a graph is NP-hard. In the following, we introduce three classic graph coloring algorithms.

(1) Contracting Vertex and Adding Edge (CVAE) [70]
Given a graph G, let $u, v \in V(G)$, $uv \notin E(G)$. We use the notation $G+uv$ to denote the resulting graph obtained from G by adding an the edge uv and use $G \circ \{u, v\}$ to denote the contracted graph on $\{u, v\}$.

Theorem 1.23 ([70]) *Let G be a graph with two nonadjacent two vertices u and v. Then,* $\chi(G) = \min\{\chi(G + uv), \chi(G \circ \{u, v\})\}$

By Theorem 1.23 there is an algorithm for graph coloring problem, named as "**Contracting Vertex and Adding Edge (CVAE)**".

Let G be a graph with two nonadjacent vertices v_i, v_j. Here we simply refer to the operation of identifying $\{v_i, v_j\}$ as **contracting-vertex** and the operation of adding the edge $v_i v_j$ as **adding-edge**. Starting with G, we can obtain a complete graph by iteratively conducting contracting-vertex and adding-edge. By Theorem 1.23 the chromatic number of the obtained complete graphs with the minimum order is the chromatic of G. Figure 1.25 presents an illustration of computing the chromatic number of 5-cycle by CVAE.

(2) Independent-Set (IS) [5]
Let S be a independent set of a graph G, if every vertex in $V(G) \setminus S$ is adjacent to at least one vertex in S in G, then S is called a **maximal independent set** of G. If there does not exist any independent set S' of G such that $|S'| > S$, then S is called

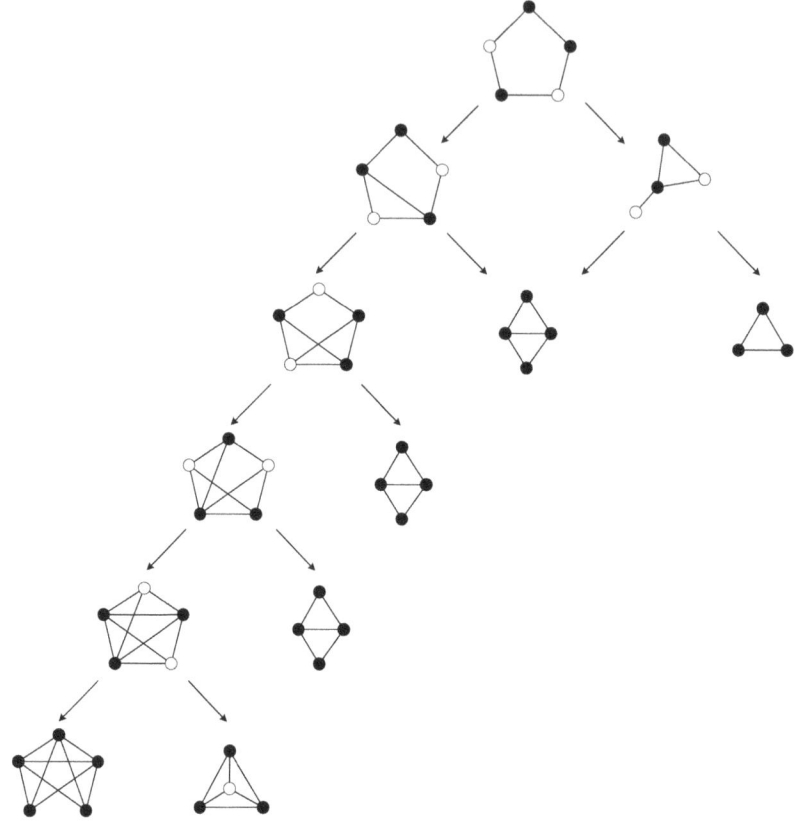

Fig. 1.25 A illustration of computing C_5 by CVAE

a **maximum independent set** of G. A **covering** of G is a subset $K \subseteq V(G)$ such that every edge of G is incident with a vertex of K. We say that K is **minimal** if none of proper subsets of K is a covering of G, and a **minimum covering** if G has no covering K' with $|K'| < |K|$.

Observe that a k-coloring of a graph G is a partition of $V(G)$ into k independent sets; we have that the chromatic number of G is the minimum such a number k. Therefore, one can construct a k-coloring of G by finding independent sets of G. Since each independent set is a subset of some maximal independent set, it is sufficient to find all maximal independent sets. In addition, by the definition of coverings, we have that the complement set of every maximal independent set of G is a minimal covering of G. The following depicts a method of finding maximal independent sets by seeking minimal coverings.

Let v be a vertex of a graph G. When constructing a minimal coverings, one should select either v or all of the neighbors of v. In the following, we model the process of finding minimal coverings into an algebraic expression, in which

1.7 Graph Coloring

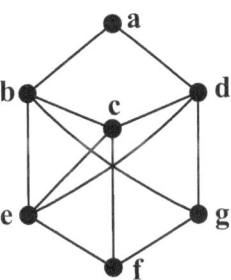

Fig. 1.26 An example of computing chromatic number based on minimal covering

denote 'the action of selecting vertex v' by the notation 'v' simply, denote by '+' the logical expression 'or', and denote by '×' the logical expression 'and'. Thus, finding minimal coverings of Fig. 1.26 can be expressed as the following algebraic expression.

$(a+bdfbd)(b+aceg)(c+bdef)(d+aceg)(e+bcdf)(f+ceg)(g+bdf) = aceg + bcdeg + bdef + bcdf$

From this, we derive that $\{a, c, e, g\}$, $\{b, c, d, e, g\}$, $\{b, d, e, f\}$ and $\{b, c, d, f\}$ are the minimal covering of Fig. 1.26, and their complement sets $\{b, d, f\}$, $\{a, f\}$, $\{a, c, g\}$ and $\{a, e, g\}$ are the maximal independent sets of G.

(3) Powell's Algorithm [59]

Powell's Algorithm is based on a greedy heuristic, as follows. Let G be a graph with $V(G)=\{v_1, v_2, \ldots, v_n\}$ such that $d_G(v_1) \geq d_G(v_2) \geq \ldots \geq d_G(v_n)$. In the process of coloring vertices, at each stage let v_i be a vertex uncolored and let V_{v_i} be the independent set defined by the following procedure: let $v_i \in V_{v_i}$ first; then add v_j to V_{v_i} one by one for each v_j such that $i' < j \leq n$, i' is the maximum subscript in V_{v_i}, v_j is not colored at the stage, and v_j is not adjacent to vertices in V_{v_i} in G.

INPUT: a graph G of order n
OUTPUT: a coloring of G

1. Arrange the vertices of G in a linear order: $v_1, v_2, \ldots, v_n$ such that $d_G(v_1) \geq d_G(v_2) \geq \ldots \geq d_G(v_n)$.

2. Let v_i be the first uncolored vertex of G (in the order $v_1, v_2, \ldots, v_n$), and color v_i with the smallest positive integer not yet assigned to vertices at the current stage.

As an example, consider the graph shown in Fig. 1.26. We first arrange the vertices in the order: c, e, b, d, f, g, a.

(1) For the first vertex v, it has that $V_c = \{c, g, a\}$ and then color vertices of V_c with color 1.

(2) After step (1), the first uncolored vertex (in the order c, e, b, d, f, g, a) is e and $V_e = \{e\}$. We then color vertices of V_e with color 2.

(3) After step (2), the first uncolored vertex (in the order c, e, b, d, f, g, a) is b and $V_b = \{b, d, f\}$. We then color vertices of V_b with color 3.

After step (3), all vertices have been colored. Therefore, $\chi(G) = 3$.

In addition to the above three graph coloring algorithms, there are also other algorithms, such that sequential coloring, strong SEQ algorithm, DSATUR algorithm, etc. Moreover, many algorithms based on bionic computation and biocomputing have been proposed; see literature [29, 66].

1.7.4 Applications of Graph Coloring

Graph coloring problem has attracted extensive attention of the society, not only for its theoretical value but also for its wide applications. Here are three simple practical applications of graph coloring.

(1) Phasing of Traffic Lights
Consider an urban intersection where two or more roads either meet or cross at the same level; traffic lights needs to be installed to adjust traffic streams. Observe that the path used by a traffic stream to traverse the intersection, may cross the one used by another traffic stream. In this case, these streams are in conflict and cannot simultaneously get the right of way. To ensure safety and same money, it is asked what is the minimum number of phasing of traffic lights.

This problem can be formulated as a graph theoretic model with vertex coloring approach. Define a graph G, in which each vertex represents a traffic stream and two vertices are adjacent if and only if there exists a confliction between corresponding traffic streams. Thus, the chromatic number of the defined graph is the minimum number of phasing of traffic lights.

(2) Chemical Storage
A company manufactures some distinct chemicals. Certain pairs of these chemicals are incompatible and would cause explosions if brought into contact with each other. As a precautionary measure, the company wishes to divide its warehouse into compartments, and store incompatible chemicals in different compartments. What is the minimum number of compartments into which the warehouse should be partitioned?

This problem can also be formulated as a graph coloring problem. Specifically, one gets a graph such that vertex-set represents the chemicals and two vertices are adjacent if and only if their corresponding chemical are incompatible. One can readily check that the least number of compartments into which the warehouse should be partitioned is equal to the chromatic number of the defined graph.

(3) Timetable Scheduling
When designing schedule of courses for students in some classes at a college, it requires that courses taught by the same teacher and courses that require same classroom must be scheduled at different time slots. In such case, courses need to be scheduled in a way to avoid conflicts. Thus, the problem of determining minimum number of time slots that can successfully schedule all the courses subject to the restriction can be translated into the edge-coloring problem of bipartite graph, as follows.

Define a bipartite graph $G[X, Y]$ such that $X=\{t_1, t_2, \ldots, t_m\}$ represents the set of teachers and $Y=\{c_1, c_2, \ldots, c_n\}$ the set of classes. If the teacher t_i teach p_{ij} lessons to class c_j, there are p_{ij} edges between t_i and c_j. Thus, the minimum number of time slots is the edge-chromatic number of the graph $G[X, Y]$. In real life, the timetable has to satisfy other certain conditions (such as the number of classrooms). In this case, this problem will become more complex; see literature [10, 60].

References

1. L Andersen. *Total colouring of simple graphs (in Danish)*. Master's thesis, University of Aalborg, 1993.
2. G D Battista, P Eades, R Tamassia, and et al. Algorithms for drawing graphs: an annotated bibliography. *Computational Geometry*, 4(5):235–282, 1994.
3. M Behzad. *Graphs and their chromatic numbers*. Doctoral thesis, Michigan State University, 1965.
4. J A Bondy and U S R Murty. *Graph theory with applications*. New York, USA, Springer, 2008.
5. R Boppana. Approximating maximum independent sets by excluding subgraphs. *Springer Berlin Heidelberg*, 32(2):13–25, 1990.
6. O V Borodin. On the total coloring of planar graphs. *Journal Fur Die Reine Und Angewandte Mathematik*, 394:180–185, 1989.
7. R L Brooks. On colouring the nodes of a network. *Proc. Cambridge Philos. Soc.*, 37:194–197, 1941.
8. P A Catlin. Hajós' graph-coloring conjecture: variations and counterexamples. *J. Combin. Theory Ser. B*, 26:268–274, 1979.
9. G Demoucron, Y Malgrange, and R Pertuiset. Graphes planaires: reconnaissance et construction des representations plenaries topologiques. *Revue Francaise de Recherche Operationnelle*, 8:33–47, 1964.
10. M A H Dempster. Two algorithms for the time-table problem. *Combinatorial Mathematics and its Applications (ed. D. J. A. Welsh), Academic Press, New York*, pages 63–65, 1971.
11. R Diestel. *Graph theory*. Higher Education Press, 2013.
12. G A Dirac. A property of 4-chromatic graphs and some remarks on critical graphs. *London Math. Soc.*, 27:85–92, 1952.
13. R B Eggleton. Graphic sequences and graphic polynomials–a report. *Colloq. Math. Soc. J. Bolyai*, 10:385–392, 1975.
14. T Eloranta and E Mäkinen. Timga: a genetic algorithm for drawing undirected graphs. *Divulgaciones Matematicas*, 9(2):155–171, 2001.
15. P Erdos and G Katona. Theory of graph. *New York: Academic Press*, pages 265–269, 1968.
16. L Gao, J Xu, and J Y Zhang. A novel neural network algorithm for plane testing problem. *Journal of xidian university (natural science edition)*, 28(2):245–248, 2001.
17. R P Gupta. The chromatic index and the degree of a graph. *Notices Amer. Math. Soc.*, 13:66T–429, 1966.
18. G Hajos. Uber eine konstruktion nicht n-farbbarer graphes. *Wiss. Z. Martin-Luther-Univ. Halle-Wittenberg. Math. Naturwiss Reihe.*, 10:116–117, 1961.
19. S L Hakimi. On realizability of a set of integers and the degrees of the vertices of a linear graph. i. *SIAM J. Appl. Math.*, 10:496–506, 1962.
20. S L Hakimi. On realizability of a set of integers and the degrees of the vertices of a linear graph. *SIAM J. Appl. Math.*, 11:135–147, 1963.
21. J E Hopcroft and R E Tarjan. Efficient planarity testing of graphs. *Journal of the ACM*, 21(4):549–568, 1974.

22. G Z Hu and Z F Zhang. Total coloring of the side-face of planar graph. *Journal of tsinghua university (natural science edition)*, 32(3):18–23, 1992.
23. J W Huang, L S Kang, and Y P Chen. Binary tree drawing algorithm based on genetic algorithm. *Journal of Software*, 11(8):1–8, 2000.
24. Z J Huang, X M Li. *Number of trees in the figure: calculation and its role in network reliability*. Harbin Institute of Technology press, 1993.
25. R H Johnson. The diameter and radius of simple graphs. *J. Combinatorial Theory, Ser. B*, 17:188–198, 1974.
26. R H Johnson. Simple separable graphs. *Pacific J. Math*, 56:143–158, 1975.
27. R H Johnson. Simple directed trees. *Discrete Math*, 14:257–264, 1976.
28. M P Kennedy and L O Chun. Neural computation of decisions in optimization problems. *IEEE Trans. On CAS*, pages 554–562, 1988.
29. Z Kokosinski, K Kwarciany, and M Kolodziej. Efficient graph coloring with parallel genetic algorithms. *Computing and Informatics*, 24:123–147, 2005.
30. D Konig. Uber graphen und ihre anwendung auf determinantentheorie und mengenlehre. *Math. Ann.*, 77:453–465, 1916.
31. M Koren. Extreme degree sequence of simple graphs. *Combinatorial Theory, Ser. B*, 15:213–224, 1973.
32. M Koren. Pairs of sequences with a unique realization by bipartite graphs. *Combinatorial Theory, Ser. B*, 21:224–234, 1976.
33. M Koren. Pairs of sequences with a unique realization by bipartite graphs. *Combinatorial Theory, Ser. B*, 21:235–244, 1976.
34. A V Kostochka. The total coloring of a multigraph with maximal 4. *Discrete Math.*, 17:161–163, 1977.
35. A V Kostochka. The total chromatic number of any multigraph with maximum degree five is at most seven. *Discrete Math.*, 162:199–214, 1996.
36. H V Kronk and J Mitchem. A seven-color theorem on the sphere. *Discrete Math.*, 5:253–260, 1973.
37. K Kuratowski. Sur le probleme des courbes gauches en topologie. *Fundamenta Mathematicae*, 15:271–283, 1930.
38. A Lempel, S Even, and I Cederbaum. An algorithm for planarity testing of graphs. *Theory of Graph*, 5(2):215–232, 1967.
39. J S Li. Degree sequence of graphs. *Mathematical development*, 23(8):193–204, 1994.
40. Y P Liu. Module 2 programming and planar embedding. *Journal of applied mathematics*, 1(4):321–329, 1978.
41. L Lovasz. On the shannon capacity of a graph. *on Information Theory*, 25(1):1–7, 1979.
42. B D McKay and Z K Min. The value of the ramsey number r (3, 8). *Journal of Graph Theory*, 16(1):99–105, 1992.
43. B D McKay and S P Radziszowski. A new upper bound for the ramsey number r (5, 5). *Australasian J Combinatorics*, 5:13–20, 1992.
44. B D McKay and S P Radziszowski. R (4, 5)=25. *Journal of Graph Theory*, 19(3):309–322, 1995.
45. E M Reingold, J Nievergelt, and N Deo. Combinatorial algorithms: Theory and practice. *New Jersey: Prentice-hall*, 9(5):1054, 1977.
46. P Rosenstiehl. Preuve algebrique du critere de planarite de wu-liu. *Annals of Discrete Mathematics*, 9:67–78, 1980.
47. D P Sanders and Y Zhao. On total 9-coloring planar graphs of maximum degree seven. *Graph Theory*, 31:67–73, 1999.
48. J Serre. *Trees*. Springer-Verlag, Berlin Heidelberg, New York, 1980.
49. C E Shannon. The zero-error capacity of a noisy channel. *Information Theory*, 3:8–19, 1956.
50. W K Shih and W L Hsu. A simple test for planar graphs. proceedings of the international workshop on discrete mathematics and algorithms. *Proceedings of the International Workshop on Discrete Mathematics and Algorithms*, pages 110–122, 1993.

References

51. Y Takefuji and K C Lee. A near-optimum parallel planarization algorithm. *Science*, 245(4922):1221–1223, 1989.
52. R Tanese. Parallel genetic algorithms for a hypercube. in proceedings of the second international conference on genetic algorithms. *L. Erlbaum Associates*, pages 177–183, 1987.
53. N Vijayaditya. On total chromatic number of a graph. *London Math. Soc.*, 3:405–408, 1971.
54. V G Vizing. On an estimate of the chromatic class of a p-graph (russian). *Diskret. Analiz.*, 3:25–30, 1964.
55. V G Vizing. Some unsolved problems in graph theory. *Russ Math. Surv.*, 23:125–142, 1968.
56. K Wagner. Beweis einer abschwachung der hadwiger-vermutung. *Math. Ann.*, 153:139–141, 1964.
57. Y K Wang, K C Fan, and J T Horng. Genetic-based search for error-correcting graph isomorphism. *IEEE Transactions on Systems*, 27(4):588–597, 1997.
58. P D Wasserman. *Neural computing theory and practice*. Van Nostrand Reinhold, New York, 1989.
59. D J A Welsh and M B Powell. An upper bound on the chromatic number of a graph and its application to timetabling problems. *The Computer Journal*, 10:85–87, 1967.
60. D de Werra. On some combinatorial problems arising in scheduling. *INFOR*, 8:165–175, 1970.
61. W J Wu. Planar embedding of a linear graph. *Chinese science bulletin*, 19(5):226–228, 1974.
62. J Xu. *Theory and application of kernel and degree of system*. Xi'an jiaotong university press, 1987.
63. J Xu. Counting formula of supporting tree of several kinds of graphs. *Journal of northwest university*, 4(19):23–31, 1989.
64. J Xu. *Self-complementing theory and its application*. xidian university press, 1999.
65. J Xu, Z P Li, and E Q Zhu. Advances in the theory of maximum plane graphs. *Journal of computer science*, 38(8):1680–1704, 2015.
66. J Xu, X Qiang, K Zhang, C Zhang, J Yang, and et al. Two algorithms for the time-table problem. In *IEEE Fifth International Conference on Bio-inspired Computing: Theories and Applications*, pages 231–235, 2010.
67. B Yao and Z F Zhang (translate). *The theory, algorithm and application of directed graph*. Science press, 2009.
68. H P Yap. *Total-colourings of graphs*. Manuscript, 1989.
69. J Y Zhang and J Xu. *Binary forward artificial neural network: theory and application*. xidian university, 2001.
70. A A Zykov. On some properties of linear complexes (russian). *Math. Sbornik*, 24:163–188, 1949.

Open Access This chapter is licensed under the terms of the Creative Commons Attribution 4.0 International License (http://creativecommons.org/licenses/by/4.0/), which permits use, sharing, adaptation, distribution and reproduction in any medium or format, as long as you give appropriate credit to the original author(s) and the source, provide a link to the Creative Commons license and indicate if changes were made.

The images or other third party material in this chapter are included in the chapter's Creative Commons license, unless indicated otherwise in a credit line to the material. If material is not included in the chapter's Creative Commons license and your intended use is not permitted by statutory regulation or exceeds the permitted use, you will need to obtain permission directly from the copyright holder.

Chapter 2
Discharging and Structure of Maximal Planar Graphs

Abstract Recall that the maximal planar graphs are a class of planar graphs with the maximum number of edges, which have been studied extensively since the late 19th century due to the fact that the Four-Color Conjecture can be studied sufficiently for maximal planar graphs. In the subsequent chapters, we will present a series of results related to maximal planar graphs. This chapter mainly discusses the structures of maximal planar graphs by using the proof technique–**discharging**.

2.1 Discharging

Let $G = (V, E)$ be a maximal planar graph with n vertices, m edges, and r faces. Let F be the set of faces of G. Since every face of G has degree 3, we have

$$3r = 2m = \sum_{v \in V} d_G(v) \tag{2.1}$$

By Euler's Formula (1.9) and Formula (1.11),

$$3n - 3m + 3r = 3n - m = 3n - \frac{1}{2}\sum_{v \in V} d_G(v) = 6$$

That is,

$$\sum_{v \in V}(d_G(v) - 6) = -12 \tag{2.2}$$

In the context of planar graphs, **discharging** is an effective way of using Euler's Formula, for which each vertex v, each edge e and each face f of a planar graph is initially assigned a weight $c(v)$, $c(e)$ and $c(f)$, respectively, where c is a function from $V \cup E \cup F$ to the set of nonnegative numbers. We call $c(x)$ the **initial charge** of x for $x \in V \cup E \cup F$. Alternatively, the planar graph can be viewed as a weighted graph with weight on its vertices, edges and faces. The **initial charge of** G is defined as

$$c(G) = \sum_{v \in V} c(v) + \sum_{e \in E} c(e) + \sum_{f \in F} c(f) \tag{2.3}$$

When initially assigning charge to a planar graph G, we mainly depend on the Euler's Formula (1.9) and its invariants. For example, based on Formula (2.2), the charges assigned to each vertex v, each edge e and each face f should be

$$c(v) = d_G(v) - 6, \, c(e) = c(f) = 0 \tag{2.4}$$

In this case, $c(G) = -12$. After the assignment of initial charge to G, we attempt to **discharge** G by redistributing the charge (in some methodical fashion) on the premise that the charge of G remain unchanged. Formally, the discharging can be defined as a sequence of functions $\varphi = (\varphi_1, \varphi_2, \ldots, \varphi_k)$ which transfer an amount of charge from one element x to another element y, $(x, y \in (V \cup E \cup F))$, where each φ_i for $i = 1, , 2, \ldots, k$ corresponds to one certain rule and the resulting charge of the graph remains constant throughout. We use $\varphi_i(c(x), c(y)) = (c(x) - a, c(y) + a)$ to denote this process for $i = 1, 2, \ldots, k$, i.e., x transfers an amount of charge a to y. We call $\varphi = (\varphi_1, \varphi_2, \ldots, \varphi_k)$ a **discharging transformation**.

The **basic idea** of studying structures of maximal planar graphs G via discharging method is to show that a desired local structure (configurations) is unavoidable. For this, we, by way of contradiction, suppose that some structures are absent; then we show that there exists a "discharging rules" which allows charges to be moved so that the **final charge** of G is not equal to the initial charge of G. This results in a contradiction and hence the desired structure must occur.

Let G be a maximal planar graph with $\delta(G) = 5$. Denote by V^i the set of vertices of degree i. We are interest in the structures of $G[V^5 \cup V^6 \cup V^7]$. Currently, the main study is focused on structures of paths and triangles, as well as cycles and stars, in $G[V^5 \cup V^6 \cup V^7]$. To present a review of developments in this research more comprehensively, we, in the following, extend maximal planar graphs to general planar graphs whose (vertex and face) degrees are at least 3.

2.2 Structure of Path

Let G be a graph. A k-**vertex** (or k-face) is a vertex (or face) of degree k. By k^+ or k^- we denote any integer not smaller or not greater that k, respectively. The **girth** of G, denoted by $g(G)$, is the length of a smallest cycle of G. An edge $xy \in E(G)$ is called an (a, b)-**edge** if $d_G(x) = a, d_G(y) = b$; a path xyz is an (a, b, c)-path of G if $d_G(x) = a, d_G(y) = b, d_G(z) = c$; a 3-face $\triangle \, xyz$ is an (a, b, c)-face if $d_G(x) = a, d_G(y) = b, d_G(z) = c$; and so are the other structures. We denote by w_k the minimum degree sum of a k-path in G, by $e_{i,j}$ the number of edges incident

2.2 Structure of Path

with a i-vertex and a j-vertex in G, and by $f_{i,j,k}$ the number of triangles incident with a i-vertex, a j-vertex and a k-vertex in G.

2.2.1 Edges

Theorem 2.1 *Let G be a planar graph with $\delta(G) \leq 5$. Then, G contains a $(5,5)$-edge or a $(5,6)$-edge.*

Proof This theorem follows directly from Theorem 2.2. So, we omit the proof here. ∎

Remark 2.1 There are planar graphs of minimum degree 5, which contains only $(5, 5)$-edges (see Fig. 2.1a, the icosahedron), or both $(5, 5)$-edges and $(5, 6)$-edges (see Fig. 2.1b; this graph has two 6-vertices of distance 2 and twelve 5-vertices), or only $(5, 6)$-edge (see Fig. 2.1c).

Indeed, the content of Theorem 2.1 was considered by many scholars. In 1904, Wernicker [60] proved that every planar graph with minimum degree 5 has a $(5,6^-)$-edge. In 1940, Lebesgue [55] showed that every planar graph contains a $(3,11^-)$-edge, $(4,7^-)$-edge, or $(5,6^-)$-edge, where the parameters 6 and 7 are tight. In 1955, Kotzig [52] proved that for any 3-connected planar graph, $w_2 \leq 13$. Afterward, in 1972, Erdös (see [41]) conjectured that for every graph of minimum degree at least 3, it has that $w_2 \leq 13$, which was first confirmed by Borodin [4] who showed that every planar graph contains a $(3,10^-)$-edge, $(4,7^-)$-edge, or $(5,6^-)$-edge [6, 11, 12]. In 1992, Borodin [8] strengthened this to the following inequality:

$40e_{3,3} + 25e_{3,4} + 16e_{3,5} + 10e_{3,6} + \frac{20}{3}e_{3,7} + 5e_{3,8} + \frac{5}{2}e_{3,9} + 2e_{3,10} + \frac{50}{3}e_{4,4} + 11e_{4,5} + 5e_{4,6} + \frac{5}{3}e_{4,7} + \frac{16}{3}e_{5,5} + 2e_{5,6} \geq 120$

This inequality was further improve by Fabrici and Jendrol' [48] in 1996, who proved that

$20e_{3,3} + 25e_{3,4} + 16e_{3,5} + 10e_{3,6} + \frac{20}{3}e_{3,7} + 5e_{3,8} + \frac{5}{2}e_{3,9} + 2e_{3,10} + \frac{50}{3}e_{4,4} + 11e_{4,5} + 5e_{4,6} + \frac{5}{3}e_{4,7} + \frac{16}{3}e_{5,5} + 2e_{5,6} \geq 120$

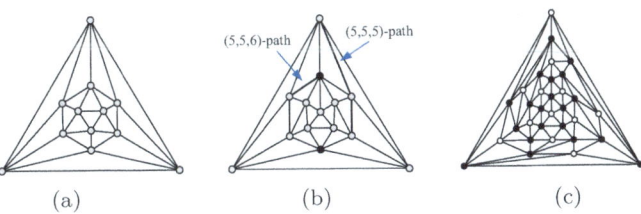

(a)   (b)   (c)

Fig. 2.1 Illustration for Remark 2.1

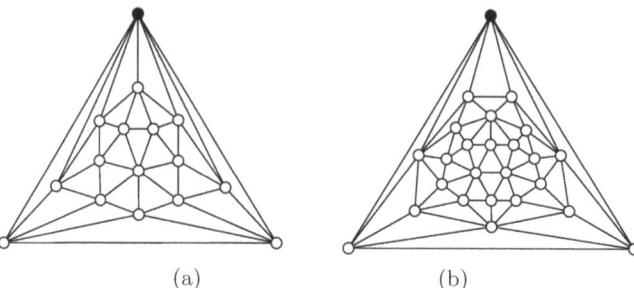

Fig. 2.2 Two maximal planar graphs: (a) $e_{5,5} = 28$, $e_{5,6} = 0$; (b) $e_{5,5} = 24$, $e_{5,6} = 4$

Notice that the above two inequalities are different only at the coefficient of $e_{3,3}$. Borodin proved that the result of by Fabrici and Jendrol' was also true for other planar graphs, except for a special multigraph.

In [8], Borodin also discussed the structure of paths in planar graphs with minimum degree 4. In addition, much more related results have been obtained for planar graphs with minimum degree 5. In 1973, Grünbaum [38] proved that if $e_{5,5} = 0$ then $e_{5,6} \geq 60$, and proposed the following conjecture.

Conjecture 2.1 $2e_{5,5} + e_{5,6} \geq 60$.

Unfortunately, Conjecture 2.1 was disproved by Fisk (see [42]), who constructed a counterexample, as shown in Fig. 2.2a, in which $e_{5,5} = 28$ and $e_{5,6} = 0$ (this implies that the coefficient before $e_{5,5}$ is at least $\frac{15}{7}$). In 1982, Grünbaum and Shephard [42] asserted that $4e_{5,5} + e_{5,6} \geq 60$. The best result on Conjecture 2.1 was given by Borodin and Sander [34], who proved that $\frac{7}{3}e_{5,5} + e_{5,6} \geq 60$; this can not be improved further (see Fig. 2.2b, in which $e_{5,5} = 24$ and $e_{5,6} = 4$). A more detailed study on Conjecture 2.1 is given in literature [16, 39].

The proof of the following theorem, due to Borodin [9] in 1992, illustrates the idea that studies structural properties of maximal planar graphs of minimum degree 5 through discharging technique.

Theorem 2.2 *Let G be a planar graph with $\delta(G) = 5$. Then,*

(1) $\frac{18}{7}e_{5,5} + e_{5,6} \geq 60$;
(2) $2e_{5,5} + e_{5,6} + \frac{2}{7}e_{5,7} \geq 60$.

Proof By way of contradiction. To (1), let G be a counterexample, i.e., $\frac{18}{7}e_{5,5} + e_{5,6} < 60$ in G. Notice that the same is true for $G + e$ for every diagonal e of a face in G. Thus, a finite number of steps result in a maximal planar graph G' that dissatisfies (1). We assign every vertex v a charge of $c(v) = d_{G'}(v) - 6$ and every element $x \in E(G') \cup F$ a charge of $c(x) = 0$, where F is the set of faces of G'. By Formula (2.2), the initial charge $c(G') = -12$. Evidently, only 5-vertices have negative amounts of initial charge. To arrive at a contradiction eventually, we have

2.2 Structure of Path

to define discharging transformation $\varphi = (\varphi_1, \varphi_2, \varphi_3, \varphi_4)$ such that the final charge of G' is changed.

(1) φ_1: for every (5, 5, 7)-face of G', transfer a charge of $\frac{2}{35}$ from its (5,5)-edge to its 7-vertex; formally, let $\triangle uu'v$ be a (5, 5, 7)-face of G',

$$\varphi_1(c(uu'), c(v)) = (c(uu') - \frac{2}{35}, c(v) + \frac{2}{35})$$

(2) φ_2: for every $(5, 8^+)$-edge of G', transfer a charge of $\frac{1}{4}$ from the 8^+-vertex to this edge; formally, let uv be a $(5, 8^+)$-edge of G',

$$\varphi_2(c(v), c(uv)) = (c(v) - \frac{1}{4}, c(uv) + \frac{1}{4})$$

(3) φ_3: for every (5, 7)-edge of G', transfer a charge of $\frac{1}{5}$ from the 7-vertex to this edge; formally, let uv be a (5, 7)-edge of G',

$$\varphi_3(c(v), c(uv)) = (c(v) - \frac{1}{5}, c(uv) + \frac{1}{5})$$

(4) φ_4: every 5-vertex receives a charge of $\frac{1}{5}$ from each of its incident edges; formally, let v be a 5-vertex and uv an edge incident with v,

$$\varphi_4(c(uv), c(v)) = (c(uv) - \frac{1}{5}, c(v) + \frac{1}{5})$$

Denote by c' the resulting charge of elements (vertices, edges and faces) of G' after discharging φ. Let v be a k-vertex of G'. When $k \geq 8$, v transfers at most $\frac{k}{4}$ to its incident edges (by φ_2); therefore, $c'(v) \geq c(v) - \frac{k}{4} = \frac{3k-24}{4} \geq 0$. When $k = 7$, if v is incident with at most five (5, 7)-edges, then $c'(v) \geq c(v) - \frac{5}{5} = 0$ ((by φ_3)); if v is incident with six (5, 7)-edges, then v is incident with five (5,5,7)-faces and hence $c'(v) \geq c(v) - \frac{6}{5} + \frac{2 \times 5}{35} = \frac{3}{35} > 0$. When $k = 6$, $c'(v) = c(v) = 0$ (by φ_1 and φ_3). Finally, when $k = 5$, $c'(v) = c(v) + \frac{1}{5} \times 5 = 0$ (by φ_4).

Let $e = uv$ be an edge of G'. If e is a $(5, 7^+)$-edge, then by φ_2, φ_3 and φ_4 we have $c'(e) \geq c(e) + \frac{1}{5} - \frac{1}{5} = 0$. If e is a (5,6)-edge, then by φ_4 it has that $c'(e) \geq c(e) - \frac{1}{5} = -\frac{1}{5}$. If e is a (5,5)-edge, then e is incident with at most two (5,5,7)-faces, and by φ_1 and φ_4 we have $c'(e) \geq c(e) - 2 \times \frac{2}{35} - 2 \times \frac{1}{5} = -\frac{18}{35}$.

In addition, by $\varphi_1, \varphi_2, \varphi_3$ and φ_4 we have $c'(f) = c(f) = 0$ for every $f \in F$. Therefore, by the assumption of $\frac{18}{7} e_{5,5} + e_{5,6} < 60$, the final charge

$$c'(G) = \sum_{v \in V(G)} c'(v) + \sum_{e \in E(G)} c'(e) + \sum_{f \in F} c'(f)$$

$$\geq -\frac{18}{35}e_{5,5} - \frac{1}{5}e_{5,6}$$
$$= -\frac{1}{5}(\frac{18}{7}e_{5,5} + e_{5,6}) > -12 \neq c(G).$$

This gets a contradiction and completes the proof of (1).

In the following, we prove (2) through a similar line of thought. Suppose that G' is a counterexample for which $2e_{5,5} + e_{5,6} + \frac{2}{7}e_{5,7} < 60$. We initially assign every vertex v a charge of $c(v) = d_{G'}(v) - 6$ and every element $x \in E(G') \cup F$ a charge of $c(x) = 0$, where F is the set of faces of G'. By Formula (2.2), the initial charge of $c(G') = -12$. Then, we define a discharging transformation $\varphi = (\varphi_2, \varphi'_3, \varphi_4)$, where φ_2 and φ_4 are defined in (1) and

φ'_3: for every $(5, 7)$-edge of G', transfer a charge of $\frac{1}{7}$ from the 7-vertex to this edge; formally, let uv be a $(5, 7)$-edge of G',

$$\varphi'_3(c(v), c(uv)) = (c(v) - \frac{1}{7}, c(uv) + \frac{1}{7})$$

Let c' be the final charge after discharging $\varphi = (\varphi_2, \varphi'_3, \varphi_4)$, and similarly we have $c'(v) \geq 0$ for every $v \in G'$ and $c'(e) \geq 0$ for every e is not a $(5, 5)$-edge, $(5, 6)$-edge or $(5, 7)$-edge. Further, by φ_4, when e is a $(5,5)$-edge, $c'(e) = -\frac{2}{5}$; when e is a $(5,6)$-edge, $c'(e) = -\frac{1}{5}$; when e is a $(5,7)$-edge, $c'(e) = \frac{1}{7} - \frac{2}{5} = -\frac{2}{35}$. Therefore, the final charge of G' is

$$c'(G') \geq -\frac{2}{5}e_{5,5} - \frac{1}{5}e_{5,6} - \frac{2}{35}e_{5,7} = -\frac{1}{5}(2e_{5,5} + e_{5,6} + \frac{2}{7}) > -12 \neq c(G')$$

This gets a contradiction. ∎

2.2.2 3-Path

In 1922, Frankin [37] proved the following theorem, which is fundamental in the structural theory of planar graphs.

Theorem 2.3 *Every planar graph G with $\delta(G) = 5$ has a $(6^-, 5, 6^-)$-path.*

Remark 2.2 There are planar graphs of minimum degree 5, which contains only $(5,5,5)$-paths (see the icosahedron in Fig. 2.1a), contains both $(5,5,5)$-paths and $(5,5,6)$-paths (see Fig. 2.1b), and contains $(6,5,6)$-paths (see Fig. 2.3).

In planar graphs, many conclusions on w_3 have been observed. Ando et al. [1] proved that every 3-connected planar graph satisfies $w_3 \leq 21$, which is sharp. In 1999, Jendrol' [46] showed that each 3-connected planar graph has a 3-path uvx such that $\max\{d_G(u), d_G(v), d_G(x)\} \leq 15$ (the bound is precise) and a 4-path $uvxy$ such that $\max\{d_G(u), d_G(v), d_G(x), d_G(y)\} \leq 23$. Further, Jendrol' [45] obtained

2.2 Structure of Path

Fig. 2.3 Illustration for Remark 2.2

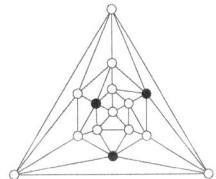

Fig. 2.4 The Jendrol'construction containing only $(3^+, 15^+, 3^+)$-path, which confirms the tightness of $w_3 \leq 21$

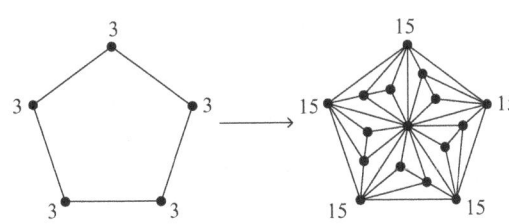

Fig. 2.5 The graph $K_{2,2t}^*$ containing only $(3, 3, \infty)$-paths and $(3, \infty, 3)$-paths

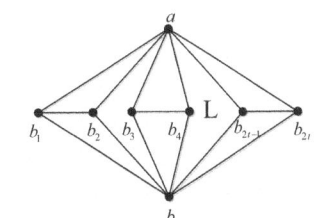

a more strong result, showing that a 3-path must belong to one of 10 types, in which $d_G(u) + d_G(v) + d_G(w)$ varies from 23 to 16. In addition, Jendrol' [45] also constructed a 3-connected planar graph which contains only an (a, b, c)-path that satisfies $a + b + c \geq 21$; see Fig. 2.4. This indicates that the result $w_3 \leq 21$ is sharp.

Remark 2.3 The requirement of 3-connectedness is essential for the finiteness of w_3, as shown by the construction $K_{2,2t}^*$ in Fig. 2.5. Clearly, every 3-path in $K_{2,2t}^*$ must contain vertices a and b, and w_3 will increase when the value of t increases.

In 1997, Borodin [13] obtained a refinement of the result $w_3 \leq 21$, obtained by Ando et al. [1].

Theorem 2.4 ([13]) *Let G be a planar graph with $\delta(G) \geq 3$. If G contains no $K_{2,4}^*$, then*

(1) either $w_3 \leq 18$ or a vertex of degree 15 adjacent to two 3-vertices,
(2) either $w_3 \leq 17$ or $w_2 \leq 7$.

∎

By Theorem 2.4, there are the following corollaries.

Corollary 2.1 ([13]) s Let G be a planar graph with $\delta(G) \geq 3$. Then

(1) if $w_2 > 6$, then $w_3 \leq 21$,
(2) if $\delta(G) \geq 4$, then $w_3 \leq 17$,
(3) if G is 3-connected and $\delta(G) \geq 4$, then G has a path uvx such that $\max\{d_G(u), d_G(v), d_G(x)\} \leq 9$.

■

Observe that $w_3 \leq 21$ and $w_3 \leq 17$ are tight; the fact that $w_3 \leq 18$ is tight is proved by Borodin until 2013 [29].

Theorem 2.5 ([29]) Let G be a planar graph with $\delta(G) \geq 3$ and without $K_{2,4}^*$. Then, G has a 3-path of one of the following types: $(3, 4^-, 11^-), (3, 7^-, 5^-)$, $(3, 10^-, 4^-), (3, 15^-, 3), (4^-, 4^-, 9^-), (6^-, 4^-, 8^-), (7^-, 4^-, 7^-), (6^-, 5^-, 6^-)$, which description is tight. Where a description is called **tight** if none of its parameters can be strengthened and no term dropped.

Clearly, Theorem 2.5 extends the conclusions of Franklin's [37] and Ando, Iwasaki, Kanekos' [1], but does not imply Theorem 2.4. In 2016, Borodin, Ivanova, Kostochka [32] gave a tight refinement of Theorem 2.4.

The proofs of Theorems 2.3, 2.4 and 2.5 are hidden in the proof of the following theorem (Theorem 2.6). So, we omit these proofs here.

Theorem 2.6 ([32]) Let G be a planar graph with $\delta(G) \geq 3$ and without two adjacent 3-vertices lying in two common 3-faces. Then, G has a 3-path of one of the following types: $(3, 15^-, 3), (3, 10^-, 4^-), (3, 8^-, 5^-), (4^-, 7^-, 4^-), (5^-, 5^-, 7^-)$, $(6^-, 5^-, 6^-), (3, 4^-, 11^-), (4^-, 4^-, 9^-), (6^-, 4^-, 7^-)$, which description is tight.

Proof The tightness is verified by the following planar graphs.

- $(3, 15^-, 3)$-path. Figure 2.4 is a planar graph containing only 3-vertices, 4-vertices and 15-vertices. From the structure one can see that every 3-path goes through a 15-vertex, which proves the tightness of $(3, 15^-, 3)$-paths.
- $(3, 10^-, 4^-)$-path. The graph of Fig. 2.6a is a planar graph whose internal vertices have degree 3,4, or 10 only, and 3-vertices is not adjacent to 4^--vertices. The vertices on its boundary have degree-sequence (in clockwise direction) 97569756. Take two copies of this graph and glue them along the boundary such that every equatorial vertex in the resulting graph has degree at least 11 and is not adjacent to 3-vertices. Thus, the resulting graph contains only $(3^+, 10^+, 4^+)$-path. Thus, this type of 3-paths are sharp.
- $(3, 8^-, 5^-)$-path. Take two copies of Fig. 2.6b, and glue them along the boundary to form a maximal planar graph in which no two 4-vertices are at distance at most 2 and no 3-path containing a 7-vertices. Therefore, the resulting graph contains no 3-path other than $(3^+, 8^+, 5^+)$-path. This confirms the tightness of $(3, 8^-, 5^-)$-paths.

2.2 Structure of Path

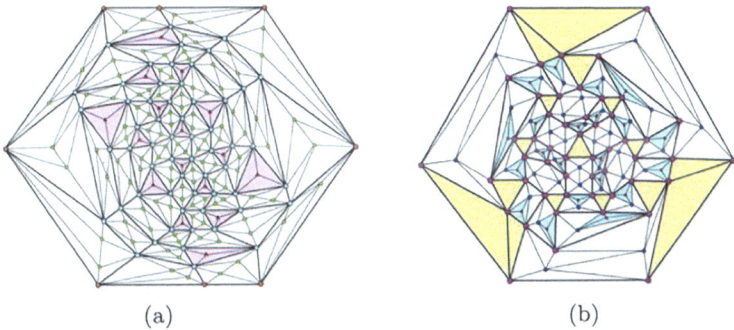

Fig. 2.6 (**a**) A half of triangulation containing only $(3^+, 10^+, 4^+)$-paths among the 3-paths mentioned in Theorem 2.6, which confirms the tightness of $(3, 10^-, 4^-)$-path; (**b**) a half of triangulation containing only $(3^+, 8^+, 5^+)$-paths among the 3-paths mentioned in Theorem 2.6, which confirms the tightness of $(3, 8^-, 5^-)$-path

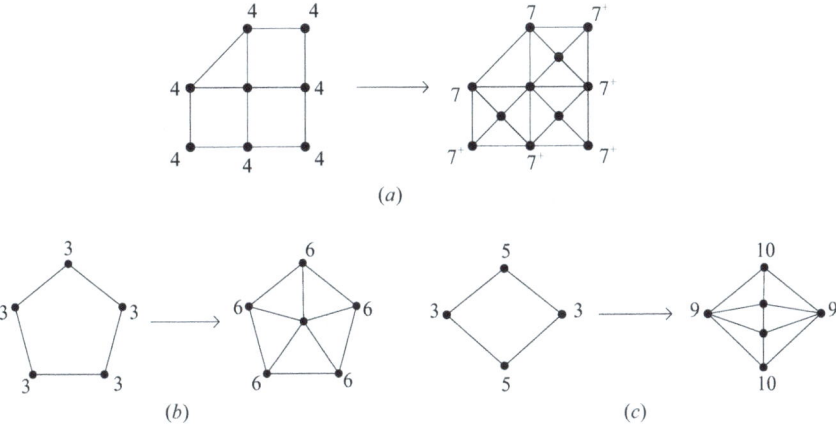

Fig. 2.7 Constructions pertaining to $(4^-, 7^-, 4^-)$-path, $(5^-, 5^-, 7^-)$-path, and $(6^-, 5^-, 6^-)$-path

- $(4^-, 7^-, 4^-)$-path, $(5^-, 5^-, 7^-)$-path, and $(6^-, 5^-, 6^-)$-path. Figure 2.7a shows an operation of constructing, from the dual of the (3,4,4,4)-Archimedean solid, a maximal planar graph containing only 4-vertices and 7-vertices; Fig. 2.7b shows how to transform the dodecahedron to a triangulation, in which each 5-vertex is surrounded by 6-vertices and there are no 4^--vertices. by the operation of Fig. 2.7c one can construct a maximal planar graph, in which each 4-vertex is surrounded by three 9^+-vertices and there are no 3^--vertices. There three Fig. 2.7a–c confirm the tightness of $(4^-, 7^-, 4^-)$-paths, $(5^-, 5^-, 7^-)$-paths, and $(6^-, 5^-, 6^-)$-paths.
- $(5^-, 5^-, 7^-)$-path. Take two copies of the semi-maximal planar graphs shown in Fig. 2.8a, and glue them along the boundary to form a maximal planar graph in

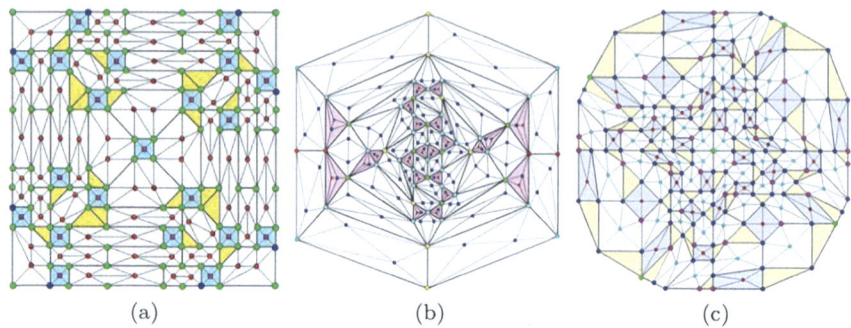

Fig. 2.8 (a) A half of the maximal planar graph with only $(5^+, 5^+, 7^+)$-paths proving the tightness of $(5^-, 5^-, 7^-)$-paths; (b) a bit more than a half of a maximal planar graph with only $(3^+, 4^+, 11^+)$-paths among those mentioned in Theorem 2.6, which implies the sharpness of $(3, 4^-, 11^-)$-paths; (c) a half of the maximal planar graph with only $(6^+, 4^+, 7^+)$-paths which confirms the tightness of $(6^-, 4^-, 7^-)$-paths

which there are no 3-vertex, each 4-vertex is surrounded by 7^+-vertices, and each 5-vertex is adjacent to four 7^+-vertices. Thus, $(5^-, 5^-, 7^-)$-paths are sharp.

- $(3, 4^-, 11^-)$-path. Take two copies of the semi-maximal planar graphs shown in Fig. 2.8b, and glue them along the boundary to form a maximal planar graph in which there are only 3-,4-, and 11^+-vertices, and no vertex is adjacent to two 3-vertices. Thus, there are only $(3, 4^-, 11^-)$-paths among the 3-paths in Theorem 2.6.
- $(6^-, 4^-, 7^-)$-path. Take two copies of the semi-maximal planar graphs in Fig. 2.8c, and glue them along the boundary to form a maximal planar graph in which there are only $(6^-, 4^-, 7^-)$-paths among those mentioned in Theorem 2.6.

The following presents the main proof of the theorem. We distinguish three parts.

Part I. Counterexample to Theorem 2.6

The proof of the main statement of Theorem 2.6 proceeds by way of contradiction. Let G be a counterexample to Theorem 2.6 with the maximum edges, i.e., G is a planar graph satisfies: (1) $\delta(G) \geq 3$; (2) G contains no two adjacent 3-vertices lying in two common 3-faces; (3) G contains no 3-paths of the types among those mentioned in Theorem 2.6; (4) for every planar graph G' such that $|V(G')|=|V(G)|$ and $|E(G')| > |E(G)|$, if G' satisfies (1) and (2), then G' contains a type of 3-paths mentioned in Theorem 2.6.

Claim 1 G is a maximal planar graph

It is enough to show that every face of G is a 3-face. Suppose to the contrary that G contains a 4^+-face, say $f = abc \ldots$. Without loss of generality, we assume that b is a vertex of the minimum degree among all vertices incident with f and, moreover, $d_G(a) \leq d_G(c)$. To get a contradiction, we would prove that $G + ac$ is also a counterexample to Theorem 2.6.

2.2 Structure of Path

Since $\delta(G) \geq 3$ and G contains no two adjacent 3-vertices lying in two common 3-faces, $G + ac$ does not contain $K_{2,4}^*$. By the assumption of G, $G + ac$ has a forbidden 3-path which is zac or acz. If $z \neq b$, then the 3-path zab or bcz is a forbidden 3-path of G, since $d_G(b) \leq d_G(a) \leq d_G(c)$, a contradiction. Therefore, we may assume that $z = b$. To complete the proof of Claim A, the following three cases should be considered. In either case, a contradiction will be obtained by showing zac and acz are not forbidden.

Case 1 $d_G(b) = 3$. If $d_G(a) = 3$, then $d_G(c) \geq 12$ since G contains no $(3, 4^-, 11^-)$-path. Therefore, in $G + ac$, the 3-path bac and acb are either $(3^+, 13^+, 4^+)$-paths or $(3^+, 4^+, 13^+)$-paths, i.e., they are not forbidden. If $d_G(a)$ $=4$, then $d_G(c) \geq 10$ by the assumption that G contains no $(4^-, 4^-, 9^-)$-path. So, bac and acb in $G + ac$ are either $(3^+, 11^+, 5^+)$-paths or $(3^+, 5^+, 11^+)$-paths, and also they are not forbidden. Analogously, if $d_G(a) \in \{5, 6\}$, then $d_G(c) \geq 7$ by the nonexistence of $(6^-, 5^-, 6^-)$-path. This means that bac and acb in $G + ac$ are either $(3^+, 6^+, 8^+)$-paths or $(3^+, 8^+, 6^+)$-paths, and are not forbidden. The same is true if $7 \leq d(a) \leq d(c)$.

Case 2 $d_G(b) = 4$. If $d_G(a) = 4$, then $d_G(c) \geq 10$ by nonexistence of $(4^-, 4^-, 9^-)$-path in G, and bac and acb in $G + ac$ are $(4^+, 11^+, 5^+)$-paths or $(4^+, 5^+, 11^+)$-paths, which are admissible. If $5 \leq d_G(a) \leq 6$, then $d_G(c) \geq 8$ by nonexistence of $(6^-, 4^-, 7^-)$-path in G. So, bac and acb in $G + ac$ are $(4^+, 6^+, 9^+)$-paths or $(4^+, 9^+, 6^+)$-paths, which are admissible. If $d_G(a) \geq 7$ then $d_G(c) \geq 7$ by the assumption of $d_G(a) \leq d_G(c)$. As a result, bac and acb in $G + ac$ are $(8^+, 4^+, 8^+)$-paths or $(4^+, 8^+, 8^+)$-paths, which are admissible again.

Case 3 $d_G(b) \geq 5$. In this case, bac and acb in $G + ac$ are $(5^+, 6^+, 8^+)$-paths or $(5^+, 8^+, 6^+)$-paths, which are again not forbidden, as desired.

This completes the proof of Claim 1. The following property follows immediately from Claim 1: G does not contain any pair of adjacent 3-vertices.

Part II. Discharging
Initially, assign every vertex v a charge of $c(v) = d_G(v) - 6$ and every element $x \in E(G) \cup F$ a charge of $c(x) = 0$, where F is the set of faces of G. By Formula (2.2), the initial charge $c(G) = -12$. Clearly, only the charges of 5^--vertices are negative. To get a contradiction, we define a discharging transformation $\varphi = (\varphi_1, \varphi_2, \varphi_3)$, by which the final charge c' of G is nonnegative.

In what follows, we denote the vertices adjacent to a vertex v in a cyclic order by $v_1, v_2, \ldots, v_{d_G(v)}$. The rules of discharging $\varphi_1, \varphi_2, \varphi_3$ are as follows.

φ_1. Let v be a 3-vertex of G. If $4 \leq d_G(v_1) \leq 6$, then each of v_2, v_3 gives $\frac{3}{2}$ to v, i.e., for $i = 2, 3$,

$$\varphi_1(c(v_i), c(v)) = (c(v_i) - \frac{3}{2}, c(v) + \frac{3}{2});$$

if $d_G(v_i) \geq 7$, $1 \leq i \leq 3$, then each v_i gives 1 to v, i.e., for $i = 1, 2, 3$,

$$\varphi_1(c(v_i), c(v)) = (c(v_i) - 1, c(v) + 1);$$

Notices that $d_G(v_2) \geq 12$ and $d_G(v_3) \geq 12$ if $d_G(v_1) = 4$ due to the nonexistence of $(3, 4^-, 11^-)$-paths in G, $d_G(v_2) \geq 9$ and $d_G(v_3) \geq 9$ if $d_G(v_1) = 5$ due to the nonexistence of $(3, 8^-, 5^-)$-paths in G, and $d_G(v_2) \geq 8$ and $d_G(v_3) \geq 8$ if $d_G(v_1) = 6$ due to the nonexistence of $(6^-, 4^-, 7^-)$-path in G. Therefore, in either of cases, it holds that $c'(v) = c(v) + 3 = 0$ after φ_1.

φ_2. Let v be a 4-vertex of G.

(a) If $d_G(v_1) = 3$, then v receives 1 from v_3, and receives $\frac{1}{2}$ from each of v_2, v_4, i.e.,

$$\varphi_2(c(v_3), c(v)) = (c(v_3) - 1, c(v) + 1),$$

and for $i = 2, 4$,

$$\varphi_2(c(v_i), c(v)) = (c(v_2) - \frac{1}{2}, c(v) + \frac{1}{2});$$

(b) If $d_G(v_1) = 4$, then:

(b1) if $d_G(v_3) \leq 11$, then v receives $\frac{4}{5}$ from v_3 and $\frac{3}{5}$ from each of v_2, v_4, i.e., i.e.,

$$\varphi_2(c(v_3), c(v)) = (c(v_3) - \frac{4}{5}, c(v) + \frac{4}{5}),$$

and for $i = 2, 4$,

$$\varphi_2(c(v_i), c(v)) = (c(v_i) - \frac{3}{5}, c(v) + \frac{3}{5});$$

(b2) if $d_G(v_3) \geq 12$, $d_G(v_2) \leq 11$, and $d_G(v_4) \leq 11$, then v receives $\frac{4}{5}$ from v_3 and $\frac{3}{5}$ from each of v_2, v_4, i.e.,

$$\varphi_2(c(v_3), c(v)) = (c(v_3) - \frac{4}{5}, c(v) + \frac{4}{5}),$$

and for $i = 2, 4$,

$$\varphi_2(c(v_i), c(v)) = (c(v_i) - \frac{3}{5}, c(v) + \frac{3}{5});$$

(b3) if $d_G(v_3) \geq 12$, $d_G(v_2) \geq 12$, and $d_G(v_4) \leq 11$, then v receives $\frac{9}{10}$ from v_3, $\frac{1}{2}$ from v_2, and $\frac{3}{5}$ from v_4.

2.2 Structure of Path

$$\varphi_2(c(v_3), c(v)) = (c(v_3) - \frac{9}{10}, c(v) + \frac{9}{10}),$$

$$\varphi_2(c(v_2), c(v)) = (c(v_2) - \frac{1}{2}, c(v) + \frac{1}{2}),$$

and

$$\varphi_2(c(v_4), c(v)) = (c(v_4) - \frac{3}{5}, c(v) + \frac{3}{5});$$

(b4) if $d_G(v_3) \geq 12$, $d_G(v_2) \geq 12$, and $d_G(v_4) \geq 12$, then v receives 1 from v_3 and $\frac{1}{2}$ from each of v_2, v_4.

$$\varphi_2(c(v_3), c(v)) = (c(v_3) - 1, c(v) + 1)$$

and for $i = 2, 4$,

$$\varphi_2(c(v_i), c(v)) = (c(v_i) - \frac{1}{2}, c(v) + \frac{1}{2});$$

(c) If $5 \leq d_G(v_1) \leq 6$, then v receives $\frac{3}{4}$ from each of v_2 and v_4, and receives $\frac{1}{2}$ from v_3, i.e., for $i = 2, 4$,

$$\varphi_2(c(v_i), c(v)) = (c(v_i) - \frac{3}{4}, c(v) + \frac{3}{4});$$

and

$$\varphi_2(c(v_3), c(v)) = (c(v_3) - \frac{1}{2}, c(v) + \frac{1}{2});$$

(d) If $d_G(v_1) > 6$, then v receives $\frac{1}{2}$ from each of v_1, v_2 and v_3, i.e., for $i = 1, 2, 3$,

$$\varphi_2(c(v_i), c(v)) = (c(v_i) - \frac{1}{2}, c(v) + \frac{1}{2}).$$

Notices that G containing no $(3, 4^-, 11^-)$-paths implies that $d_G(v_i) \geq 12$ for $i = 2, 3, 4$ if $d_G(v_1) = 3$; G containing no $(4^-, 4^-, 9^-)$-paths implies that $d_G(v_i) \geq 10$ for $i = 2, 3, 4$ if $d_G(v_1) = 4$; G containing no $(6^-, 4^-, 7^-)$-paths implies that $d_G(v_i) \geq 8$ for $i = 2, 3, 4$ if $d_G(v_1) \in \{5, 6\}$; otherwise, $d_G(v_i) \geq 7$ for $i = 1, 2, 3, 4$. Therefore, for each 4-vertex, it has that $c'(v) = c(v) + 2 = 0$ after φ_2.

φ_3. Let v be a 5-vertex of G. If $d_G(v_1) \leq 5$, then v receives $\frac{1}{2}$ from each of v_3, v_4, i.e., for $i = 3, 4$,

$$\varphi_3(c(v_i), c(v)) = (c(v_i) - \frac{1}{2}, c(v) + \frac{1}{2})$$

otherwise, v receives $\frac{1}{4}$ from each of its neighbors of degree at least 7, i.e., for every $v' \in N_G(v)$ such that $d_G(v') \geq 7$,

$$\varphi_3(c(v'), c(v)) = (c(v') - \frac{1}{4}, c(v) + \frac{1}{4})$$

In φ_3, if $d_G(v_1) \leq 5$, then $d_G(v_i) \geq 8$ for $i = 2, 3, 4, 5$ since G contains no $(5^-, 5^-, 7^-)$-paths; otherwise, it has that $d_G(v_1) \geq 6$ and $d_G(v_i) \geq 7$ for $i = 2, 3, 4, 5$ since G contains no $(6^-, 5^-, 6^-)$-paths. This implies that $c'(v) = c(v) + 1 = 0$ after φ_3.

Part III. Checking $c'(G) \geq 0$

By the discharging rule $\varphi = (\varphi_1, \varphi_2, \varphi_3)$ given in Part II, we see that $c'(x) = c(x) = 0$ for every $x \in E(G) \cup F$. In addition, it has been proved that $c'(v) \geq 0$ for every vertex v of degree at most 5. Therefore, we need to prove $c'(v) \geq 0$ for every vertex v of degree at least 6. To do this, a lot of cases have to be discussed (in [32] the authors distinguished eight cases). This is a simple but a tedious work, so we leave it to the readers.

Thus, we have proved $c'(v) \geq 0$ for every $v \in V(G)$ and hence $c'(G) \geq 0 > -12$. This gets a contradiction and completes the proof of Theorem 2.6. ∎

Remark 2.4 By Theorem 2.6, every planar graph contains a 2^--vertices, a $(3, 3, \infty)$-path, or a type of 3-paths mentioned in Theorem 2.6.

Based on the results in Theorems 2.5 and 2.6, Borodin, et al. proposed a challenging problem as follows.

Problem 2.1 ([32]) Describe all tight descriptions of 3-paths in planar graphs G with $\delta(G) \geq 3$ and $g(G) \geq 3$.

Remark 2.5 To make modest contribution to Problem 2.1, the authors in [32] gave a description of all one-term descriptions in an arbitrary planar graph: there exist precisely three one-term tight descriptions of 3-paths: $(10^-, 5^-, \infty)$, $(5^-, 10^-, \infty)$, and $(5^-, \infty, 6^-)$.

From the above conclusions, one can see that it is hard to characterize the structure of 3-paths in planar graphs. Therefore, scholars turn to the study of 3-paths in planar graphs with some forbidden properties. In 2015, Borodin and Ivanova [20] proved the following theorem.

2.2 Structure of Path

Theorem 2.7 ([20]) *Let G be a planar graph with $\delta(G) \geq 3$ and $g(G) \geq 4$. Then, the following seven descriptions of 3-paths are tight.*

(1) $(5^-, 3, 6^-) \cup (4^-, 3, 7^-);$
(2) $(3, 5^-, 3) \cup (3, 4^-, 4^-);$
(3) $(5^-, 3, 6^-) \cup (3, 4^-, 3);$
(4) $(3, 5^-, 3) \cup (4^-, 3, 4^-);$
(5) $(5^-, 3, 7^-);$
(6) $(3, 5^-, 4^-);$
(7) $(5^-, 4, 6^-).$

In [24], Borodin and Ivanova observed an analogous result as that by Franklin [37] (Theorem 2.3).

Theorem 2.8 ([24]) *Every 3-connected planar graph of minimum degree 5 has a $(5, 6^-, 6^-)$-path, which is tight.*

Proof The tightness is verified by the graph obtained by replacing each face of the icosahedron by the configuration shown in Fig. 2.9 (since the resulting graph contains neither $(5, 6^-, 5)$-paths nor $(5, 5, 6^-)$-paths).

The proof of the main statement of this theorem is analogous to that of Theorem 2.6, which is not so complicated. Let G be a counterexample to Theorem 2.8 having the most edges. One can readily check that G is a maximal planar graph.

Let the initial charge c be: $c(v) = d(v) - 6$ and $c(x) = 0$ for $x \in E(G) \cup F$ where F is the set of faces of G. Thus, only 5-vertices have a negative initial charge and by Formula (2.2) $c(G) = -12$.

Define a discharging $\varphi = (\varphi_1, \varphi_2)$ as follows:

φ_1. Every 6^+-vertex gives $\frac{1}{4}$ to its every adjacent 5-vertex.

φ_2. Every 7^+-vertex gives $\frac{1}{8}$ to its every adjacent 6-vertex.

By $\varphi = (\varphi_1, \varphi_2)$, one can check that the final charge c' satisfies that $c'(v) \geq 0$ for $v \in V(G)$ and $c'(x) = c(x) = 0$ for $x \in E(G) \cup F$. This implies that $c'(G) \geq 0 > -12 = c(G)$, and arrives at a contradiction. ∎

For the detailed proof of Theorem 2.8, one can refer to [24] (Theorem 2). The authors in [24] also made a modest contribution to Problem 2.1 by the following theorem.

Fig. 2.9 A construction showing the tightness of Theorem 2.8

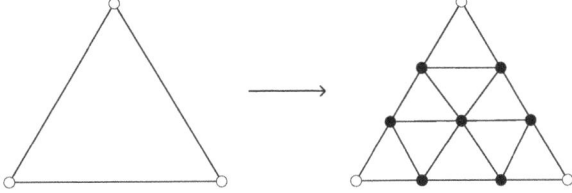

Theorem 2.9 ([24]) *Let G an arbitrary 3-connected planar graph with minimum degree 5. Then, G contains no tight descriptions of 3-paths other than $(5, 6^-, 6^-)$-paths and $(6^-, 5, 6^-)$-paths.*

Proof Let $\mathcal{D}$ be the set of 3-connected planar graph with minimum degree 5. Suppose $D = \{(x_1, y_1, z_1), \ldots, (x_k, y_k, z_k)\}$ is a tight description of 3-paths in $\mathcal{D}$. Then,

(1) every graph in $\mathcal{D}$ contains a (x_i, y_i, z_i)-path for at least one i such that $1 \leq i \leq k$, and

(2) if we delete any term (x_i, y_i, z_i) from D or decrease any parameter in D by one without changing the other $3k - 1$ parameters, then the new description is not satisfied by at least one $D \in \mathcal{D}$.

Clearly, all parameters are at least 5. Observer that, by its tightness, the description D cannot have triplets (x_j, y_j, z_j) and $(x_{j'}, y_{j'}, z_{j'})$ such that $x_j \leq x_{j'}, y_j \leq y_{j'}, z_j \leq z_{j'}$ (otherwise $D = D \setminus \{(x_j, y_j, z_j)\}$ is equivalent to D but shorter).

Case 1. D has a term $(5^+, 6^+, 6^+)$. By Theorem 2.8, D is true and not stronger than the tight description $(5, 6^-, 6^-)$, which implies that $D = \{(5, 6^-, 6^-)\}$.

Case 2. D has a term $(6^+, 5^+, 6^+)$. By Theorem 2.3, D is true and not stronger than the tight description $(6^-, 5, 6^-)$, so $D=(6^-, 5, 6^-)$.

Case 3. Every term in D has at most one parameter greater than 5.

Such a D is not a description at all, since all 3-paths in the graph partly shown in Fig. 2.9 go through at most one 5-vertex. This proves that there are precisely two tight descriptions of 3-paths in $\mathcal{D}$, as desired. ∎

The above presents a review on the problem of describing all tight descriptions of 3-paths in planar graphs, by in contrast there are few literature that discuss tight descriptions of 4-paths in planar graphs, even restricted to 3-connected planar graphs with minimum degree 5. In 1996, Jendrol' and Madaras [49] proved that every connected planar graph of minimum degree 5 contains a 4-path of weight at most 23, which is tight. In 2016, Borodin and Ivanova [25], by Theorem 2.7, proved that every 3-connected planar graph with minimum degree 5 contains $(6^-, 5, 6^-, 6^-)$-paths or $(5, 5, 5, 7^-)$-paths, and Ivanova [44] confirmed the existence of tight descriptions of 4-paths: $(5, 6^-, 6^-, 6^-)$-paths or $(5, 5, 5, 7^-)$-paths.

In 2000, Madaras [56] proved that every maximal planar graph with minimum degree 4 satisfies $w_4 \leq 31$ and constructed a graph with $w_4 = 27$. In 2016, Borodin and Ivanova [27] improved this result; they proved that every maximal planar graph with minimum degree at least 4 satisfies $w_4 \leq 27$, which is tight.

In 2017, Batueva, Borodin and Ivanova [3] gave all tight descriptions of 4-paths in 3-connected planar graphs with minimum degree 5.

Theorem 2.10 *There exist precisely ten tight descriptions of 4-paths in 3-connected planar graphs with minimum degree 5.*

(1) $(5, 6^-, 6^-, 6^-) \cup (5, 5, 5, 7^-)$,
(2) $(6^-, 5, 6^-, 6^-) \cup (5, 5, 5, 7^-)$,
(3) $(5, 6^-, 6^-, 6^-) \cup (5, 5, 7^-, 5)$,

(4) $(6^-, 5, 6^-, 6^-) \cup (5, 5, 7^-, 5)$,
(5) $(5, 6^-, 6^-, 7^-)$,
(6) $(6^-, 5, 6^-, 7^-)$,
(7) $(6^-, 6^-, 5, 7^-)$,
(8) $(5, 6^-, 7^-, 6^-)$,
(9) $(5, 7^-, 6^-, 6^-)$,
(10) $(6^-, 5, 7^-, 6^-)$.

2.3 Faces

Let G be a planar graph with $\delta(G) \geq 3$ and $3 \leq g(G) \leq 5$. The **weight** $w(f)$ of a face f in G is the sum of degrees of its incident vertices. The **weight** $w(G)$ (or simply w) of G is the minimum weight of 5^--faces in G. Let $v_1, v_2, \ldots, v_\ell$ be the vertices in the boundary of f, and let $d_G(v_i) = k_i$ for $i = 1, 2, \ldots, \ell$. If $k_1 \leq k_2 \leq \ldots \leq k_\ell$, then we say that f is a **face of type** $(k_1, k_2, \ldots, k_\ell)$ or simply $(k_1, k_2, k_3, \ldots, k_\ell)$-face.

A 3-face is **pyramidal** if it is incident with at least two 4^--vertices, and a 4-face is **pyramidal** if it is incident with at least three 3-vertices. Observe that if G contains pyramidal faces, then $w(G)$ can be arbitrarily large [26].

Lebesgue [55] in 1940 described the structure of 5^--faces in a planar graph G with $\delta(G) \geq 3$ and $g(G) \geq 3$.

Theorem 2.11 ([55]) *Let G be a planar graph G such that $\delta(G) \geq 3$ and $g(G) \geq 3$. Then, G has a 5^--face belonging to one of the following types:* $(3, 6, \infty)$, $(3, 7, 41^-)$, $(3, 8, 23^-)$, $(3, 9, 17^-)$, $(3, 10, 14^-)$, $(3, 11, 13^-)$, $(4, 4, \infty)$, $(4, 5, 19^-)$, $(4, 6, 11^-)$, $(4, 7, 9^-)$, $(5, 5, 9^-)$, $(5, 6, 7^-)$, $(3, 3, 3, \infty)$, $(3, 3, 4^-, 11^-)$, $(3, 3, 5^-, 7^-)$, $(3, 4, 4^-, 5^-)$, $(3, 3, 3, 3, 5^-)$.

For special classes of planar graphs, some parameters in Theorem 2.11 have been improved. In 1963, Kotzig [53] proved that every planar graph G with $\delta(G) = 5$ satisfied $w(G) \leq 18$, and conjectured that $w(G) \leq 17$. Afterward in 1989, Borodin [5] confirmed this conjecture.

Theorem 2.12 ([5]) *Every planar graph of minimum degree 5 has a $(5, 5, 7^-)$-face or $(5, 6, 6^-)$-face, where all parameters are best possible.*

Theorem 2.12 also prove a conjecture proposed by Grünbaum [40] in 1975, which is stated that the **cyclic connectivity** (i.e., the minimum number of edges in a graph whose removal results in two components each of which has a cycle) of every 5-connected planar graph is at most 11, where bound is sharp.

In 1992, Borodin [7] improved this result by analyzing the number of $(5, 5, 5)$-, $(5, 5, 6)$-, $(5, 5, 7)$-, and $(5, 6, 6)$-faces.

Theorem 2.13 ([7]) *Every planar graph of minimum degree 5 satisfies that*

$$18f_{5,5,5} + 9f_{5,5,6} + 5f_{5,5,7} + 4f_{5,6,6} \geq 144 \tag{2.5}$$

Moreover, there are maximal planar graph, in which all coefficients in (2.5), except possibly the third one, are tight, while the third can not be less than 3.

Proof By way of contradiction and using the discharging technique. Let G be a counterexample to Theorem 2.13 which contains the maximum number of edges, i.e.,

$$18f_{5,5,5} + 9f_{5,5,6} + 5f_{5,5,7} + 4f_{5,6,6} < 144 \tag{2.6}$$

Then, every 6^+-vertex of G is incident with only 3-faces; since if there is a 6^+-vertex incident with a 4^+-face, then we can add a diagonal edge incident with the 6^+-vertex in the 4^+-face such that no new $(5, 5, 5)$-, $(5, 5, 6)$-, $(5, 5, 7)$-, or $(5, 6, 6)$-face is produced. Observe that the coefficients in (2.6) monotonically decrease; one can check that (2.6) still holds if some $(5, 5, 5)$-face turns into a $(5, 5, 6)$-face, or if some $(5, 5, 6)$-face turns into a $(5, 5, 7)$- or a $(5, 6, 6)$-face.

We may assume that G is connected. Let V, E, F denote the set of vertices, edges, and faces of G, respectively, and let F_i denote the set of faces of degree i. By the Euler's Formula (Formula (1.12)) and the observation that $2|E| = \sum_{v \in V} d_G(v) = \sum_{i \geq 3} i |F_i|$, one gets

$$\sum_{v \in V}(d_G(v) - 6) + \sum_{i \geq 4}(2i - 6)|F_i| = -12 \tag{2.7}$$

Let $t(v)$ be the number of 3-faces incident with v. Since $2i - 6 \geq \frac{i}{2}$ when $i \geq 4$, it follows from Formula (2.7) that $\sum_{v \in V}(d_G(v) - 6) + \sum_{i \geq 4} \frac{i|F_i|}{2} \leq -12$, and hence, by the observation that $\sum_{i \geq 4} i|F_i| = \sum_{i \geq 3} i|F_i| - 3|F_3| = \sum_{v \in V} d_G(v) - \sum_{v \in V} t(v)$, we have

$$\sum_{v \in V}(d_G(v) - 6 + \frac{d_G(v) - t(v)}{2}) \leq -12 \tag{2.8}$$

Let the initial charge c of G be: $c(v) = d_G(v) - 6 + \frac{d_G(v) - t(v)}{2}$ for every $v \in V$ and every element $x \in E \cup F$ a charge of $c(x) = 0$. By Formula (2.7), the initial charge $c(G) \leq -12$, i.e.,

$$\sum_{v \in (V \cup E \cup F)} c(x) \leq -12 \tag{2.9}$$

2.3 Faces

Now, we redistribute the charge by the following discharging transformation $\varphi = (\varphi_1, \varphi_2)$ as follows.

φ_1. Let v be a 7^+-vertex of G. Then, v is incident with only 3-face. Transfer each 3-face f that is incident with v and incident with at least one 5-vertex, from v, an amount of charge equal to

(a) $\frac{d_G(v)-6}{d_G(v)}$, if $d_G(v) \geq 8$; that is, $\varphi_1(c(v), c(f)) = (c(v) - \frac{d_G(v)-6}{d_G(v)}, c(f) + \frac{d_G(v)-6}{d_G(v)})$;

(b) $\frac{1}{6}$, if $d_G(v) = 7$ but f is not a (5,5,7)–face; that is, $\varphi_1(c(v), c(f)) = (c(v) - 16, c(f) + \frac{1}{6})$.

φ_2. Let v be a 5-vertex and $f = \triangle\ uvw$ be a 3-face incident with v. Then, f transfers to v an amount of charge as follows:

(a) $\frac{1}{2}$ if f is a (5,5,5)-face, i.e., $\varphi_2(c(f), c(v)) = (c(f) - \frac{1}{2}, c(v) + \frac{1}{2})$;
(b) $\frac{3}{8}$ if f is a (5,5,6)-face, i.e., $\varphi_2(c(f), c(v)) = (c(f) - \frac{3}{8}, c(v) + \frac{3}{8})$;
(c) $\frac{5}{24}$ if f is a (5,5,7)-face, i.e., $\varphi_2(c(v), c(v)) = (c(f) - \frac{5}{24}, c(v) + \frac{5}{24})$;
(d) $\frac{1}{3}$ if f is a (5,6,6)-face, i.e., $\varphi_2(c(f), c(v)) = (c(f) - \frac{1}{3}, c(v) + \frac{1}{3})$;
  let c_x be the charge which is transferred from x to f by φ_1, if $d_G(x) \geq 6$ for $x \in \{u, w\}$.
(e) $c_u + c_w$ if $d_G(u) \geq 6$ and $d_G(w) \geq 6$, i.e., $\varphi_2(c(f), c(v)) = (c(f) - (c_u + c_w), c(v) + (c_u + c_w))$;
(f) $\frac{1}{2}c_w$ if $d_G(u) = 5$ and $d_G(w) \geq 8$, i.e., $\varphi_2(c(f), c(v)) = (c(f) - \frac{c_w}{2}, c(v) + \frac{c_w}{2})$.

Observe that, by φ_1 and φ_2, every 3-face i transfers at least $\frac{1}{8}$ to each of its incident 5-vertices, and the lower bound is tight for $(5, 5, 8)$-faces.

We now show that the final charge of every vertex $v \in V$ is nonnegative. If $d_G(v) = 6$ or $d_G(v) \geq 8$, it is easy to see that $c'(v) \geq 0$. If $d_G(v) = 7$, then v is incident with at most six $(5, 6^+, 7)$-faces and hence by $\varphi_1(a)$ $c'(v) \geq c(v) - 1 \geq 0$. In the following, we may assume $d_G(v) = 5$. Let v_1, v_2, v_3, v_4, v_5 are the neighbors of v lying around v in a clockwise order.

- $t(v) \leq 3$. Then, it is direct to see that $c'(v) \geq c(v) \geq -1 + \frac{2}{2} = 0$.
- $t(v) = 4$. Since v receives at least $\frac{1}{8}$ from each its incident 3-face, it has that $c'(v) \geq c(v) + \frac{4}{8} \geq= 0$.
- $t(v) = 5$. In this case, if v is incident with at least one $(5, 5, 5)$-face, then $c'(v) \geq -1 + \frac{1}{2} + \frac{4}{8} = 0$. Therefore, we may assume that v is not incident with $(5, 5, 5)$-faces. Then, if v is adjacent to two 5-vertex, $c'(v) \geq -1 + \frac{1}{4} + \frac{3}{4} = 0$; if v is adjacent to one 5-vertex, then $c'(v) \geq -1 + \frac{3}{4} + \frac{1}{4} = 0$; if v is not adjacent to 5-vertex, then $c'(v) \geq -1 + 3 \cdot \frac{1}{3} = 0$.

For a more detailed discussion of checking $c'(v) \geq 0$ for $d_G(v) = 5$, see the proof of Theorem 2 in [7]. So, we have proved that $c'(v) \geq 0$ for each $v \in V$. Then, by Formula (2.9) and the observation that $c'(e) = c(e) = 0$ for each $e \in E$, we have
$$\sum_{f \in F} c'(f) \leq -12.$$

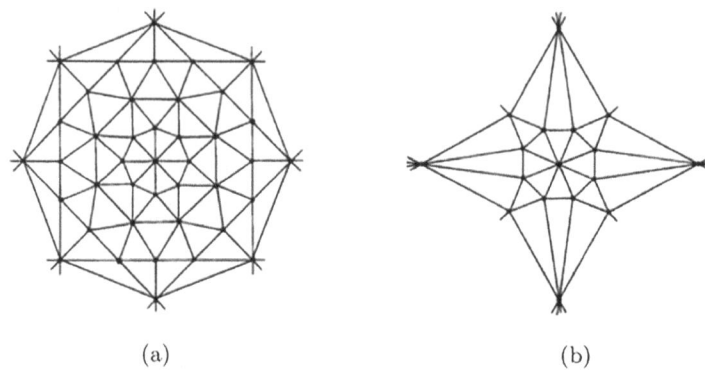

Fig. 2.10 (a) A maximal planar graph with only (5,5,7)-faces, (b) a maximal planar graph with only (5,5,5)-faces

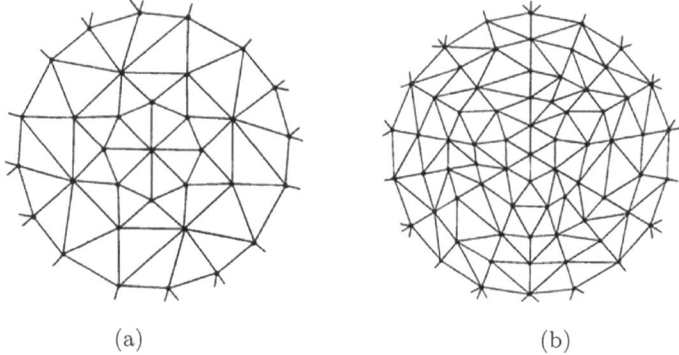

Fig. 2.11 (a) a maximal planar graph with only (5,5,6)-faces, (b) a maximal planar graph with only (5,6,6)-faces

Let f be a face of G. By discharging transformation φ, $c'(f) = 0$ for each face if f is not a $(5, 5, 5)$-, $(5, 5, 6)$-, $(5, 5, 7)$- or $(5, 6, 6)$-face. In addition, by φ_2 $(a) \sim (d)$, $c'(f) = -\frac{3}{2}$, $c'(f) = -\frac{3}{4}$, $c'(f) = -\frac{5}{12}$ and $c'(f) = -\frac{1}{3}$ when f is a $(5, 5, 5)$-, $(5, 5, 6)$-, $(5, 5, 7)$- and $(5, 6, 6)$-face, respectively. Therefore,

$$-\frac{3}{2} f_{5,5,5} - \frac{3}{4} f_{5,5,6} - \frac{5}{12} f_{5,5,7} - \frac{1}{3} f_{5,6,6} \leq -12$$

that is, $18 f_{5,5,5} + 9 f_{5,5,6} + 5 f_{5,5,7} + 4 f_{5,6,6} \geq 144$, a contradiction.

The tightness of coefficients in (2.5) are illustrated in Figs. 2.10 and 2.11. Particularly, in Fig. 2.10a it has that $f_{5,5,7} = 48$, $f_{5,5,5} = f_{5,5,6} = f_{5,6,6} = 0$. This shows that the third coefficients in 2.5 can not be less than 3. ∎

2.3 Faces

In addition to Borodin's work (Theorem 2.13), many improved results of Lebesgue's work (Theorem 2.11) have been done since; see [14, 35, 43]. In 2002, Borodin [15] improved nine parameters in Theorem 2.11 while others were retained.

Theorem 2.14 *Every planar graph has a 5^--face belonging to one of the following types, where the parameters remarked by $*$ are tight. These include* $(3, 6^-, \infty^*)$, $(3, 7^*, 22^-)$, $(3, 8^*, 22^-)$, $(3, 9^*, 15^-)$, $(3, 10^*, 13^-)$, $(3, 11^*, 12^-)$, $(4, 4, \infty^*)$, $(4, 5^*, 17^-)$, $(4, 6^*, 11^-)$, $(4, 7^*, 8^-)$, $(5, 5^*, 8^-)$, $(5, 6, 6^*)$, $(3, 3, 3, \infty^*)$, $(3, 3, 4^{-*}, 11^-)$, $(3, 3, 5^{-*}, 7^-)$, $(3, 4, 4^-, 5^{-*})$, *and* $(3, 3, 3, 3, 5^{-*})$.

By Theorem 2.11, we see that every planar graph of minimum degree at least 4 contains either a $(4, 4, \infty)$ or a 3-face with an infinite weight. For the 3-faces of planar graphs without 3-vertices, Borodin, et al. [15] in 2013 proved the following result.

Theorem 2.15 ([15]) *Let G be a planar graph without 3-vertices. Then, G contains a 3-face belonging to one of the following types, where every parameter is tight:* $(4, 4, \infty)$, $(4, 5, 14^-)$, $(4, 6, 10^-)$, $(4, 7, 7)$, $(5, 5, 7^-)$, $(5, 6, 6)$.

For maximal planar graph, Theorem 2.11 has been improved significantly. By arguing the characteristic of face in maximal planar graph, Jendrol' [47] in 1999 optimized all of the descriptions in Theorem 2.11, except $(4, 4, \infty)$ and $(4, 6, 11^-)$.

Theorem 2.16 ([47]) *Every maximal planar graph with order at least 5 contains a face of one of the following types:* $(3, 4, 35^-)$, $(3, 5, 21^-)$, $(3, 6, 20^-)$, $(3, 7, 16^-)$, $(3, 8, 14^-)$, $(3, 9, 14^-)$, $(3, 10, 13^-)$, $(4, 4, \infty)$, $(4, 5, 13^-)$, $(4, 6, 17^-)$, $(4, 7, 8^-)$, $(5, 5, 7^-)$, $(5, 6, 6)$.

Moreover, Jendrol' [47] conjectured that

Conjecture 2.2 ([47]) Every maximal planar graph with order at least 5 contains a face belonging to one of the following types: $(3, 4, 30^-)$, $(3, 5, 18^-)$, $(3, 6, 20^-)$, $(3, 7, 14^-)$, $(3, 8, 14^-)$, $(3, 9, 12^-)$, $(3, 10, 12^-)$, $(4, 4, \infty)$, $(4, 5, 10^-)$, $(4, 6, 15^-)$, $(4, 7, 7)$, $(5, 5, 7^-)$, $(5, 6, 6)$.

Unfortunately, this conjecture was disproved by Borodin and Ivanova [19] in 2014 by showing that (4,5,11)-face is reachable. They further proved the following theorem.

Theorem 2.17 ([19]) *Let G be a maximal planar graph with $\delta(G) \geq 4$. Then, G contains a face of one of the following types, where every parameter is tight:* $(4, 4, \infty)$, $(4, 5, 11^-)$, $(4, 6, 10^-)$, $(4, 7, 7)$, $(5, 5, 7^-)$, $(5, 6, 6)$.

Clearly, we can see from Theorems 2.17 and 2.15 that the descriptions of 3-face in maximal planar graphs are more specific than that in general planar graphs. Also in 2014, Borodin, Ivanova and Kostochka [30] obtained a more clear description of faces in maximal planar graphs, which is viewed as the best result so far in the literature.

Theorem 2.18 ([30]) *Every maximal planar graph with order at least 5 contains a face of one of the following types, where every parameter is tight:* $(3, 4, 31^-)$, $(3, 5, 21^-)$, $(3, 6, 20^-)$, $(3, 7, 13^-)$, $(3, 8, 14^-)$, $(3, 9, 12^-)$, $(3, 10, 12^-)$, $(4, 4, \infty)$, $(4, 5, 11^-)$, $(4, 6, 10^-)$, $(4, 7, 7)$, $(5, 5, 7^-)$, $(5, 6, 6)$.

Proof We first show the tightness by the following constructions. Take two copies of the semi-maximal planar graphs shown in Fig. 2.10a, and glue them along the boundary to form a maximal planar graph. One can see that the resulting graph contains no faces of types other than (5,5,7) among those mentioned in the theorem. Thus, (5,5,7) is sharp. The sharpness of other types are illustrated in Figs. 2.12, 2.13, 2.14, 2.15, 2.16, and 2.17.

Now, we turn to the proof of the main statement of Theorem 2.18. By way of contradiction. A face is **hard** if it is not incident with a 3-vertex. Suppose that G^* is a counterexample to Theorem 2.18 with the fewest hard faces. Let V, E, F denote the set of vertices, edges, and faces of G^*, respectively. The proof will proceed by observing some structural properties of G^* first, then presenting a discharging

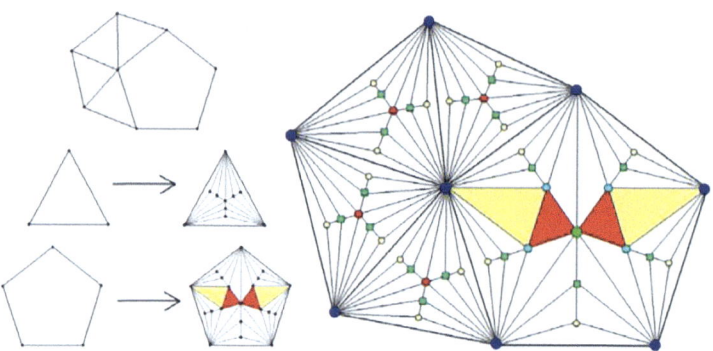

Fig. 2.12 A construction with no faces of types other than (3,4,31) in Theorem 2.18, showing the tightness of (3,4,31)

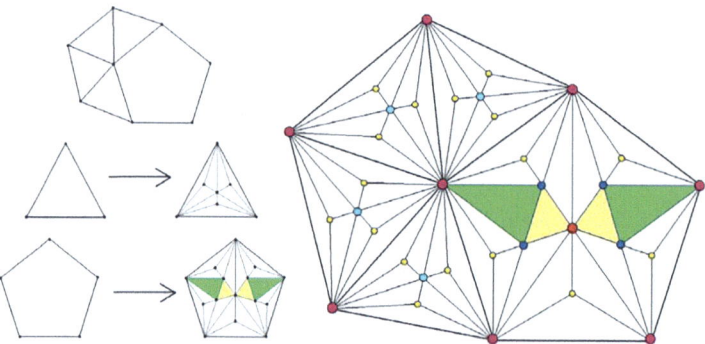

Fig. 2.13 A construction with no faces of types other than (3,5,21) in Theorem 2.18, showing the tightness of (3,5,21)

2.3 Faces

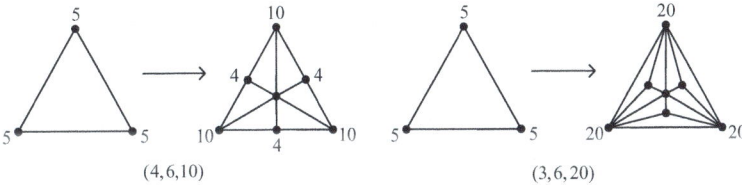

Fig. 2.14 Starting with the icosahedron, a construction showing the tightness of (4,6,10) is obtained by implementing the left-hand side operation, and a construction showing the tightness of (3,6,20) is obtained by implementing the right-hand side operation

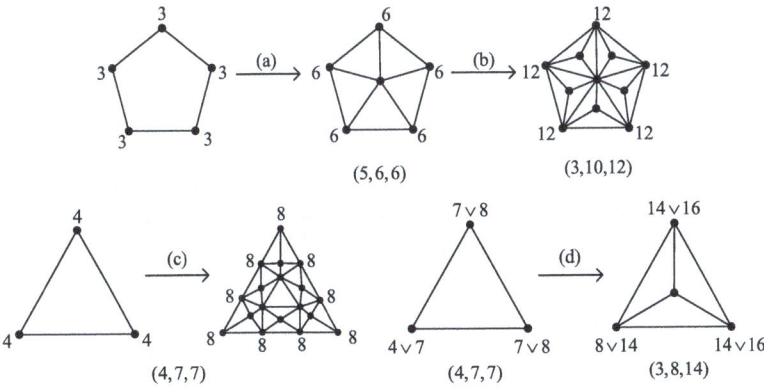

Fig. 2.15 Starting with the dodecahedron, constructions showing the tightness of (5,6,6) and (3,10,12) are obtained by implementing operation (**a**) followed by (**b**); starting with the octahedron, constructions showing the tightness of (4,7,7) and (3,8,14) are obtained by implementing operation (**c**) followed by (**d**)

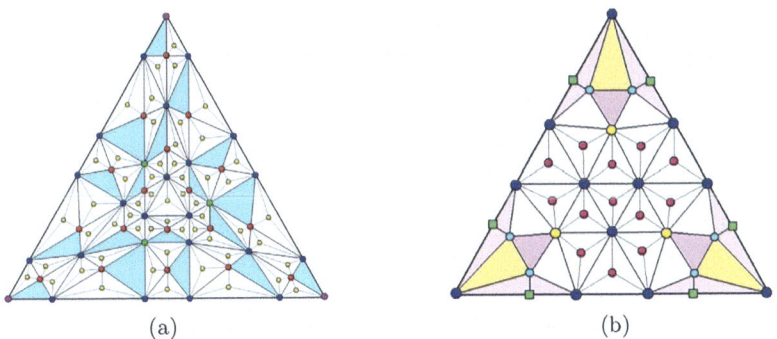

Fig. 2.16 (**a**) A construction with only (3, 7, 13)-faces among those mentioned in Theorem 2.18, confirming the tightness of (3, 7, 13); (**b**) a construction with only (3, 9, 12)-faces among those mentioned in Theorem 2.18, confirming the tightness of (3, 9, 12)

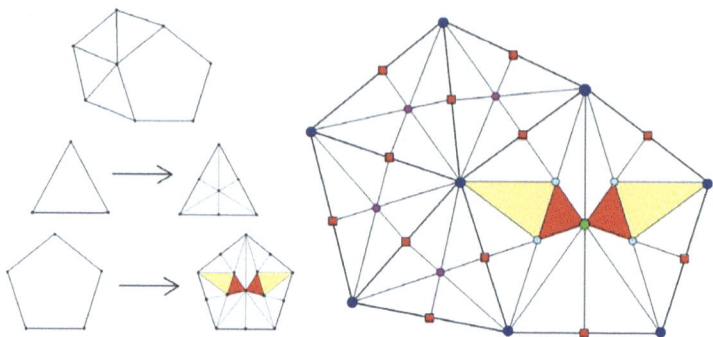

Fig. 2.17 A construction with only (4, 5, 11)-faces among those mentioned in Theorem 2.18, confirming the tightness of (4, 5, 11)

transformation, and finally checking the final charge to be nonnegative and hence a contradiction.

(I). Structural Properties of G^* Given a vertex v, let $v_1, v_2, \ldots, v_{d_G(v)}$ be the neighbors of v in a cyclic order. Then, G^* has the following simple structural properties.

(1) G^* does not contain two adjacent 3-vertices, since $G^* \not\cong K_4$ and G^* contains no multiple edges.
(2) A 4-vertex is adjacent to at most one 3-vertex, since G^* is simple graph.
(3) For a $(2k + 1)$-vertex v such that $2 \le k \le 5$, v_1 or v_{2k-1} is not a 3-vertex. Otherwise, if $d_{G^*}(v_1) = d_{G^*}(v_{2k-1}) =$, then $d_{G^*}(v_{2k})$ and $d_{G^*}(v_{2k+1})$ are sufficiently large since G^* contains no $(3, 5, 21^-)$-faces, $(3, 7, 13^-)$-faces, $(3, 9, 12^-)$-faces, and $(3, 10, 12^-)$-faces. Then, by adding a vertex x in the face $vv_{2k}v_{2k+1}$ followed by joining it to v, v_{2k}, and v_{2k+1}, we will obtain a new counterexample with fewer hard faces than G^*, a contradiction.
(4) A $(2k + 1)$-vertex v such that $2 \le k \le 5$ has at most $k - 1$ neighbors of degree 3.

II. Discharging

By Euler's Formula (1.9 in Theorem 1.12), we have

$$\sum_{v \in V} (d_{G^*}(v) - 6) + \sum_{f \in F} (2d_{G^*}(f) - 6) = -12 \tag{2.10}$$

Let the initial charge c of G^* be: $c(v) = d_{G^*}(v) - 6$ for every $v \in V$, $c(x) = 0$ for every element $x \in E \cup F$. Clearly, only 5^--vertices have a negative charge. We will redistribute the charges of vertices to elements of $V \cup F$ by a discharging transformation so that the final charge c' of G is nonnegative. This contradicts the fact that the sum of the new charges is, Formula (2.10), equal to -12.

2.3 Faces

A more specific definition concerning 7-vertices should be defined in terms of the degree of its neighbors. Let v be a 7-vertex of G^*. If $d_{G^*}(v_1) = 4$, $4 \leq d_{G^*}(v_3) \leq 5$, and $d_{G^*}(v_5) = 5$, then v is called a **poor vertex**, denoted by 7_p-vertex. By 7_p^4-**vertex** or 7_p^5-**vertex** we denote a 7_p-vertex v such that $d_{G^*}(v_3) = 4$ or $d_{G^*}(v_3) = 5$, respectively. Two adjacent 7_p-vertices are said to be **coupled** each other. Furthermore, we call a 7-vertex v a **bad** vertex if $d_{G^*}(v_7) = 7$, $d_{G^*}(v_2) = 5$, $d_{G^*}(v_4) = d_{G^*}(v_6) = 3$, and there is a face $\triangle v_2 v_3 z$ with $z \neq v$ and $d_{G^*}(z) \geq 5$. Clearly, if v is a bad vertex, then $d_{G^*}(v_3) \geq 14$ and $d_{G^*}(v_7) \geq 14$ since G^* contains no $(3, 7, 13)$-face.

We use the following discharging transformation $\varphi = (\varphi_1, \varphi_2, \varphi_3, \varphi_4, \varphi_5)$.

φ_1. **Every 3-vertex v receives the following charge from its neighbors v_1, v_2 and v_3:**

(a) $\frac{3}{2}$ from each of v_2 and v_3 if $d_{G^*}(v_1) \leq 6$;
(b) $\frac{2}{3}$ from v_1 and $\frac{7}{6}$ from each of v_2 and v_3 if $d_{G^*}(v_1) = 7$;
(c) $\frac{1}{2}$ from v_1 and $\frac{5}{4}$ from each of v_2 and v_3 if $d_{G^*}(v_1) = 8$;
(d) $\frac{3}{4}$ from v_1 and $\frac{9}{8}$ from each of v_2 and v_3 if $d_{G^*}(v_1) = 9$;
(e) $\frac{4}{5}$ from v_1 and $\frac{11}{10}$ from each of v_2 and v_3 if $d_{G^*}(v_1) = 9$;
(f) 1 from each of v_1, v_2 and v_3 if v has no 10^--neighbors.

φ_2. **For each face $\triangle uvw$ such that $d_{G^*}(v) = 4$ and $d_{G^*}(u) \geq 8$, v receives the following charge:**

(a) $\frac{1}{2}$ from u through $\triangle uvw$ if $d_{G^*}(w) \leq 6$;
(b) $\frac{1}{4}$ from u through $\triangle uvw$ and $\frac{1}{2}$ from w (along the edge wv) if $d_{G^*}(w) = 7$;
(c) $\frac{1}{4}$ from each of u and w through $\triangle uvw$ if $d_{G^*}(w) \geq 8$ with the following exception (c^*);
(c^*) $\frac{1}{2}$ from v_3 though each of the faces $\triangle v_2 v v_3$ and $\triangle v_3 v v_4$, and nothing from v_2 and v_4 through these faces, if $d_{G^*}(v_1) = 3$, $d_{G^*}(v_2) \geq 32$, $d_{G^*}(v_3) \geq 13$, and $d_{G^*}(v_4) \geq 32$.

φ_3. **For each face $\triangle uvw$ such that $d_{G^*}(v) = 5$ and $d_{G^*}(u) \geq 8$, v receives the following charge from u through $\triangle uvw$:**

(a) $\frac{1}{8}$ if $d_{G^*}(w) = 5$ and $d_{G^*}(u) \leq 11$;
(b) $\frac{1}{4}$ if $d_{G^*}(w) \geq 6$ and $d_{G^*}(u) \leq 11$;
(c) $\frac{1}{4}$ if $d_{G^*}(w) = 5$ and $d_{G^*}(u) \geq 12$;
(d) $\frac{1}{2}$ if $d_{G^*}(w) \geq 6$ and $d_{G^*}(u) \geq 12$, except for the following (d^*);
(d^*) $\frac{1}{4}$ if $d_{G^*}(w) = 7$ and there is a face $\triangle uv'w$ such that $d_{G^*}(v') = 3$.

φ_4. Let v be a 7-vertex. If v_2 is a 5-vertex, then v gives to v_2 the following charge:

(a) If $d_{G^*}(v_1) \geq 6$ and v is neither bad nor coupled poor, then

(a1) $\frac{1}{4}$ if $d_{G^*}(v_3) \geq 8$;
(a2) $\frac{1}{3}$ if $d_{G^*}(v_3) \leq 7$ and $d_{G^*}(v_1) \leq 7$;

(b) If v and v_1 are coupled poor 7-vertices (and hence $d_{G^*}(v_6) = 4$), then

  (b1) $\frac{1}{8}$ if $d_{G^*}(v_4) = 4$;
  (b2) $\frac{3}{8}$ if $d_{G^*}(v_4) = 5$; in this case, v_4 also receives $\frac{1}{4}$ from v;

(c) $\frac{1}{6}$ if v is a bad vertex.

φ_5. Let v be a 7-vertex. If v_2 is a 8^+-vertex, then v receives the following charge from v_2 through $\triangle v_1 v_2$:

(a) $\frac{1}{4}$ if $d_{G^*}(v_1) = 4$;
(b) Suppose that $d_{G^*}(v_3) = 3$, $d_{G^*}(v_1) = 5$, and there is a face $\triangle v_1 v' v_2$ with $v' \neq v$. Then,

  (b1) $\frac{1}{3}$ if $d_{G^*}(v') \leq 4$;
  (b2) $\frac{1}{4}$ if $d_{G^*}(v_4) \geq 5$;

(c) Suppose that $d_{G^*}(v_1) = 6$ or $d_{G^*}(v_1) \geq 8$. Then,

  (c1) $\frac{1}{4}$ if $d_{G^*}(v_2) \leq 13$;
  (c2) $\frac{1}{3}$ if $d_{G^*}(v_2) \geq 14$;

(d) $\frac{1}{4}$ if $d_{G^*}(v_1) = 7$ and $d_{G^*}(v_2) \geq 12$;
(e) Suppose that $d_{G^*}(v_1) = 7$ or $d_{G^*}(v_2) \geq 11$. Then,

  (e1) $\frac{1}{4}$ if v_1 is poor but not coupled;
  (e2) $\frac{1}{8}$ otherwise.

III. Proving the Final Charge of G^* to be Nonnegative

Let c' be the final charge of G^*. By $\varphi_1, \varphi_2, \varphi_3, \varphi_4, \varphi_5$, it is enough to show that for every $x \in V \cup F$, $c'(x) \geq 0$. This checking process is too long and complicated to be presented here. In [30], the authors confirmed this fact by arguing fourteen cases (using about seven journal pages). For more detailed discussion of this proof, see [30] (Theorem 8). ∎

From the above discussion, one can clearly depict the structure of faces in planar graphs, especially in maximal planar graphs. In addition to these result, a series of works have been done to characterize the weight w of a 5^--face in planar graphs.

By Theorem 2.12, every 3-connected planar graph with maximum degree 5 satisfies $w \leq 17$ and the bound is sharp. For maximal planar graphs without 4-vertices, Kotzig [54] in 1979 proved that $w \leq 39$; this bound was improved, by Borodin [10] in 1992, to 29 and the bound is sharp, which also confirmed a conjecture proposed by Kotzig in [54]. In 1998, Borodin [14] further proved that if a maximal planar graph contains no adjacent 4-vertices, then $w \leq 37$ and the bound is tight; if a maximal planar graph without two adjacent vertices whose degrees are 4 and 4 or 4 and 3, then $w \leq 29$ and it is tight.

2.3 Faces

In 1940, Lebesgue [55] proved that every 3-connected planar graph such that every face is a 4-face satisfies $w \leq 21$. Since then, Avgustinovich and Borodin [2] in 1995 improved this bound to 20; further, in 2015, Borodin and Ivanova [22] again improved this bound by showing that $w \leq 18$ and the bound is sharp. For triangle-free 3-connected planar graph, Borodin and Ivanova [23] in 2016 obtained that $w \leq 20$ and the bound is tight. In addition to these result, there are results on planar graphs with some restrictions. In 1998, Borodin and Woodall [35] proved that every planar graph without $(3, 5, \infty)$-faces contains either a $(3, 6, 20^-)$-face or a 5^--face with weight at most 25, where the parameters are tight. In 1996, Horňák and Jendrol' [43] proved that the weight of every 5^--face in a planar graph with a $(3, 5, \infty)$-face is at least 38, and there exists a 5^--face such that $w(f) \leq 47$; moreover, they proved that every 3-connected planar graph satisfies that $w \leq 32$. This result is improved by Borodin and Ivanova in 2016 [26], which is depicted as follows.

Theorem 2.19 ([26]) *Let G be a planar graph without pyramidal faces. Then, $w \leq 30$ and the bound is tight (see Fig. 2.18).*

By Theorem 2.11, one can see that every triangle-free 3-connected planar graph without pyramidal faces contains a 4-face of weight at most 21, or a 5-face of weight at most 17. For a long time, the tightness of these bounds can not be determined, and were confirmed by Borodin and Ivanova [23] until 2016.

Theorem 2.20 ([23]) *Every triangle-free 3-connected planar graph without pyramidal faces contains a 4-face of weight at most 20, or a 5-face of weight at most 17, where the parameters are tight.*

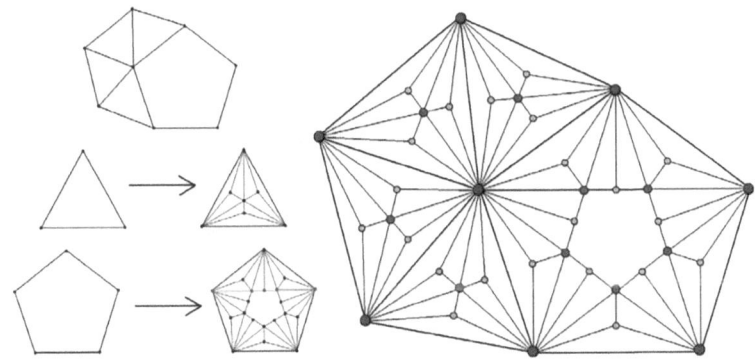

Fig. 2.18 A maximal planar graph each of which face has weight at least 30

2.4 Cycle and Star

This section depicts the structures of cycles and stars in planar graphs. Recall that the **weight** of a subgraph H of a graph G is the sum of degrees of the vertices of H in G. For convenience, here we denote by $\mathbf{M}_5$ the set of planar graphs of minimum degree 5, by $\mathbf{P}_5$ the set of 3-connected planar graphs of minimum degree 5, and by $\mathbf{T}_5$ the set of maximal planar graphs of minimum degree 5. Clearly, both $\mathbf{P}_5$ and $\mathbf{T}_5$ are subset of $\mathbf{M}_5$. A k-**star** is a complete bipartite graph $K_{1,k}$ with partition $(\{v\}, \{x_1, x_2, \ldots, x_k\})$, denoted by $S_k(v) = [v, x_1, x_2, \ldots, x_k]$, where v is called the **center** of $S_k(v)$. This section only considers stars with center of degree at most 5. A $(5; a, b, c)$-**star** of a graph G is a 3-star whose center is a 5-vertex in G and is adjacent to an a-vertex, a b-vertex, and a c-vertex in G.

Given a graph H, $w_\mathbf{M}(H)$ is defined as follows:

$$w_M(H) = \max\{\min\{\sum_{v \in V(H^*)} d_G(v) | H^* \subseteq G, H^* \cong H\} | G \in \mathbf{M}_5\}$$

Where $H^* \subseteq G$ denotes H^* is a subgraph of G. Analogously, $w_\mathbf{P}(H)$ and $w_\mathbf{T}(H)$ can be defined in the say way. Let $\varphi_\mathbf{M}(H)$(resp. $\varphi_\mathbf{P}(H)$ and $\varphi_\mathbf{T}(H)$) be the minimum integer k for which every planar graph of minimum degree 5 (resp. 3-connected planar graphs and maximal planar graphs) contains a copy of H whose maximum degree at most k.

2.4.1 The Weight of Cycle and the Restriction on the Degree

By Theorem 2.11, we have $w_\mathbf{T}(C_3) \leq 18$. In 1963, Kotzig [53] proved this result by another approach, and he conjectured that $w_\mathbf{T}(C_3) \leq 17$ and the bound is tight. In 1989, Borodin proved this conjecture by showing that $w_\mathbf{M}(C_3) = 17$ and $\varphi_\mathbf{M}(C_3) = 7$. In 1996, Jendrol' and Madaras [49] proved that $\varphi_\mathbf{M}(S_4) = 10$, $\varphi_\mathbf{T}(C_4) = \varphi_\mathbf{T}(C_5) = 10$. In a private communication, Soták proved that $\varphi_\mathbf{P}(C_4) = 11$ and $\varphi_\mathbf{P}(C_5) = 10$; see the survey [51]. In 1999, Jendrol', et al. [50] obtained that $10 \leq \varphi_\mathbf{T}(C_6) \leq 11$, $15 \leq \varphi_\mathbf{T}(C_7) \leq 17$, $15 \leq \varphi_\mathbf{T}(C_8) \leq 29$, $19 \leq \varphi_\mathbf{T}(C_9) \leq 41$, and when $k \geq 11$, $\varphi_\mathbf{T}(C_k) = \infty$. Madaras and Soták [58] proved that $20 \leq \varphi_\mathbf{T}(C_{10}) \leq 415$. For general $\mathbf{P}_5$, Mohar, et al. [59] proved that $10 \leq \varphi_\mathbf{P}(C_6) \leq 107$. In 2014, Borodin, Ivanova and Kostochka [31] proved that $\varphi_\mathbf{P}(C_6) = \varphi_\mathbf{T}(C_6) = 11$, and obtained the following conclusion.

Theorem 2.21 ([31]) *Every 3-connected planar graph G of minimum degree 5 contains a 6-cycle whose vertices with degree at most 11 in G, and this bound is sharp.*

2.4 Cycle and Star

In addition to the conclusion $15 \leq \varphi_T(C_7) \leq 17$ obtained by Jendrol' et al. [50], for C_7 Madaras, et al. [57] proved that $\varphi_P(C_7) \leq 359$. In 2015, Borodin and Ivanova [21] proved $\varphi_P(C_7) = \varphi_T(C_7) = 15$.

Theorem 2.22 ([21]) *Every 3-connected planar graph G of minimum degree 5 contains a 7-cycle such that each vertex on it has degree at most 15 in G, and this bound is sharp.*

For $\mathbf{T}_5$, Jendrol' and Madaras [49] in 1996 obtained the following conclusion.

Theorem 2.23 ([49]) $\varphi_T(C_3) \leq 18$, $\varphi_T(C_4) \leq 35$, and $\varphi_T(C_5) \leq 45$.

In 1998, Borodin and Woodall [36] improved the result in Theorem 2.23; they proved that $\varphi_T(C_4) = 25$, and $\varphi_T(C_5) = 30$. In 2014, Borodin, Ivanova and Woodall [33] proved that for any 3-connected planar graph of minimum degree 5, $\varphi_P(C_4) = 26$ and $\varphi_P(C_5) = 30$. As a corollary, they confirmed that $\varphi_P(C_4) = 11$ and $\varphi_P(C_5) = 10$, which is first observed by Soták but not published.

2.4.2 Stars

As for the research on structure of Star in $\mathbf{M}_5$, Wernicke [60] proved that $w(S_1) \leq 11$ and Franklin [37] proved that $w(S_2) \leq 17$, and these bounds are tight. In 1940, Lebesgue [55] showed that $w(S_3) \leq 24$. This bound was improved by Jendrol' and Madaras [49] in 1996; they obtained that $w(S_3) \leq 23$ and characterized the 3-star in $\mathbf{M}_5$.

Theorem 2.24 ([49]) *Let G be a planar graph of minimum degree 5. Then, G contains a 3-star $S_3 = [v, x_1, x_2, x_3]$ such that $d_G(v) = 5$ and*

(1) $d_G(x_1) = 5, d_G(x_2) \leq 6, d_G(x_3) \leq 7$, or
(2) $d_G(x_1) = d_G(x_2) = d_G(x_3) = 6$,

where the parameters are tight.

Theorem 2.25 ([49]) *Let G be a planar graph of minimum degree 5. Then, G contains a 4-star $S_4 = [v, x_1, x_2, x_3, x_4]$ such that $d_G(v) = 5$ and $d_G(x_i) \leq 10$ for $i = 1, 2, 3, 4$, where the parameter 10 is tight.*

In addition, Jendrol' and Madaras [49] considered the wight of a 4-path; they proved that every connected planar graph of minimum degree 5 contains a 4-path P_4 such that $w(P_4) \leq 23$, which is sharp.

It is easy to see that Theorem 2.23 can be derived from Theorems 2.24 and 2.25.

For maximal planar graphs of minimum degree 5, Jendrol' and Madaras [49] obtained the following results.

Theorem 2.26 ([49]) *Let G be a maximal planar graphs of minimum degree 5. Then, G contains*

(1) a 3-star $S_3 = [v, x_1, x_2, x_3]$ such that $d_G(v) \leq 8$ and $d_G(x_i) \leq 6$ for $i = 1, 2, 3$;
(2) a 4-star $S_4 = [v, x_1, x_2, x_3, x_4]$ such that $d_G(v) \leq 11$ and $d_G(x_i) \leq 7$ for $i = 1, 2, 3, 4$.

In 1940, Lebesgue [55] also proved that every planar graph of minimum degree 5 contains a 5-vertex v such that the sum of degrees of any four neighbors of v is at most 26; that is, every planar graph of minimum degree 5 contains a 4-star with center of degree 5 and with weight at most 31. In 1998, Borodin and Woodall [36] improved this bound from 31 to 30. In 2013, Borodin and Ivanova [17] argued the tightness of the bound 30. They obtained the following result.

Theorem 2.27 ([17]) *Let G be a planar graphs of minimum degree 5. Then, G contains a 4-star of center of degree 5 belong to one of the following types:*

$$(5, 5, 5, 10), (5, 5, 6, 9), (5, 5, 7, 8), (5, 6, 6, 8), (5, 6, 7, 7), (6, 6, 6, 7)$$

More specifically, they in [17] constructed six planar graphs of minimum degree 5 such that (1) every 4-star with center of degree 5 has weight at least 30, and (2) each 4-star of weight 30 belonging one of the types mentioned in Theorem 2.27 belongs to one the planar graphs they constructed.

In 2013, Borodin and Ivanova [18] clearly depicted the structure of $(d-2)$-star with a d-vertex as center, for $d \leq 5$, in planar graphs.

Theorem 2.28 ([18]) *Every planar graph contains a star of one of the following types: (1) $(3, 10^-)$-edge, (2) $(5^-, 4, 9^-)$-path, (3) $(6, 4, 8^-)$-path, (4) $(7, 4, 7)$-path, (5) $(5; 4, 5, 5)$-star, (6) $(5; 5, b, c)$-star for $5 \leq b \leq 6$ and $5 \leq c \leq 7$, (7) $(5; 6, 6, 6)$-star. These parameters are all sharp.*

Observe that there exists a planar graph of minimum degree 5, which contains a 5-star S_5 with center of degree 5 and with minimum wight such that $w(S_5)$ is sufficiently large. Let v be a 5-vertex of a planar graph G, and its neighbors v_1, v_2, v_3, v_4, v_5 are arranged in this order. If there is an integer $k(\leq 5)$ such that $d_G(v_{k+1}) = d_G(v_{k+4}) = 5$, $d_G(v_{k+2}) \leq 6$, and $d_G(v_{k+3}) \leq 6$, then v is called a **cyclic (5,6,6,5)-vertex**. In 1940, Lebesgue [55] proved that if a planar graph of minimum degree 5 contains no 4-star with a cyclic (5,6,6,5)-vertex as center, then $w(S_5) \leq 68$. In 2014, Borodin, Ivanova and Jensen [28] improved this bound from 68 to 55, and constructed a planar graph of minimum degree 5 without cyclic (5,6,6,5)-vertex in which $w(S_5) = 48$.

References

1. K Ando, S Iwasaki, and A Kaneko. Every 3-connected planar graph has a connected subgraph with small degree sum. 1993.
2. S V Avgustinovich and O V Borodin. Neighborhoods of edges in normal cards. *Diskretn.anal.issled.oper*, pages 3–9, 1995.
3. Ts Ch D Batueva, O V Borodin, and A O Ivanova. All tight descriptions of 4-paths in 3-polytopes with minimum degree 5. *Graphs and Combinatorics*, 33:53–62, 2017.
4. O V Borodin. On the total coloring of planar graphs. *Journal Für Die Reine Und Angewandte Mathematik*, 1989(394):180–185, 1989.
5. O V Borodin. Solving the kotzig and grünbaum problems on the separability of a cycle in planar graphs. *Mat Zametki*, (5):9–12, 1989.
6. O V Borodin. Joint generalization of the theorems of lebesgue and kotzig on the combinatorics of planar maps. *Diskr.mat*, (4):24–27, 1991.
7. O V Borodin. Structural properties of planar maps with the minimal degree 5. *Mathematische Nachrichten*, 158(1):109–117, 1992.
8. O V Borodin. Precise lower bound for the number of edges of minor weight in planar maps. *Mathematica Slovaca*, 42(2), 1992.
9. O V Borodin. Structural properties of planar maps with the minimal degree 5. *Mathematische Nachrichten*, 158(1):109–117, 1992.
10. O V Borodin. Minimal weight of a face in planar triangulations without 4-vertices. *Mat Zametki*, (1):16–19,160, 1992.
11. O V Borodin. Joint extension of two theorems of kotzig on 3-polytopes. *Combinatorica*, 13(1):121–125, 1993.
12. O V Borodin. The structure of neighborhoods of an edge in planar graphs and the simultaneous coloring of vertices, edges and faces. *Mathematical Notes*, 53(5):483–489, 1993.
13. O V Borodin. Minimal vertex degree sum of a 3-path in plane maps. *Discussiones Mathematicae Graph Theory*, 17(2):279–284, 1997.
14. O V Borodin. Triangulated 3-polytopes without faces of low weight. *Discrete Mathematics*, 186(1-3):281–285, 1998.
15. O V Borodin. Strengthening lebesgue's theorem on the structure of the minor faces in convex polyhedra. *Diskretn.anal.issled.oper.ser*, (3):29–39, 2002.
16. O V Borodin. Structural properties of planar maps with the minimal degree 5. *Mathematische Nachrichten*, 158(1):109–117, 2010.
17. O V Borodin and A O Ivanova. Describing 4-stars at 5-vertices in normal plane maps with minimum degree 5. *Discrete Mathematics*, 313(17):1710–1714, 2013.
18. O V Borodin and A O Ivanova. Describing (d-2)-stars at d-vertices, $d \leq 5$, in normal plane maps. *Discrete Mathematics*, 313:1700–1709, 2013.
19. O V Borodin and A O Ivanova. Combinatorial structure of faces in triangulated 3-polytopes with minimum degree 4. *Siberian Mathematical Journal*, 55(1):12–18, 2014.
20. O V Borodin and A O Ivanova. Describing tight descriptions of 3-paths in triangle-free normal plane maps. *Discrete Mathematics*, 338(11):1947–1952, 2015.
21. O V Borodin and A O Ivanova. Each 3-polytope with minimum degree 5 has a 7-cycle with maximum degree at most 15. *Siberian Mathematical Journal*, 56(4):612–623, 2015.
22. O V Borodin and A O Ivanova. The vertex-face weight of edges in 3-polytopes. *Siberian Mathematical Journal*, 56(2):275–284, 2015.
23. O V Borodin and A O Ivanova. On the weight of minor faces in triangle-free polytopes. *Discussiones Mathematicae Graph Theory*, 36(3):603–619, 2016.
24. O V Borodin and A O Ivanova. *An analogue of Franklin's Theorem*. Elsevier Science Publishers B. V., 2016.
25. O V Borodin and A O Ivanova. Describing 4-paths in 3-polytopes with minimum degree 5. *Siberian Mathematical Journal*, 57(5):764–768, 2016.

26. O V Borodin and A O Ivanova. The weight of faces in normal plane maps. *Discrete Mathematics*, 339(10):2573–2580, 2016.
27. O V Borodin and A O Ivanova. Every triangulated 3-polytope of minimum degree 4 has a 4-path of weight at most 27. *The electronic journal of combinatorics*, 23(3), 2016.
28. O V Borodin, A O Ivanova, and T R Jensen. 5-stars of low weight in normal plane maps with minimal degree 5. *Discussiones Mathematicae Graph Theory*, 34(3), 2014.
29. O V Borodin, A O Ivanova, T R Jensen, A V Kostochka, and M P Yancey. Describing 3-paths in normal plane maps. *Discrete Mathematics*, 313(23):2702–2711, 2013.
30. O V Borodin, A O Ivanova, and A V Kostochka. *Describing faces in plane triangulations*. Elsevier Science Publishers B. V., 2014.
31. O V Borodin, A O Ivanova, and A V Kostochka. *Every 3-polytope with minimum degree 5 has a 6-cycle with maximum degree at most 11*. Elsevier Science Publishers B. V., 2014.
32. O V Borodin, A O Ivanova, and A V Kostochka. Tight descriptions of 3-paths in normal plane maps. *Journal of Graph Theory*, 2016.
33. O V Borodin, A O Ivanova, and D R Woodall. *Light C4 and C5 in 3-polytopes with minimum degree 5*. Elsevier Science Publishers B. V., 2014.
34. O V Borodin and D P Sanders. On light edges and triangles in planar graphs of minimum degree five. *Mathematische Nachrichten*, 170(1):19–24, 1994.
35. O V Borodin and D R Vudal. Weight of faces in plane maps. *Mathematical Notes*, 64(5):562–570, 1998.
36. O V Borodin and D R Woodall. Short cycles of low weight in normal plane maps with minimum degree 5. *Discussiones Mathematicae Graph Theory*, 3(3):159–164, 1998.
37. P Franklin. The four color problem. *American Journal of Mathematics*, 44(3):225–236, 1922.
38. B Grünbaum. Acyclic colorings of planar graphs. *Israel Journal of Mathematics*, 14(4):390–408, 1973.
39. B Grünbaum. New views on some old questions of combinatorial geometry. *New Views on Some Old Questions of Combinatorial Geometry*, pages 451–468, 1973.
40. B Grünbaum. Polytopal graphs. *Studies in Graph Theory Part II*, 12:201–224, 1975.
41. B Grünbaum. New views on some old questions of combinatorial geometry. *Colloquio Internazionale sulle Teorie Combinatorie (Rome, 1973)*, Tomo I:451–468. Atti dei Convegni Lincei, No. 17, Accad. Naz. Lincei, Rome, 1976.
42. B Grünbaum and G C Shephard. Analogues for tilings of kotzig's theorem on minimal weights of edges. *North-Holland Mathematics Studies*, 60(08):129–140, 1982.
43. M Horňák and S Jendrol'. Unavoidable sets of face types for planar maps. *Discuss.math.graph Theory*, (16):123–141, 1996.
44. A O Ivanova. Tight description of 4-paths in 3-polytopes with minimum degree 5. *M.K. Ammosov North-Eastern Federal University*, 23(1):46–55, 2016.
45. S Jendrol'. A structural property of convex 3-polytopes. *Geometriae Dedicata*, 68(1):91–99, 1997.
46. S Jendrol'. Paths with restricted degrees of their vertices in planar graphs. *Czechoslovak Mathematical Journal*, 49(3):481–490, 1999.
47. S Jendrol'. Triangles with restricted degrees of their boundary vertices in plane triangulations. *Discrete Mathematics*, 196(196):177–196, 1999.
48. S Jendrol' and I Fabrici. An inequality concerning edges of minor weight in convex 3-polytopes. *Discussiones Mathematicae Graph Theory*, 16(1):81–87, 1996.
49. S Jendrol' and T Madaras. On light subgraphs in plane graphs of minimum degree ve. *Discussiones Mathematicae Graph Theory*, 16(2):207–217, 1996.
50. S Jendrol, T Madaras, R Sotak, and Z Tuza. On light cycles in plane triangulations. *Discrete Mathematics*, 197-198(1-3):453–467, 1999.
51. S Jendrol and H J Voss. Light subgraphs of graphs embedded in the plane—a survey. *Discrete Mathematics*, 313(4):406–421, 2013.
52. A Kotzig. Contribution to the theory of eulerian polyhedra. pages 101–113, 1955.
53. A Kotzig. From the theory of eulerian polyhedra. *Mat. casopis SAV13*, pages 20–34, 1963.
54. A Kotzig. Extremal polyhedral graphs. *Ann. New York Acad. Sci.*, 319:569–570, 1979.

References

55. H Lebesgue. Quelques consequences simples de la formule deuler. *Journal De Mathématiques Pures Et Appliqués*, pages 27–43, 1940.
56. T Madaras. Note on the weight of paths in plane triangulations of minimum degree 4 and 5. *Discussiones Mathematicae Graph Theory*, 20(2), 2000.
57. T Madaras, R Škrekovski, and H J Voss. The 7-cycle c7 is light in the family of planar graphs with minimum degree 5. *Discrete Mathematics*, 307(11):1430–1435, 2007.
58. T Madaras and R Soták. The 10-cycle csb 10 is light in the family of all plane triangulations with minimum degree five. *Tatra Mt.math.publ*, 18:35–56, 1999.
59. B Mohar, R Skrekovski, and H J Voss. *Light subgraphs in planar graphs of minimum degree 4 and edge-degree 9*. John Wiley and Sons, Inc., 2003.
60. P Wernicke. Uber den kartographischen vierfarbensatz. *Mathematische Annalen*, 58(3):413–426, 1904.

Open Access This chapter is licensed under the terms of the Creative Commons Attribution 4.0 International License (http://creativecommons.org/licenses/by/4.0/), which permits use, sharing, adaptation, distribution and reproduction in any medium or format, as long as you give appropriate credit to the original author(s) and the source, provide a link to the Creative Commons license and indicate if changes were made.

The images or other third party material in this chapter are included in the chapter's Creative Commons license, unless indicated otherwise in a credit line to the material. If material is not included in the chapter's Creative Commons license and your intended use is not permitted by statutory regulation or exceeds the permitted use, you will need to obtain permission directly from the copyright holder.

Chapter 3
Computer-Based Proofs of Four Color Conjecture

Abstract This section introduces the research course of proving Four Color Conjecture using a computer, which mainly focus on the construction of an unavoidable set of reducible configurations. Those include works that have been done by Heesch, Haken & Appel, and Simon, etc.

3.1 Four Color Conjecture

It is well known, in the field of mathematics, that there are three proverbial conjectures, including Fermat's Conjecture (Fermat's Last Theorem), Goldbach's Conjecture, and Four Color Conjecture. Just as one has observed, all of these conjectures are easily perceived, even by junior middle school students, which makes them known to every household. Fermat's Conjecture states that no three positive integers x, y, and z can satisfy the equation $x^n + y^n = z^n$ for any integer $n \geq 3$; understanding this conjecture requires only the mathematics foundation of junior high school. Goldbach's Conjecture states that every even integer greater than 2 can be expressed as the sum of two primes; understanding this conjecture requires only the mathematics foundation of primary school. The Four Color Conjecture states that every map of the world can be colored with at most four colors such that no two countries sharing a common boundary curve segment receive the same color; evidently, almost every one can understand this conjecture, even an uneducated people.

The adjacency relation among each pair of countries in a map can be depicted by a graph, in which vertices represent the countries and two vertices are adjacent if and only if the two countries corresponding them in the map share a common boundary curve segment. Clearly, the graph corresponding to the map is a plane graph. In 1852, Guthrie [4] observed that four colors are enough to properly color a planar graph; this is the so called Four Color Conjecture. To prove this conjecture, one can only consider maximal planar graphs.

Conjecture 3.1 (Guthrie's Conjecture) Every maximal planar graph is 4-colorable.

3.2 Kempe's Proof and Heawood's Counterexample

On July 17, 1879, almost a year to the day after Cayley's article regarding the Four-Color Problem appeared in the journal "Nature", A. B. Kempe (a lawyer and mathematician) [13] first published a paper in the American Journal of Mathematics, which gave a proof of the Four Color Conjecture; we here call it Kempe's proof.

Kempe's proof proceeds by induction on the number of vertices, which can be briefly described as follows.

Suppose that every maximal planar graph (and so planar graph) of order less than n is 4-colorable and consider a maximal planar graph G of order n. The case of $n \leq 4$ is trivial and suppose that $n \geq 5$. His approach was to reduce G into a smaller maximal planar graph G' of order less than n; by the induction hypothesis, G' is 4-colorable and Kempe attempted to derive a 4-coloring of G from a 4-coloring of G' [7, 13].

By Theorem 1.15, it follows that $3 \leq \delta(G) \leq 5$, by which we consider the following three cases.

Case 1. $\delta(G) = 3$ Let $x \in V(G)$, $d_G(x) = 3$, and $N_G(x) = \{v_1, v_2, v_3\}$. Let $G' = G - x$; by the induction hypothesis, G' has a 4-coloring f'. Let $f'(N_G(x)) = \{1, 2, 3\}$. Then, f' can be extended to a 4-coloring f of G by, for every $u \in V(G)$, letting

$$f(u) = \begin{cases} f'(u), & u \neq x \\ 4, & u = x \end{cases} \quad (3.1)$$

Case 2. $\delta(G) = 4$ Let $x \in V(G)$, $d_G(x) = 4$, and $N_G(x) = \{v_1, v_2, v_3, v_4\}$. Let $G' = G - x$; by the induction hypothesis, G' has a 4-coloring f'. Then, $2 \leq |f'(N_G(x))| \leq 4$. If $2 \leq |f'(N_G(x))| \leq 3$, f' can be easily extended to a 4-coloring of G by assigning x a color properly. Therefore, suppose that $|f'(N_G(x))| = 4$ and without loss of generality assume that $f'(v_i) = i$ for $i = 1, 2, 3, 4$; see Fig. 3.1a. With respect to f', if v_1 and v_3 are not in the same 13-component, we can obtain a 4-coloring f of G by first interchanging the colors of the 13-component containing

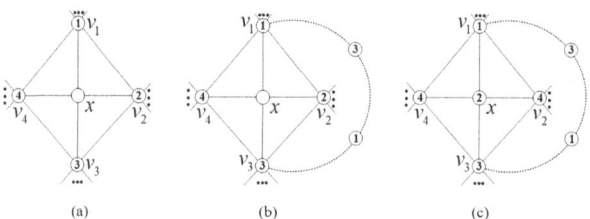

(a) (b) (c)

Fig. 3.1 Illustration for $\delta(G) = 4$

3.2 Kempe's Proof and Heawood's Counterexample

v_1 and then for every $u \in V(G)$ letting

$$f(u) = \begin{cases} f'(u), & u \neq x, v_1 \\ 3, & u = v_1 \\ 1, & u = x \end{cases} \quad (3.2)$$

Therefore, assume that v_1 and v_3 belong to the same 13-component with respect to f'; see Fig. 3.1b. Then, v_2 and v_4 are not in the same 24-component with respect to f'. Therefore, we can obtain a 4-coloring f of G by first interchanging the colors of the 24-component containing v_2 and then for every $u \in V(G)$ letting

$$f(u) = \begin{cases} f'(u), & u \neq x, v_2 \\ 4, & u = v_2 \\ 2, & u = x \end{cases} \quad (3.3)$$

Figure 3.1c illustrates this fact.

Case 3. $\delta(G) = 5$ Let $x \in V(G)$, $d_G(x) = 5$, and $N_G(x) = \{v_1, v_2, v_3, v_4, v_5\}$. Let $G' = G - x$; by the induction hypothesis, G' has a 4-coloring f'. Then, $3 \leq |f'(N_G(x))| \leq 4$. If $|f'(N_G(x))| = 3$, then similarly f' can be easily extended to a 4-coloring of G. Therefore, suppose that $|f'(N_G(x))| = 4$ and without loss of generality assume that $f'(v_i) = i$ for $i = 1, 2, 3, 4$ and $f'(v_5) = 2$; see Fig. 3.2a.

With respect to f', if v_1 and v_3 are not in the same 13-component (or v_1 and v_4 are not in the same 14-component), we can obtain a 4-coloring f of G by first interchanging the colors of the 13-component (or 14-component) containing v_1 and then for every $u \in V(G)$ letting

$$f(u) = \begin{cases} f'(u), & u \neq x, v_1 \\ 3 \text{ (or } 4), & u = v_1 \\ 1, & u = x \end{cases} \quad (3.4)$$

Therefore, assume that v_1 and v_3 belong to the same 13-component and v_1 and v_4 belong to the same 14-component with respect to f'; see Fig. 3.2b. Then, with respect to f', v_2 and v_4 are not in the same 24-component and v_3 and v_5 are

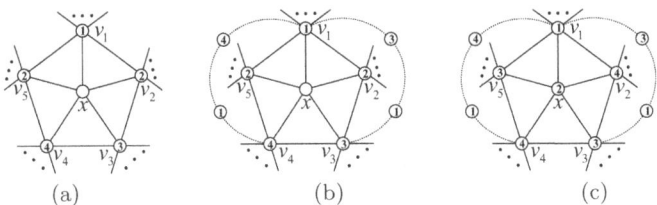

Fig. 3.2 Illustration for $\delta(G) = 5$

not in the same 23-component. Therefore, we can obtain a 4-coloring f of G by first interchanging the colors of the 24-component containing v_2, interchanging the colors of the 23-component containing v_5, and then for every $u \in V(G)$ letting

$$f(u) = \begin{cases} f'(u), & u \neq x, v_2, v_5 \\ 4, & u = v_2 \\ 3, & u = v_5 \\ 2, & u = x \end{cases} \quad (3.5)$$

Figure 3.2c illustrates this fact.

The above describes the skeleton of Kempe's proof. Unfortunately, Heawood [11] discovered a flaw in Kempe's proof: when $\delta(G) = 5$, if the 13-component containing v_1 and v_3 and the 14-component containing v_1 and v_4 share at least two vertices with color 1 (see Fig. 3.3a), then after interchanging the colors of the 24-component containing v_2, whether or not v_3 and v_5 belong to the same 23-component can not be determined. This makes it infeasible to further interchange colors; see Fig. 3.3b.

Figure 3.4 illustrates the Heawood's counterexample. Neither Heawood nor Kempe can modify the mistake of Kempe's proof to gain a correct proof of the Four Color Conjecture. But, by using Kempe's approach, one can obtained the following theorem.

Theorem 3.1 (Five Color Theorem [11]) *Every maximal planar graph is 5-colorable.*

Although Kempe can not prove the Four Color Conjecture eventually, the idea implied in Kempe's proof turns out to be rather important to graph coloring theory and even to the computing theory. By Kempe's method, one can readily induce a new coloring from a given one. This approach is called **Kempe Change**, i.e., interchanging the colors of some bichromatic component with respect to a given 4-coloring of G. The complexity of finding all colorings of a graph can be greatly reduced by using Kempe Change. Since graph coloring problem is NP-complete

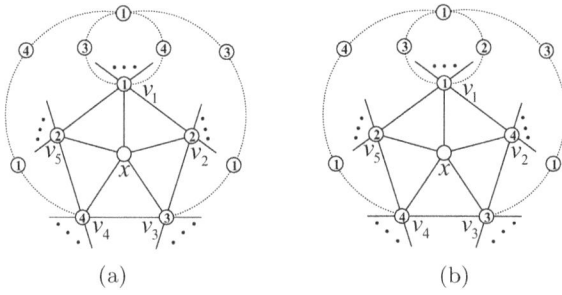

Fig. 3.3 Illustration for the flaw in Kempe's proof

3.2 Kempe's Proof and Heawood's Counterexample

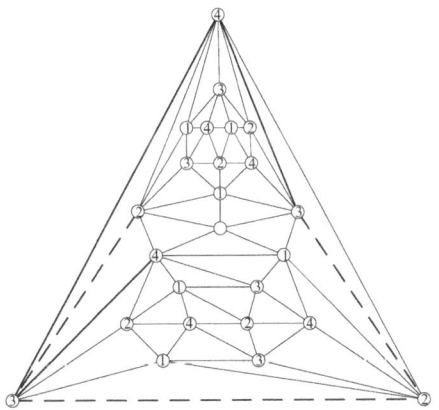

Fig. 3.4 Heawood's Counterexample

and Cook [8] in 1971 proved that all NP-complete problems are equivalent in polynomial time, Kempe's work contributes a lot to the research of computational complexity.

After Heawood and Kempe's proof, many scholars have studied the Four Color Conjecture. Since 1890, although no mathematical proof of the Four Color Conjecture has been obtained, a series of theories and methods have been put forward in the course of research. For example, in 1912, Birkhoff [5] introduced the technique of chromatic polynomial, which is not only an enumeration tool of graph colorings, but also an approach of connecting colorings to structures of graphs. In Chap. 7, we will discuss the recursion formulae of chromatic polynomial of maximal planar graphs and propose a new idea of proving Four Color Conjecture.

Before 1976, the main idea of proving the Four Color Conjecture (to modify the flaw of Kempe's proof), adopted by mathematics, is to find **unavoidable sets of reducible configurations** for maximal planar graphs with minimum degree 5. However, it requires great efforts to prove a configuration to be reducible or a set of reducible configurations to be unavoidable. For this, in 1969, Heesch [17] proposed the method of "discharging transformation" at an academic conference and applied computer to search for the unavoidable sets of reducible configurations. After listening to Heesch's report, Haken [2, 3] was greatly inspired, and finally in 1976, together with Appel, et al., gave a computer-based proof of Four Color Conjecture. Haken and Appels' work caused great influence in the field of computer. This sets a precedent of logical reasoning with machines. However, as a mathematician, it is natural to expect to give a rigorous and brief mathematical proof for the Four Color Conjecture. Unfortunately, **the mathematical proof has not come out yet**.

Many scholars have also expressed doubts on the reliability of the computer-assisted proof. Indeed, Haken and Appel had modified their work several times before they published their proof in 1976, and finally determined 1936 reducible unavoidable configurations. In 1996, 20 years later, Thomas, et al. [16], gave another proof, still using a computer, in which the number of reducible configurations in the unavoidable set was reduced to 633. Since the approach adopted by Thomas, et al.

is the same as that of Haken and Apple, it doesn't make much sense (which only implies that the computer in 1996 is superior to the one in 1976).

Nevertheless, the work of Haken and Appel is great, so this chapter will give a detailed description of their work.

3.3 Reducible Unavoidable Set

3.3.1 Basic Definition

To set forth Kempe's approach clearly, we first present some notations and terminologies.

Recall that a **configuration** is a semi-maximal planar graph G^C on the outer cycle C which has no inner chords. The subgraph induced by the vertices not on C is called the **interior** of the configuration and the length of C is called the **length** of the configuration. Let U be a set of configurations. We say U to be **unavoidable** if every maximal planar graph contains at least one member of U.

For example, the wheel W_k with $k(k \geq 2)$ spokes is a configuration of length k whose interior is an isolated vertex; Fig. 3.5 illustrates W_2, W_3, W_4, and W_5, which are used in Kempe's proof. Since every maximal planar graph contains a 2-vertex (here suppose that multiple edges are permitted), 3-vertex, 4-vertex, or 5-vertex, it follows that $\{W_2, W_3, W_4, W_5\}$ is an unavoidable set.

Suppose that a maximal planar graph G of order n is not 4-colorable. If every maximal planar graph of order less than n is 4-colorable, then G is called a **minimum counterexample** to the Four Colour Conjecture. A configuration is **reducible** if it is not contained in any minimum counterexample. Clearly, given an arbitrary planar graph G containing a configuration G^C, let G' be the graph obtained from G by deleting the interior of G^C. If G' contains a 4-coloring which can be extended to a 4-coloring of G, then G^C is **reducible**. **An unavoidable set of reducible configurations** refers to a set of reducible configuration such that every maximal planar graph contains at least one configuration.

From the reducibility and unavoidability point of view, the basic idea of proving the Four Color Conjecture is to find an unavoidable set of reducible configurations

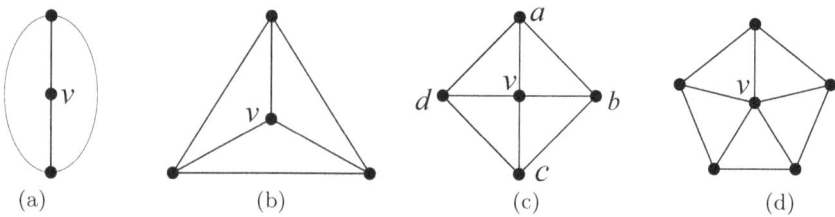

Fig. 3.5 The four unavoidable configurations in Kempe's proof

3.3 Reducible Unavoidable Set

U. If such a set is found, then by contradiction the minimum counterexample does not exist and the Four Color Conjecture is confirmed.

3.3.2 Unavoidable Set

In Kempe's work, the unavoidable set consists of four configurations, but the reducibility of the last configuration (Fig. 3.5d) can not be proved. Therefore, we have to attempt to explore new avoidable set. In 1904, Wernicke [19] found an unavoidable set consisting of the five configurations in Fig. 3.6, which just replaces Fig. 3.5d with Fig. 3.6d, e.

In 1922, Franklin [9] proved that any minimum counterexample to the Four Color Conjecture contains one of the six situations in Fig. 3.7, by which he derived a series of reducible configurations and constructed an unavoidable set of reducible configuration of maximal planar graph of order less than 26. In his work, he proposed a graph parameter, called **Birkhoff number**, which was the maximum integer n such that every maximal planar of order at most n contains an unavoidable set of reducible configurations; thus, Franklin proved that Birkhoff number was at least 26.

The ultimate aim of Franklin is to find an unavoidable set of reducible configurations for every maximal planar graph, i.e., extending the Birkhoff number to infinity. However, with the increasing of the number of vertices, finding an unavoidable set and proving them to be reducible become very difficult. This is mainly due to the fact that the number of 4-colorings of a cycle increase rapidly with the increase of the cycle's length. To illustrate this, we see that the number of (distinct) 4-colorings of 6-cycle is 31 while that of 12-cycle is 22144. Hence, this checking process is far more difficult and complicated.

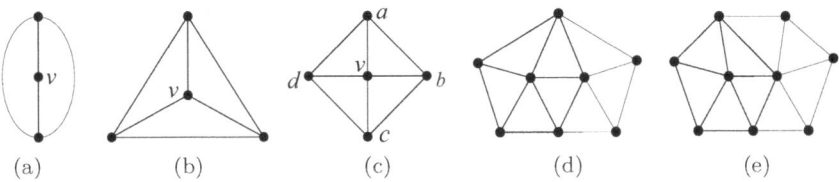

Fig. 3.6 Wernicke's unavoidable set

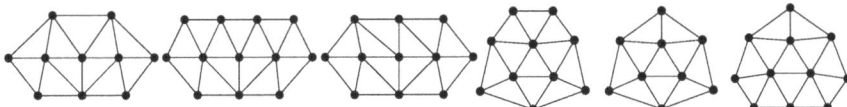

Fig. 3.7 Six situations observed by Franklin

Table 3.1 The historical development of Birkhoff number

	Time	Birkhoff number
P. Franklin	1922	26
C.N. Reynolds	1926	28
P. Franklin	1938	32
C.E. Winn	1940	36
O. Ore and J.G. Stemple	1968	41
WR. Stromquist	July 2 1973	45
J. Mayer	September 1973	48
WR. Stromquist	spring 1974	52
J. Mayer	1975	96

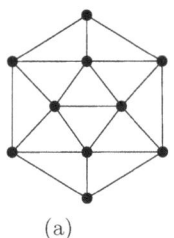 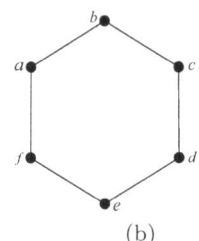

Fig. 3.8 The Birkhoff diamond and a 6-cycle

(a)　　　　　　(b)

Since it was proposed, a great many works have been made to study Birkhoff number. Table 3.1 presents the historical development of the Birkhoff number [10].

In 1948, the German mathematician Heinrich Heesch constructed an unavoidable set consisting of about 10,000 configurations, which contains large configurations of length 18. Most notably, he was the first one who proposed the "**discharging transformation**" to search for unavoidable set of configurations [17].

In Chap. 2, we have depicted the principle of discharging transformation explicitly. To prove a set of configurations is unavoidable, we first suppose that a counterexample contains no configuration of the set; then we construct a discharging transformation φ, by which the final charge is not equal to the initial charge, and arrive at a contradiction [14, 17].

3.3.3 Reducibility

The reliability of configurations was first studied in 1913 by Birkhoff, who proved the configuration in Fig. 3.8a (called Birkhoff diamond) is reducible [6]. In this section, we wish to depict the method of proving Fig. 3.8a to be reducible, which is due to Birkhoff and thenceforth is improved by Heesch.

Theorem 3.2 *Birkhoff diamond is reducible.*

3.3 Reducible Unavoidable Set

Proof Suppose that G is a minimum counterexample and G contains a Birkhoff diamond, say G^C, as shown in Fig. 3.8a. Let G' be the graph obtained from G by removing the interior of G^C; see Fig. 3.8b. By the minimality, G' has a 4-coloring f'. To show that G^C is reducible, we need to prove that f' can be extended to a 4-coloring of G.

Observe that under f' there are in total 31 possible 4-colorings of the six vertices a, b, c, d, e, f on the outer cycle of C. Those include

1 2 1 2 1 2	1 2 1 3 2 4 $\checkmark$	1 2 3 1 4 3	1 2 3 4 1 2
1 2 1 2 1 3 $\checkmark$	1 2 1 3 4 2 $\checkmark$	1 2 3 2 1 2 $\checkmark$	1 2 3 4 1 3
1 2 1 2 3 2	1 2 1 3 4 3 $\checkmark$	1 2 3 2 1 3 $\checkmark$	1 2 3 4 1 4 $\checkmark$
1 2 1 2 3 4 $\checkmark$	1 2 3 1 2 3	1 2 3 2 1 4 $\checkmark$	1 2 3 4 2 3
1 2 1 3 1 2 $\checkmark$	1 2 3 1 2 4	1 2 3 2 3 2 $\checkmark$	1 2 3 4 2 4 $\checkmark$
1 2 1 3 1 3	1 2 3 1 3 2 $\checkmark$	1 2 3 2 3 4	1 2 3 4 3 2 $\checkmark$
1 2 1 3 1 4	1 2 3 1 3 4	1 2 3 2 4 2	1 2 3 4 3 4 $\checkmark$
1 2 1 3 2 3 $\checkmark$	1 2 3 1 4 2	1 2 3 2 4 3	

The above lists all of the possible 4-colorings of vertices a, b, c, d, e, f in Fig. 3.8b. Among them, if a 4-coloring can be extended to a 4-coloring of G directly, then we remark $\checkmark$ after it and call it a **reasonable coloring**; otherwise an **unreasonable coloring**. For example, '1 2 1 2 1 3' is a reasonable coloring since it can be extended to a 4-coloring of G directly (see Fig. 3.9). To show that f' can be extended to a 4-coloring, we must prove that each of the above 31 colorings can be extended to a 4-coloring of G. However, this is not an easy task indeed. We need to use Kempe changes to transform unreasonable colorings into reasonable colorings. For example, '1 2 1 3 1 3' can be transformed into '1 2 1 2 1 2' by Kempe change on 14-component; analogously, '1 2 1 3 1 4' can be transformed into '1 2 1 3 2 4' by Kempe change on 12-component. If each unreasonable coloring can be transformed into a reasonable one by Kempe changes, then G^C is called D-**reducible**.

As described above, to show that a configuration is reducible, we first determine whether it is D-reducible. If not, we may use another strategy. In fact, it is not necessary to consider all of the 31 4-colorings. Since every planar graph of order less than $|V(G)|$ is 4-colorable, G^C can be replaced by a configuration $G^{C'}$ containing less number of vertices than G^C, such as Fig. 3.9b. Thus, we can obtain another 4-

Fig. 3.9 A reasonable coloring of G^C and a replacement of Birkoff diamond

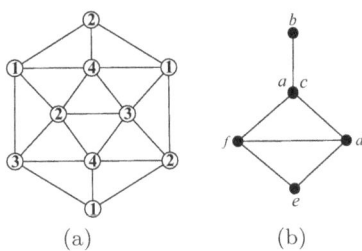

(a)   (b)

colorable planar graph G'' from G by replacing G^C with $G^{C'}$. Let f'' be a 4-coloring of G''. It is enough to consider the cases that $f''(a) = f''(c)$ and $f''(d) \neq f''(f)$. There are in total six such 4-colorings: 1 2 1 2 1 3, 1 2 1 2 3 4, 1 2 1 3 1 2, 1 2 1 3 1 4, 1 2 1 3 2 4, and 1 2 1 3 4 2, in which only '1 2 1 3 1 4' is unreasonable but it can be transformed into a reasonable coloring by Kempe change. Therefore, G has a 4-coloring and C is reducible. ∎

Indeed, there are many configurations which can replace G^C, provided that their outer cycle is complete and they contains less number of vertices than C. If C could be replaced by something smaller one, thereby producing a maximal planar graph by which C can be shown to be reducible, then C is called C-**reducible**.

The following presents some classic results on reducibility [10]. In a minimum counterexample to the Four Colour Conjecture, the following cannot occur.

- **Birkhoff 1913**: a vertex all of whose neighbors have degree 5.
- **Birkhoff 1913**: a vertex of even degree all of whose neighbors have degree 6.
- **Franklin 1922**: a 5-5-5-chain whose vertices are neighbors of one and the same 6-vertex.
- **Franklin 1922**: a 5-vertex whose neighbors can be arranged into a 5-5-6-6-6-chain.
- **Errera 1925**: only vertices of degree 5 and 6.
- **Winn 1937**: a 5-vertex all of whose neighbors have degree 6.
- **Chojnacki-Hanani 1942**: only vertices with degrees not equal to 6 or 7.
- **Heesch 1958**: only vertices of degrees 5 and 7, but without a 7-7-7-triangle.
- **Stanik 1973**: only vertices having degrees not equal to 6, but without a 5-5-5-triangle.
- **Osgood 1974**: only vertices with degrees 5, 6 and 8.
- **Allaire 1976**: only vertices with degrees not equal to 6.

In 1965, Heesch, with the help of Karl Dṙre, designed the first algorithm to check the reducibility of configurations by using computer [10]. At that time, only configurations of length less than 12 could be tested for reducibility, due to limitations of computer memory modules. But, the unavoidable set constructed by Heesch contains configurations of length more than 14, even larger. Therefore, the reducibility can also not be tested quickly by the computer [15].

In the algorithm of Appel and Haken [1–3], they first test whether a configuration is D-reducible; if not, then test whether it is C-reducible by several times of attempts. If it can not be proved to be C-reducible in a short time, then the configuration will be discarded and the unavoidable set will be modified accordingly. Heesch observe that when a configuration contains some special structures, its reducibility can not be proved by all known method. Haken and Appel refer to these structures as **decks**, as shown in Fig. 3.10. They set the modification rule as follows: if some configuration contains one of these decks or has length at lest 14, then it will be discarded [10].

3.4 Proof by Computer

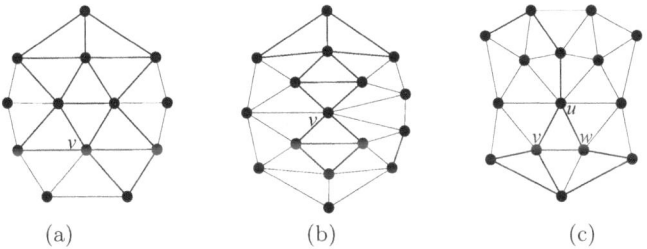

Fig. 3.10 Three decks of Appel and Haken

3.4 Proof by Computer

In 1976, Haken [1] developed a new discharging procedure which contains 487 rules, by which in March 1976 he constructed an unavoidable set consisting of 1936 configurations. By the method mentioned in Sect. 3.3.3, they proved that these configurations are reducible with the help of an IBM 360 in Urbana (University of Illinois), taking about 1200 hours, and eventually completed the computer-based proof of the Four Color Conjecture.

On June 22, 1976, Haken and Appel first announced their result at the Summer Meeting of American Mathematical Society, organized by Mathematical Association of America at university of Toronro. In September, the same year, the news of proving the Four Color Conjecture by them was published in the bulletin column of American Mathematical Society [1]. In 1977, they published the two-part article, titled "Every planar map is four colorable", in "Illinois Journal of Mathematics"[2, 3].

Now, we turn our attention to the detailed description of the Haken and Appels' work.

Let G be a minimum counterexample to the Four Color Conjecture. Let V, E, F be the set of vertices, edges, and faces of G, respectively. We may assume that $\delta(G) = 5$. We first assign an initial charge c to G such that $c(v) = 60(6 - d_G(v))$ for every $v \in V$ and $c(x) = 0$ for every $x \in E \cup F$. Here, setting the coefficient to 60 is just to minimize the number of fractional arithmetics. By Euler's Formula (Formula (1.9) in Theorem 1.12), we infer that

$$\sum_{v \in V} c(v) = 720 \tag{3.6}$$

Observe that $c(v)$ is negative for all vertices of degree at least 7, zero for all 6-vertices, and positive for all 5-vertices.

To simplify description, we describe **configurations** mainly by drawings where **degree specifications of the vertices** follows Fig. 3.11. A configuration G^C is said to be **contained in** G if there is an embedded mapping $f: G^C \to G$ which remains the degree of vertices of G^C unchanged.

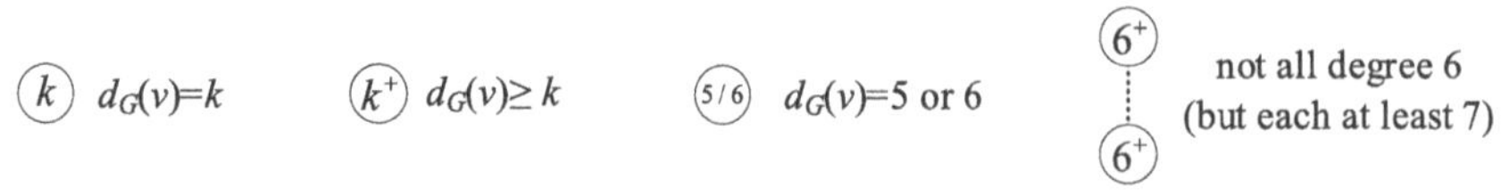

ⓚ $d_G(v)=k$ ⓚ⁺ $d_G(v) \geq k$ ⑤/⑥ $d_G(v)=5$ or 6 not all degree 6 (but each at least 7)

Fig. 3.11 Degree specifications of the vertices introduced by Heesch

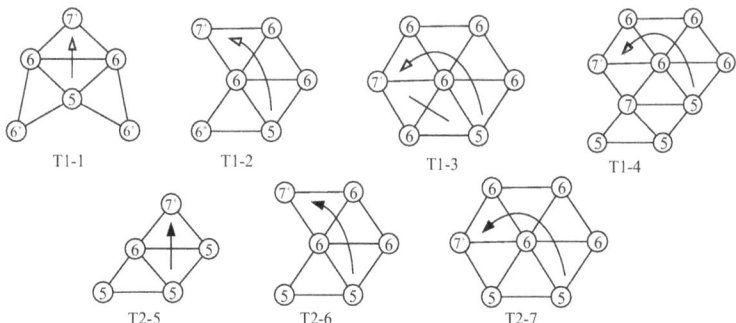

Fig. 3.12 T-discharging

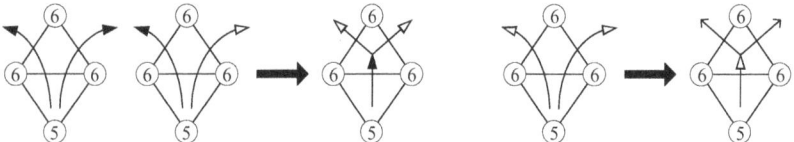

Fig. 3.13 T-discharging correction diagram

Now, we define a **discharging transformation** φ, which transfers the charge of each 5-vertex to its neighbors with a negative charge. The specific rules are as follows:

(1) short-range discharging: transfer charge along edges of G whose ends are 5-vertex and 7^+-vertex;
(2) transversal discharging (abbreviated T-discharging): transfer charge from a 5-vertex through one, two, or three 6-6 edges to a 7^+-vertex.

First, if one of the seven configurations shown in Fig. 3.12 (which are called **T-discharging seven situations**, or simply **T-situations**), is contained in G, then the charge is transferred as indicated by the arrows, in which solid arrow means to transfer a charge of 20 and the open arrow means to transfer a charge of 10.

In addition, if a 5-vertex transfers charge to two 7^+-vertices along the same (6,6)-edge, then the discharging rules are modified as follows: if at least one of the two arrows is solid, then a charge of 10 is transferred along each of the arrows; if both of the arrows are open, then a charge of 5 is transferred along each of them; see Fig. 3.13.

3.4 Proof by Computer

According to the value of charge a T-discharging transfer, T-dischargings are classified into two classes. A T-discharging arrow of value 5 or 10 is called a **T1-discharging** and that of value 20 is called a **T2-discharging** (correspondingly, the seven T-situations in Fig. 3.12 are named as T1-1, T1-2, T1-3, T1-4, T2-5, T2-6, T2-7). In addition, we occasionally draw an "arrow without head" to indicate the path of a T-discharging whose value we do not choose to specify. For instance, in the configuration T1-3 in Fig. 3.12 the unspecified T-discharging will be T2-discharging if the vertex without degree-specification (at the bottom of the drawing) is mapped to a 5-vertex of G and will be T1-discharging otherwise.

Now, we define short-range discharging, including small discharging and large discharging. The "situations of small dischargings", abbreviated S-**situations**, are illustrated in Figs. 3.28, 3.29, 3.30, 3.31, 3.32, 3.33, and 3.34 (by individual drawings). Most of the configurations in Figs. 3.28 3.29, 3.30, 3.31, 3.32, 3.33, and 3.34 include some vertices of partially specified degrees (≥ 6 or ≥ 7) which are separated from the configuration by "clip marks"; see Fig. 3.14. The configurations without these "clipped off" vertices are the S-situations. The full configurations are called **enlarged** S-**situations** and will be explained later. In addition, each of these configurations has a **distinguished edge**, which is drawn vertically and marked by a number (0, 5, 10, 15, 20, or 25), representing its discharging value. Compared with the S-situations, the "situations of large discharging", abbreviated L-**situations**, which are similarly illustrated in Figs. 3.35, 3.36, 3.37, 3.38, 3.39, 3.40, 3.41, and 3.42. Again, the discharging values (35, 40, 50, or 60) are marked at the distinguished edges.

For convenience, the special abbreviations in Fig. 3.15 are used in the proof, which are explained by examples in Fig. 3.16.

Figure 3.15a, b represent part of T-situations which are expanded in Fig. 3.16. Figure 3.15c represents a 7^+-vertex v satisfying that v is not a 7-vertex adjacent to a 5-vertex which does not belong to the configuration containing v but is adjacent to a vertex of the configuration. Figure 3.15d illustrates a 7^+-vertex v with an the exception that v is a 7-vertex which is adjacent to a 5-vertex whose neighbors

Fig. 3.14 Clip marks

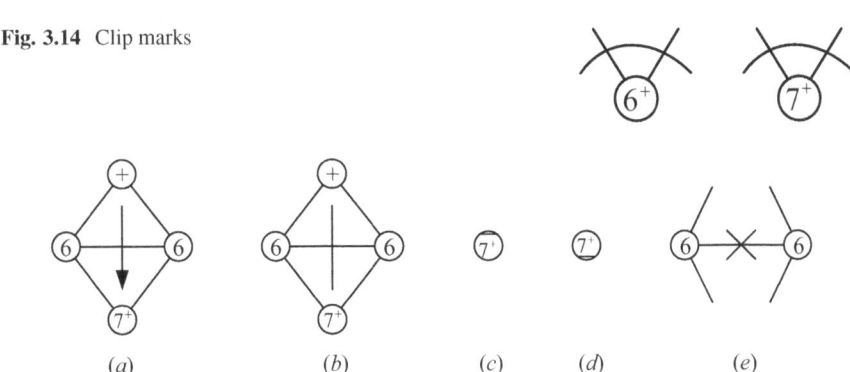

Fig. 3.15 Special abbreviations

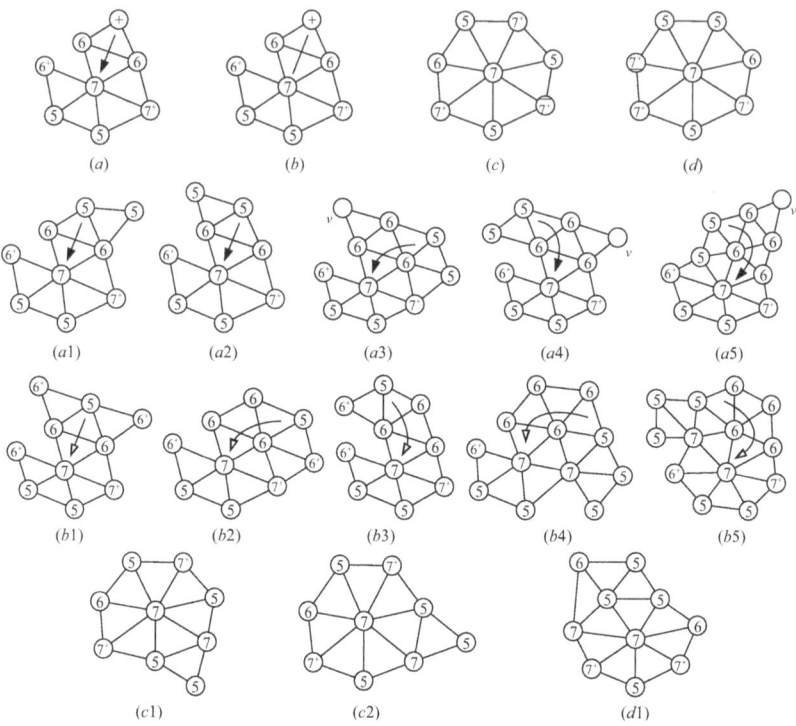

Fig. 3.16 Examples for the explanation of special abbreviations in 3.15

have degree 6,7,7,5, and 5 in the clockwise order. Figure 3.15e illustrates that no T-discharging crosses the marked (6,6)-edge.

Figure 3.16a illustrates one of the five configurations of Fig. 3.16a1–a5, provided that the T2-discharging arrows do not split (i.e., $d_G(v) \leq 6$ in the configurations Fig. 3.16a3–a5). Figure 3.16b illustrates one of the ten configurations of Fig. 3.16a1–a5 and b1–b5. In this case, all T-discharging arrows may or may not split; that is, $d_G(v)$ is arbitrary above). Figure 3.16c excludes Fig. 3.16c1, c2. Figure 3.16d excludes Fig. 3.16d1.

Regarding the edge e, there are three possibilities (see Fig. 3.17 for examples).

(1) No S-situation or L-situation is attached at e. Then, e is called a **regular discharging edge** or **R-edge** and the discharging value $t(e)$ of e is defined to be 30.
(2) There are $k \geq 1$ S-situations and zero L-situations that are attached at e. In this case, e is called a **small discharging edge** or **S-edge** and the discharging value $t(e)$ is defined to be the smallest of the discharging values of the attached S-situations.
(3) There are $k \geq 1$ L-situations and $\ell \geq 0$ S-situations that are attached at e. In this case, we refer to e as a **large discharging edge** or **L-edge** and the discharging

3.4 Proof by Computer

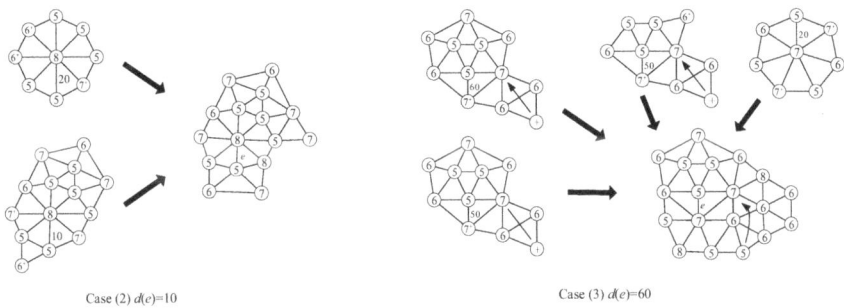

Case (2) $d(e)=10$ Case (3) $d(e)=60$

Fig. 3.17 Illustration for transferring charge of an $(5, 7^+)$-edge e

value $t(e)$ is defined to be the largest of the discharging values of the attached L-situations.

From the forgoing discussion, every $(5, 7^+)$-edge e of G has a uniquely defined discharging value $t(e)$. To all other edges, we assign the discharging value zero. Then, a new charge distribution c' from c can be obtained by (simultaneously) transferring the charge $t(e)$ from the 5-vertex to the 7^+-vertex along each edge e and carrying out the T-discharging. The charge transferred along R-, S-, and L-edges are called **R-**, **S-**, or **L-discharging**, respectively. By implementing short range discharging and T-charging simultaneously, we obtain the new charge distribution c'. By now, the definition of the discharging transformation φ has been defined completely.

For S-edge and L-edge, the following abbreviations are introduced.

- S0: discharging value 0 or 5;
- S1: discharging value 10 or 15;
- S2: discharging value 20 or 25;
- L4: value of the distinguished edge is 40 or 35;
- L5: value of the distinguished edge is 50;
- L6: value of the distinguished edge is 60.

Observe that the discharging transformation φ depends essentially on the set $\mathcal{T}$ of T-discharging situations in Fig. 3.12, on the set $\mathcal{S}$ of S-situations in Figs. 3.28, 3.29, 3.30, 3.31, 3.32, 3.33, and 3.34, and on the set $\mathcal{L}$ of L-situations in Figs. 3.35, 3.36, 3.37, 3.38, 3.39, 3.40, 3.41, and 3.42. For convenience, denote the discharging transformation by $\varphi = (\mathcal{T}, \mathcal{S}, \mathcal{L})$ which means that different discharging transformation can be constructed by using different sets of T-, S-, or L-situations. Then, the following theorem holds (discharging theorem).

Theorem 3.3 (Discharging Theorem) *If G contains no element of the set U, then $c'(v) \leq 0$ for every $v \in V(G)$ after the discharging transformation $\varphi=(\mathcal{T}, \mathcal{S}, \mathcal{L})$, where U is too complicated to be presented here (one can refer to [2, 3]).*

Fig. 3.18 Illustration for Lemma 3.1

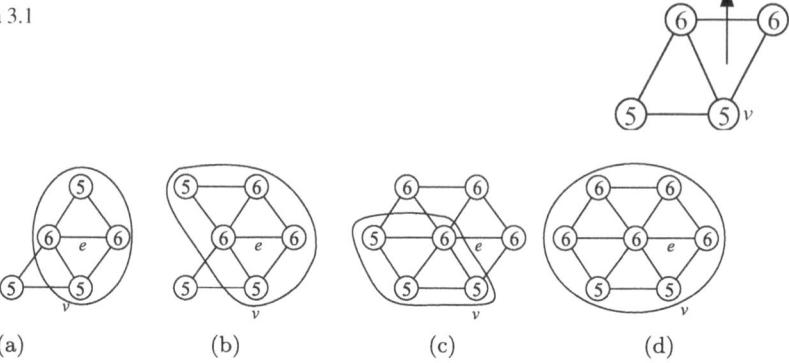

Fig. 3.19 Illustration for the proof of Lemma 3.1. (**a**) 1–3. (**b**) 1–6. (**c**) 1–2. (**d**) 1–10

To prove Theorem 3.3, we may show that $c'(v) \leq 0$ for every $v \in V$. Clearly, $c'(v) = 0$ for any 6-vertex v. Therefore, it remains to proved that

(***1**) for every 5-vertex v, $c'(v) \leq 0$, and
(***2**) for every 7^+-vertex v, $c'(v) \leq 0$.

First, we prove (***1**). For this, we need some preliminary lemmas based on T-discharging.

Lemma 3.1 (5-6-6) *If G contains a 5-vertex v which has three consecutive neighbors of degrees 5, 6, 6, respectively, then a T-discharging of value 20 leaves v across the $(6, 6)$-edge (see Fig. 3.18).*

Proof Clearly, no T2-discharging leaves v across the (6,6)-edge. Then, by definition of the T-discharging, none of the T2-situations T2-5, T2-6, T2-7 is contained in G so as to induce a T-discharging from v across the (6,6)-edge. Thus G contains one of the four configurations of Fig. 3.19 and hence one of the four members of U which are circled in Fig. 3.19. ∎

The proofs of the following three lemmas can be proved with a similar line of thought.

Lemma 3.2 (6-6-6) *If G contains a 5-vertex v which has three consecutive neighbors of degrees 6, 6, 6, respectively, then a T-discharging of value at least 10 leaves v across the $(6, 6)$-edge (see Fig. 3.20a).*

Lemma 3.3 (5^5-7-6-6) *If G contains a 5-vertex v which has four consecutive neighbors of degrees 5,7, 6, 6, respectively, such that another 5-vertex is adjacent to the 5- and 7-vertices, then a T-discharging of value at least 10 leaves v across the $(6, 6)$-edge (see Fig. 3.20b).*

3.4 Proof by Computer

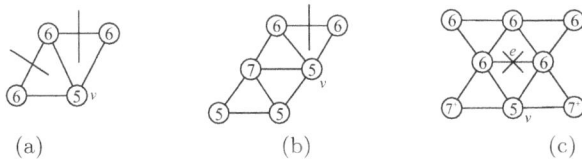

Fig. 3.20 Illustration for Lemma 3.2 (**a**), 3.3 (**b**), and 3.4 (**c**)

Lemma 3.4 (6-6) *If G contains a 5-vertex v which is adjacent to a $(6, 6)$-edge e so that no T-discharging leaves v across e, then G contains the configuration of Fig. 3.20c.*

The following lemma following from inspection of Figs. 3.28, 3.29, 3.30, 3.31, 3.32, 3.33, and 3.34 and the set U.

Lemma 3.5 (S^+) *If $f: S \to G$ is an embedded mapping of an S-situation S into G (which respects the degree specifications), then f can be extended to an embedded mapping from the enlarged S-situation S^+ to G (which respects the degree specifications).*

Now, we consider the discharging transformation $\varphi = (\mathcal{T}, \mathcal{S}, \mathcal{L})$ (which uses the T- and S-situations but no L-situations) and denote also by c' the final charge after this procedure. Then, we have the following conclusion.

Lemma 3.6 (c'(v_5)) *If v is a 5-vertex of G so that $c'(v) > 0$, then one of the cases indicated in Fig. 3.43, applies, that is, one of the configurations CTS-01, ..., CTS-33 drawn in Fig. 3.43 is contained in G with its central 5-vertex identified to v and so that S-situations are attached to the edges marked e, f, g, or h as indicated in Fig. 3.43.*

Proof This can be proved by straightforward enumeration of all possible cases of $c'(v) > 0$ for 5-vertex v of G. ∎

Thus, one see that G contains no element of U. The remaining cases are found in Fig. 3.43.

Let μ be the number of 7^+-vertices adjacent to v in G. We need to consider the cases μ=0, 1,2,3,4,5.

If $\mu = 0$, then v is surrounded by 6^--vertices, which yields a member of U in every case. If $\mu = 1$, the only cases in which no member of U occurs are CTS-01, CTS-02, and CTS-03, where the T2-dischargings in CTS-01 and CTS-03 are T-discharging in Lemma 3.1.

If $\mu = 2$, then at least one S-situation must be attached (otherwise two R-dischargings would yield $c'(v) \leq 0$); moreover, if only one S-situation is attached, then the sum of its discharging value $t(e)$ and the values of the T-dischargings which may be derived by Lemmas 3.1, 3.2, or 3.3, must be smaller than 30 (otherwise the remaining R-discharging would yield $c'(v) \leq 0$).

If $\mu=3$, then G contains at least two S-situations and at least one of them is S0-situation or S1-situation. But if the sum of the discharging values $t(e)+t(f)$ is not smaller than 30, then a third S-situation must be attached. All those cases which do not yield configurations of U involve either an S0- or two S1-situations.

If $\mu = 4$, then G contains two S-situations and there are consecutive edges e, f so that $t(e)+t(f) < 30$. A third S-situation must be attached at an edge g, and if $t(e)+t(f)+t(g) \geq 30$, then a fourth S-situation is required. All cases which do not yield configurations of U involve either two S0- and one S2-situations, or one S0- and two S1-situations.

Finally, if $\mu = 5$, we consider all adjacent attachments of an S0 and an S1 or S2. Clearly, only a few of them do not yield configurations of U. Then one finds that all consecutive triplets (S0, S0, S0), (S0, S0, S1), and (S1, S0, S1) yield configurations of U. It is then easy to enumerate the remaining cases; the only one which does not yield configuration of U involves four consecutive S-situations (S0, S1, S1, S0).

We then completes the proof of (*1) by the following Lemma 3.7.

Lemma 3.7 (L) *Each of the configurations CTS-01, ..., CTS-33 in Fig. 3.43 contains an L-situation in which the discharging edge is marked x and the discharging value is large enough to yield $c'(v) \leq 0$ for the central 5-vertex v.*

Proof The proof of this lemma can be illustrated immediately by Fig. 3.43. ∎

In the following, we turn to the proof of (**2**), before which we need some simple lemmas (without detailed proof).

Lemma 3.8 (T) *Let v be a 7^+-vertex of G. If v is adjacent to a (6,6)-edge e, then v receives at most one T-discharging across e.*

Lemma 3.9 (T1,T2) *Let v be a 7^+-vertex of G. If v receives T2-dischargings across two consecutive (6,6)-edges e and f, then one of the two configurations of Fig. 3.21 is contained in G.*

Lemma 3.10 (T2,T2,T2) *Let v be a 7^+-vertex of G. Then, v does not receive T2-discharging across three consecutive (6,6)-edges.*

Lemma 3.11 (T,T2,T2,T) *Let v be a 7^+-vertex of G. If v receives T-dischargings across four consecutive (6,6)-edges e, f, g, h, then the dischargings across the second and third edges, f and g, are not both T2-dischargings.*

Fig. 3.21 Illustration for Lemma 3.9

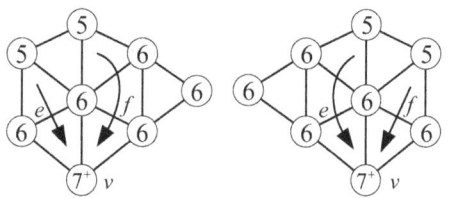

3.4 Proof by Computer

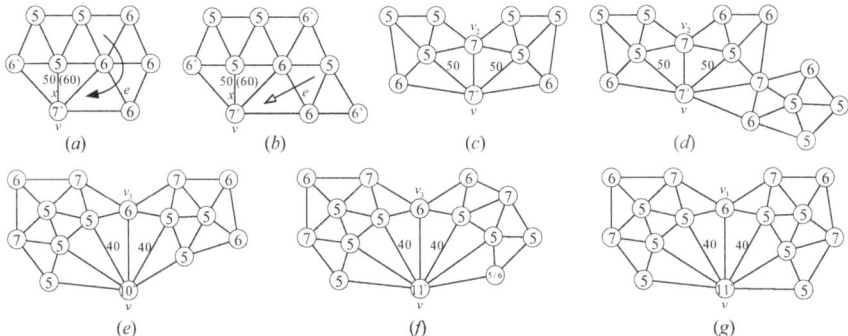

Fig. 3.22 (**a**) one of 411, 441, 491, ..., 495 at x; (**b**) one of 411, 441, 492, 493, 494 at x; (**c**) twice 441; (**d**) 441 and one of 551, 552, 720; (**e**) 432 and 403; (**f**) 432 and 431 or 465; (**h**) twice 432

Lemma 3.12 (60/50, T) *Let v be a 7^+-vertex of G. If v receives an L-discharging of value 60 or 50 along an edge x and a T-discharging across a (6,6)-edge e next to x (that is, the 5-vertex of x and the 6-vertices of e are consecutive), then Fig. 3.22a or b occurs.*

Lemma 3.13 (60/50, T2, T2) *Let v be a 7^+-vertex of G. If v receives an L-discharging of value 60 or 50 and a T2-discharging across a (6,6)-edge e next to x, then v can not receive a second T2-discharging across a (6,6)-edge f consecutive to e.*

Lemma 3.14 (60/50, ·, 60/50) *Let v be a 7^+-vertex of G with three consecutive neighbors v_1, v_2, v_3 such that $d_G(v_1) = d_G(v_3) = 5$. If v receives an L6- or L5-discharging from each of v_1 and v_3, then Fig. 3.22c or d occurs.*

Lemma 3.15 (5, L, ·, L, 5) *Let v be a 7^+-vertex of G with five consecutive neighbors v_1, v_2, v_3, v_4, v_5 such that $d_G(v_1) = d_G(v_2) = d_G(v_4) = d_G(v_5) = 5$. If v receives an L-discharging from each of v_2 and v_4, then Fig. 3.22e, f, or g occurs.*

Lemma 3.16 (5, L, 5) *Let v be a 7^+-vertex of G with five consecutive neighbors v_1, v_2, v_3 such that $d_G(v_1) = d_G(v_2) = d_G(v_3) = 5$. Then, no L-discharging can go from v_2 to v.*

Lemma 3.17 (5, L) *Let v be a 7^+-vertex of G with two consecutive neighbors v_1, v_2 such that $d_G(v_1) = d_G(v_2) = 5$. Then, no L5- or L6-discharging can go from v_1 or v_2 to v.*

Lemma 3.18 (5, L, T2) *Let v be a 7^+-vertex of G with five consecutive neighbors v_1, v_2, v_3, v_4 such that $d_G(v_1) = d_G(v_2) = 5$ and $d_G(v_3) = d_G(v_4) = 6$. If v receives an L-discharging from v_2 and a T2-discharging across the edge v_3v_4, then Fig. 3.23 occurs.*

Fig. 3.23 Illustration for Lemma 3.18

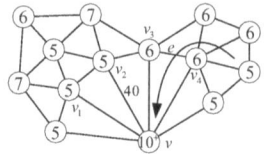

Lemma 3.19 (5, L, ·, 60/50) *Let v be a 7^+-vertex of G with four consecutive neighbors v_1, v_2, v_3, v_4 such that $d_G(v_1) = d_G(v_2) = d_G(v_4) = 5$. If v receives an L-discharging from v_2 and a L6- or L5-discharging from v_4, then the discharging from v_4 is induced by the L-situation 50-441 (i.e., L5) so that $d_G(v_3) = 7$.*

Lemma 3.20 (50/60, T, 50/60) *Let v be a 7^+-vertex of G with four consecutive neighbors v_1, v_2, v_3, v_4 such that $d_G(v_1) = d_G(v_4) = 5$ and $d_G(v_2) = d_G(v_3) = 6$. If v receives an L-discharging of value greater than 40 from each of v_2 and v_4, and a T-discharging across the edge $e = v_2 v_3$, then T1-1 is attached at e.*

According to the above lemmas, one can compute an upper bound for the sum of all dischargings which go to a 7^+-vertex v of G, denoted by $up(v)$. By $n(v)$ we denote the number of neighbors of v with degree 5 in G.

Lemma 3.21 (Upper Bound Lemma) *Let v be a k-vertex of G such that $k \geq 7$. Then,*

$$up(v) \leq 30k - 7.5(k - n(v)) \qquad (3.7)$$

if G does not contain the configuration of Fig. 3.23, then

$$up(v) \leq 30k - 10(k - n(v)) \qquad (3.8)$$

Proof Let $v_1, v_2, \ldots, v_k$ be the neighbors of v in some clockwise cyclic order. Assign to each v_i for $i = 1, 2, \ldots, k$ a **contribution value** c_i such that

$$c_i = \begin{cases} 30, & if \ d_G(v_i) = 5 \\ c_i^* + c_i^{**}, & if \ d_G(v_i) > 5 \end{cases} \qquad (3.9)$$

where c_i^* and c_i^{**} are defined as follows (with subscripts modulo k).

(1) If v_j is a 5-vertex which accepts an L4-, L5-, or L6-discharges and if neither of v_{j-1} nor v_{j+1} is a 5-vertex, then $c_{j-1}^{**} = c_{j+1}^{**} = 5$, 10, or 15, respectively, with the three exceptions in Fig. 3.24, where c_{j-1}^{**} and c_{j+1}^* are defined as indicated below the drawings.

(2) If v_j and v_{j+1} are 5-vertices such that v receives an $L4$-discharges from v_j, then $c_{j-1}^{**} = 10$. Correspondingly, if v_{j-1} and v_j are 5-vertices such that v receives an L4-discharges from v_j, then $c_{j+1}^* = 10$.

(3) If v_j and v_{j+1} are 6-vertices such that v receives a Tl-discharging across the (6,6)-edge $v_j v_{j+1}$, then $c_j^{**} = c_{j+1}^* = 5$.

3.4 Proof by Computer

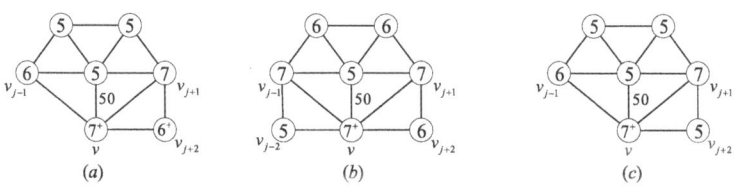

Fig. 3.24 (a) $c^{**}_{j-1} = 0$, $c^*_{j+1} = 20$; (b) $c^{**}_{j-1} = 0$, $c^*_{j+1} = 20$; (c) $c^{**}_{j-1} = 15$, $c^*_{j+1} = 5$

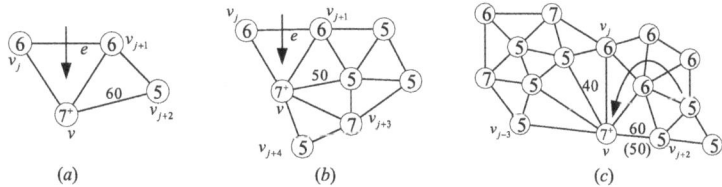

Fig. 3.25 (a) c^{**}_j=15, v^*_{j+1}=5; (b) c^{**}_j=15, c^*_{j+1}=5; (c) c^{**}_j=12.5, c^*_{j+1}=7.5

(4) If v_j and v_{j+1} are 6-vertices such that v receives a T2-discharging across the edge (6,6)-edge $v_j v_{j+1}$, then $c^{**}_j = c^*_{j+1} = 10$, with the three exceptions in Fig. 3.25, where c^{**}_j and v^*_{j+1} are defined as indicated below the drawings.

(5) If c^*_i or c^{**}_i is not defined by the above (1), (2), (3), or (4) for some $i \in \{1, 2, \ldots, k\}$, then it is defined to be zero.

Then, by the above lemmas, it follows that

$$\sum_{i=1}^{k} c_i \geq d(v) \tag{3.10}$$

where

$$c_i \leq \begin{cases} 22.5, d_G(v_i) \neq 5 \\ 20, \ d_G(v_i) \neq 5 \text{ and } d_G(v_i) \neq 6 \end{cases} \tag{3.11}$$

This completes the proof of this lemma. ∎

Corollary 3.1 *If the configuration of Fig. 3.23 does not occur and if there is some i for which $c_i < 20$, then*

$$up(v) \leq 30k - 10(k - n(v)) - 10 \tag{3.12}$$

Proof This follows from Lemma 3.21, since $\sum_{i=1}^{k} c_i$ is an integral multiple of 10. ∎

Observe that

$$c'(v) = up(v) - 60(k - 6) \tag{3.13}$$

One can deduce that (*2) holds when $k \geq 11$. This is because by Lemma 3.21 when $k \geq 12$, $c'(v) \leq 0$; when $k = 11$, if $c'(v) > 0$ then $n(v) \geq 8$ (but if $n(v) = 8$, the configuration of Fig. 3.23 must occur). Moreover, $n(v) \geq 10$ is ruled out in G because of 15-34 in U. Now, in the remaining cases one can readily check that either $c'(v) \leq 0$ or 15-34 (or 15-35) in U occur.

Regarding to the cases $k = 7, 8, 9, 10$, we need to consider the discharging transformation $\varphi = (\mathcal{T}, \emptyset, \mathcal{L})$ (i.e., we ignore the S-situations) and we denote by c' also the corresponding final charge distribution. Then, the following holds.

Lemma 3.22 *Let v be a 7^+-vertex of G such that $c'(v) > 0$. Then, one of the cases CTL-1, ..., CTL-152 in Figs. 3.44, 3.45, 3.46, and 3.47 occurs, where the central 7^+-vertex is v and the L-situations are attached as indicated to those edges which are marked by large discharging values but to no other edges incident to v.*

Proof The proof proceeds by straightforward case enumeration for $k = 7, 8, 9$, and 10. ∎

When $k = 7$, one need to consider cases in terms of the neighborhoods of v.

(a) No neighbor of v with degree 5 but T-dischargings of total value greater than 60.
(b) One neighbor of v with degree 5, which is R-, L4-, L5-, or L6-discharging to the v and T-dischargings of total value greater than 30, 20, 10, or 0, respectively.
(c) Two neighbors of v with degree 5 and a T- or L-discharging.
(d) Three or more neighbors of v with degree 5.

Those cases in which no member of U occurs are listed in Figs. 3.44, 3.45, 3.46, and 3.47. Observe that all cases in which an L-situation of width $w \geq 4$ occurs yield likely to be reducible configurations if the pivot is a v; but some of these configurations have length greater than 14. For this reason, the unavoidable set is modified by including the cases CTL-76, CTL-77 in Fig. 3.43, instead of the attempt of reducing the corresponding configurations of length 15 in order to include them in U.

When $k = 8$, it is the case of greatest combinatorial complexity. The following cases need to consider in terms of the neighborhoods of v.

(a') v has no neighbor of degree 5;
(b') One, two, or three neighbors of v with degree 5 and correspondingly strong T- and/or L-dischargings.
(c') Four neighbors of v with degree 5 and a T- or L-discharging.
(d') Five or more neighbors of v with degree 5.

The case (a') follows from Lemmas 3.8, 3.10, and 3.11. For (b'), (c'), and (d'), the only cases for which G contains no configuration of U are CTL-138 and CTL-139 in Fig. 3.47.

For $k = 9$ and $k = 10$, we can prove that $c'(v) \leq 0$ with a similar line of thought.

The following lemma can be proved immediately by inspection, and then complete the proof of (*2) and thus the proof of the Discharging Theorem (Theorem 3.3).

Lemma 3.23 (S) *In all cases CTL-1, ..., CTL-152 in Figs. 3.44, 3.45, 3.46, and 3.47, we have $c'(v) \leq 0$ for every central vertex v.*

Hence, by Formula (3.6) we obtain a contradiction. Therefore, the following holds.

Corollary 3.2 *G contains a configuration of U.*

By Theorem 3.3, the Four Color Conjecture can be proved if the configurations in the unavoidable set U can be shown to be reducible. This process is checked using computer.

3.5 Discussion and Conclusion

To dispel any remaining doubts about A-H proof which is extremely long and complicated, Haken, et al., attempted to refine their proof by constructing a smaller unavoidable set of configurations whose reducibility are more easily verifiable. They soon afterward reduced the size of unavoidable set of reducible configurations to 1476, and later to 633 by Robertson, et al. in 1994 [16]. To confirm the validity, mathematicians examined the proof in detail and found a large number of flaws and errors this time. Fortunately, these defects can be modified. However, the revision also lasted a number of years before it was finally completed [10].

While Robertson, et al. [16] used the same general approach as A-H proof to prove the reducibility of configurations, they simplified the process of the unavoidability of the set of configurations by improving the discharging transformation (reduced to 32 rules; see Fig. 3.26). In addition, they also described an $O(n^2)$ algorithm of finding 4-coloring of planar graphs, which improved the $O(n^4)$ algorithm generated from A-H proof.

It has been proved, by Birkhoff, that every configuration of length 4, or of length 5 with two vertices in its interior, is reducible. That is,

Theorem 3.4 *Let G be a smallest counterexample to the Four Color Conjecture. Then, G does not contain a 4-cycle or a 5-cycle with two vertices in its interior.*

By Theorem 3.4, one see that in every smallest counterexample to the Four Color Conjecture there are only a few types of cycles with smaller length. Figure 3.27 illustrates two nontrivial case of them. The **trivial cycles** include two types: one is the 3-cycle; the other is the 5-cycle induced by five neighbors of a 5-vertex.

To describe Thomas's work clearly, we introduce the following definitions: given a maximal planar graph G, a cycle C of G is called **short** if the length of C is at most 5. If every short cycle of G is trivial, then G is called **essentially 6-connected**. Thomas's proof is based on the following three theorems.

Fig. 3.26 Thomas's 32 discharging rules

Fig. 3.27 Two nontrivial short cycles

3.5 Discussion and Conclusion

Thomas et al. [16] proved the following three theorems.

Theorem 3.5 *Let G be a essentially 6-connected maximal planar graph. Then, G contains at least one configuration of the set of 633 configurations.*

Proof Suppose that G does not contain any configuration of the set of 633 configurations. Then, according to the discharging transformation shown in Fig. 3.26, the final charge is not equal to the initial charge and arrive at a contradiction. Therefore, the set of the 633 configurations is unavoidable (Figs. 3.28, 3.29, 3.30, 3.31, 3.32, 3.33, and 3.34). ∎

Theorem 3.6 ([16]) *Every minimum counterexample to the Four Color Conjecture is essentially 6-connected.*

Proof In [16], Thomas, et, al. described an algorithm of finding a 4-coloring of maximal planar graph, which starts with a short cycle and all 4-coloring of maximal planar graphs with small order. For a smallest counterexample G to the Four Color Conjecture, since every maximal planar graph with order less than $|V(G)|$ is 4-colorable. Suppose that G contains a nontrivial short cycle, then one can construct a 4-coloring of G by the Algorithm, a contradiction. Hence, G contains no nontrivial short cycle and is essentially 6-connected. ∎

Theorem 3.7 *Every minimum counterexample to the Four Color Conjecture contains no configuration of the set of 633 configurations.*

Theorem 3.7 shows the reducibility (Figs. 3.35, 3.36, 3.37, 3.38, 3.39, 3.40, 3.41, and 3.42).

By Theorems 3.5, 3.6, and 3.7, Thomas, et al. proved that there does not exist any counterexample to the Four Color Conjecture, and proved the Four Color Conjecture (Figs. 3.43, 3.44, 3.45, 3.46, and 3.47).

The Four Color Theorem was the first major mathematical theorem to be proved using computer. This proof has not been fully accepted by mathematician in the beginning. In 1979, Thomas Tymoczko [18] argued that whether or not the Four Color Theorem and its computer-assisted proof (Appel-Haken proof, abbreviated A-H proof) can be considered as a "Theorem" or "Proof" in the original sense is still involved in doubt, and the definitions of their proof need also examining and verifying. There are basically two reasons: (1) no mathematician can survey the whole proof mainly because there was no printout of the computer calculations, and it is likely that there never will be; (2) the computer-assisted proof can not form logical statements [12]. Also, many mathematicians believe that the computer-aided proofs are only an extension of human calculations, since the computer merely conduct the operation (every step) according to the instructions of the human; it only saves the working time [17].

For more than a century, to obtain a mathematical proof of the Four Color Conjecture, mathematicians have made a great effort. In the process of proving, many novel concepts and methods are introduced in succession, which greatly promoted the development of topology, graph theory, and computer science, etc. The research on the Four Color Conjectures is still on the way.

Appendix

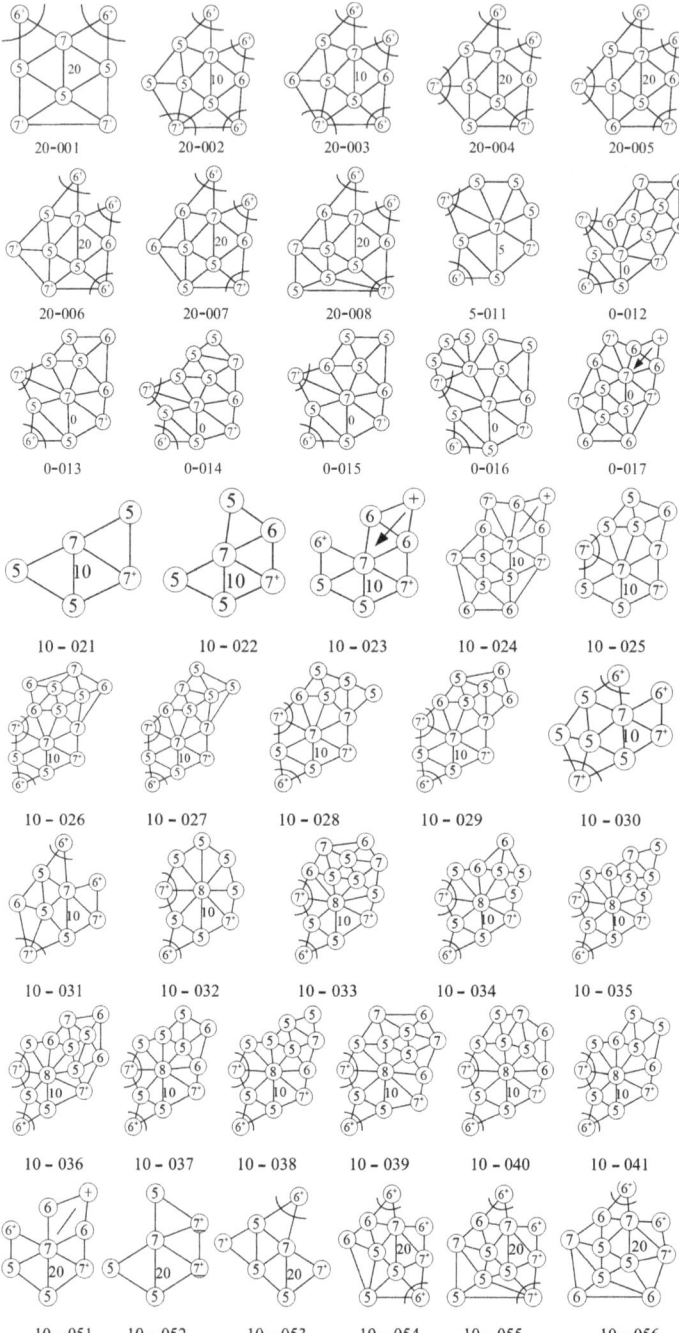

Fig. 3.28 S-situations: page 1

Appendix

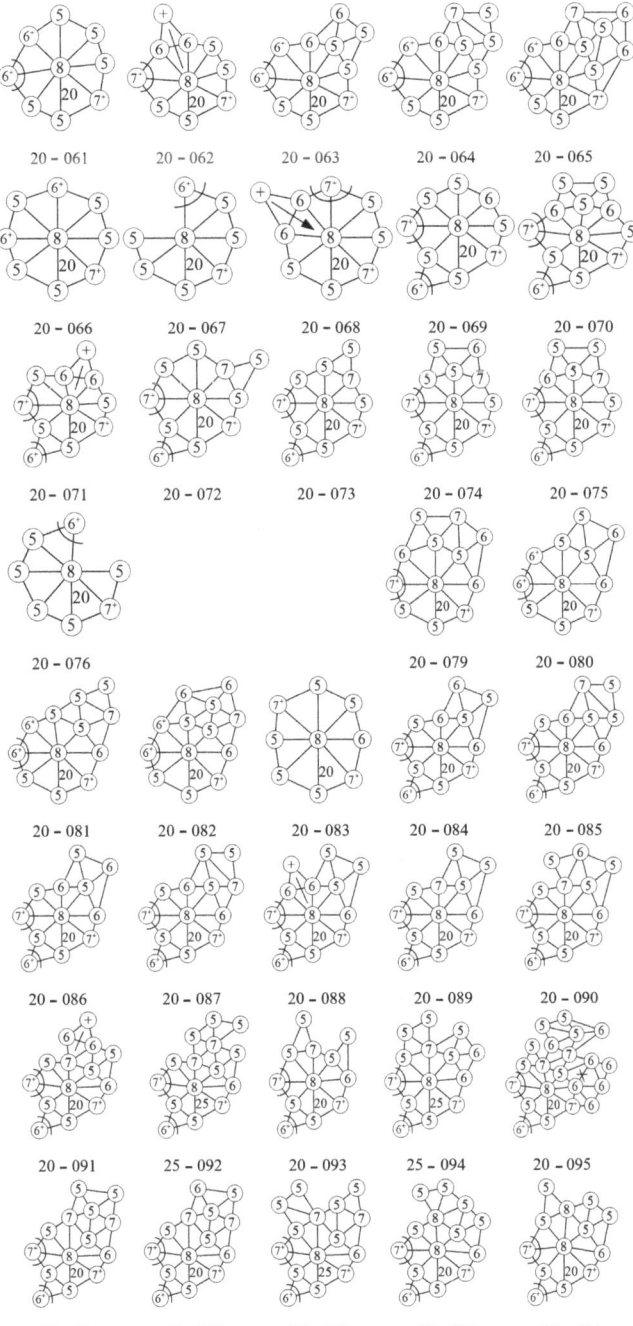

Fig. 3.29 S-situations: page 2

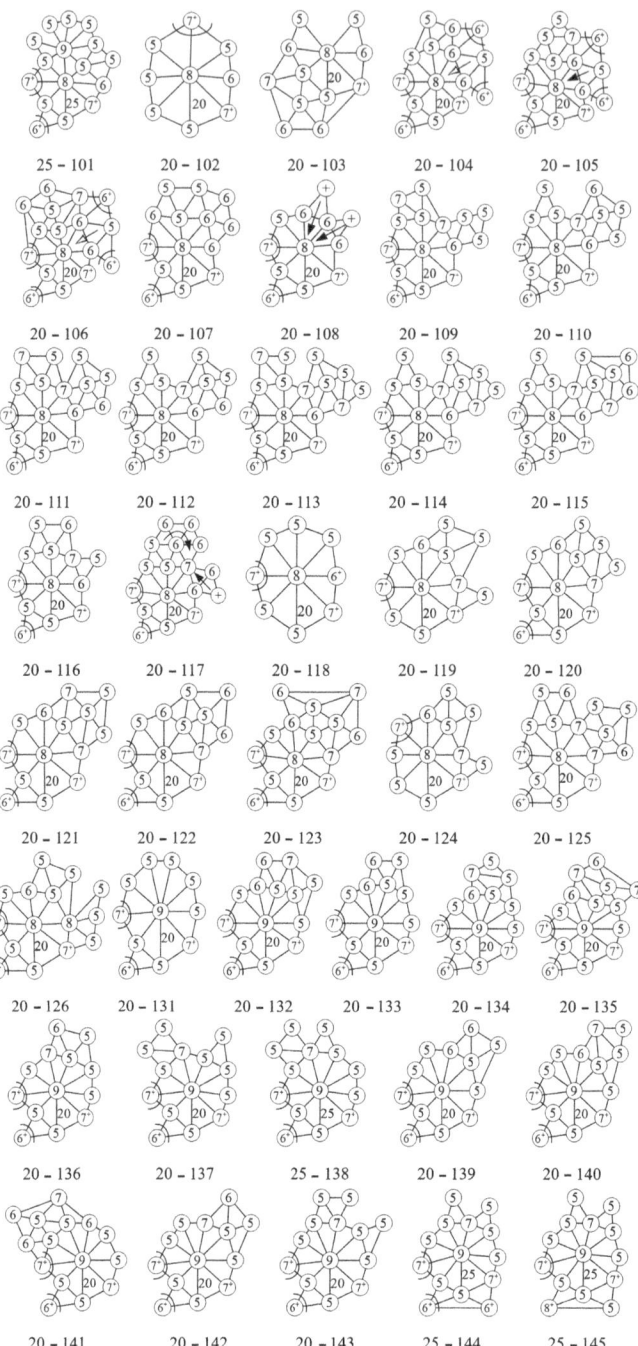

Fig. 3.30 S-situations: page 3

Appendix

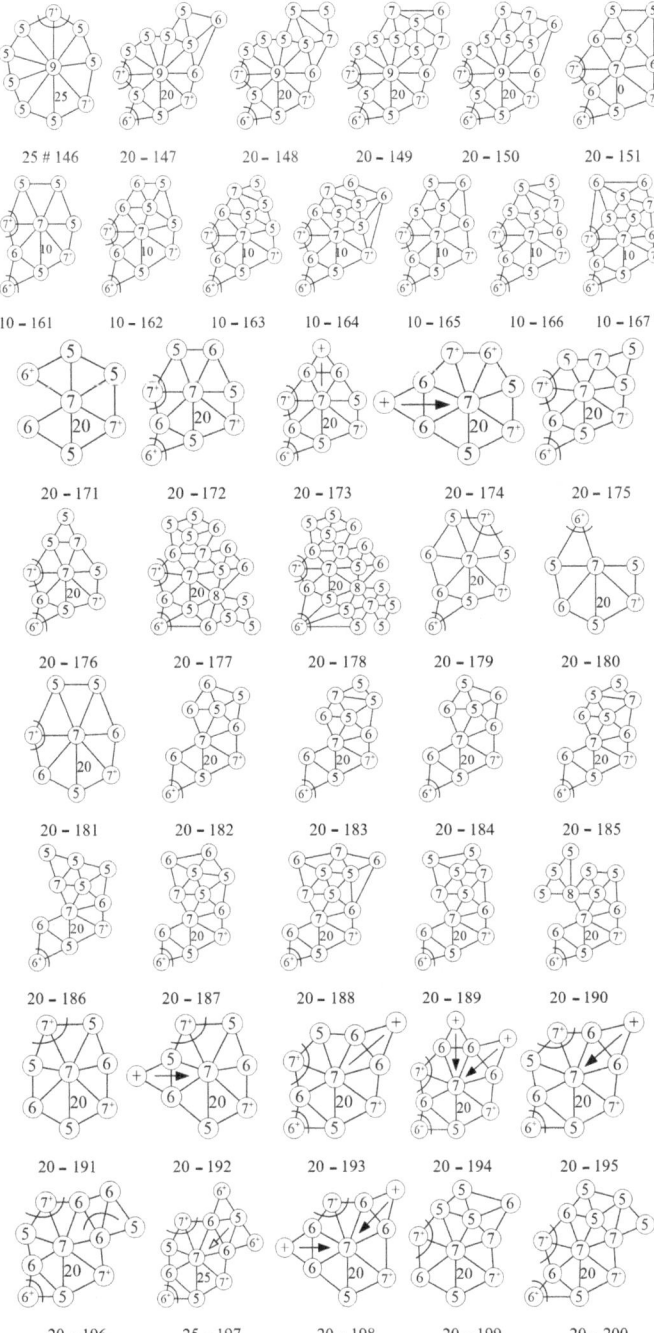

Fig. 3.31 S-situations: page 4

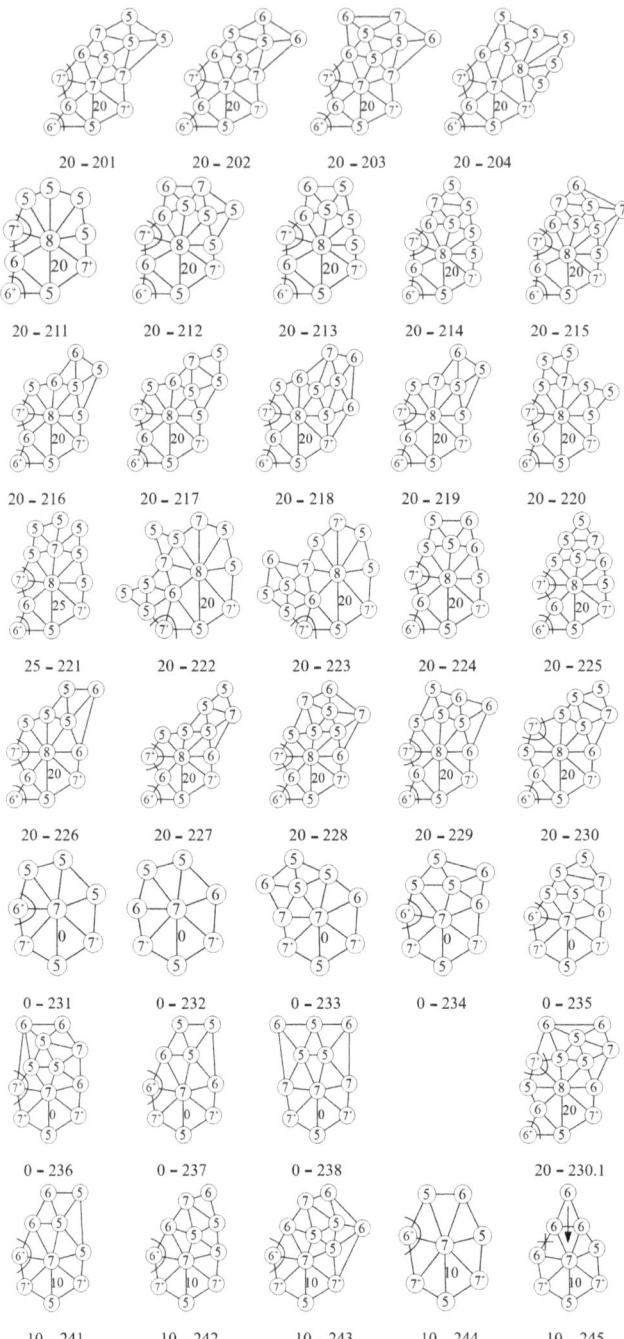

Fig. 3.32 S-situations: page 5

Appendix 101

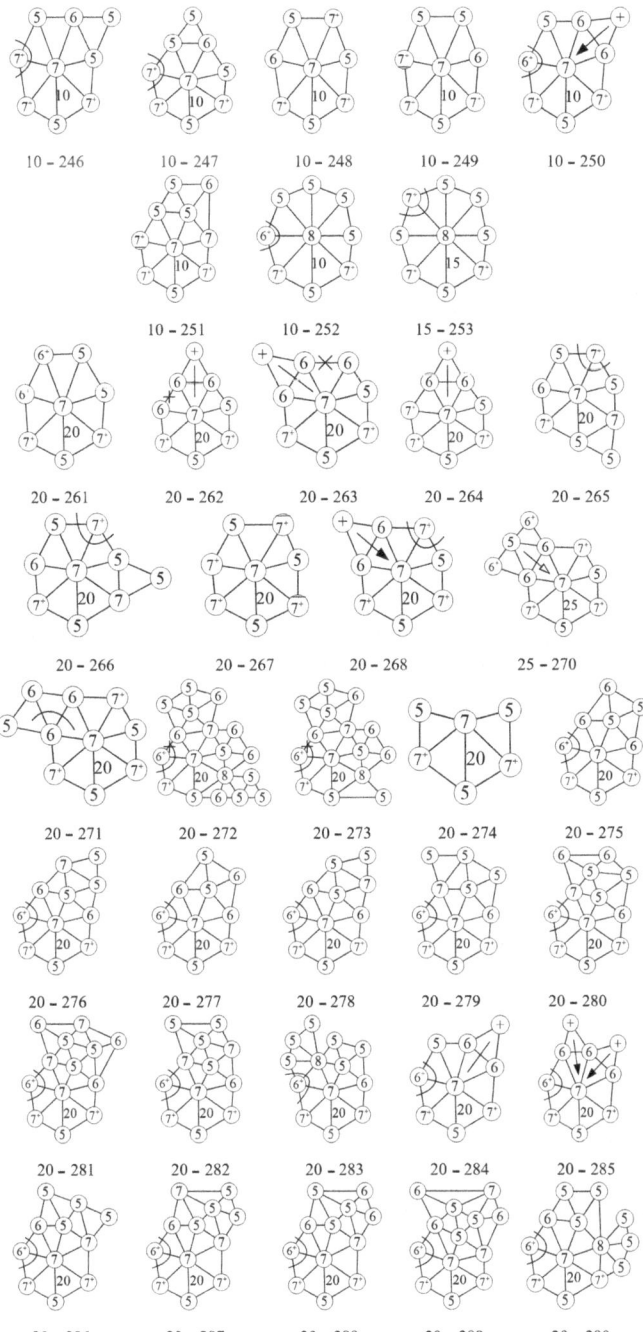

Fig. 3.33 S-situations: page 6

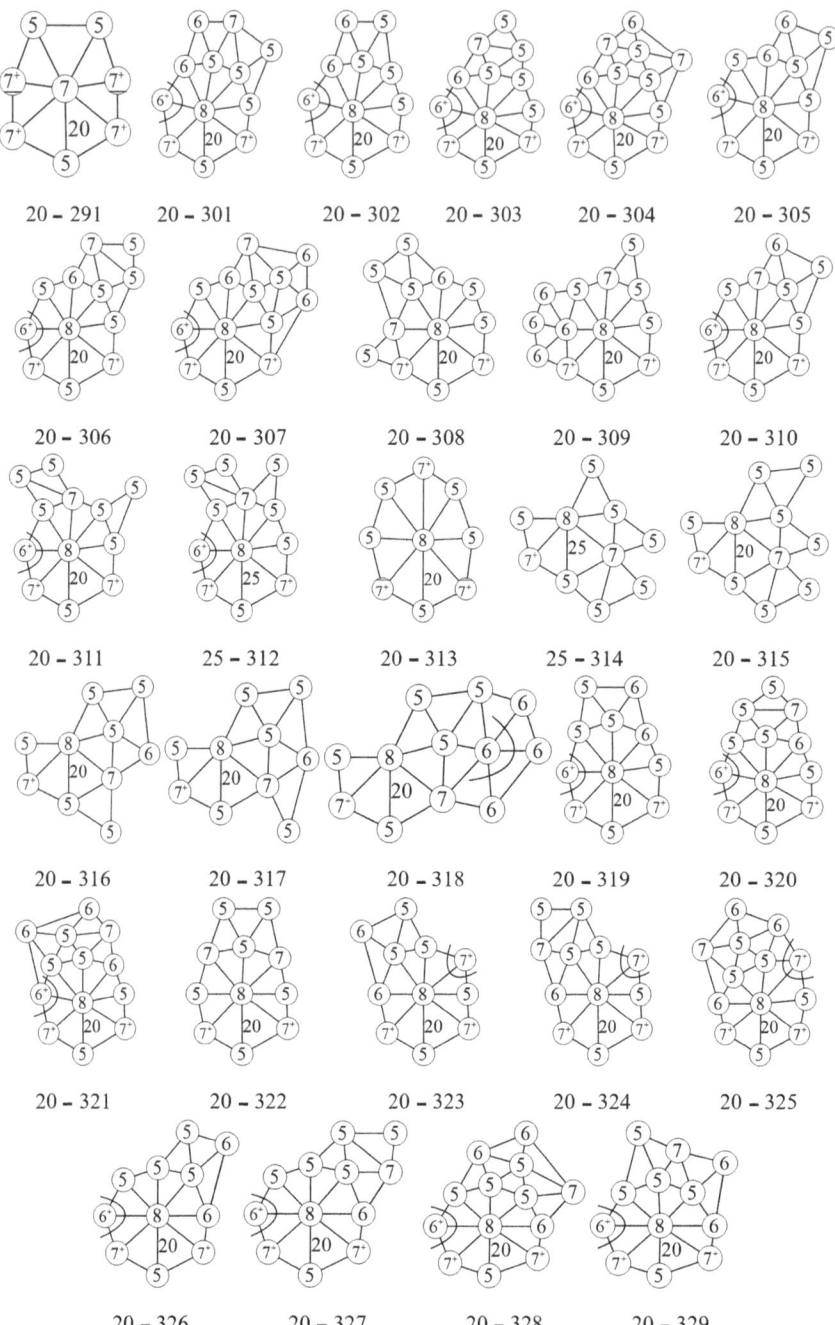

Fig. 3.34 S-situations: page 7

Appendix

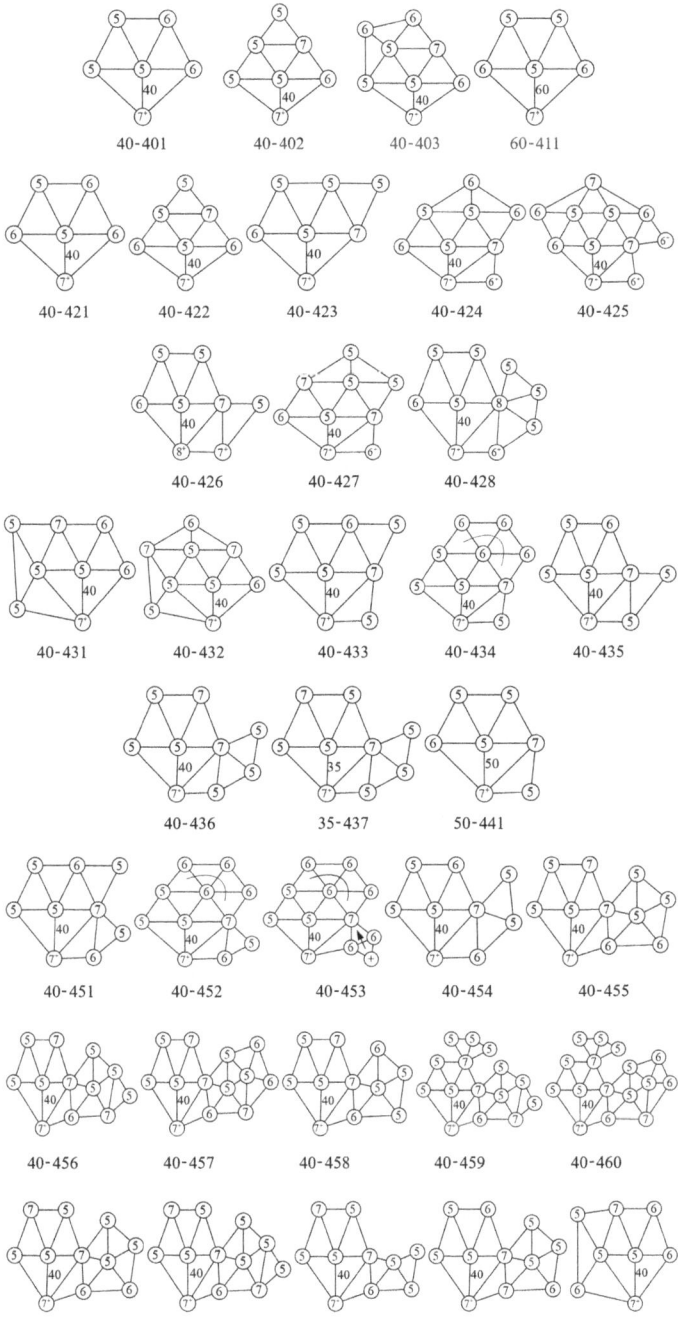

Fig. 3.35 L-situations: page 1

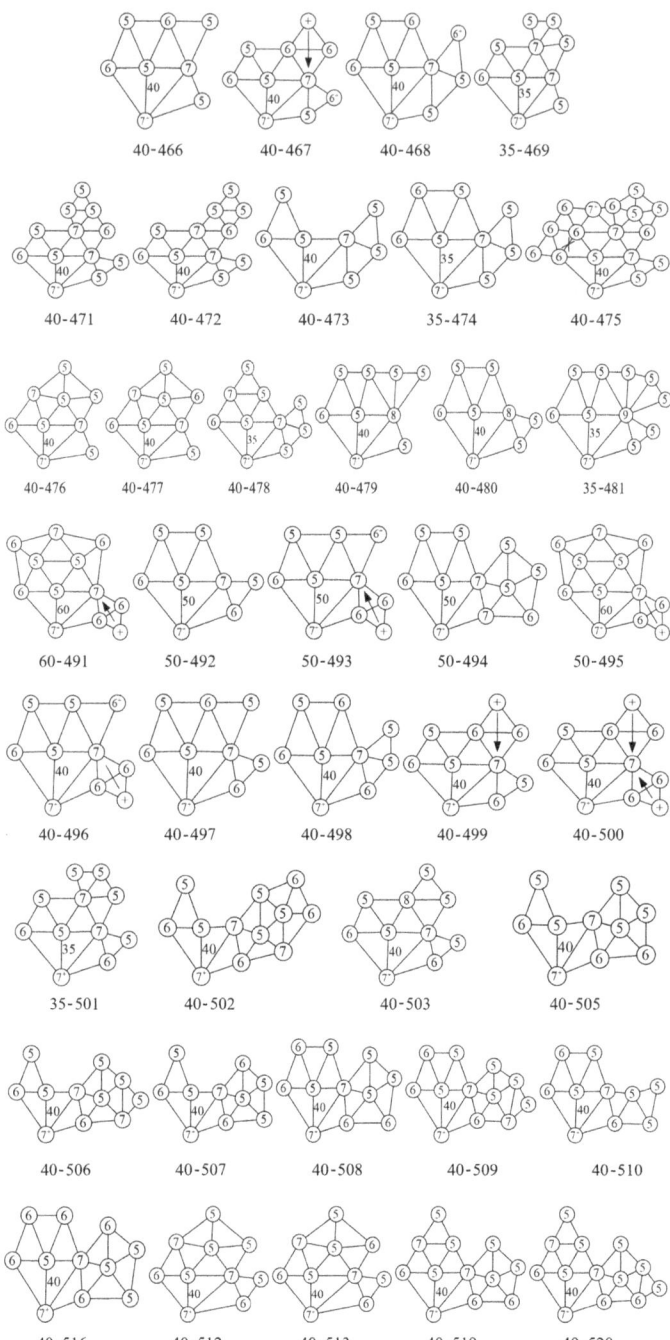

Fig. 3.36 L-situations: page 2

Appendix

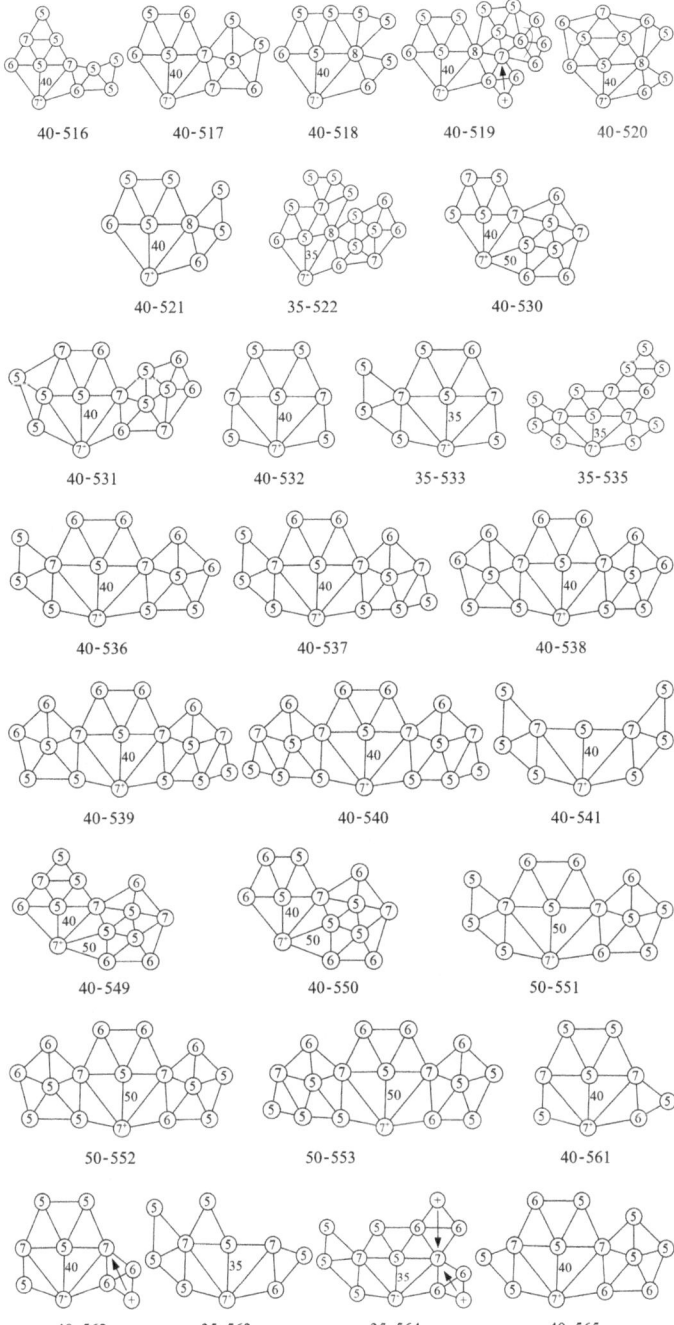

Fig. 3.37 L-situations: page 3

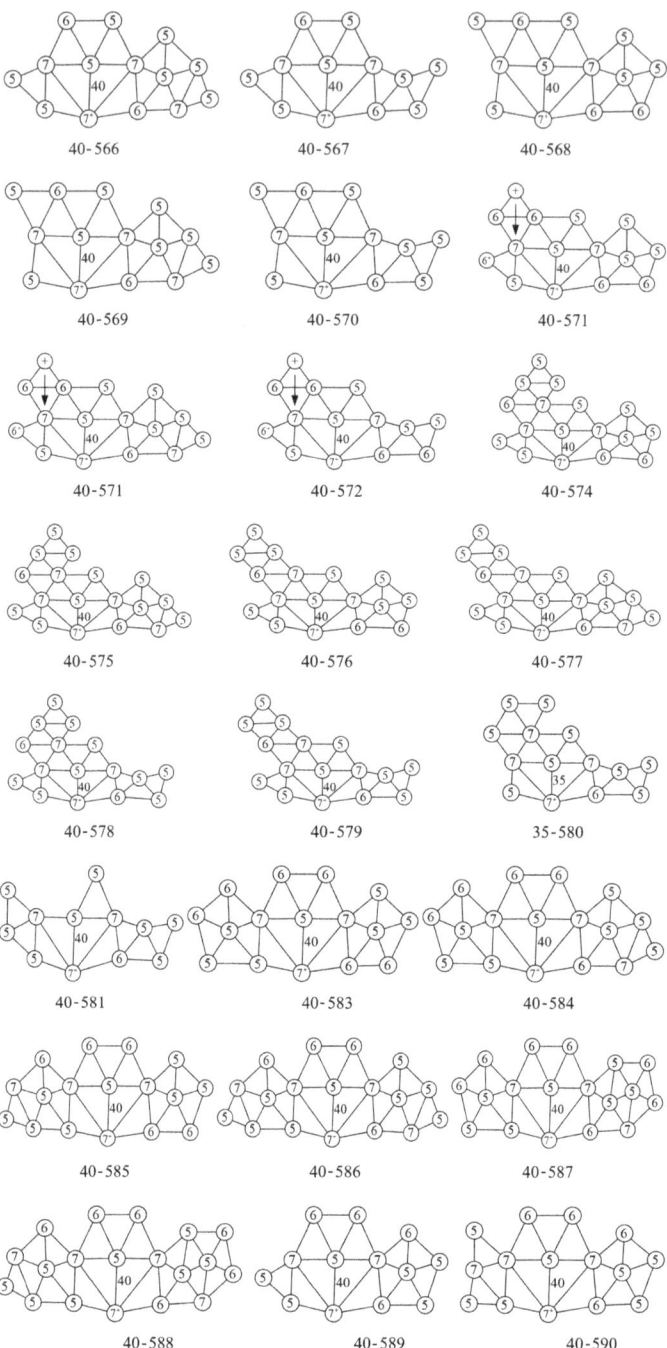

Fig. 3.38 L-situations: page 4

Appendix

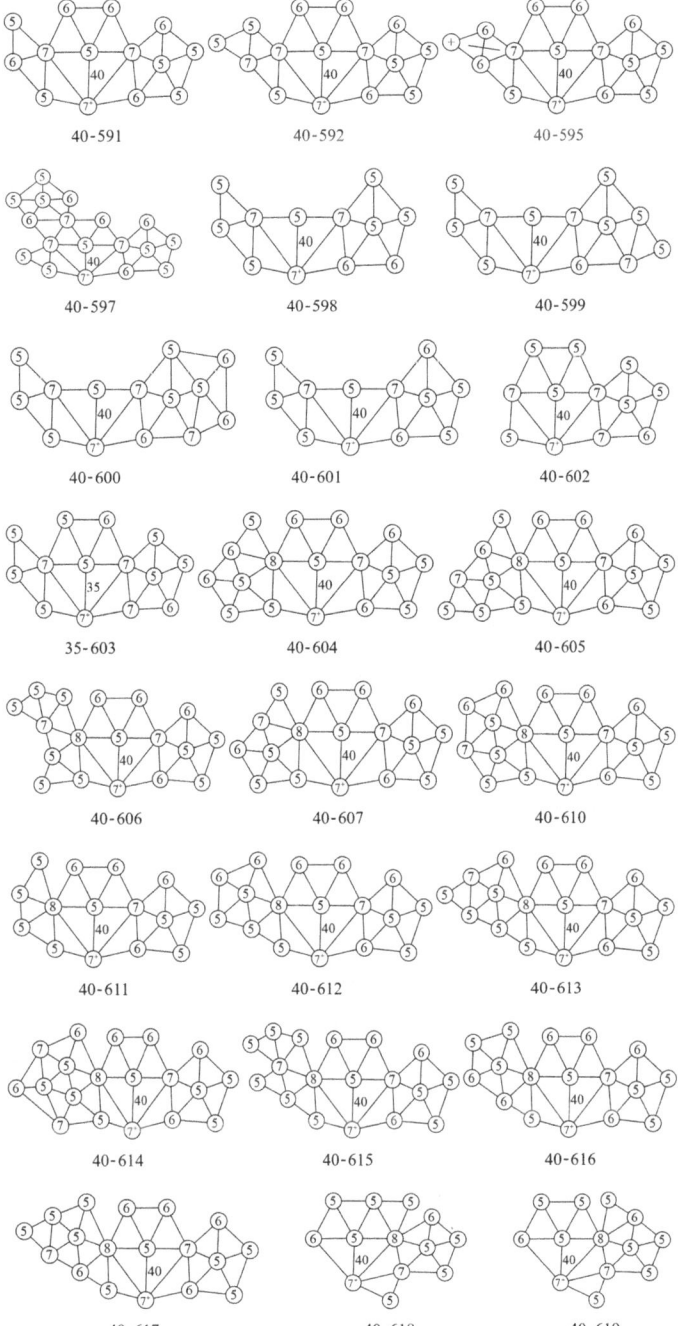

Fig. 3.39 L-situations: page 5

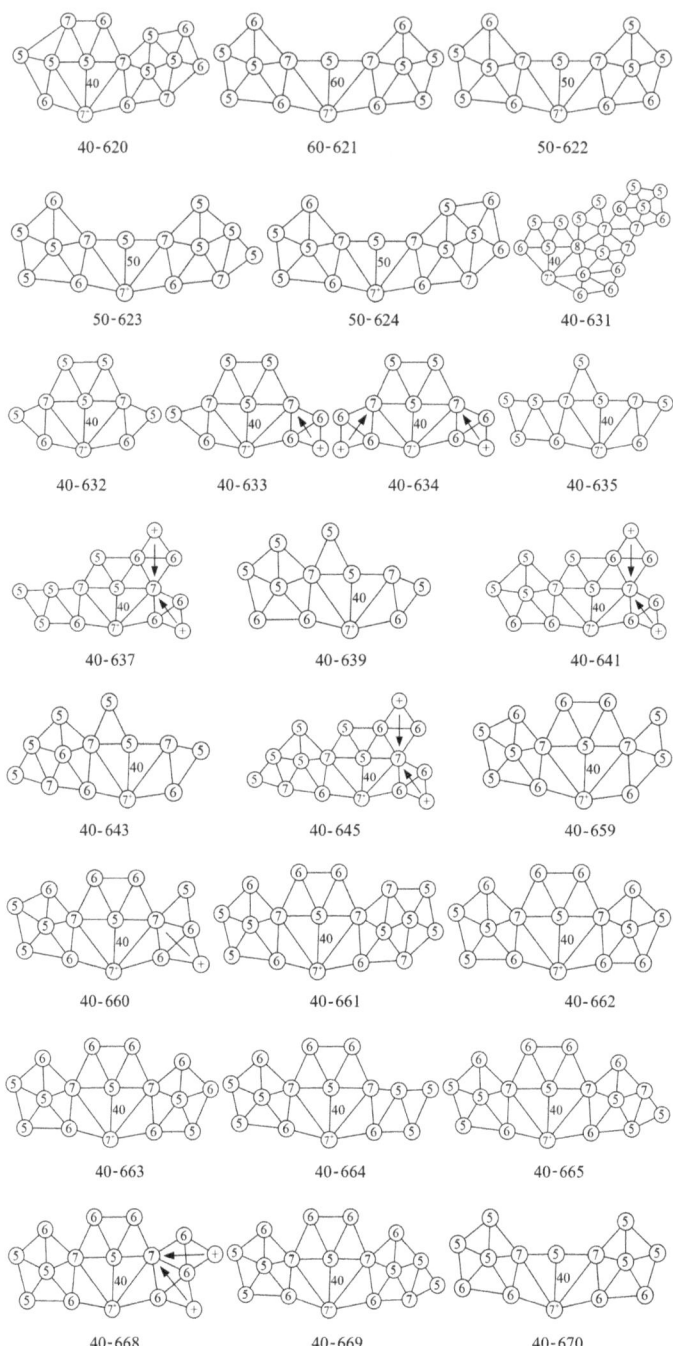

Fig. 3.40 L-situations: page 6

Appendix

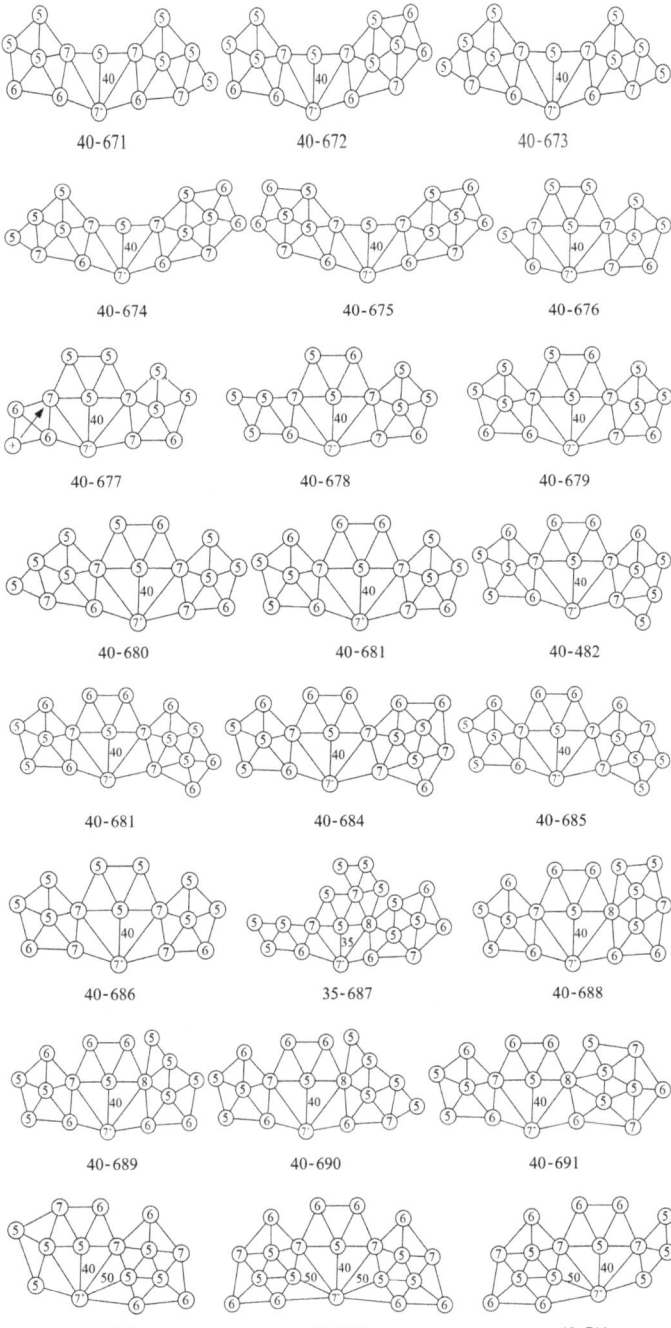

Fig. 3.41 L-situations: page 7

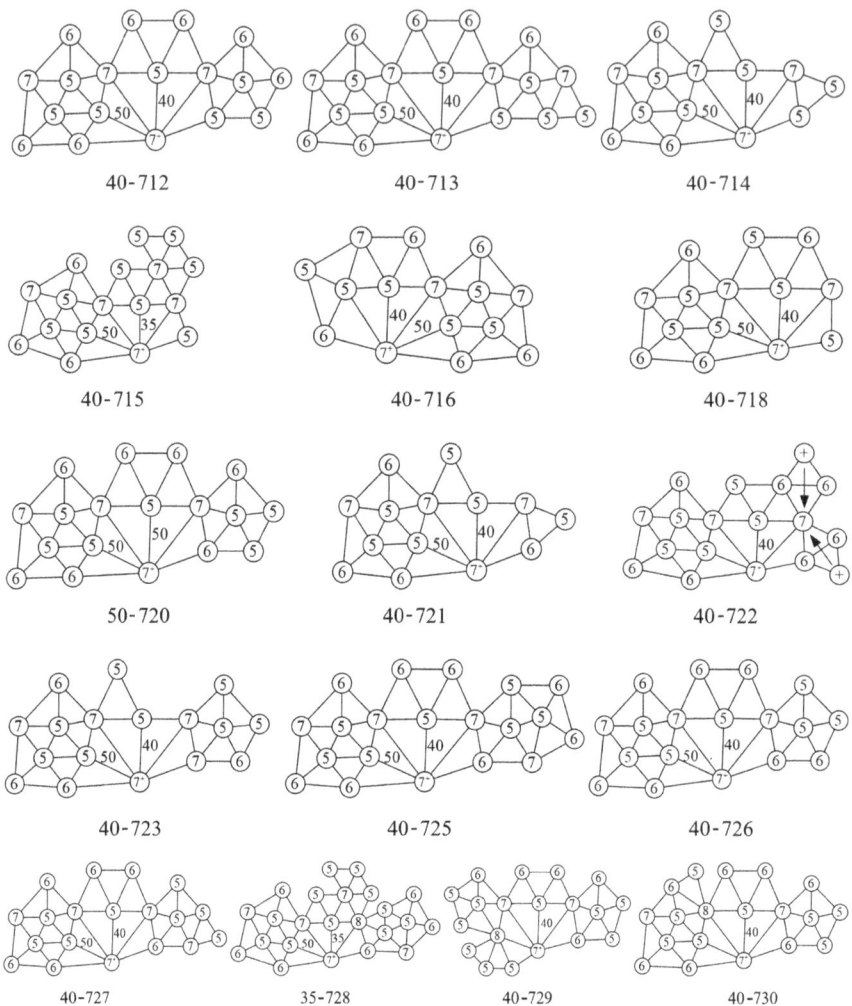

Fig. 3.42 L-situations: page 8

Appendix

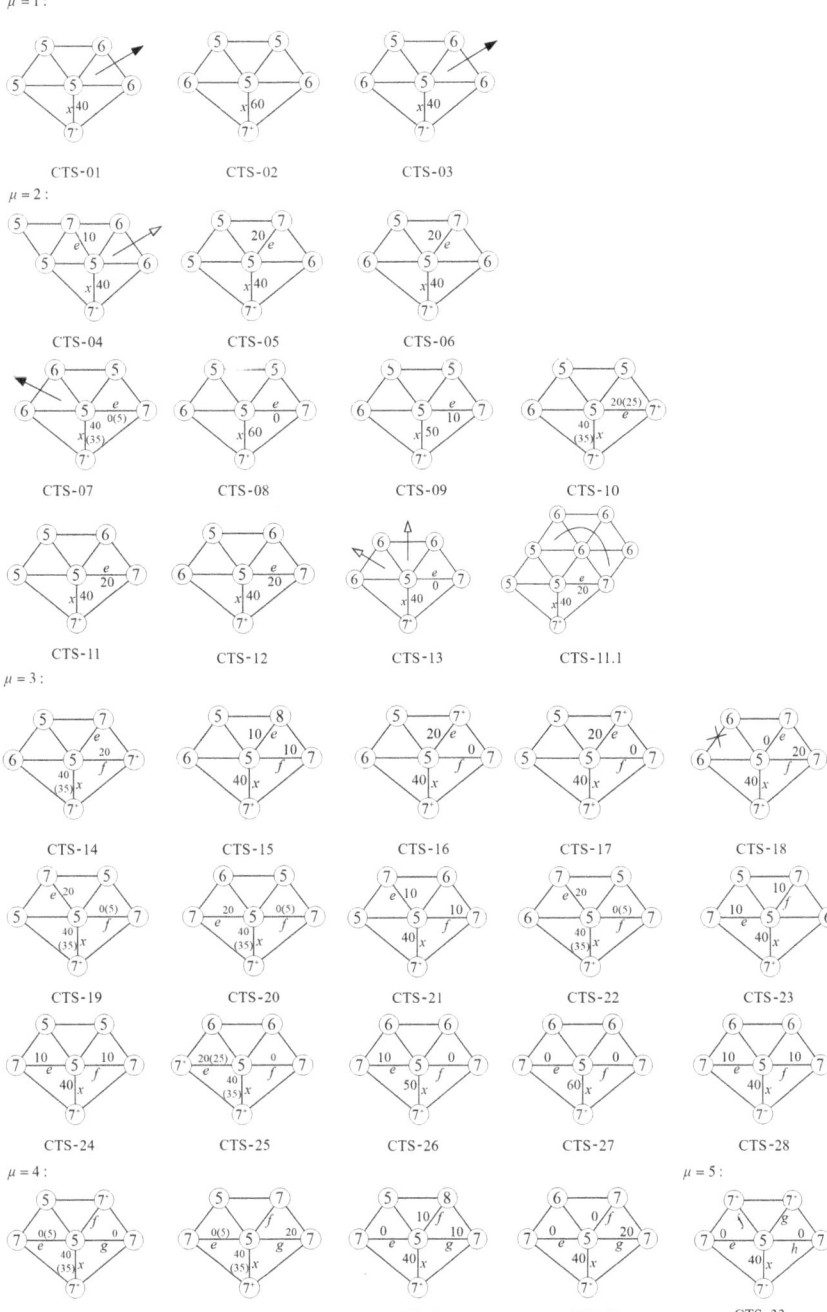

Fig. 3.43 Configurations mentioned in Lemma 3.6

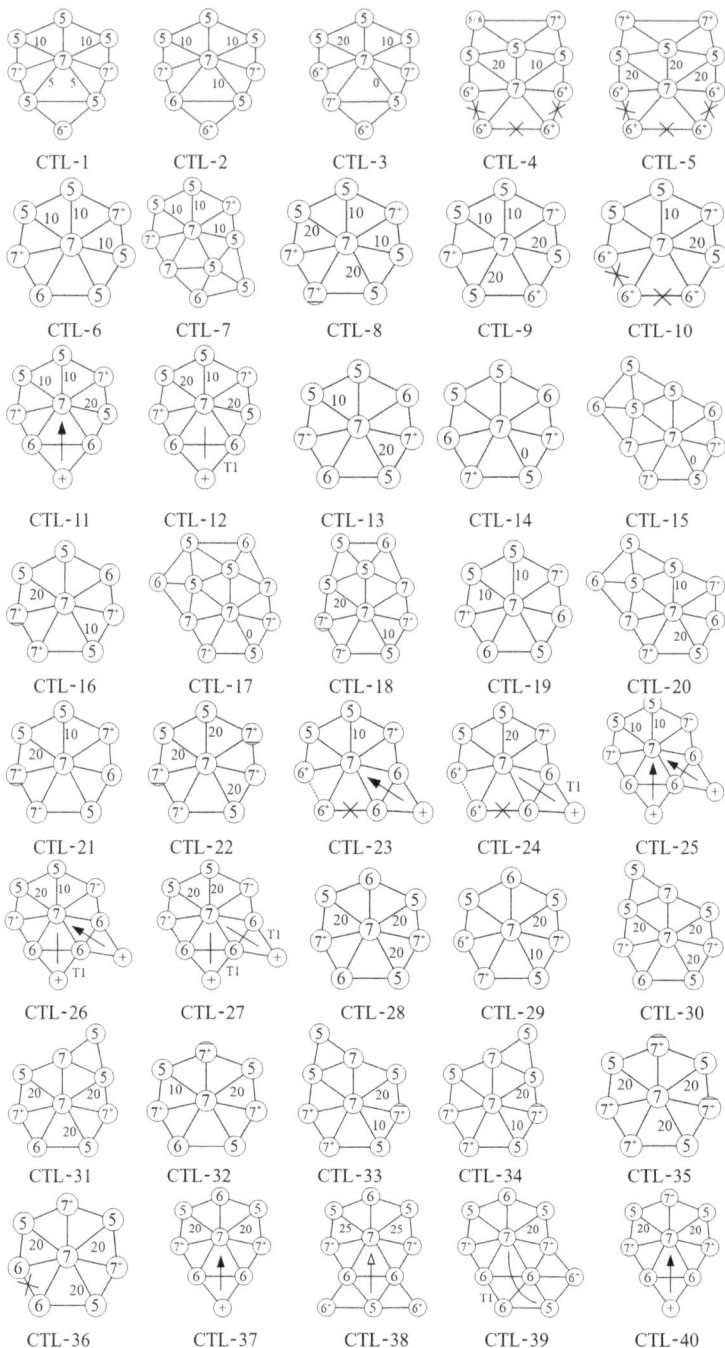

Fig. 3.44 Page 1

Appendix

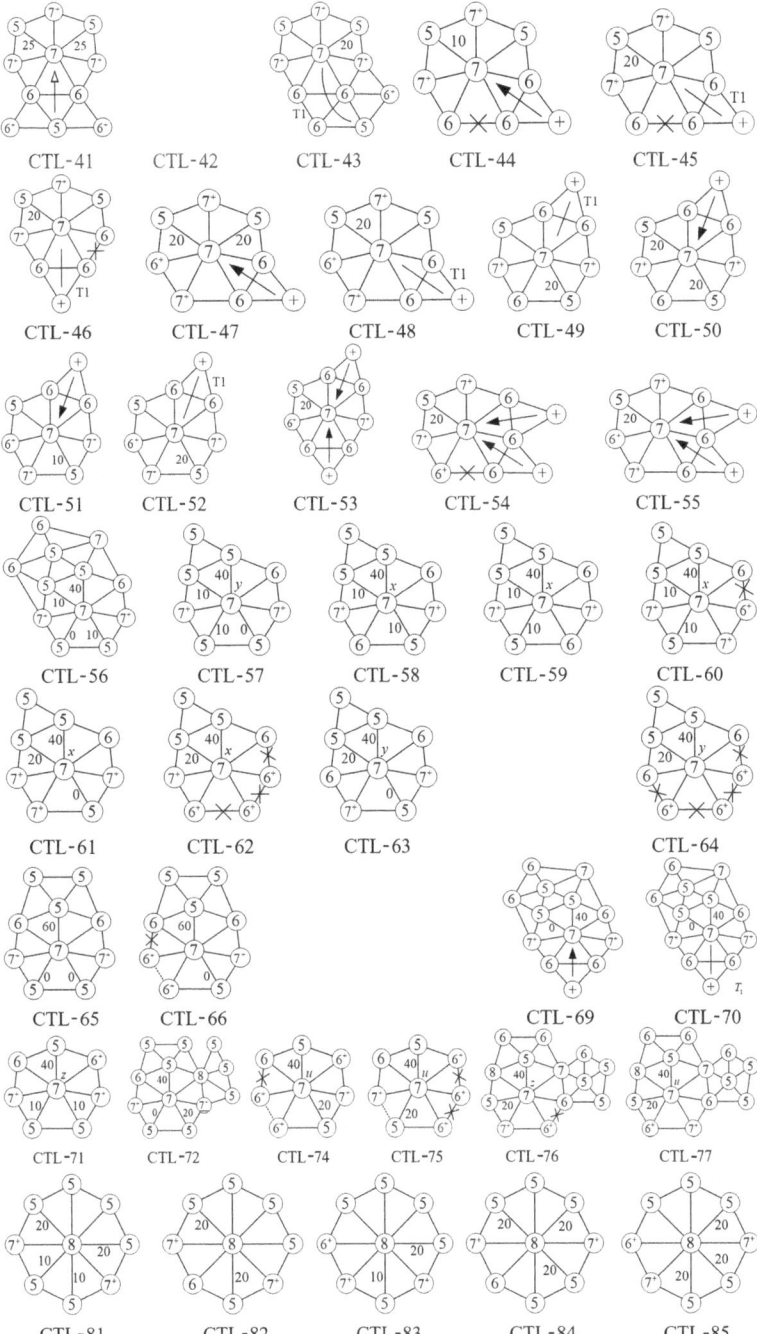

Fig. 3.45 Page 2

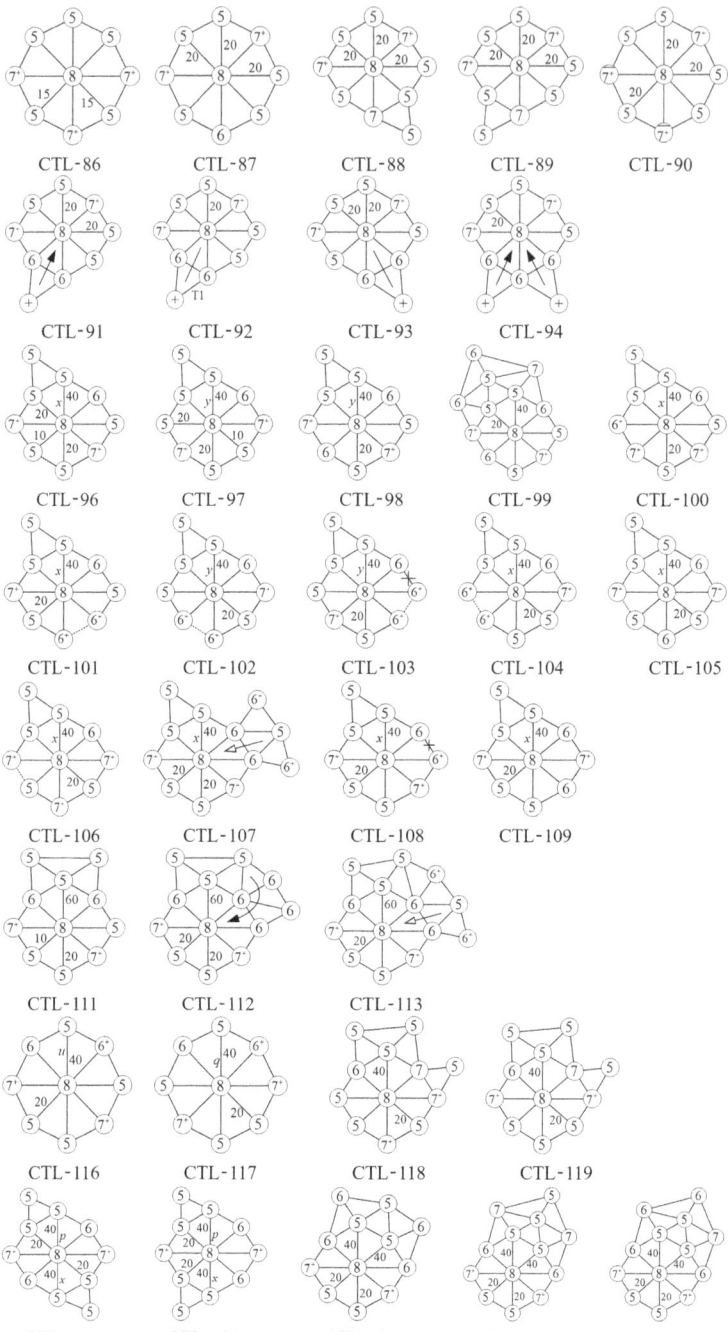

Fig. 3.46 Page 3

Appendix

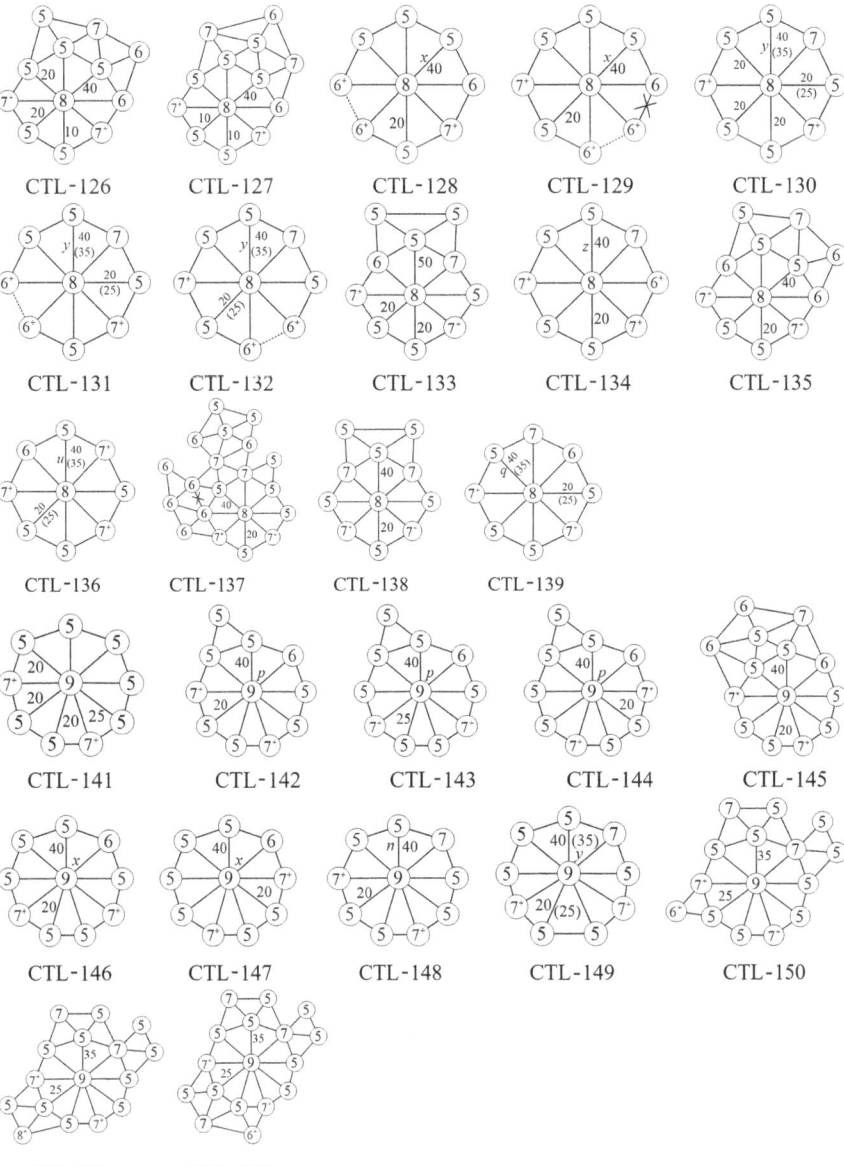

Fig. 3.47 Page 4

References

1. K Appel and W Haken. Research announcement: Every planar map is four colorable. *Bulletin of the American mathematical Society*, 82(5): 711–712, 1976.
2. K Appel and W Haken. Every planar map is four colorable. part i: Discharging. *Illinois Journal of Mathematics*, 21(3): 429–490, 1977.
3. K Appel, W Haken, and J Koch. Every planar map is four colorable. part ii: Reducibility. *Illinois Journal of Mathematics*, 21(3): 491–567, 1977.
4. L W Beineke and R J Wilson. *Selected topics in graph theory*. Academic Press, 1978.
5. G D Birkhoff. A determinantal formula for the number of ways of coloring a map. *Annals of Mathematics*, 14: 42–46, 1912.
6. G D Birkhoff. The reducibility of maps. *American Journal of Mathematics*, 35: 115–128, 1913.
7. R Bravaco and S Simonson. The four-color theorem. *Mathematica in Education and Research*, 6(1).
8. S A Cook. The complexity of theorem-proving procedures. *Proceedings of the third annual ACM symposium on Theory of computing*, 151–158, 1871.
9. P Franklin. The four color problemz. *American Journal of Mathematics*, 44(4): 225–236, 1922.
10. R Fritsch and G Fritsch. The Four-Color Theorem: History, Topological Foundations, and Idea of proof. *Springer*, 1998.
11. P J Heawood. Map-colour theorem. *Quarterly Journal of Mathematics*, 24:332–338, 1890.
12. T Herczeg and B Booss-Bavnbek. The Effect of Computers on Pure Mathematics. *Roskilde University*, 2009.
13. A B Kempe. On the geographical problem of the four colors. *American Journal of Mathematics*, 2(3): 193–200, 1897.
14. J P Magee. Reducible configurations and so on: The final years of the four color theorem. *Dissertations and Theses–Gradworks*, 2008.
15. J J O'Connor and E F Robertson. The four colour theorem. *University of St. Andrews, Scotland*, 1996.
16. N Robertson, D Sanders, P Seymour, and R Thomas. The four-colour theorem. *Journal of Combinatorial Theory, Series B*, 70: 2–44, 1997.
17. A Soifer. The Mathematical Coloring Book: Mathematics of Coloring and the Colorful Life of Its Creators. *Springer, New York Berlin Heidelberg*, 2009.
18. T Tymoczko. The four-color problem and its philosophical significance. *The Journal of Philosophy*, 76(2): 57–83, 1979.
19. P Wernicke. Üober den kartoyraphischen vierfarbensatz. *Math. Ann.*, 58(3): 413–426, 1904.

Open Access This chapter is licensed under the terms of the Creative Commons Attribution 4.0 International License (http://creativecommons.org/licenses/by/4.0/), which permits use, sharing, adaptation, distribution and reproduction in any medium or format, as long as you give appropriate credit to the original author(s) and the source, provide a link to the Creative Commons license and indicate if changes were made.

The images or other third party material in this chapter are included in the chapter's Creative Commons license, unless indicated otherwise in a credit line to the material. If material is not included in the chapter's Creative Commons license and your intended use is not permitted by statutory regulation or exceeds the permitted use, you will need to obtain permission directly from the copyright holder.

Chapter 4
Construction of Maximal Planar Graphs with the Same Order

Abstract From this chapter, we will present a series of methods to construct maximal planar graphs. In this chapter, we first introduce a simple but useful operation, called **diagonal flip** (or edge-flipping), by a finite sequence of which any two maximal planar graphs with the same order can be transformed into each other.

4.1 Definitions and Notation

To study the transformation between two maximal planar graphs with the same order, Wagner [8] in 1936 proposed the concept of **diagonal flip** (also called **edge-flipping**), which is a local deformation of a maximal planar graph G that replaces a diagonal edge ac with the other edge bd in a quadrilateral region obtained from two 3-faces abc and acd (see Fig. 4.1). If the resulting graph has no multiple edges, i.e., $bd \notin E(G)$, then we call it the **diagonal flip on** ac **in** G (or **flip** ac for short) and ac a **flippable** edge of G; otherwise (i.e., ac is not flippable), we do not preform this operation.

Recall that an n-order maximal planar graph has totally $3n - 6$ edges (see Formula (1.11) in Theorem 1.13). It is natural to ask what is the maximum number of flippable in a maximal planar graph. Hurtado, et al. [4] proved that every n-order maximal planar graph contains at least $\lceil \frac{n-4}{2} \rceil$ flippable edges. Gao, et al. [3] improved this result by confirming that the number of flippable edges in an arbitrary n-order maximal planar graph G is at least $n - 2$ and, in particular, at least $2n + 3$ when $\delta(G) \geq 4$, and these bounds are sharp.

Theorem 4.1 ([3]) *Every maximal planar graph of order $n (n > 4)$ has at least $n - 2$ flippable edges, and the bound is tight.*

Proof Let G be a maximal planar graph of order $n(> 4)$. Suppose that there exists a face $v_1 v_2 v_3$ incident without flippable edges. Observe that each edge $v_i v_j$, $i \neq j, i, j \in \{1, 2, 3\}$, is exactly incident with two faces. Let $v_1 v_2 v_4$ be another face incident with $v_1 v_2$ where $v_4 \neq v_3$. Since $v_1 v_2$ is not flippable, it has that $v_3 v_4 \in E(G)$. Since $n > 4$, it follows that v_1 or v_2 is a 4^+-vertex. Without loss of generality,

Fig. 4.1 Diagonal flip

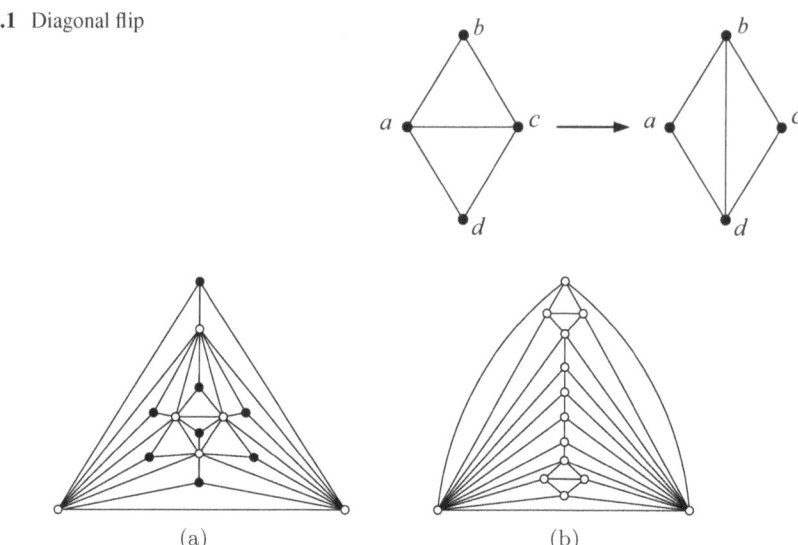

Fig. 4.2 (**a**) A 14-order maximal planar graph with 12 flippable edges, (**b**) a 14-order maximal planar graph of minimum degree 4 with 31 flippable edges

we may assume that $d_G(v_1) \geq 4$. Then, v_1v_3 is a flippable edge, a contradiction. Therefore, each face is incident with at least one flippable edge. By Euler's Formula (Formula (1.9) in Theorem 1.12), it has that G has exactly $2(n-2)$ faces. Hence, the number of flippable edges in G is at least $\frac{2(n-2)}{2} = n-2$.

To show the sharpness, it is enough to construct a class of n-order maximal planar graphs which has exactly $n-2$ flippable edges. Let G' be a t-order maximal planar graph. Clearly, G' has $2t-4$ 3-faces. Let G'' be a graph obtained from G' by adding a vertex on every 3-face and connecting it to the three vertices incident with the face. One can readily check that $|V(G'')| = 3t - 4$ and the number of flippable edges in G'' is equal to the number of edges of G', i.e., $3(t-2)$. Figure 4.2a illustrates this resulting graph G'' for $t = 6$. ∎

Theorem 4.2 ([3]) *Every n-order maximal planar graph G with $\delta(G) \geq 4$ has at least* $\min\{2n + 3, 3n - 6\}$ *flippable edges, and the bound is tight.*

Proof By Theorem 4.1 it is enough to consider the case that G is separating triangle. Since $\delta(G) \geq 4$, it follows from the proof of Theorem 4.1 that each nonflippable edge is related to exactly four fippable edges. Additionally, if $v_1v_2v_3$ be a face of G such that v_1v_2 is a flippable edge, then at least one of v_1v_3 and v_2v_3 is flippable (otherwise, v_3 has degree 3). Therefore, each fippable edge is related to at most two nonfippable edges.

In the following, we show that G contains at least fourteen faces with 3 flippable edges. Let $u_1u_2u_3$ be a separating cycle of G such that the maximal planar graph $T(u_1u_2u_3)$ consisting of $u_1u_2u_3$ and all its interior vertices, contains no separating triangles. Since G contains no 3-vertex, $T(u_1u_2u_3)$ contains at least 7 inner faces and at least 6 vertices. Since $T(u_1u_2u_3)$ is not separating, every edge of $T(u_1u_2u_3)$ is a flippable edge. Similarly, one can deduce that the maximal planar graph consisting of $u_1u_2u_3$ and all its exterior vertices, contains at least 7 inner faces each of which contains 3 flippable edges. Therefore, the number of the flippable edges of G is at least

$$\frac{14 + (2n - 4 - 14) \times 2}{2} = 2n + 3.$$

Maximal planar graphs that achieve this bound can be obtained as follows. Let G' be an $(n-6)$-order maximal planar graph which contains two adjacent $(n-7)$-vertices, say u and v. Insert a triangle in each of the two faces incident with u and v in such a way that the degree of the six new vertices is four; see Fig. 4.2b. One can easily verify that the resulting maximal planar graph achieves the bound, as desired. ∎

4.2 Transformation Between Two Maximal Planar Graphs with the Same Order

Through diagonal flip, one can obtain a new maximal planar graph G' form an original maximal planar graph G. It is possible that G' and G are isomorphic. Therefore, it is essential to determine whether or not an n-order maximal planar graph can be transformed into a distinct one with the same order (up to isomorphism), by a series of diagonal flips. In 1936, Wagner [8] answer this question 'yes'. Although the number of maximal planar graphs of order n is exponential in n, Wanger [8] proved that every maximal planar graph can be transformed into the **standard form of n-order maximal planar graphs**, by which they showed that the number of diagonal flips for transforming two maximal planar graphs of order n is at most $2n^2$. This approach cleverly avoided the isomorphism problem.

The **standard form of n-order maximal planar graphs**, denoted by $\triangle_n$, is the unique n-order maximal planar graph containing two $(n-1)$-vertices; see Fig. 4.3.

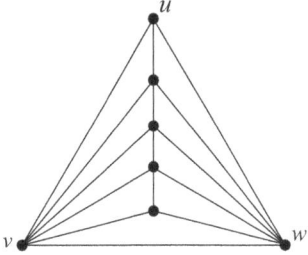

Fig. 4.3 The standard form of 7-order maximal planar graphs

There are several papers that focus on how many diagonal flips are needed to transform two maximal planar graphs into each other, which improve the upper bound given by Wagner. In 1993, Negami and Nakamoto [7] proved that every n-order maximal planar graph can be transformed into $\triangle_n$ by $O(n^2)$ diagonal flips. In 1997, Komuro [5] proved that any two n-order maximal planar graphs can be transformed into each other by at most $8n - 54$ (or $8n - 48$) if $n \geq 13$ (or $n \geq 7$). For convenience of the reader, the remainder of this section is to depict the proof of this result, for which two lemmas are needed. Let G be a maximal planar graph. For any two vertices order u, v, let

$$\omega_G(u, v) = 3d_G(u) + d_G(v) \tag{4.1}$$

Lemma 4.1 ([5]) *Let G be a maximal planar graph of order n and v, w two adjacent vertices of G. Then, G can be transformed into $\triangle_n$ by $4n - 4 - \omega_G(v, w)$ diagonal flips.*

Proof Let uvw be a face of G incident with v and w, and $w, w_1, \ldots, w_t, v$ are the neighbors of u lying around u in this order. Suppose that $d_G(u) = 4$. If $w_2 w \notin E(G)$, then replace uw_1 with ww_2; otherwise, replace uw with vw_1. In both of these two cases, $\omega_G(v, w)$ increases by 1 and 2, respectively, with one diagonal flip.

Now, suppose that $d_G(u) = 3$. Let $N_G(u) = \{v, w, u_0\}$. Then, $\{u, v, w\} \subseteq N_G(u_0)$. If $d_G(u_0) \geq 5$, let $u, w, u_1, u_2, \ldots, u_k, v$ be the neighbors of u_0 lying around u_1 in this order. If $u_2 w \notin E(G)$, then replace $u_0 u_1$ with $w u_2$ and $\omega_G(v, w)$ increases by 1 with one diagonal flip; otherwise if $u_2 w \in E(G)$, then $v u_1 \notin E(G)$. In this case, replace $u_0 w$ with $u u_1$, and $u u_0$ with $v u_1$. Then, $\omega_G(v, w)$ increases by 2 with one diagonal flip.

Further, if $d_G(u_0) = 3$ then G is isomorphic to $\triangle_4$; if $d_G(u_0) = 4$, then there is another common neighbor $u_1 (\neq u)$ of u_0, v and w. Then, we can do the same deformation insider the triangle $u_0 v w$ as we did for the triangle uvw.

Repeating these deformations, we shall have a sequence of vertices $u, v_1, v_2, \ldots, v_{n-3}$ so that they form a path and are adjacent to both v and w. This algorithm stops when the degree of u_{n-3} is 3, and then the resulting maximal planar graph is isomorphic to $\triangle_n$, in which both v and w are $(n - 1)$-vertices and $\omega_{\triangle_n}(v, w) = 4n - 4$. Since $\omega_G(v, w)$ increases by 1 or 2 by one diagonal flip through the above deformations, the total number of those diagonal flips is at most $\omega_{\triangle_n}(v, w) - \omega_G(v, w) = 4n - 4 - \omega_G(v, w)$. ∎

It is clear from Theorem 4.1 that the bigger the value of $\omega_G(v, w)$ is, the smaller the number of diagonal flips is. Therefore, we would like to find two adjacent vertices with large degree.

Lemma 4.2 ([5]) *Let G be a maximal planar graph of order $n (\geq 6)$. If $G \not\cong C_{n-2} + \overline{K_2}$, then every 5^+-vertex in G is adjacent to another 5^+-vertex.*

Proof Let u be a k-vertex in G, $k \geq 5$, and $u_1, u_2, \ldots, u_k$ be its neighbors lying around u in this order. Suppose that $d_G(u_i) \leq 4$ for all $i \in \{1, 2, \ldots, k\}$. If $d_G(u_3) = 3$, then $u_2 u_4 \in E(G)$ and $u_2 u_3 u_4$ is a face of G. In this case, $d_G(u_2) = d_G(u_4) = 4$, and hence $u_1 = u_5$ and $u_1u_2u_4$ is a face, a contradiction. Thus, we may assume that $d_G(u_i) = 4$ for all $i \in \{1, 2, \ldots, k\}$. Then, all u_i are adjacent to a common vertex $v \neq u$, i.e., G is isomorphic to $G \not\cong C_{n-2} + \overline{K_2}$. ∎

It is clear from Lemma 4.2 that all 5^+-vertices induce a connected subgraph in every maximal planar graph.

Theorem 4.3 *The number of diagonal flips to transform two maximal planar graphs of order n into each other is at most $8n - 54$ if $n \geq 13$ and at most $8n - 48$ if $7 \leq n \leq 12$.*

Proof It is enough to show that every maximal planar graph of order n can be transformed into $\triangle_n$ by at most $4n - 27$ diagonal flips if $n \geq 13$ and at most $4n - 24$ if $7 \leq n \leq 12$.

Observe that if $G \cong C_{n-2} + \overline{K_2}$, then G can be transformed into $\triangle_n$ by only one diagonal flip. Thus, we may suppose that G is not isomorphic to $C_{n-2} + \overline{K_2}$.

When $n \geq 13$, by Formula (2.2) G has at least one 6^+-vertex, say v. By Lemma 4.2 v is adjacent to a 5^+-vertex, say w, in G. Thus, $\omega_G(v, w) \geq 3 \times 6 + 5 = 23$ and by Lemma 4.1 the number of diagonal flips does not exceed $4n - 4 - 23 = 4n - 27$.

When $7 \leq n \leq 12$, G may contain no 6^+-vertex. If G contains only 4^--vertex, then it has that $n = 6$. Therefore, G has a 5^+-vertex, say v, which is adjacent to another 5^+-vertex w in G, by Lemma 4.2. Thus, $\omega_G(v, w) \geq 3 \times 5 + 5 = 20$ and by Lemma 4.1 the number of diagonal flips does not exceed $4n - 4 - 20 = 4n - 24$. ∎

4.3 Upper Bounds of the Number of Diagonal Flips

In Sect. 4.2, it has shown that every two maximal planar graphs with the same order can be transformed into each other by a finite sequence of diagonal flips, up to isomorphism. In 2000, Mori, et al. [6] prove that every n-order maximal planar graph can be transformed into a 4-connected one by at most $n - 4$ diagonal flips. In 2011, Bose, et al. [2] improved this upper bound. In this section, we will focus on these problems.

Let G be a maximal planar graph and $e \in E(G)$ an arbitrary edge. We call e a **free edge** if e does not belong to any separating triangle of G.

Lemma 4.3 ([2, 6]) *In a maximal planar graph of order $n \geq 6$, flipping every edge of a separating triangle D will remove that separating triangle. This never introduces a new separating triangle, provided that the selected edge belongs to multiple separating triangles or none of the edges of D belong to multiple separating triangles.*

Lemma 4.4 ([2]) *Let G be a maximal planar graph. If a vertex $v \in V(G)$ belongs to a separating triangle D of G, then v is incident with at least one free edge inside D.*

Proof Let e_1 be an edge of D incident to v. Since D is separating, its interior contains at least one vertex and there is a face T_1 inside D that is incident with e_1. Let e_2 be the other edge incident with face T_1 and vertex v.

The remainder of the proof proceeds by induction on the number of separating triangles contained in D. The base case holds, since e_2 is a free edge if there are not any separating triangles inside D.

Now, suppose that e_2 belongs to a separating triangle, say D'. Clearly, the number of separating triangles contained in D' is strictly smaller than that in D. Since v is also incident with D', by induction hypothesis, there is a free edge incident to v inside D'. Since D' is contained in D, this free edge is also inside D. ∎

Observe that a separating triangle may be inside another separating triangle in a maximal planar graph. A separating triangle of a maximal planar graph G is called **deepest** if it is contained by the largest number of separating triangles in G. By repeatedly flipping an edge of a deepest separating triangle, Bose, et al. [2] observed the following theorem. Their proof is interesting, so we present it in the following.

Theorem 4.4 ([2]) *Let G be a maximal planar graph of order $n \geq 6$. Then, G can be transformed into a 4-connected one by at most $\frac{3n-6}{5}$ diagonal flip.*

Proof By charging scheme. First, place a coin on every edge of G; then, flip an edge of a deepest separating triangle (preferring edges that belong to multiple separating triangles) until no separating triangles are left. We pay five coins for every flip. During the process, we maintain the following two invariants.

(1) Every edge of a separating triangle has a coin.
(2) Every vertex of a separating triangle is incident with a free edge that is inside the triangle and has a coin.

There are four types of edges we need to consider to pay for flipping an edge of a deepest separating triangle D.

Type I The flipped edge e. By Lemma 4.3 e cannot belong to any separating triangle after the flip. So, the first invariant holds if we remove e's coin. Observe that e is not a free edge before flip and no new separating triangle is introduced; so by Lemma 4.4 the second invariant was satisfied.

Type II A non-flipped edge e of D that is not shared with any other separating triangle. In this case, the flip removed D and did not introduce any new separating triangles. Therefore e cannot belong to any separating triangle after the flip. So, the two invariants hold if we remove e's coin.

Type III A free edge e incident with a vertex v of D that is not shared with any containing separating triangle. Since e did not belong to any separating triangle and the flip did not introduce any new ones, the first invariant holds if we remove e's coin. Moreover, since the flip removed D and e is not incident with a vertex of another separating triangle that contains D, it is no longer required to have a coin to satisfy the second invariant. Therefore, the second invariant holds if we remove e's coin.

4.3 Upper Bounds of the Number of Diagonal Flips

Type IV A free edge e incident with a vertex v of D, where v is an endpoint of an edge e' of D that is shared with a non-containing separating triangle D' (provided that we flip e'). Observe that every separating triangle containing D but not D' must share e' (Lemma 10 in [2]) and is therefore removed by the flip. Hence, every separating triangle after the flip containing D contains D' as well. This also holds for containing triangles incident with v. Since the second invariant requires only one free edge with a coin for each vertex, we can safely charge the one inside D, as long as we do not charge the free edge in D'.

In order to select edges we flip and determine how to pay for each flip, we consider the following five cases, in terms of the number of edges shared with other separating triangles and whether any of these triangles contain D. These cases are illustrated in Figs. 4.4 and 4.5.

Case 1 D does not share any edges with other separating triangles (see Fig. 4.4a). In this case, we flip any edge of D edges. By the first invariant, each edge of D has a coin. These edges all fall into Types I and II, so we use their coins to pay for the flip. Since D can share at most one vertex with a containing triangle (by Lemma 8 in [2]), we charge two free edges, each incident to one of the other two vertices (Type III).

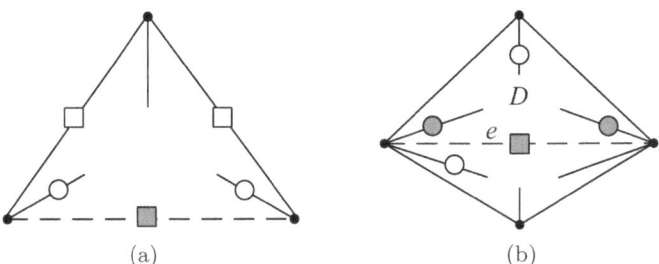

Fig. 4.4 (a) The edges that are charged if the deepest separating triangle does not share any edges with other separating triangles. The flipped edge is dashed and the charged edges are marked with black boxes (Type I), white boxes (Type II), white disks (Type III) or black disks (Type IV), (b) the edges that are charged if the deepest separating triangle only shares edges with non-containing separating triangles

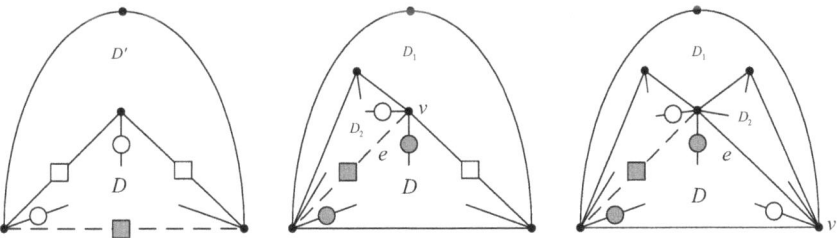

Fig. 4.5 The edges that are charged if the deepest separating triangle shares an edge with a containing triangle

Case 2 D share no edge with separating triangles containing D, but share an edges (one or more) with separating triangles that do not contain D (see Fig. 4.4b). Let D' be a separating triangles that do not contain D and share an edge e with D. We flip e and charge e (Type I) and two free edges inside D that are incident with the vertices of e (Type IV). Moreover, consider the quadrilateral Q formed by D and D', i.e., $Q = (D \cup D') - e$. Since D does not share an edge with a separating triangle containing D, there are at most two vertices of Q that are inside separating triangles containing D. Therefore, we charge two free edges, each incident to one of the other two vertices, for the last two coins (Type III).

Case 3 D shares an edge e with a separating triangle D' containing D, but does not share the other edges with any separating triangle (see Fig. 4.5a). In this case, we flip e and charge all of edges of D. Observe that edges of D that are not incident with D' are not incident with other separating triangles, and after flip at most one vertex incident with e is inside separating triangles. Therefore, we charge two free edges, each incident with a vertex not in separating triangles.

Case 4. D shares an edge with a separating triangle D_1 containing D and shares one other edge e with a separating triangle D_2 that do not contain D (see Fig. 4.5b). In this case, we flip e. Let v be the vertex of D that is not shared with D_1. We charge the flipped edge e (Type I), the unshared edge of D (Type II), and two free edges inside D that are incident to the vertices of the flipped edge (Type II). We charge the last coin from a free edge e' in D_2 that is incident to v. Since D is deepest, D_2 is also deepest. In addition, every triangle containing D also contains D_2. Therefore, vertex v is not inside any separating triangle incident with e', and hence we can charge it.

Case 5. D shares one edge with a separating triangle D_1 containing D and the other two edges of D are incident with two separating triangles that do not contain D (see Fig. 4.5c). Let e be the common edge of D and one of separating triangle D_2 that do not contain D. Let v be the vertex that is shared by D_1, D_2 and D. In this case, we flip edge e. The charged edges are identical to Case 4, except that there is no unshared edge any more. Instead, we charge the last free edge in D. The reason that we can charge in this way is that there is a free edge inside D_2 incident with v.

From the foregoing discussion, we have proved that we can charge 5 coins for every flip, while maintaining the two invariants. To complete the proof, it is now enough to show that after performing these flips we have indeed removed all separating triangles. As long as our triangulation has a separating triangle, we can always find a deepest separating triangle D. Since D shares at most one edge with separating triangles (by Lemma 7 in cite4-7), one of the cases (Case1 $\sim$ Case 5) must apply to D. This gives us an edge of D to flip and five edges to charge, each of which is guaranteed by the invariants to have a coin. Therefore the process stops only after all separating triangles have been removed. ∎

A graph is **outerplanar** if it has a planar embedding in which all vertices lie on the boundary of its outer face. An outerplanar graph is **maximal** if the addition of an edge between any pair of nonadjacent vertices destroys outerplanarity. A Hamilton

4.3 Upper Bounds of the Number of Diagonal Flips

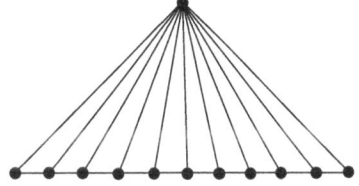

Fig. 4.6 Standard maximal outerplane graph H_n

cycle in a graph is a cycle passing through all vertices of the graph exactly once. We say that G is Hamiltonian if G has a Hamilton cycle. In the following, we present results on the number of diagonal flips, for which a Hamilton maximal planar graph and a 4-connected maximal planar graph can be transformed into the standard form. There are some simple facts.

Lemma 4.5 ([6])

(1) Up to isomorphism, there exists only one maximal planar graph of order 4 and 5, which are $\triangle_4$ and $\triangle_5$.
(2) Every maximal outerplanar graph has a 2-vertex.
(3) Every maximal outerplanar graph of order at least 5 contains a 4^+-vertex.
(4) Let G be a maximal outerplanar graph with outer cycle C and e an edge of G. If $e \notin E(C)$, then, e is flippable.

Proof The proofs of these results are straightforward. We here omit them. ∎

We refer to the maximal outerplane graph of order n isomorphic to $P_{n-1} + K_1$ as the **standard maximal outerplane graph of order** n, denoted H_n. The unique $(n-1)$-vertex in H_n is called the **apex** of H_n (see Fig. 4.6)

Theorem 4.5 ([6]) *Let G be a Hamiltonian maximal planar graph of order n. Then, up to isomorphism, G can be transformed into $\triangle_n$ by at most $\max\{2n-10, 0\}$ diagonal flips. Moreover, if g is 4-connected, then at most $\max\{2n-11, 0\}$ diagonal flips are sufficient.*

Proof By Lemma 4.5 (1) we may assume that $n \geq 6$. Let C be a Hamilton cycle of G. Then, G can be decomposed into two maximal outerplane graphs G_1 and G_2 such that $G_1 \cap G_2 = C$. By Lemma 4.5 (1), G_1 contains a 2-vertex, say v. Let $N_{G_1} = \{v_1, v_2\}$.

Observe that G is 3-connected, i.e., $d_G(v) \geq 3$; it follows that $d_{G_2}(v) \geq 3$ (here, if G is 4-connected, $d_{G_2}(v) \geq 4$). If G_2 has a 3-face $\triangle\text{-}vxy$ such that $xy \notin E(C)$, then by Lemma 4.5 (4) xy is flippable in G_2 (in the quadrilateral $vxzy$ formed by two 3-faces $\triangle\text{-}vxy$ and $\triangle\text{-}zxy$ of G_2). In addition, since $d_{G_1}(v) = 2$, it has that $vz \notin E(G_1)$. Therefore, xy is flippable in G. Thus, G_2 can be transformed into the standard maximal outerplane graph H_n with apex v by at most $n-4$ diagonal flips (if G is 4-connected, then at most n-5 diagonal flips are enough), since $d_{H_n} = n-1$ and $d_{G_2}(v) \geq 3$ (if G is 4-connected, $d_{G_2}(v) \geq 3$). Let G' be the Hamiltonian plane triangulation obtained from G by the sequence of diagonal flips transforming G_2 into H_n.

Let $G'_1 = G_1 - v$, the subgraph of G_1 obtained by deleting v and its incident edges. Clearly, G'_1 is a maximal outerplane graph of order $n-1$ such that $G' = G'_1 + \{v\}$. Denote by C' the outer cycle of G'_1. Since two nonadjacent vertices of G'_1 is by no means adjacent in G', every flippabe edge of G'_1 is also flippable in G', i.e., by Lemma 4.5 (4) every edge not in $E(C')$ is a flippable edge of G'.

Observe that $|V(G'_1)| \geq 5$; by Lemma 4.5 (3) G'_1 has a vertex 4^+-vertex. Then, we can transform G'_1 into the standard maximal outerplane graph H_{n-1} with apex u by at most $n-6$ diagonal flips, since $d_{G'_1}(u) \geq 4$ and $d_{H_{n-1}}(u) = n-2$. Thus, we obtain $\triangle_n$ by at most $n-4+n-6=2n-10$ diagonal flips (if G is 4-connected, then at most $n-5+n-6=2n-11$ diagonal flips). ∎

The following result follows from Theorem 4.5 directly.

Corollary 4.1 ([6]) *Any two 4-connected maximal planar graphs of order n can be transformed into each other by at most* $\max\{4n-22, 0\}$ *diagonal flips, up to isomorphism.*

Theorem 4.6 ([2]) *Any two maximal planar graphs of order n can be transformed into each other by at most* $5.2n - 24.4$ *diagonal flips, up to isomorphism.*

Proof By Theorem 4.5, any two 4-connected maximal planar graphs can be transformed into each other by at most $4n-22$ diagonal flips. By Theorem 4.4, every maximal planar graph of order n can be transformed into a 4-connected one by at most $\lfloor \frac{3n-6}{5} \rfloor$ diagonal flips. Hence, one can transform any maximal planar graph into any other by at most $\lfloor \frac{3n-6}{5} \rfloor + 4n - 22 = 5.2n - 24.4$ diagonal flips. ∎

4.4 Lower Bounds of the Number of Diagonal Flips

As for the lower bound on the number of diagonal flips that are required to transform two maximal planar graphs into each other, Komuro [5] proved the following theorem in the maximum degree respective of view, which was by far the best result.

Theorem 4.7 ([5]) *let G be a maximal planar graph of order n. Then, G can be transformed into* $\triangle_n$ *by at least* $2n - 2\Delta(G) - 3$ *diagonal flips.*

Proof Let u and v be the two $(n-1)$-vertices in $\triangle_n$ obtained from G by a sequence of diagonal flips. Observe that each diagonal flip can make the degree of u or v increase 1, and at most one diagonal flip that can make the degree of u and v increase 1 simultaneously. Therefore, the total sequence includes at least $2(n-1) - 2\Delta(G) - 1 = 2n - 2\Delta(G) - 3$ diagonal flips. ∎

By Theorem 4.7, every n-order maximal planar graph with maximum degree 6 can be transformed into $\triangle_n$ by at least $2n - 15$ diagonal flips. This implies that any two n-order maximal planar graphs with maximum degree 6 can be transformed into each other by at least $4n - 30$ diagonal flips if we use $\triangle_n$ as a transformation.

Komuro [5] also obtained a lower bound in terms of degree-sequence.

4.4 Lower Bounds of the Number of Diagonal Flips

Theorem 4.8 ([5]) *Let G and G' be two maximal planar graphs of order n. Let $V(G) = \{v_1, v_2, \ldots, v_n\}$ and $V(G') = \{v'_1, v'_2, \ldots, v'_n\}$, where $d_G(v_i) \le d_G(v_j)$ and $d_{G'}(v'_i) \le d_{G'}(v'_j)$ for $i < j, i, j \in \{1, 2, \ldots, n\}$. Then, it requires at least $\frac{1}{4} D(G, G')$ diagonal flips to transform G into G', where*

$$D(G, G') = \sum_{i=1}^{n} |d_G(v_i) - d_{G'}(v'_i)|$$

Proof Let σ be a bijection from $V(G)$ to $V(G')$ such that for every $v_i \in V(G)$, $\sigma(v_i) = v'_i$ if and only if v_i corresponds to v'_i when G is transformed into G' by a sequence of diagonal flips. Since each diagonal flip can change the degree of vertex by 1, it observe that at least $|d_G(v_i) - d_{G'}(\sigma(v_i))|$ diagonal flips are required to transformed v_i to $\sigma(v_i)$. In addition, each diagonal flip changes the degrees of four vertices simultaneously. Thus, the minimum number of diagonal flips which transform G to G' is at least $\frac{1}{4} \sum_{i=1}^{n} (d_G(v_i) - d_{G'}(\sigma(v_i)))$.

Indeed, one can check that when $\sigma(v_1), \sigma(v_2), \ldots, \sigma(v_n)$ are arranged in non-decrease order, the value of $\frac{1}{4} \sum_{i=1}^{n} (d_G(v_i) - d_{G'}(\sigma(v_i)))$ is the minimum. Therefore, the lower bound on diagonal flips which transform G to G' is at least $\frac{1}{4} D(G, G')$. ∎

Observe that there are Hamiltonian maximal planar graphs with maximum degree 6. By Theorem 4.4 it requires at least $2n - 15$ diagonal flips to transform a n-order Hamiltonian maximal planar graph to $\triangle_n$. In addition, by Theorem 4.5 the number of diagonal flips which transform a n-order Hamiltonian maximal planar graph to $\triangle_n$ is at most $2n - 10$. Therefore, the upper bound in Theorem 4.5 obtained by Mori, et al. [6] is almost attained.

As for the number of diagonal flips which transform a maximal planar graph into a 4-connected one, Bose, et al. [2] gave a tight lower bound.

Theorem 4.9 ([2]) *There exist maximal planar graphs of order n which can be transformed into a 4-connected one by exactly $\lceil \frac{3n-10}{5} \rceil$ diagonal flips.*

Proof Figure 4.7 illustrates the construction scheme, which is based on the recursive method to construct edge-disjoint separating triangles. The construction starts with an empty triangle (see Fig. 4.7a). The recursive step consists of adding an inverted triangle in the interior of the triangle and connecting each vertex of the new triangle to the two vertices (see Fig. 4.7b). This is recursively applied to the three new triangles that share an edge with the inserted triangle, but not to the inserted triangle itself (see Fig. 4.7c). After k iterations, instead of applying the recursive step again, we add a single vertex in the interior of each triangle we are recursing on and connect this vertex to every vertex of the triangle. We also add a single vertex in the exterior face so that the original triangle becomes separating (see Fig. 4.7d).

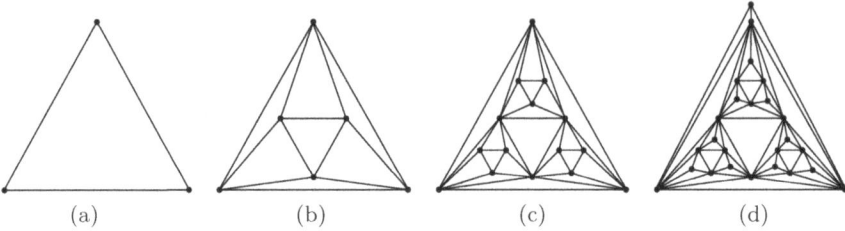

Fig. 4.7 Recursive construction of maximal planar graphs which contains lots of edge-disjoint separating triangles

By this construction, we see that the resulting graph, say G, has $\lceil \frac{3n-10}{5} \rceil$ edge-disjoint separating triangles, where $n = |V(G)|$. To make G become 4-connected, we have to remove all separating triangles; that is, at least $\lceil \frac{3n-10}{5} \rceil$ diagonal flips are required. Since the number of diagonal flips is integer, it has that $\lceil \frac{3n-10}{5} \rceil = \lfloor \frac{3n-6}{5} \rfloor$, and hence the conclusion holds. ∎

Here, we shall notice by Theorem 4.9 that the method of Mori, et al. has reached its limit, i.e., to transform a maximal planar graph G into the standard form, we first transform G into a 4-connected one, and then transform it into the standard form. However, the 4-connected is just a sufficient condition for a maximal planar graph to be Hamiltonian, but it is not necessary since there are many Hamiltonian maximal planar graphs which is not 4-connected. Therefore, there may exist other efficient approach to construct a Hamiltonian maximal planar graphs by using less number of diagonal flips. At present, the best lower upper on this number is given by Aichholzer, Huemer and Krasser [1].

References

1. O Aichholzer, C Huemer, and H Krasser. Triangulations without pointed spanning trees. *Computational geometry*, 40(1):79–83, 2008.
2. P Bose, D Jansens, A van Renssen, M Saumell, and S Verdonschot. Making triangulations 4-connected using flips. In *the 23rd Canadian Conference on Computational Geometry*, pages 241–247, 2011.
3. Z Gao, J Urrutia, and J Wang. Diagonal flips in labelled planar triangulations. *Graphs and Combinatorics*, 17(4):647–657, 2001.
4. F Hurtado, M Noy, and J Urrutia. Flipping edges in triangulations. In *Proceedings of the twelfth annual symposium on Computational geometry*, pages 214–223. ACM, 1996.
5. H Komuro et al. The diagonal flips of triangulations on the sphere. 1997.
6. R Mori, A Nakamoto, and K Ota. Diagonal flips in hamiltonian triangulations on the sphere. *Graphs and Combinatorics*, 19(3):413–418, 2003.
7. S Negami, A Nakamoto, et al. Diagonal transformations of graphs on closed surfaces. 1993.
8. K Wagner. Bemerkungen zum vierfarbenproblem. *Jahresbericht der Deutschen Mathematiker-Vereinigung*, 46:26–32, 1936.

References

Open Access This chapter is licensed under the terms of the Creative Commons Attribution 4.0 International License (http://creativecommons.org/licenses/by/4.0/), which permits use, sharing, adaptation, distribution and reproduction in any medium or format, as long as you give appropriate credit to the original author(s) and the source, provide a link to the Creative Commons license and indicate if changes were made.

The images or other third party material in this chapter are included in the chapter's Creative Commons license, unless indicated otherwise in a credit line to the material. If material is not included in the chapter's Creative Commons license and your intended use is not permitted by statutory regulation or exceeds the permitted use, you will need to obtain permission directly from the copyright holder.

Chapter 5
Construction of Maximal Planar Graphs with the Different Order

Abstract Chapter 4 introduces the operation of diagonal flip, by which one can transform a pair of maximal planar graphs with the same order into each other. In this chapter, we fucus on the methods of constructing a maximal planar graph from another one with different order; that is, start with a small order maximal planar graph, e.g., tetrahedron, octahedron or icosahedron, one can obtain a maximal planar graph with a give order by a serious of operations. This can be represented as a **generating system**, denoted by $< G; \Phi >$, where G is the **starting graph** and Φ is a set of operations, called **operators**. The generating systems of constructing maximal planar graphs, in particular, those of minimum degree 5 or of even number order, will be argued in detail in the following.

5.1 Pure Chord-Cycle Construction

Before we present the detail of this method, we introduce the definition of pure chord-cycles. Let G be a maximal planar graph and C is a cycle of G. If there are no vertices in the interior of C, then C is called a **pure chord-cycle** of G. For convenience, the triangle of G is also viewed as a pure chord-cycle.

In 1891, Eberhard [7] first studied the construction problem of maximal planar graphs. He established a generating system which can construct all maximal planar graphs, denoted $< K_4 : \{\phi_1, \phi_2, \phi_3\} >$, where K_4 is the starting graph and ϕ_1, ϕ_2, ϕ_3 are operators; see Fig. 5.1.

Observe that Eberhard's method, in essence, is to find a chord-cycle C of length 3, 4 or 5, delete all of the chords of C, add a new vertex v inside C and connect v to every vertex of C. The proof of the following theorem is due to Eberhard, written in German. Recall that a k-vertex is a vertex of degree k, and k^+ and k^- denote any integer not smaller or not greater that k, respectively.

Theorem 5.1 ([7]) *Every maximal planar graph G of order n can be generated from an $(n - 1)$-order one by using operators $\phi_1, \phi_2,$ and ϕ_3.*

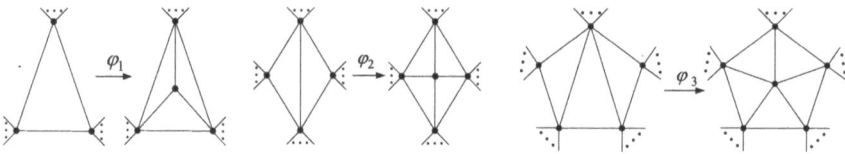

Fig. 5.1 The three operators proposed by Eberhard

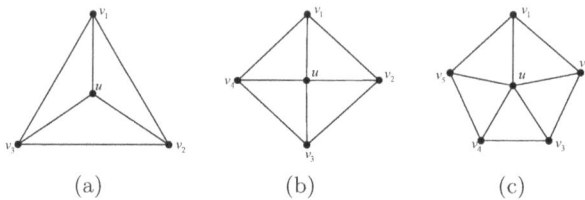

Fig. 5.2 Illustration for the proof of Theorem 5.1

Proof By n, e, and f we denote the number of vertices, edges, and faces of G. We suppose that $n \geq 5$ since $n \leq 4$ is trivial. Let X_k be the number of k-vertices. Let u be a minimum degree vertex of G. By Theorem 1.15, $3 \leq d_G(u) \leq 5$.

Case 1. $d_G(u) = 3$. Let $N_G(u) = \{v_1, v_2, v_3\}$; see Fig. 5.2a. Delete u and its incident edges and the resulting graph G' is an $(n-1)$-order maximal planar graph. Therefore, G can be generated from G' by ϕ_1.

Case 2. $d_G(u) = 4$. Let $N_G(u) = \{v_1, v_2, v_3, v_4\}$; see Fig. 5.2b. By Jordan curve theorem, either $v_1v_3 \notin E(G)$ or $v_2v_4 \notin E(G)$. Without loss of generality, we assume that $v_1v_3 \notin E(G)$. Delete u and its incident edges and connect v_1v_3. Then, the resulting graph G' is an $(n-1)$-order maximal planar graph (Observe that when $v_1v_3 \in E(G)$, G' is not a maximal planar graph). Therefore, G can be generated from G' by ϕ_2.

Case 3. $d_G(u) = 5$. Let $N_G(u) = \{v_1, v_2, v_3, v_4, v_5\}$; see Fig. 5.2c. By Jordan curve theorem, one can see that there exists some $i \in \{1, 2, 3, 4, 5\}$ such that $|N_G(v_i) \cap \{v_1, v_2, v_3, v_4, v_5\}| = 2$. Without loss of generality, we assume that $v_1v_3 \notin E(G)$ and $v_1v_4 \notin E(G)$. Delete u and its incident edges and connect v_1v_3 and v_1v_3. Then, the resulting graph G' is an $(n-1)$-order maximal planar graph. Consequently, G can be generated from G' by ϕ_3. This completes the proof. ∎

The following corollary follows from Theorem 5.1.

Corollary 5.1 *All maximal planar graphs can be generated by generating system* $< K_4; \{\phi_1, \phi_2, \phi_3\} >$.

In 1967, Bowen and Fisk [4] published an article in "Mathematics of Computation" which described an identical method as Eberhard to construct maximal planar graphs. They obtained the exact number of maximal planar graphs of orders $6 \sim 12$ with minimum degree at least 3, up to isomorphism, which are shown in Table 5.1,

5.2 Generating 5-Connected Maximal Planar Graphs

Table 5.1 The number of 6 ~ 12 maximal planar graphs of minimum degree 3 and 4

Order	6	7	8	9	10	11	12
Number							
$t_n(3)$	2	5	14	50	233	1429	7595
$t_n(4)$	1	1	2	5	12	34	130

where $t_n(\ell)$ denotes the number of maximal planar graphs of minimum degree at least ℓ for $\ell = 3, 4$.

5.2 Generating 5-Connected Maximal Planar Graphs

After Eberhard's work, Barnette [1] and Butler [6] in 1974 presented a method of constructing all 5-connected maximal planar graphs. For a change, in their generating systems, the starting graph is icosahedron and the operators are ϕ_4, ϕ_5 and ϕ_6, which are illustrated in Fig. 5.3, where edges and half edges drawn are always required to be presented while ellipsis next to each vertex corresponds to any number (zero or nonzero) of edges incident with the vertex, just assuring that the vertex has degree at least 5.

Before we present some facts needed for the proof that every 5-connected maximal planar graph can be generated from the icosahedron by using ϕ_4, ϕ_5, and ϕ_6, repeatedly, we introduce some terminology and notation.

Let G be a maximal planar graph and C a cycle without chords in G. If C consists of the neighbors of some vertex v, i.e., $C=G[N_G(v)]$, then we say that C **surrounds** v. If C is a separating cycle and does not surround any vertex, then C is called a **proper separating cycle**. If G is k-connected and every separating k-cycle is not proper, then G is called k^*-**connected**. Let e be an edge of G. If $G \circ e$, the resulting graph by contracting e, is k-connected, then we call e k-**contractible**.

Lemma 5.1 ([1]) *Let G be a 5-connected maximal planar graph without 5-contractible edge. If G is not isomorphic to icosahedron, then the resulting graph G' obtained from G by the inverse of ϕ_6 (which is illustrated in Fig. 5.4) is still 5-connected.*

Proof To the contrary, suppose that G' is not 5-connected. Then G' has a separating 4-cycle C which contains v'. We may assume, without loss of generality, that C

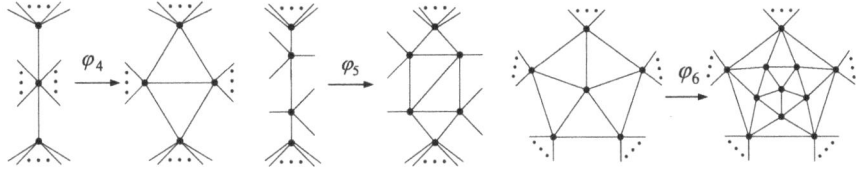

Fig. 5.3 The three operators proposed by Barnette and Butler

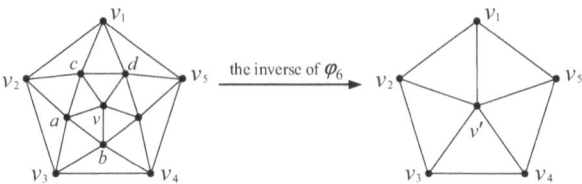

Fig. 5.4 The inverse of ϕ_6

Fig. 5.5 Illustration for Lemma 5.5

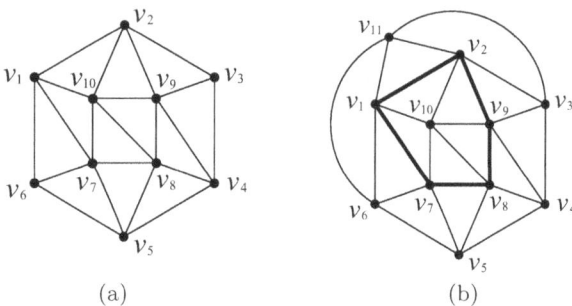

(a)   (b)

contains v_1 and v_3. Suppose that $C = v_1v'v_3v_6v_1$. Since $v_1v_2v_3v_6v_1$ is a 4-cycle in G, it must have a chord v_2v_6 (observe that G is 5-connected, which implies that $v_1v_3 \notin E(G)$). To round off the proof, we will get a contradiction by showing that v_2v_6 is a 5-contractible edge of G. Suppose not, then v_2v_6 belongs to a separating 5-cycle of G, which can only possible be $v_6v_2abv_4v_6$ and $v_6v_2cdv_5v_6$. This implies that either $v_6v_5 \in E(G)$ or $v_6v_4 \in E(G)$. Suppose that $v_6v_4 \in E(G)$. Then $v_6v_1v_5v_4v_6$ is a 4-cycle which must has a chord v_5v_6. But now G is isomorphic to the icosahedron, a contradiction. A similar line of though leads to a contradiction if we assume that $v_6v_5 \in E(G)$. ∎

Lemma 5.2 ([1]) *Let G be a 5-connected maximal planar graph with exact four 5-vertices which is not isomorphic to icosahedron; see Fig. 5.5a. Then, unless there is a vertex v_{11} such that $v_{11}v_1v_{10}v_9v_4v_{11}$ (or $v_{11}v_2v_{10}v_7v_5v_{11}$) is a separating 5-cycle, then we can implement the inverse of ϕ_5 on the pair $v_{10}v_9$, v_7v_8 or the pair v_7v_{10}, v_8v_9; or the inverse of ϕ_4 or ϕ_6.*

Proof Suppose that $v_{10}v_9$ or v_7v_8 is not contractible. Then, at least one edge of them is in a separating 5-cycle other than $v_{10}v_9v_4v_5v_7v_{10}$ and $v_1v_2v_9v_8v_7v_1$. By symmetry, we may assume that $v_{10}v_9$ is in a separating 5-cycle C of G.

Case 1. $C = v_3v_9v_{10}v_7v_6v_3$. In this case, $v_3v_2v_1v_6$ is 4-cycle with a chord. Then, $d_G(v_1) < 5$ or $d_G(v_2) < 5$, a contradiction.

Case 2. $C = v_1v_{10}v_9v_3v_{11}v_1$ for some $v_{11} \notin \{v_i | i = 1, 2, \ldots, 10\}$. Suppose that v_7v_{10} and v_9v_8 are not contractible. With the same argument we may assume that v_7v_{10} is in a separating 5-cycle C' other those surrounding v_8 or v_{10}.

Case 2.1 $C' = v_3v_9v_{10}v_7v_6v_3$. This is the same as Case 1.

Case 2.2 $C' = v_2v_{10}v_7v_5v_{12}v_2$ for some $v_{12} \notin \{v_i | i = 1, 2, \ldots, 10\}$. By symmetry, this is the type of circuit mentioned in the hypothesis.

Case 2.3 $C' = v_2v_{11}v_6v_7v_{10}v_2$. In this case, v_{10} is adjacent to only 5-vertices. Since G is 5-connected, every vertex of $\{v_3, v_4, v_5, v_6, v_{11}\}$ has degree at least 5. If all of these vertices have degree at least 6, then we can implement the inverse of ϕ_6 on the cycle $v_1v_7v_8v_9v_2v_1$; if there is a 5-vertex in $\{v_3, v_4, v_5, v_6, v_{11}\}$, say v_5, then we can implement the inverse of ϕ_4 on the edge v_5v_{12}.

Case 3. $C = v_1v_{11}v_4v_9v_{10}v_1$. This is the type of cycle in the hypothesis. ∎

Theorem 5.2 ([1]) *Let G be a 5^*-connected maximal planar graph, other than the icosahedron. Then, we can obtain a 5-connected maximal planar graph from G by using once the inverse operation of ϕ_4, ϕ_5 or ϕ_6.*

Proof Let v_0 be an arbitrary 5-vertex of G. If $N_G(v_0)$ does not contain three consecutive 5-vertices, then there exists an edge e with one end v_0 which does not belong to any 5-cycle surrounding a vertex. Therefore, the resulting graph obtained from G by implementing the inverse of ϕ_4 on e. If there are three consecutive 5-vertices adjacent to v_0, then G contains a subgraph isomorphic to Fig. 5.5a, where v_0 corresponds to v_8 and its three consecutive 5-vertices are v_7, v_{10}, v_9. By Lemma 5.2, either we can obtain a 5-connected maximal planar graph from G by using once the inverse operation of ϕ_5 on the pair $v_{10}v_9$, v_7v_8 or the pair v_7v_{10}, v_8v_9, or G contains a 5-cycle $v_1v_{10}v_9v_4v_{11}v_1$ which means that $v_1v_{10}v_8v_4v_{11}v_1$ is a proper separating cycle, a contradiction with the assumption that G is 5^*-connected. ∎

Theorem 5.3 ([1]) *Let G be a 5-connected maximal planar graph, other than the icosahedron. Then, we can obtain a 5-connected maximal planar graph from G by using once the inverse operation of ϕ_4, ϕ_5 or ϕ_6.*

Proof By Theorem 5.2 we may assume that G is not 5^*-connected, that is, G contains a proper separating cycle. If G contains 5-contractible edge, then we can get the desired graph by the inverse of ϕ_4. Therefore, we suppose that G does not contain any 5-contractible edge. Let C be a smallest proper separating 5-cycle of G, i.e., if there is another proper separating 5-cycle whose one edge inside C, then this separating 5-cycle has a vertex outside C. Let $C = v_1v_2v_3v_4v_5v_1$.

Claim 1. There is no path of length 2 inside C which joints two nonadjacent vertices on C. Otherwise, suppose that there is a path $v_1v_0v_3$. Let $C' = v_1v_0v_3v_4v_5v_1$. If C' has chords, then v_0v_5 or v_0v_4 is a chord of C', say $v_0v_5 \in E(G)$. Then, the cycles $v_0v_3v_4v_5v_0$ and $v_1v_0v_3v_2v_1$ have chords v_0v_4 and v_0v_2, respectively. As a result, C is not a proper separating 5-cycle, a contradiction. If C' contains no chord, then C' surrounds a vertex by the minimality of C. However, when adding a chord for cycle $v_1v_0v_3v_2v_1$, we have that v_0 is a 4-vertex, a contradiction. Thus, every vertex of C must be incident with at least two edges inside C.

Claim 2. Every edge inside C belongs to a 5-cycle surrounding a vertex. If not, there is an edge inside C that belongs to a proper separating 5-cycle C', since G contains no 5-contractible edge. Suppose that $C' = v_6v_1v_7v_8v_3v_6$, where v_6 is outside C and v_7 and v_8 are inside C. Then, $v_6v_2 \in E(G)$. If the cycle $v_2v_1v_7v_8v_3v_2$ contains a chord, then there is only one vertex v_2 inside C' and C' is not a proper separating cycle, a contradiction. Therefore, the cycle $v_2v_1v_7v_8v_3v_2$ contains no chord, and by the minimality of C, it surrounds a vertex, say v_9. Then, $v_1v_9v_3v_6v_1$ is a separating 4-cycle, a contradiction.

Claim 3. G contains a subgraph isomorphic to the graph in Fig. 5.5a, and the four 5-vertices are on or inside C. Let H be a graph which consists of C, the interior of C and a vertex w outside C that is connected to every vertex of C. Let n_i denote the number of i-vertices of G. Then, by Euler's Formula (1.9) in Theorem 1.12, it follows that $\sum(6-i)n_i=12$. Since $\delta(G) \geq 5$, $n_5 \geq 12$. Therefore, there are at least six 5-vertices. By the definition of C and the structure of H, we see that H is 5^*-connected. Then, with a similar line of thought of the proof of Theorem 5.2, we deduce that G contains the desired subgraph.

Claim 4. G can implement the inverse operation of ϕ_5 on the pair $v_{10}v_9$, v_7v_8 or v_7v_{10}, v_8v_9. If not, without loss of generality we may assume that G contains the path $v_1v_{11}v_4$, where $v_{11} \notin \{v_i | i = 1, 2, \ldots, 10\}$. Clearly, $v_1v_{10}v_8v_4v_{11}v_1$ is a proper separating 5-cycle with at least one vertex outside C. If v_1 is outside C, then both v_{10} and v_{11} on C. Consider the possibility of C; there are four separating 5-cycles, $v_2v_{10}v_8v_5v_{11}v_2$, $v_2v_{10}v_8v_4v_{11}v_2$, $v_2v_{10}v_7v_6v_{11}v_2$, and $v_2v_{10}v_7v_5v_{11}v_2$, which contains v_{10}, v_{11} but no v_1. For the first two cases, the cycles separate v_7 and v_9; for the third case, the cycle surrounds v and is not a proper separating cycle; for the fourth case, $v_2v_{111} \in E(G)$ and $v_2v_9v_4v_{12}v_2$ is a separating 4-cycle. Thus, in either case, we derive a contradiction. So, v_1 is not outside C. Similarly, we have that v_4 is also not outside C. Thus, V_{11} is outside C and both v_1 and v_4 are on C. Now, we consider other vertices.

If $v_{10} \in V(C)$, then $v_8 \notin V(C)$. In this case, since $v_8v_{10} \in E(C)$, C separates v_9 and v_7. Moreover, $v_9 \notin V(C)$; otherwise $v_{10}v_8v_4$ is a path connect two nonadjacent vertices of C, a contradiction with Claim 1; neither v_7 nor v_2 lie on C; otherwise, C contains a chord and v_{10} is adjacent to one vertex of C, a contradiction. Consequently, $V_{10} \notin V(C)$. Analogously, $v_8 \notin V(C)$.

If $v_9 \in V(C)$, then $v_1v_{10}v_9$ is a path connect two nonadjacent vertices of C, a contradiction with Claim 1. Therefore, $V_9 \notin V(C)$. Analogously, $v_7 \notin V(C)$.

Obviously, $v_2v_4 \notin E(G)$; otherwise v_3 will be a 3-vertex. If $v_2 \in V(C)$, $v_2v_9v_4$ is a path connect two nonadjacent vertices of C, a contradiction with Claim 1. Therefore, $v_2 \notin V(C)$. Since $v_2v_{10} \in E(G)$ and v_{10} is inside C, v_2 is not outside C. Analogously, $v_5 \notin V(C)$.

Since $d_G(v_2) \geq 5$, $v_1v_3 \notin E(G)$. If $v_3 \in V(C)$, $v_1v_2v_3$ is a path connect two nonadjacent vertices of C, a contradiction with Claim 1. Therefore, $v_3 \notin V(C)$. Analogously, $v_6 \notin V(C)$.

From the above, we see that a subgraph isomorphic to Fig. 5.5a inside C, except the two vertices v_1 and v_4 which lie on C. Let v_{12} be a vertex of C which is adjacent to both v_1 and v_4. Then, the cycle $C'' = v_{12}v_1v_6v_5v_4v_{12}$ contains no vertex outside C, which shows that C'' surrounds a vertex or contains a chord. If C'' has a chord, then $d_G(v_6) \leq 4$ or $d_G(v_5) \leq 4$, a contradiction; if C'' surrounds a vertex, then v_6 is a 4-vertex, a contradiction. This completes the proof of the theorem. ∎

By Theorem 5.3, the following result holds.

Corollary 5.2 *Starting from the icosahedron, one can generate all 5-connected maximal planar graphs by using ϕ_4, ϕ_5, and ϕ_6. That is, every 5-connected maximal planar graph can be generated by the system $< Z_{20;\Phi} >$, where Z_{20} is the icosahedron and $\Phi = \{\phi_4, \phi_5, \phi_6\}$.*

5.3 Generating 3-, 4-Connected Maximal Planar Graphs of Minimum Degree 5

In Sect. 5.2 we present the methods of constructing 5-connected maximal planar graphs. To generate 3-,4-connected maximal planar graphs of minimum degree 5, in 1983, Batagelj [2] extended generating system $< Z_{20}; \{\phi_4, \phi_5, \phi_6\} >$ to $< Z_{20}; \{\phi_4, \phi_5, \phi_7\} >$, where ϕ_7 is the diagonal flip (see Fig. 4.1). All graph considered in this section are maximal planar graphs with minimum degree 5.

For $k \in \{3, 4\}$ a separating k-cycle is called **deepest** if no edge of other separating k-cycles is inside (or outside) it. One can readily check that if a maximal planar graph contains separating 3-cycle, then it must contain a deepest separating 3-cycle. If a maximal planar graph contains a separating 4-cycle but no separating 3-cycle, then it must contains a deepest separating 4-cycle.

For convenience, we denote by ϕ_7^t a diagonal flip such that the flipped edge does not belong to any separating cycle of length at most $(t-1)$ in the resulting graph.

Theorem 5.4 ([5])

(a) Every n-order 3-connected maximal planar graph of minimum degree 5 with a separating 3-cycle can be generated from an n-order 3-connected maximal planar graph of minimum degree 5 that contains fewer separating 3-cycles by ϕ_7.

(b) Every n-order 4-connected maximal planar graph of minimum degree 5 with a separating 4-cycle can be generated from an n-order 4-connected maximal planar graph of minimum degree 5 by ϕ_7^4 or from a 4-connected maximal planar graph of minimum degree 5 with smaller order by ϕ_4.

Proof For (a), Let G be an n-order 3-connected maximal planar graph with $\delta(G) = 5$ and with a deepest separating 3-cycle C. Since C is deepest, every vertex of C is incident with at least two edges inside C. Thus, the union of C and the interior of C has the structure of Fig. 5.6a, where C is remarked by bold lines.

In addition, since C is a separating cycle, there are vertices outside C, i.e., each vertex of C is incident with an edge outside C. If C contains two vertices, say the lower two in the Fig. 5.6a, each of which is incident with only one edge outside C, then a 3-vertex would occur, a contradiction (see Fig. 5.6b). Therefore, at least two vertices $v, w \in V(C)$ such that each of them is incident at least two edges outside C, which implies that $d_G(v) \geq 6$ and $d_G(w) \geq 6$. Let G' be the resulting graph obtained from G by the inverse of ϕ_7 on vw. Clearly, $\delta(G') = 5$, C has been destroyed, and the new edge can not produced a new separating 3-cycle. Hence, G'

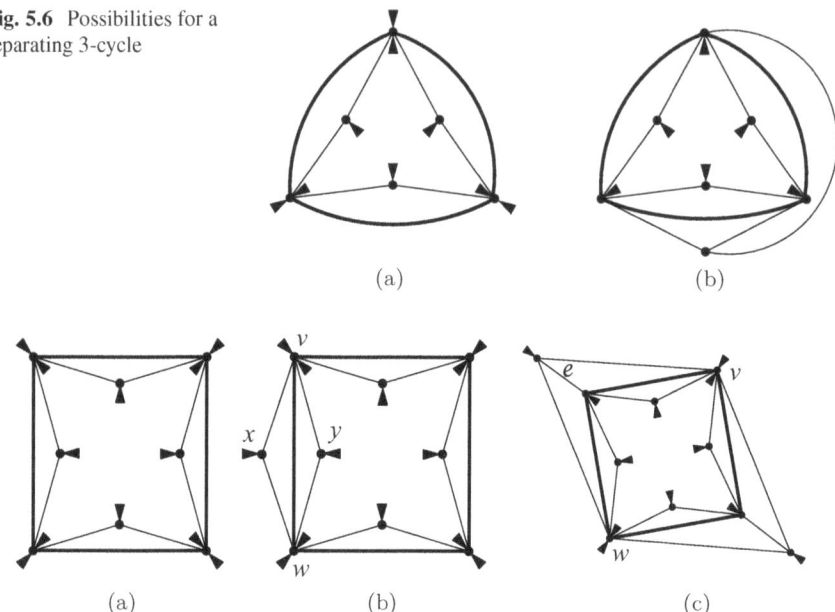

Fig. 5.6 Possibilities for a separating 3-cycle

Fig. 5.7 Possibilities for a separating 4-cycle

contains a smaller number of separating 3-cycles, and G can be generated from G by ϕ_7.

For (b), suppose that G is a graph satisfying the conditions of the theorem, i.e., G contains no separating 3-cycle but a separating 4-cycle. Let C be a deepest separating 4-cycle. Again, each vertex of C is incident with at least two edges inside C, and C and the interior of C has the structure shown Fig. 5.7a. Since C is a separating cycle and G contains no separating 3-cycle, vertices opposite on C can not be adjacent. This implies that each vertex of C is incident with at least one edge outside C. If C contains two adjacent vertices each of which is incident with only one edge outside C, then it would yield either a 4-vertex outside C or a separating 3-cycle, a contradictions. Therefore, at least two vertices of C, say v, w, each of which is incident with at least two edges outside C, i.e., $d_G(v) \geq 6$ and $d_G(w) \geq 6$.

If $vw \in E(C)$ (see Fig. 5.7b), let x and y be the common neighbors of v and w outside and inside C, respectively. Then, x and y are not adjacent to vertices in $V(C) \setminus \{v, w\}$; otherwise, a separating 3-cycle would by produced. Let G' be the resulting graph obtained from G by the reverse of ϕ_7 on vw (replaced by xy). Clearly, C is destroyed in G'. If xy lies on a new separating 4-cycle C' in G', then $v \in C'$ or $w \in C'$ which implies a separating 3-cycle in G, a contradiction. Therefore, G' is an n-order 4-connected maximal planar graph of minimum degree 5 with fewer separating 4-cycles. Therefore, G can be obtained from G' by ϕ_7^4 on xy.

5.3 Generating 3-, 4-Connected Maximal Planar Graphs of Minimum Degree 5

Otherwise, we may assume that each of vertices in $V(C) \setminus \{v, w\}$ is incident with exact one edge outside C; see Fig. 5.7. In this case, by implement the inverse of operation ϕ_4 (on the edge e) we can obtain a smaller order 4-connected maximal planar graph G' of minimum degree 5 (observe that if there is a separating 3-cycle in G', then it would have to cross the interior of C. One can easily be seen that this does not exist by checking the various possibilities). Hence, G can be obtained from G' by ϕ_4. ∎

Theorem 5.5 ([5])

(a) Every 5-connected maximal planar graph of minimum degree 5 can be generated from the icosahedron by ϕ_4, ϕ_5, and ϕ_7^5.
(b) Every 4-connected maximal planar graph of minimum degree 5 can be generated from the icosahedron graph by ϕ_4, ϕ_5, and ϕ_7^4.

Proof Let G be a maximal planar graph that can not be reduced by the inverse of operation ϕ_4 or ϕ_5. By Theorem 5.3, G can be reduced by the inverse of operation ϕ_6. Therefore, G contains the configuration on the left-hand side of operation ϕ_6 in Fig. 5.4. Therefore, for part (a), it is enough to show that a graph containing this configuration can be reduced by the inverse of operation ϕ_7^5. In Fig. 5.8, we see that the reverse of ϕ_7^5 can not produce separating 4-cycles. Therefore, the resulting graph by the reverse of ϕ_7^5 is still a 5-connected maximal planar graph of minimum degree 5. This paves the way for implementing the inverse of ϕ_5. Hence, every 5-connected maximal planar graph of minimum degree 5 that contains this configuration can be constructed from a smaller 5-connected maximal planar graph of minimum degree 5, by applying ϕ_5 followed by ϕ_7^5. This proves part (a).

Part (b) follows easily from (a) and Theorem 5.4 (b). ∎

Theorem 5.6 ([2]) *Every 3-connected maximal planar graph G of minimum degree 5 can be generated from the icosahedron graph by ϕ_4, ϕ_5, and ϕ_7.*

Proof The result follows from Theorem 5.5 and Theorem 5.4 (a). ∎

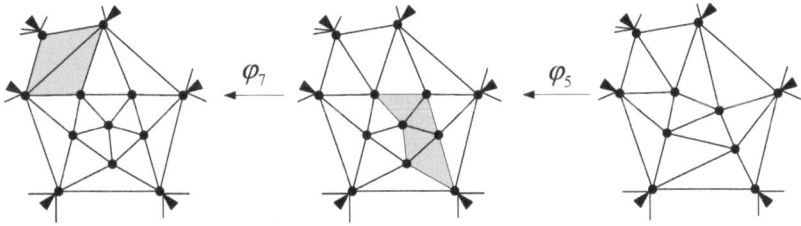

Fig. 5.8 Replacing a ϕ_6 by ϕ_5 followed by ϕ_7

5.4 Generating Maximal Planar Graphs of Minimum Degree at Least 4

In 1984, Batagelj [3] introduced a generating system, written $< Z_8; \{\phi'_4, \phi_8\} >$, for the construction of maximal planar graphs of minimum degree at least 4. Here, the starting graph is Z_8, the octahedron, and the operators are ϕ'_4 and ϕ_8 which are illustrated in Fig. 5.9. Observe that ϕ'_4 is similar to the operator ϕ_4; what makes them different is that ϕ'_4 relax the restriction that the two ends of the 3-path to be transformed must have degree at least 5 and require that the degree of the middle vertex of the 3-path is 1 or 2 in its right-hand side; see the left-hand side of Fig. 5.9a.

Theorem 5.7 ([3]) *Every maximal planar graph of minimum degree at least 4 can be generated form the octahedron by ϕ'_4 and ϕ_8.*

Proof It is enough to prove that every maximal planar graph G with $\delta(G) \geq 4$, other than the octahedron, can be reduced to a smaller maximal planar graph without 3-vertices by the inverse of ϕ'_4 or ϕ_8.

Let x be a minimum degree vertex of G. By the Euler's Formula we have $d_G(x) \leq 5$. We distinguish two cases.

Case 1. $d_G(x) = 4$. Let $N_G(x) = \{z, v, w, u\}$ and their structure is shown in Fig. 5.10a. There are two possibilities in terms of the degrees of vertices in $N_G(x)$.

Case 1.1. $N_G(x)$ contains no 4-vertex; see Fig. 5.10a. In this case, $uv \notin E(G)$ or $zw \notin E(G)$, and by symmetry we may assume that $uv \notin E(G)$. Then, G can be reduced to a smaller maximal planar graph without 3-vertices by the inverse of ϕ'_4 on xv.

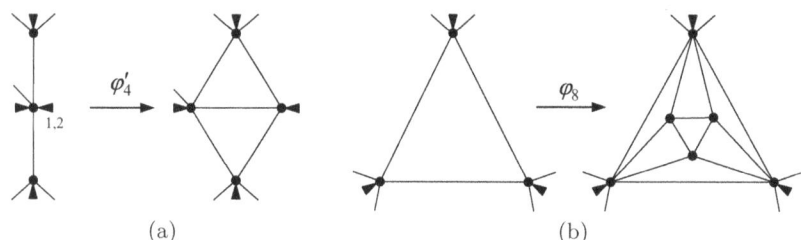

Fig. 5.9 Two operators for generating maximal planar graphs of minimum degree at least 4

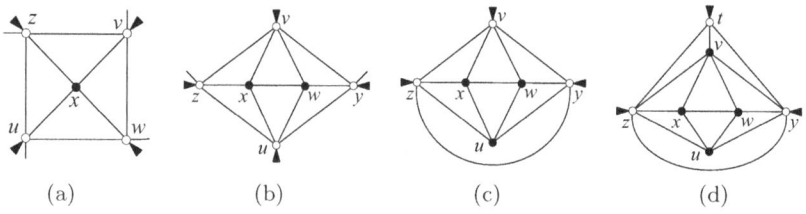

Fig. 5.10 Illustration for the case $d_G(x) = 4$

5.5 Generating Maximal Planar Graphs of Even Number Order

Fig. 5.11 Illustration for the case $d_G(x) = 5$

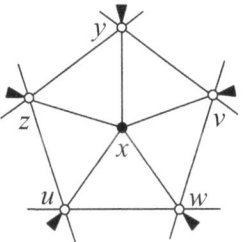

Case 1.2. $N_G(x)$ contains a 4-vertex, say w; see Fig. 5.10b. If $d_G(u) \geq 5$ and $d_G(v) \geq 5$, then G can be reduced by the inverse of ϕ'_4 on xw; otherwise, we may assume that u is a 4-vertex (see Fig. 5.10c). If all v, z, y have degree at least 6, then G can be reduced by the inverse of ϕ_8 on the triangle xwu. If $\{v, z, y\}$ contains a vertex of degree at most 5, then $\{v, z, y\}$ contains a 5-vertex (otherwise G is isomorphic to the octahedron). Without loss of generality, suppose that v is a 5-vertex (see Fig. 5.10d). Then, G can be reduced by the inverse of ϕ'_4 on vt.

Case 2. $d_G(x) = 5$. The neighborhood of x is shown in Fig. 5.11.

Observe that there exist at least one vertex in $N_G(x) = \{u, w, v, y, z\}$ such that the two vertices that are not adjacent to it on the cycle $uwvyzu$ are also not adjacent to it in G. By symmetry, we may assume that $yu \notin E(G)$ and $yw \notin E(G)$. Then, G can be reduced by the inverse of ϕ'_4 on xy. ∎

In 2005, Brinkmann and McKay [5] reviewed the research on Barnette, Butlery and Batageljs' work in detail. They described an efficient method to construct maximal planar graphs with minimum degree 5. They proved that by ϕ_4, ϕ_5, ϕ_6, and ϕ_7 one can generate maximal planar graph of minimum degree 5 with separating 3-cycles, 4-cycles, and 5-cycles, respectively, and gave the detailed algorithm to generate them. By constructive approach, they obtain the exact values of the number of $(12 \sim 40)$-orders maximal planar graphs of minimum degree 5, where the numbers of 3-, 4-, and 5-connected maximal planar graphs of order 4- with minimum degree 5 are 8469193859271, 7488436558647, and 5925181102878, respectively.

5.5 Generating Maximal Planar Graphs of Even Number Order

This section turns to the construction of maximal planar graph containing even number vertices. For this, we first introduce the concept of **even maximal planar graphs**. If a maximal planar graph contains no vertex with odd number degree, then we call it an **even maximal planar graph**. In 1984, Batagelj [3] presented a generating system, denoted $< Z_8; \{\phi_9, \phi_{10}\} >$, to construct this class of graphs,

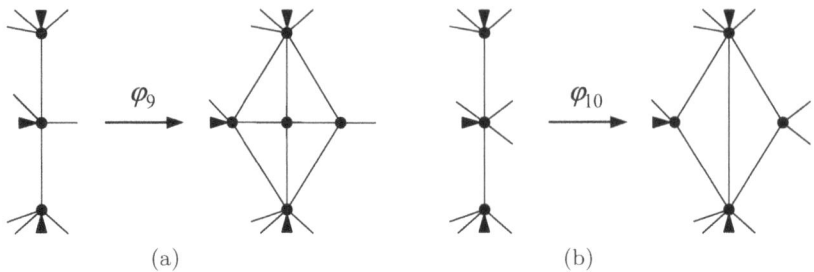

Fig. 5.12 Two operators for generating even maximal planar graphs

Fig. 5.13 Illustration for the case that every neighbor of x has degree at least 6

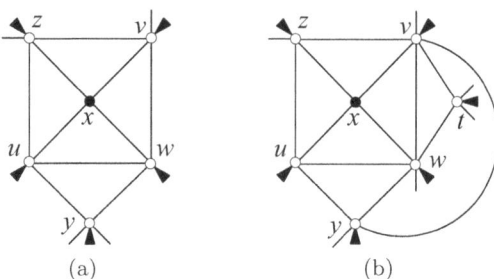

where starting graph Z_8 is the octahedron and the operators are ϕ_9 and ϕ_{10} (which illustrated in Fig. 5.12).

Theorem 5.8 ([3]) *Every even maximal planar graph can be generated from the octahedron by ϕ_9 and ϕ_{10}.*

Proof It is enough to prove that every even maximal planar graph G, other than the octahedron, can be reduced to a smaller even maximal planar graph by the inverse of ϕ_9 or ϕ_{10}. By Euler's Formula, every even maximal planar graph contains at least four 4-vertices. Let x be a 4-vertex of G and u, w, v, z are its neighbors surrounding x in this order (see Fig. 5.13a). We consider two cases.

Case 1. All u, w, v, z have degree at least 6. Let y and t the common neighbors (other than x) of the pair u, w and the pair v, w, respectively. If $yv \notin E(G)$ and $yz \notin E(G)$, then G can be reduced by the inverse of ϕ_{10} on the quadrilateral $xuyw$; otherwise, we may assume that $yv \in E(G)$ by symmetry (see Fig. 5.13b). Then, $tz \notin E(G)$ and $tu \notin E(G)$, and G can be reduced by the inverse of ϕ_{10} on the quadrilateral $xwtv$.

Case 2. There is a 4-vertex in $\{u, w, v, z\}$, say w.

5.5 Generating Maximal Planar Graphs of Even Number Order

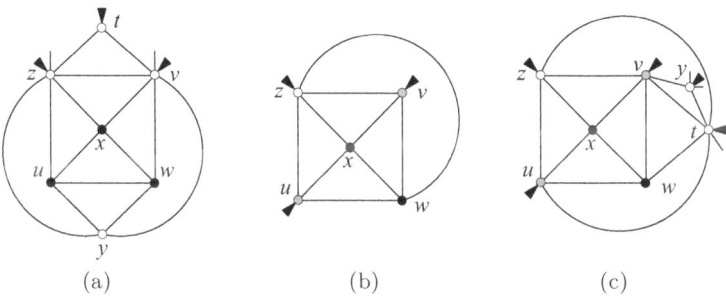

Fig. 5.14 Illustration for the case that x has at least one neighbor of degree 4

Fig. 5.15 Two maximal planar graphs for the illustration that ϕ_9 and ϕ_{10} are independent each other. (a) G_1. (b) G_2

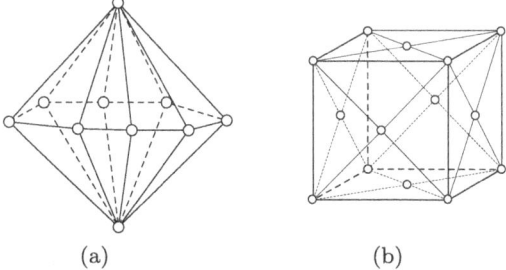

Case 2.1. $d_G(u) = 4$ or $d_G(v) = 4$. By symmetry we may assume that $d_G(u) = 4$; see Fig. 5.14a. Since G is not isomorphic to the octahedron, $d_G(z) \geq 6$ and $d_G(v) \geq 6$. Let t the common neighbor of v and z, other than x. Then, G can be reduced by the inverse of ϕ_{10} on the quadrilateral $xvtz$.

Case 2.2. $d_G(u) \geq 6$ and $d_G(v) \geq 6$. We need to further consider the following three cases.

Case 2.2.1. $N_G(w) \cap N_G(z) = \{x, u, v\}$. Then, every path connecting w and z that does not contains u, x or v contains at least four vertices. Then, G can be reduced by the inverse of ϕ_9 (contracting w and z).

Case 2.2.2. $wz \in E(G)$; see Fig. 5.14b. Clearly, this case does not exist, since $d_G(u) \geq 6$ and $d_G(w) = 4$.

Case 2.2.3. $|N_G(w) \cap N_G(z)| \geq |\{x, u, v\}| = 3$. Let $t \in (N_G(w) \cap N_G(z)) \setminus \{x, u, v\}$; see Fig. 5.14c. Then, G can be reduced by the inverse of ϕ_{10} on the quadrilateral $vwty$.

This completes the proof of the theorem. ∎

Observe that ϕ_9 and ϕ_{10} are independent each other. As an illustration, we consider the two graphs G_1 and G_2 in Fig. 5.15. Both G_1 and G_2 are even maximal planar graphs. Since G_1 does not contain any two adjacent vertices of degree at least

6, G_1 can not be reduced to a smaller even maximal planar graph by the inverse of ϕ_{10}; since G_2 contains no two adjacent 4-vertex, G_2 can not be reduced to a smaller even maximal planar graph by the inverse of ϕ_9.

5.6 Maximal Planar Graphs of Minimum Degree 5 and of Orders 12 ~ 19

By using the method introduced in Sect. 5.3, the maximal planar graphs of minimum degree 5 and of orders 12 ~ 19 are constructed [8], which is an useful reference material for interested readers. In the following, we present these graphs, in which n denotes the order of the graph and the number in the parenthesis is the degree-sequence (Figs. 5.16, 5.17, and 5.18). Notice that there does not exist any maximal planar graph of order 13.

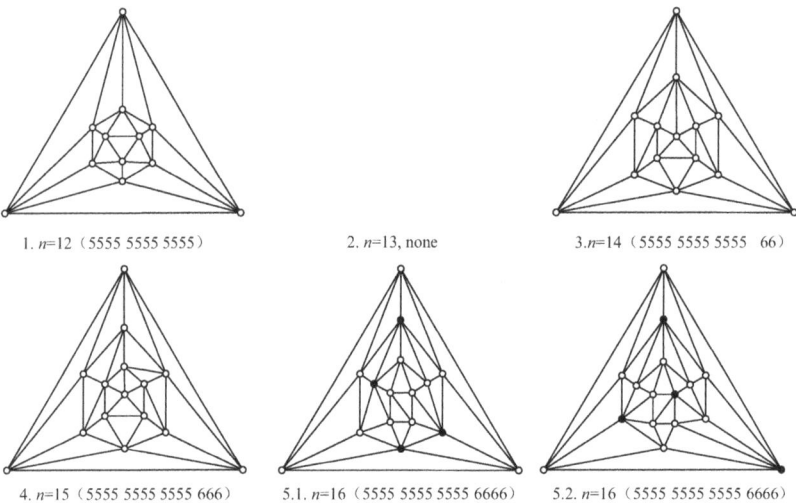

1. n=12 (5555 5555 5555)　　2. n=13, none　　3. n=14 (5555 5555 5555 66)

4. n=15 (5555 5555 5555 666)　　5.1. n=16 (5555 5555 5555 6666)　　5.2. n=16 (5555 5555 5555 6666)

Fig. 5.16 Maximal planar graphs of minimum degree 5 and of orders 12 ~ 16

5.6 Maximal Planar Graphs of Minimum Degree 5 and of Orders 12 ∼ 19   145

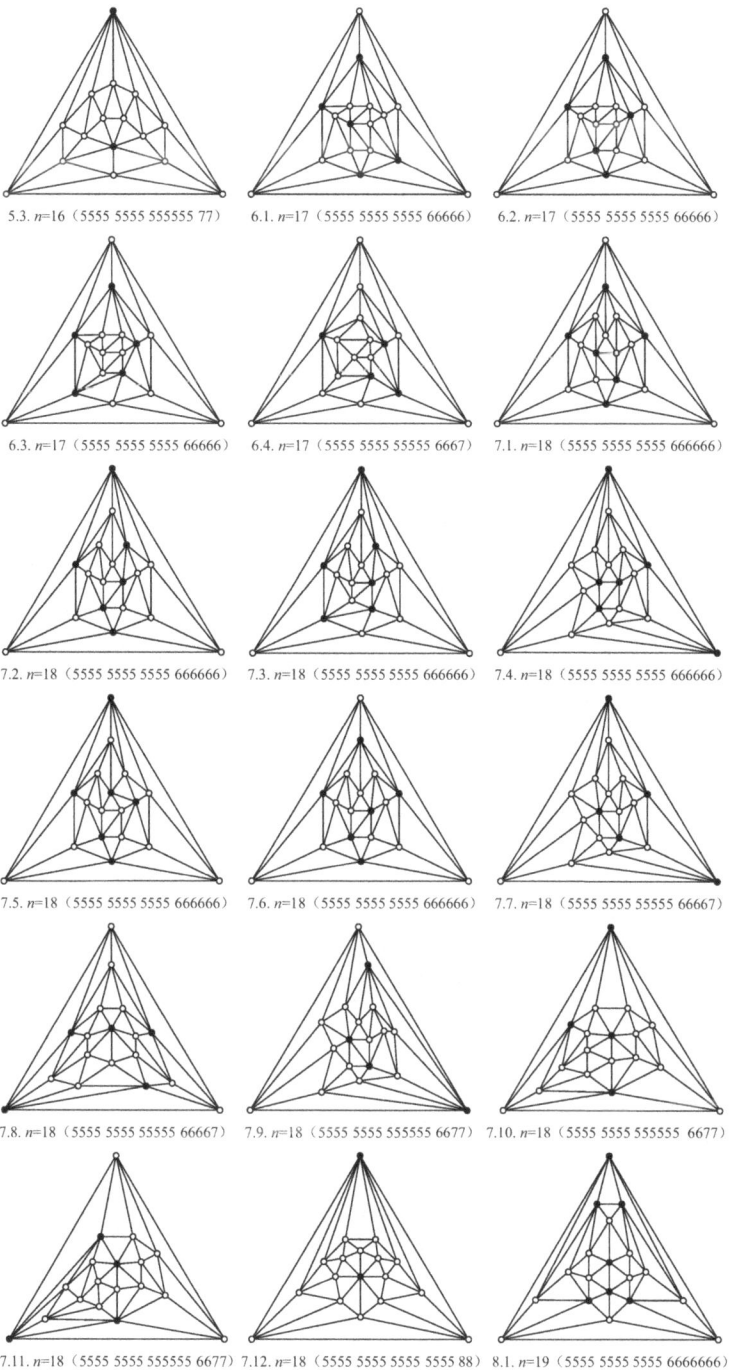

Fig. 5.17 Maximal planar graphs of minimum degree 5 and of orders 16 ∼ 19

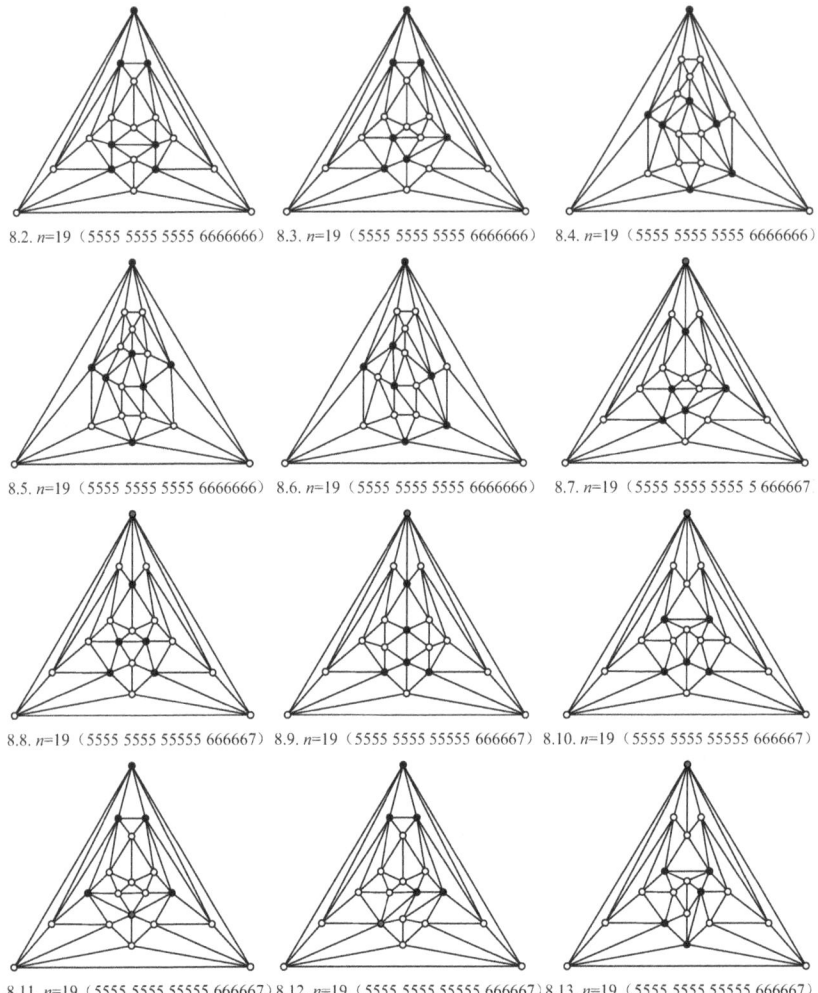

Fig. 5.18 Maximal planar graphs of minimum degree 5 and of order 19

References

1. D Barnette. On generating planar graphs. *Discrete Mathematics*, 7(3-4):199–208, 1974.
2. V Batagelj. An inductive definition of the class of all triangulations with no vertex of degree smaller than 5. In *Proceedings of the Fourth Yugoslav Seminar on Graph Theory, Novi Sad.*, 15–24, 1983.
3. V Batagelj. Inductive definition of two restricted classes of triangulations. *Discrete Mathematics*, 52(2-3):113–121, 1984.
4. R Bowen and S Fisk. Generation of triangulations of the sphere. *Mathematics of Computation*, 21(98):250–252, 1967.

References

5. G Brinkmann and B D McKay. Construction of planar triangulations with minimum degree 5. *Discrete Mathematics*, 301(2-3):147–163, 2005.
6. J W Butler. A generation procedure for the simple 3-polytopes with cyclically 5-connected graphs. *Can. J. Math.*, 26(3):686–708, 1974.
7. V Eberhard. *Zur morphologie der polyeder*. BG Teubner, 1891.
8. E Zhu. The theory on the tree-colorable maximal planar graphs. *Doctoral thesis, Peking University*, 2015.

Open Access This chapter is licensed under the terms of the Creative Commons Attribution 4.0 International License (http://creativecommons.org/licenses/by/4.0/), which permits use, sharing, adaptation, distribution and reproduction in any medium or format, as long as you give appropriate credit to the original author(s) and the source, provide a link to the Creative Commons license and indicate if changes were made.

The images or other third party material in this chapter are included in the chapter's Creative Commons license, unless indicated otherwise in a credit line to the material. If material is not included in the chapter's Creative Commons license and your intended use is not permitted by statutory regulation or exceeds the permitted use, you will need to obtain permission directly from the copyright holder.

Chapter 6
Generating System of Maximal Planar Graphs

Abstract In Chaps. 4 and 5, we depicted the methods of generating a maximal planar graph from a given one with the same and different order. This chapter will introduce another one approach, called generating system of maximal planar graphs, which can establish a connection between structures and colorings of maximal planar graphs and hence may help to the final resolution of the Four Color Conjecture by mathematical method.

6.1 Basic Extending-Contracting Operations System of Maximal Planar Graphs

In this section, we introduce the basic **extending-contracting operational system**. This system consists of two parts: operating object and basic operators, where the operating object is a maximal planar graph, and the basic operators include four pairs of operators: the extending i-wheel operation and the contracting i-wheel operations, $i = 2, 3, 4, 5$. The function of this system is: starting with K_3, one can generate any given maximal planar graph by using the four pairs of operators repeatedly.

The **extending 2-wheel operation** consists of 2 steps:

(1) add a new edge between two adjacent vertices, which will generate a 2-parallel edge (namely a 2-cycle, a cycle of order 2);
(2) add a new vertex in the face of the 2-cycle and connect the new vertex to the two vertices of the 2-cycle.

Naturally, the object of extending 2-wheel operation is an edge of a maximal planar graph; see Fig. 6.2a.

For a graph with 2-wheels, the **contracting 2-wheel operation** is to delete the wheel-center of a 2-wheel and the two edges incident with the wheel-center, and then delete one of the parallel edges of the 2-cycle. The procedures of extending and contracting 2-wheel operations are shown in Fig. 6.1.

The **extending 3-wheel operation** is to add a new vertex in a certain face of the maximal planar graph and connect it to the three vertices of the face, respectively.

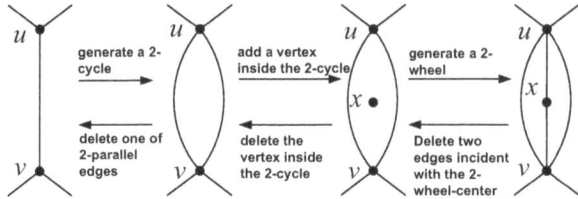

Fig. 6.1 The procedures of extending and contracting 2-wheel operations

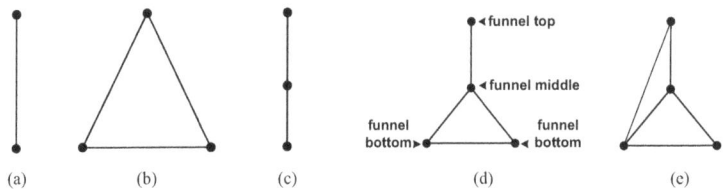

Fig. 6.2 The objects of basic extending wheel operations and semi-funnel. (**a**) edge. (**b**) triangle. (**c**) 2-path. (**d**) funnel. (**e**) semi-funnel

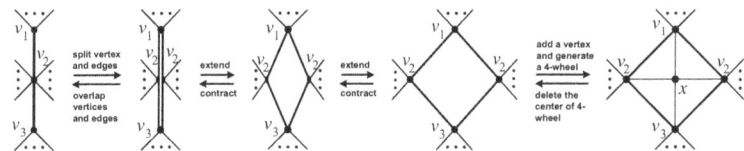

Fig. 6.3 The illustration of extending and contracting 4-wheel operations

The object of extending 3-wheel operation is a triangle of a maximal planar graph; see Fig. 6.2b. The **contracting 3-wheel operation** is to delete a certain 3-degree vertex and its incident edges.

Let G be a maximal planar graph, and $P_3 = v_1 v_2 v_3$ be a 2-path of G. The **extending 4-wheel operation on path** P_3 consists of two steps: (1) replace P_3 by a 4-cycle $v_1 v_2 v_3 v_2'$. That is, spilt the vertex v_2 into two vertices v_2 and v_2', split the edges $v_1 v_2$ into two edges $v_1 v_2$, $v_1 v_2'$, and split $v_2 v_3$ into $v_2 v_3$, $v_2' v_3$. All edges (incident with v_2) on the left of P_3 in G are incident with v_2, and all edges (incident with v_2) on the right of P_3 in G are incident with v_2' so that the obtained new graph would be planar. This process is shown in Fig. 6.3 (see the first to the fourth graph); (2) add a new vertex in the face $v_1 v_2 v_3 v_2'$, and connect it to vertices v_1, v_2', v_3, v_2 respectively, see the fifth graph in Fig. 6.3. The **contracting 4-wheel operation** includes three steps: (1) delete a certain 4-degree vertex and the edges incident with it; (2) identify a pair of the non-adjacent vertices; (3) delete one of the multiple edges if there are two multiple edges in the obtained new graph and no vertex in the face incident with the multiple edges (under the planar embedding). This procedure is shown in Fig. 6.3 (see the fifth to the first graph).

6.1 Basic Extending-Contracting Operations System of Maximal Planar Graphs

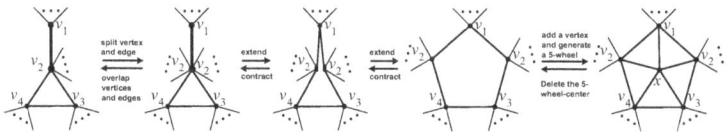

Fig. 6.4 The illustration of extending and contracting 5-wheel operations

The graph shown in Fig. 6.2d is called a **funnel**, denoted by L, where the 1-degree vertex is the **top** of the funnel, the 3-degree vertex is the **middle** of the funnel, and the two 2-degree vertices are the **bottoms** of the funnel. As the middle and two bottoms of L are vertices of a triangle, we also write L by $L = v - \Delta$, where v is the top of L. If we add an edge between the top and one of bottoms of the funnel, then we call the new graph a **semi-funnel** (see Fig. 6.2e). Let H be an induced subgraph of G. We call H a **funnel** (or **semi-funnel**) subgraph if H is isomorphic to a funnel (or a semi-funnel). The semi-funnel subgraph is one of objects to construct ancestor-graphs or descendent-graphs of a graph.

For a maximal planar graph G, the **extending 5-wheel operation** and the **contracting 5-wheel operation** are similar to the extending 4-wheel operation and the contracting 4-wheel operation. The difference between the 5-wheel and 4-wheel operations is that an extending 5-wheel operation is on a funnel, while an extending 4-wheel operation is on a 2-path. Figure 6.4 illustrates the processs of extending and contracting 5-wheel operations. Specifically, the **extending 5-wheel operation on a funnel** L includes two steps: (1) replace L by a 5-cycle $v_1 v_2 v_3 v_4 v_2'$. That is, spilt the vertex v_2 into two vertices v_2 and v_2', and split the edge $v_1 v_2$ into two edges $v_1 v_2$, $v_1 v_2'$. All edges (incident with $_2v$) on the left of L in G are incident with v_2 and all edges (incident with v_2) on the right of L in G are incident with v_2', satisfying that the obtained new graph is also planar; (2) add a new vertex in the face of the 5-cycle $v_1 v_2 v_3 v_4 v_2'$, and connect it to vertices v_1, v_2', v_3, v_4, v_2 respectively. The **contracting 5-wheel operation** is to: delete a certain 5-degree vertex and the edges incident with it; identify a pair of the non-adjacent vertices; and finally delete one of multiple edges if there are two multiple edges in the obtained new graph and no vertex in the face incident with the multiple edges (under the planar embedding).

Let ζ_i^+ and ζ_i^- denote the extending i-wheel operation and the contracting i-wheel operation for $i = 2, 3, 4, 5$, respectively, and let $\Psi = \{\zeta_2^-, \zeta_2^+, \zeta_3^-, \zeta_3^+, \zeta_4^-, \zeta_4^+, \zeta_5^-, \zeta_5^+\}$ denote the set of all the basic operators given above, where $\zeta_2^-, \zeta_2^+, \zeta_3^-, \zeta_3^+$ are called intermediate operators, $\zeta_4^-, \zeta_4^+, \zeta_5^-, \zeta_5^+$ are called final operators. For a maximal planar graph G, we denote by $\zeta_i^+(G)$ and $\zeta_i^-(G)$ the resulting graphs after implementing an extending i-wheel operation and a contracting i-wheel operation for $i = 2, 3, 4, 5$, respectively. Without taking into account the value of i in the extending and contracting i-wheel operation, we use $\zeta^-(G)$ and $\zeta^+(G)$ to replace $\zeta_i^-(G)$ and $\zeta_i^+(G)$ simply; in addition, we use $\zeta^{m+}(G)$ and $\zeta^{m-}(G)$ to denote the resulting graphs after implementing m contracting operations and m extending operations respectively, where $m \geq 2$.

Obviously, for a non-separating maximal planar graph G with $\delta \geq 4$, we can see that both $\zeta^-(G)$ and $\zeta^+(G)$ are maximal planar graph, while they are possible to be separating or they have minimum degree 2 or 3. No matter what the degrees of them are, the following result holds (we leave the proof of Theorem 6.1 to the reader).

Theorem 6.1 *Let G be an n-order maximal planar graph with $\delta(G) \geq 4$. Then*

$$|\zeta_2^-(G)| = |\zeta_3^-(G)| = |V(G)| - 1 = n - 1 \tag{6.1}$$

$$|\zeta_4^-(G)| = |\zeta_5^-(G)| = |V(G)| - 2 = n - 2 \tag{6.2}$$

6.2 Domino Extending-Contracting Operational System

6.2.1 Consecutive Extending-Contracting Operation and Domino Extending-Contracting Operation

The previous section introduces four pairs of basic extending and contracting operators, which can generate maximal planar graphs. More importantly, the method proposed can associate structure with coloring easily. Starting with K_3, we can generate any given maximal planar graph using this system. Generally, to generate a desired graph we need to implement many times of extending and contracting operations. We refer to such a sequence of extending and contracting operations as a **consecutive extending-contracting operation**.

Recall that the maximal planar graphs considered in this paper are assumed to be those with minimum degree at least 4. Therefore, if the minimum degree of $\zeta^+(G)$ or $\zeta^-(G)$ is 2 or 3, then we need to further implement extending or contracting operations repeatedly until we obtain a graph with $\delta \geq 4$ or K_4.

Let G be a maximal planar graph with $\delta \geq 4$, and W_4 (or W_5) be a 4-wheel (or 5-wheel). Let $\zeta^-(G)$ be the graph resulting from contracting 4-wheel (or 5-wheel) operation on W_4 or W_5. If $\delta_{\zeta^-(G)} \geq 4$, then we refer to such a contracting 4-wheel (or 5-wheel) operation as once **domino contracting wheel operation**; if $\delta_{\zeta^-(G)} = 2$ or 3, then we continue to implement a contracting 2-wheel or 3-wheel operation, and denote by $\zeta^{2-}(G)$ the resulting graph. If $\delta_{\zeta^{2-}(G)} \geq 4$, we refer to these two successive contracting wheel operations also as once **domino contracting wheel operation**. If $\delta_{\zeta^{2-}(G)} = 2$ or 3, then we implement contracting 2-wheel or 3-wheel operations repeatedly until a K_4 or a graph $\zeta^{m-}(G)$ with $\delta_{\zeta^{m-}(G)} \geq 4$ is obtained. If $\delta_{\zeta^{m-}(G)} \geq 4$, we refer to these m contracting wheel operations as once **domino contracting wheel operation**; if $\zeta^{m-}(G) \cong K_4$, we call G a **dominoable maximal planar graph**. Figure 6.5a shows a dominoable maximal planar graph G of order 9 and Fig. 6.5b is $\zeta^-(G)$ that is obtained from Fig. 6.5a by implementing one contracting 4-wheel operation on the 4-wheel (marked by bold lines in Fig. 6.5a), in the process of which u, v are identified. Since there exists two 2-degree vertices in

6.2 Domino Extending-Contracting Operational System

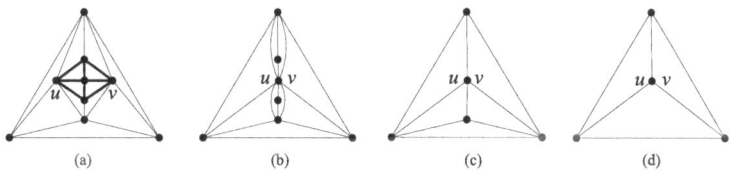

Fig. 6.5 A dominoable maximal planar graph of order 9. (**a**) G. (**b**) $\zeta^-(G)$. (**c**) $\zeta^{3-}(G)$. (**d**) $\zeta^{4-}(G)$

$\zeta^-(G)$, we implement contracting 2-wheel operations on the two 2-degree vertices respectively. The resulting graph $\zeta^{3-}(G)$ is shown in Fig. 6.5c, which has minimum degree 3. Therefore, we continually conduct contracting wheel operations till the resulting graph is K_4 or the one with minimum degree ≥ 4. The process of a domino contracting wheel operation on G is illustrated in Fig. 6.5a–d.

Let G be a maximal planar graph with $\delta \geq 4$, and P_3 (or L) be a 2-path (or funnel subgraph). If $\zeta^+(G)$ is the resulting graph by conducting an extending 4-wheel (or 5-wheel) operation on P_3 (or L), then we call the extending 4-wheel (or 5-wheel) operation once **domino extending wheel operation**. If $\zeta^+(G)$ is the resulting graph by conducting an extending 2-wheel (or 3-wheel) operation, then the minimum degree of $\zeta^+(G)$ is 2 or 3. We continue to implement an extending wheel operation on $\zeta^+(G)$, and denote the resulting graph by $\zeta^{2+}(G)$. If $\delta_{\zeta^{2+}(G)} \geq 4$, we refer to these two consecutive extending wheel operations as once **domino extending wheel operation**; if $\delta_{\zeta^{2+}(G)} = 2$ or 3, then we need to continually implement extending wheel operations. Let m be the total number of extending wheel operations. If $\zeta^{m+}(G)$ has minimum degree ≥ 4, then we refer to these m extending wheel operations as once **domino extending wheel operation**. Examples for domino extending wheel operations are given in the following subsection.

6.2.2 Domino Extending-Contracting Operations with Inner Vertices ≤ 3 and Domino Configuration

Let G be a maximal planar graph with $\delta \geq 4$, and $\zeta^{m+}(G)$ be the resulting graph by conducting one domino extending wheel operation based on G, which includes m extending wheel operations. The structural change from G to $\zeta^{m+}(G)$ is related closely with a subgraph, called domino configuration. In the following, we discuss this configuration in details for $m = 1, 2, 3$.

When $m = 1$, $\zeta^+(G)$ is obtained by one extending 4-wheel or 5-wheel operation on G. In this case, we call the 4-wheel or 5-wheel a **domino configuration**, where the object of extending wheel operations is a 2-path or funnel; see Fig. 6.6.

Suppose $\zeta^+(G)$ is a maximal planar graph of minimum degree at least 4, and $W_4 = x - v_1v_2v_3v_2'$ is a 4-wheel subgraph of $\zeta^+(G)$, shown in Fig. 6.6a, where $d_{\zeta^+(G)}(v_1), d_{\zeta^+(G)}(v_3) \geq 6$. We use G to denote the resulting graph by conducting

Fig. 6.6 Two domino configurations with one vertex inside the infinite face. (**a**) A domino configuration obtained by ζ_4^+. (**b**) A domino configuration obtained by ζ_5^+

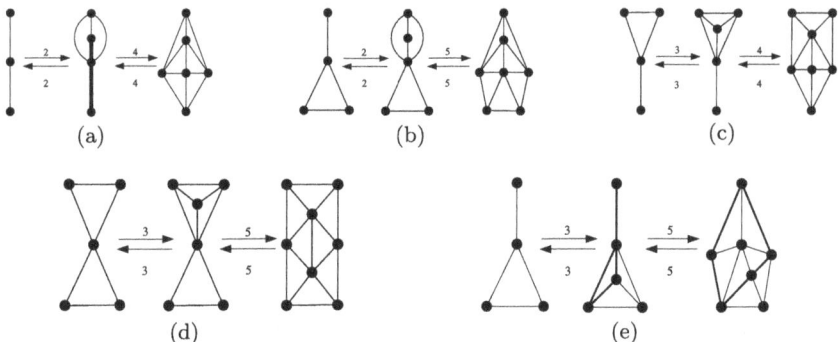

Fig. 6.7 Domino configurations with two vertices inside the infinite face. (**a**) extending, contracting 24-wheel operations. (**b**) extending, contracting 25-wheel operations. (**c**) extending, contracting 34-wheel operations. (**d**) I-type extending, contracting 35-wheel operations. (**e**) II-type extending, contracting 35-wheel operations

contracting wheel operation on W_4. Obviously, $\delta(G) \geq 4$. Therefore, we can obtain G from $\zeta^+(G)$ by conducting only one domino contracting wheel operation. We then call the W_4 in $\zeta^+(G)$ a **domino configuration**. Analogously, if $W_5 = x - v_1v_2v_3v_4v_2'$ is a 5-wheel in $\zeta^+(G)$ and $d_{\zeta^+(G)} \geq 6, d_{\zeta^+(G)}(v_3) \geq 5, d_{\zeta^+(G)}(v_4) \geq 5$, as shown in Fig. 6.6b, then one contracting wheel operation on W_5 is also a domino contracting wheel operation, where v_2, v_2' are identified. Accordingly, we call the 5-wheel W_5 in $\zeta^+(G)$ a **domino configuration**.

When $m = 2$, we can obtain $\zeta^{2+}(G)$ by implementing extending 24-wheel operation (that is, implement ζ_2^+ first and then $\zeta_4^+(G)$. Other definitions are defined in the same way), extending 34-wheel operation, extending 25-wheel operation or extending 35-wheel operation (there exist two types: one is **I-type extending 35-wheel operation**, in which the wheel-center in the process of extending 3-wheel is the top of funnel in extending 5-wheel, as shown in Fig. 6.7d; the other is **II-type extending 35-wheel operation**, in which the wheel-center in the process of extending 3-wheel is one bottom of funnel in extending 5-wheel; see Fig. 6.7e). In this case, we refer to the subgraph induced by the vertices set of two wheel-centers and their neighbors in $\zeta^{2+}(G)$ as a **domino configuration**, where the objects before extending wheel operation can be a 2-path, funnel or **dumbbell subgraph** (two triangles with exactly one common vertex); See Fig. 6.7.

6.2 Domino Extending-Contracting Operational System

Remark Domino configurations induced by extending 25-wheel, 34-wheel and 35-wheel operations, respectively, are isomorphic. Therefore, there are three domino configurations including two wheel-centers.

Analogously, the number of domino contracting wheel operations that involve two wheel-centers is in total five: contracting 24-wheel operation, contracting 25-wheel operation, contracting 34-wheel operation, I-type contracting 35-wheel operation and II-type contracting 35-wheel operation, respectively; see Fig. 6.7. It is not hard to obtain the necessary conditions for implementing these five kinds of domino contracting wheel operations. For example, the necessary condition for implementing contracting 24-wheel operation is all vertices in the outer cycle of the corresponding configuration have degree at least 6, except two ones which are identified in the process of contracting 4-wheel operation.

When $m = 3$, $\zeta^{3+}(G)$ can be obtained from G by conducting extending: 224-wheel operation; 234-wheel operation; 334-wheel operation (two types: one is **non-adjacent extending 334-wheel operation** in which two wheel-centers in the process of extending 3-wheel are not adjacent, as shown in Fig. 6.8c; the other is **adjacent extending 334-wheel operation**, in which the two wheel-centers in the process of extending 3-wheel are adjacent, as shown in Fig. 6.8d); extending 235-wheel operation (two types: one is **adjacent extending 235-wheel operation**,

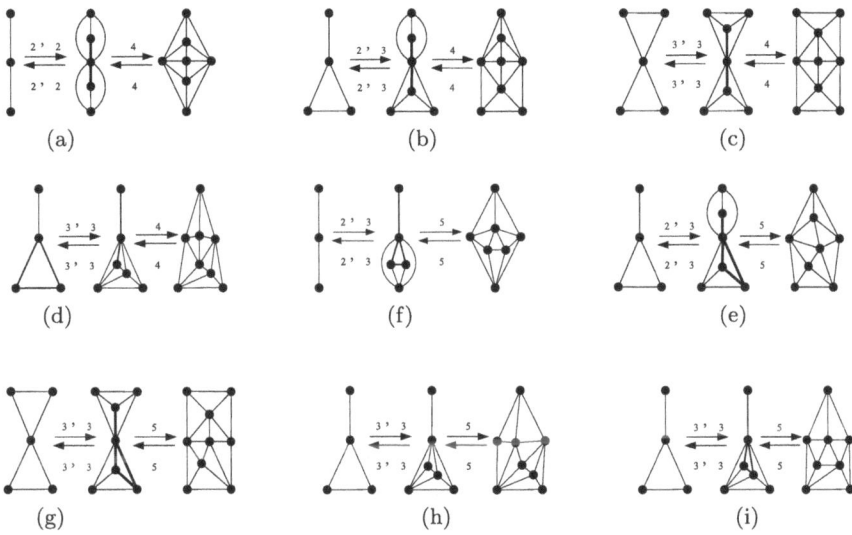

Fig. 6.8 Seven domino configurations with three vertices inside the infinite face. (**a**) extending, contracting 224-wheel operations. (**b**) extending, contracting 234-wheel operations. (**c**) non-adjacent extending, contracting 334-wheel operation. (**d**) adjacent extending, contracting 334-wheel operation. (**e**) adjacent extending, contracting 235-wheel operation. (**f**) non-adjacent extending, contracting 235-wheel operation. (**g**) non-adjacent extending, contracting 335-wheel operation. (**h**) asymmetric and adjacent extending, contracting 335-wheel operation. (**i**) symmetric and adjacent extending, contracting 335-wheel operation

in which two wheel-centers in the process of $\zeta_2^+(G)$ and $\zeta_3^+(G)$ are adjacent, as shown in Fig. 6.8e; the other is **non-adjacent extending 235-wheel operation**, in which the two wheel-centers in the process of $\zeta_2^+(G)$ and $\zeta_3^+(G)$ are not adjacent, as shown in Fig. 6.8f); or extending 335-wheel operation (three types: **non-adjacent extending 335-wheel operation, asymmetric and adjacent extending 335-wheel operation**, and **symmetric and adjacent extending 335-wheel operation**, as shown in Fig. 6.8g, h, and i, respectively). In this case, we refer to the subgraph of $\zeta^{3+}(G)$ induced by the vertex set of the three wheel-centers and their neighbors, in the process of extending wheel operation, as a **domino configuration**, where the object of the above extending operations are 2-path, funnel or dumbbell subgraph. We refer to the non-adjacent extending 334-wheel operation as dumbbell transformation, which will play a key role on the study of pure tree-coloring graphs [3]; see the Chap. 9 for the detailed information.

Remark Domino configurations induced by extending 334-wheel and 235-wheel operations are isomorphic, by extending 234-wheel and 335-wheel operations are isomorphic. Therefore, the number of domino configurations that contain three wheel-centers is 7.

Similarly, there are nine domino contracting wheel operations, involving three wheel-centers: contracting 224-wheel operation, contracting 234-wheel operation, non-adjacent contracting 334-wheel operation, adjacent contracting 334-wheel operation, adjacent contracting 235-wheel operation, non-adjacent contracting 235-wheel operation, non-adjacent contracting 335-wheel operation, asymmetric and adjacent contracting 335-wheel operation, symmetric and adjacent contracting 335-wheel operation; see Fig. 6.8. The necessary conditions for implementing these operations can be deduced easily, so we are not going to repeat them in details.

To sum up, there are in total a number of 12 domino configurations with $1 \sim 3$ wheel-centers. For convenience, we list all of them in Fig. 6.12. In what follows, the wheel-centers in a domino configuration are also called **inner vertices** of the domino configuration.

6.2.3 Set of Objects of Domino Extending Wheel Operations

Let G be a maximal planar graph with $\delta \geq 4$. Suppose that $P_3 = v_1 v_2 v_3$ is a 2-path and $L = u_1 - \Delta u_2 u_3 u_4$ is a funnel subgraph. If v_1 and v_3 are adjacent in P_3, or u_1 is adjacent to one of bottoms of L, then the resulting graph by conducting one extending 4-wheel operation on P_3 or 5-wheel operation on L is separating. So, when we only conduct one extending wheel operation, we demand that v_1 and v_3 are not adjacent in P_3, and u_1 is not adjacent to any bottom of L. However, when we conduct $m(\geq 2)$ extending wheel operations, the situation will be different.

Remark 6.1 *Let G be a maximal planar graph with $\delta \geq 4$, and $P_3 = v_1 v_2 v_3$ be a 2-path of G such that v_1 and v_3 are adjacent. For any $m \geq 1$, when implementing m*

6.2 Domino Extending-Contracting Operational System

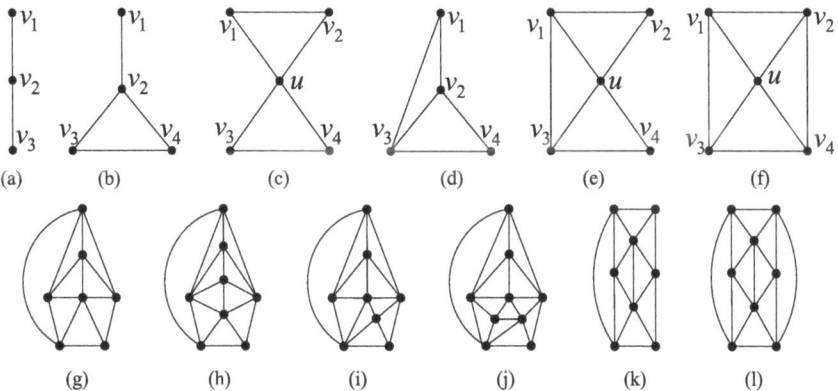

Fig. 6.9 Six object subgraphs that are extended in domino extending wheel operations and examples. (**a**) 2-path. (**b**) funnel. (**c**) dumbbell. (**d**) semi-funnel. (**e**) semi-closed dumbbell. (**f**) closed dumbbell. (**g**) $\zeta^{2+}(G)$. (**h**) $\zeta^{3+}(G)$. (**i**) $\zeta^{3+}(G)$. (**j**) $\zeta^{4+}(G)$. (**k**) $\zeta^{2+}(G)$. (**l**) $\zeta^{2+}(G)$

extending wheel operations on P_3, we obtain a separating graph $\zeta^{m+}(G)$ that has a maximal planar proper subgraph with infinite face $\Delta v_1 v_2 v_3$.

Remark 6.2 *Let G be a non-separating maximal planar graph with $\delta \geq 4$. Suppose that $GL = v_1 - \Delta v_2 v_3 v_4$ is a funnel subgraph of G, in which v_1 and v_3 are adjacent. For any $m \geq 2$, when implementing m extending wheel operations on L, we obtain a non-separating graph $\zeta^{m+}(G)$. Examples of this remark are shown in Fig. 6.9g–j.*

Remark 6.3 *Let G be a non-separating maximal planar graph with $\delta \geq 4$. Suppose that $Y = \Delta v_1 v_2 u - \Delta u v_3 v_4$ is a dumbbell of G, as shown in Fig. 6.9c. No matter whether or not v_1 is adjacent to v_3 and v_2 is adjacent to v_4, we will obtain a non-separating graph $\zeta^{m+}(G)$ by implementing $m(\geq 2)$ extending wheel operations on Y; see Fig. 6.9k and 6.9l.*

Based on these three remarks, it is easy to know that there are in total 6 objects in domino extending wheel operations; see Fig. 6.9a–f.

6.2.4 General Definition of Domino Configurations

In Sect. 6.2.2, we have showcased all domino configurations containing 1-3 inner vertices. A question naturally arises: what is the structure of a domino configuration when it contains $m \geq 4$ inner vertices? To answer this question, we give a general definition of the domino configuration, and characterize properties of such a class of graphs in this subsection. First, we give three examples to illustrate the processes of domino contracting wheel operations on domino configurations with v_2 inner vertices, as shown in Fig. 6.10.

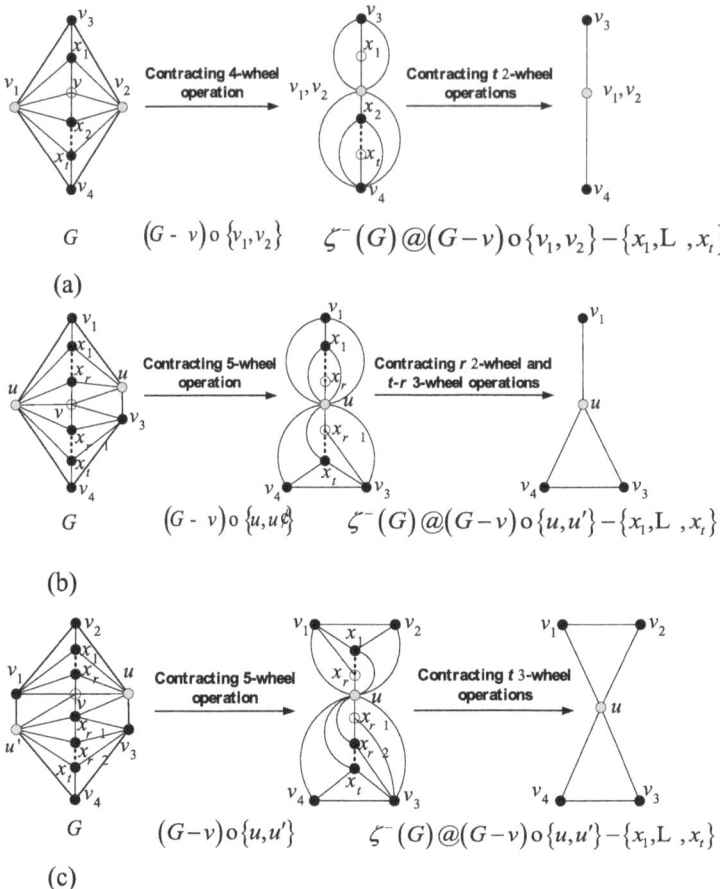

Fig. 6.10 Three domino configurations with ≥ 4 inner vertices. (**a**) a domino configuration with 4-cycle as the infinite face. (**b**) a domino configuration with 5-cycle as the infinite face. (**c**) a domino configuration with 6-cycle as the infinite face

Note that for any domino configuration with $1 \sim 3$ inner vertices given in Sect. 6.2.2 or more than 3 inner vertices obtained by implementing domino extending wheel operation, there are the following properties: At least one of 4-wheel W_4 or 5-wheel W_5 in the domino configuration satisfy:

(1) Let x be the wheel-center of W_4 or W_5. Then there exists a pair of non-adjacent vertices u, v on C^x such that $\{u, v\} \subset V(C)$;
(2) When conducting one domino contracting wheel operation on W_4 or W_5, in which u, v are identified, we can obtain a 2-path, funnel or dumbbell.

Based on the above discussions, we introduce the general definition of domino configurations as follows. Let G be a maximal planar graph with minimum degree of at least 4, and G^C be a semi-maximal planar subgraph of G with outer cycle C.

6.2 Domino Extending-Contracting Operational System

We call G^C a **domino configuration** if there exists a 4-wheel W_4 or a 5-wheel W_5 in G^C satisfying:

(1) Let x be the wheel-center of W_4 or W_5. Then there exists a pair of non-adjacent vertices u, v on C^x such that $\{u, v\} \subset V(C)$;
(2) When conducting a domino contracting wheel operation on W_4 or W_5, in which u, v are identified, we can obtain a graph without any wheels. Here, we call u, v the **contracted vertices** of G^C, and call x the **initial contracted wheel-center** of G^C.

Suppose that G^C is a domino configuration, and x is the initial contracted wheel-center. We use $X(x)$ to denote the **set of inner vertices** of G^C. Moreover, when there is no scope for confusion, we also write $X(x)$ as X simply.

It is easy to see that every domino configuration G^C can be contracted into a 2-path, a funnel or a dumbbell subgraph, which implies that the length of C is 4, 5 or 6. So, we have the following theorem.

Theorem 6.2 *Let G be a maximal planar graph with $\delta_G \geq 4$, and G^C be a domino configuration of G with contracted vertices u, v. Then,*

(1) *G^C can be contracted into a 2-path, a funnel, or a dumbbell subgraph by conducting a domino contracting operation, where u, v are contracted vertices;*
(2) *$4 \leq |C| \leq 6$.*

Based on Theorem 6.2, we further have the following result.

Lemma 6.1 *Let G^C be a domino configuration with contracted vertices u, v.*

(1) *When $|V(C)| = 4$, let $C = uz_1vz_2u$. Then $d_{G^C}(z_1) \leq 4$; $d_{G^C}(z_2) \leq 4$;*
(2) *When $|V(C)| = 5$, let $C = uz_1vz_2z_3u$. Then $d_{G^C}(z_1) \leq 4$; $d_{G^C}(z_2)$ or $d_{G^C}(z_3) = 3$;*
(3) *When $|V(C)| = 6$, let $C = uz_1vz_2z_3z_4u$. Then $d_{G^C}(z_1)$ or $d_{G^C}(z_2) = 3$; $d_{G^C}(z_3)$ or $d_{G^C}(z_4) = 3$.*

Proof For (1), to the contrary we assume $d_{G^C}(z_1) \geq 5$. Let $u, y_1, \ldots, y_l, v$ be the $l \geq 3$ neighbors of z_1 one by one in G^C. Let x be the initial contracted wheel-center of G^C. Then G^C can be contracted into a 2-path by conducting a domino contracting operation. It is easy to see that all degrees of $y_1, \ldots, y_l$ are ≥ 3 in $G^C[V(G) \cup \{y_1, \ldots, y_l\}]$. Suppose that in the process of the above domino contracting wheel operation y is the first vertex in $\{y_1, \ldots, y_l\}$ to be contracted. We use $\zeta^-(G^C)$ to denote the graph just before the wheel with wheel-center y is contracted during the domino contracting wheel operation. When $y = y_1$ or y_l, it has that y_2 or y_{l-1} is adjacent to x_v^u in $\zeta^-(G^C)$, where x_v^u is the new vertex after identifying u and v. Thus, y_2 is adjacent to u, or y_{l-1} is adjacent to v in G^C; that is, $d_{G^C}(y_2) = 3$ or $d_{G^C}(y_{l-1}) = 3$, which contradicts the fact that G^C is a domino configuration. Therefore, $d_{G^C}(z_1) \leq 4$. By the same token, we also have also $d_{G^C}(z_2) \leq 4$.

For (2), we present an analogous proof of that for (1). We have that $d_{G^C}(z_1) \leq 4$. Obviously, $d_{G^C}(z_2)$ and $d_{G^C}(z_3) \geq 3$. Assume that $d_{G^C}(z_2) \geq 4$ and $d_{G^C}(z_3) \geq 4$.

Let $u, y_1, \ldots, y_l, v$ be the l neighbors of z_2 or z_3, one by one in G^C, where y_r is the common neighbor of z_2 and z_3, $2 \leq r \leq l-1$, $l \geq 3$. Then in $G^C[V(C) \cup \{y_1, \ldots, y_l\}]$, the degree of y_r is 4, and all degrees of $\{y_1, \ldots, y_l\} \setminus \{y_r\} \geq 3$. Suppose that in the process of the above domino contracting operation y is the first vertex to be contracted in $\{y_1, \ldots, y_l\}$. Similar to the proof of (1), it follows that there is a 3-degree vertex in G^C, and a contradiction. Hence, $d_{G^C}(z_2) = 3$ or $d_{G^C}(z_3) = 3$.

For (3), analogous to the proof of (2), we can deduce that $d_{G^C}(z_1) = 3$ or $d_{G^C}(z_2) = 3$, $d_{G^C}(z_3) = 3$ or $d_{G^C}(z_4) = 3$. So, the result holds. ∎

Theorem 6.3 follows from Lemma 6.1 directly.

Theorem 6.3 *Let G^C be a domino configuration with initial contracted wheel-center x and contracted vertices u, v.*

(1) *If $P_3 = uz_1v$ is a 2-path on C, where Y and z_1 are not adjacent, then $G^C - z_1$ is a domino configuration with initial contracted wheel-center x and contracted vertices u, v;*

(2) *If $P_4 = uz_2z_3v$ is a 3-path on C, where neither z_2 nor z_3 is adjacent to x. If $d_{G^C}(z_2) = d_{G^C}(z_3) = 3$, then $G^C - \{z_2, z_3\}$ is a domino configuration with initial contracted wheel-center x and contracted vertices u, v; if $d_{G^C}(z_2) = 3$, $d_{G^C}(z_3) \geq 4$, then $G^C - z_2$ is a domino configuration with initial contracted wheel-center x and contracted vertices u, v.*

6.2.5 Properties of Domino Configurations

In order to characterize domino configurations, we first introduce four operators, $\tau_1, \tau_1', \tau_2, \tau_3, G_{v_2v_2'}^{C_5}$, called generated operations of domino configurations.

Suppose that G^C is a domino configuration with contracted vertices u, v. The τ_1 operator of G^C is to select a 2-path $P = uyv$ on C, and then add a new vertex z in the exterior of C and connect z to u, y, v respectively. The resulting graph obtained from G^C by implementing τ_1 is denoted by $\tau_1(G^C)$.

The τ_1' operator of G^C is to select a 2-path $P = xyv$ on C, where $x \notin \{u, v\}$, and then add a new vertex z in the exterior of C and connect this vertex to x, y, v respectively. The resulting graph obtained from G^C by implementing τ_1' is denoted by $\tau_1'(G^C)$.

The τ_2 operator of G^C is to select a 2-path $P = uyv$ on C, and then add two adjacent vertices z_1, z_2 in the exterior of C and connect z_1 to u, z_2 to v, and y to z_1 and z_2, respectively. The resulting graph obtained from G^C by implementing τ_2 is denoted by $\tau_2(G^C)$.

The τ_3 operator of G^C is to select a 3-path $P = uy_1y_2v$ on C, and then add a new vertex z in the exterior of C and connect this vertex to u, y_1, y_2, v respectively. The resulting graph obtained from G^C by implementing τ_3 is denoted by $\tau_3(G^C)$. The specific processes of $\tau_1, \tau_1', \tau_2, \tau_3$ are shown in Fig. 6.11a–d.

6.2 Domino Extending-Contracting Operational System

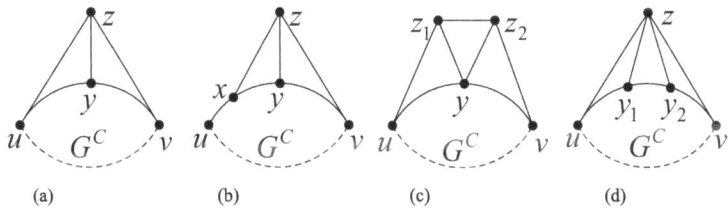

Fig. 6.11 Four kinds of generated operations of domino configurations. (a) $\tau_1(G^C)$. (b) $\tau_1'(G^C)$. (c) $\tau_2(G^C)$. (d) $\tau_3(G^C)$

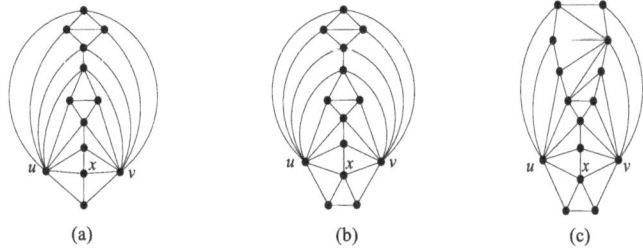

Fig. 6.12 Three domino configurations. (a) $\tau_3\tau_2\tau_1\tau_3\tau_2\tau_1(W_4)$. (b) $\tau_3\tau_2\tau_1\tau_3\tau_2\tau_1(W_5)$. (c) $\tau_1'\tau_1'\tau_1'\tau_1'\tau_1'\tau_1'\tau_2\tau_1(W_5)$

Based on the above four operators, we establish an operational system to generate domino configurations, denoted by $\langle\{W_4, W_5\}; \Gamma\rangle$, where $\Gamma = \{\tau_1, \tau_1', \tau_2, \tau_3\}$. This system aims to generate all domino configurations based on W_4 and W_5 by using $\tau_1, \tau_1', \tau_2, \tau_3$ repeatedly. For example, starting with W_4, we can obtain $\tau_3\tau_2\tau_1\tau_3\tau_2\tau_1(W_4)$, as shown in Fig. 6.12a by implementing $\tau_1, \tau_2, \tau_3, \tau_1, \tau_2, \tau_3$ successively; starting with W_5, we can obtain $\tau_3\tau_2\tau_1\tau_3\tau_2\tau_1(W_5)$ shown in Fig. 6.12b, by implementing $\tau_1, \tau_2, \tau_3, \tau_1, \tau_2, \tau_3$ successively; starting with W_5, we can obtain $\tau_1'\tau_1'\tau_1'\tau_1'\tau_1'\tau_1'\tau_2\tau_1(W_5)$ shown in Fig. 6.12c, by implementing $\tau_1, \tau_2, \tau_1', \tau_1', \tau_1', \tau_1', \tau_1', \tau_1'$ successively.

Note that for any configuration G^C with the contracted vertices u, v, there exist the following facts.

Fact 1 Implementing one τ_1 is the same as conducting one extending 2-wheel operation, thus, G^C is a domino configuration iff $\tau_1(G^C)$ is a domino configuration. The length of the boundary of infinite face of $\tau_1(G^C)$ is equal to that of G^C, that is, $|V(\tau_1(C))| = |V(C)|$, where $\tau_1(C)$ is the boundary of infinite face of $\tau_1(G^C)$, similarly hereinafter.

Fact 2 Implementing one τ_1' is the same as conducting one extending 3-wheel operation. Thus, G^C is a domino configuration iff $\tau_1'(G^C)$ is a domino configuration. The length of the boundary of infinite face of $\tau_1'G^C$ is equal to that of G^C, that is, $|V(\tau_1'(C))| = |V(C)|$.

Fact 3 Implementing once τ_2 is the same as conducting once extending 23-wheel operation. So G^C is a domino configuration iff $\tau_2(G^C)$ is a domino configuration. Here, $|V(\tau_2(C))| = |V(C)| + 1$.

Fact 4 Implementing one τ_3 operator is the same as conducting one extending 3-wheel operation. Hence, G^C is a domino configuration iff $\tau_3(G^C)$ is a domino configuration. Here, $|V(\tau_3(C))| = |V(C)| - 1$.

Theorem 6.4 *Any domino configuration can be generated by $\langle \{W_4, W_5\}; \Gamma \rangle$.*

Proof The proof is by induction on the number t of inner vertices of a domino configuration G^C.

When $t = 2, 3$, by the foregoing discussion (in Sect. 6.2.2), there are in total three domino configurations with 2 inner vertices (see Fig. 6.7 or line 2 in Fig. 6.13). Moreover, all the domino configurations with 1-3 inner vertices are illustrated in Fig. 6.13.

By implementing τ_1 and τ_2 on W_4, respectively, we obtain the first and second domino configurations with two inner vertices, shown in Fig. 6.13 line 2; by implementing τ_1, τ_1', τ_2 and τ_3 on W_5, respectively, we get the second and third domino configurations (in line 2 of Fig. 6.13) which contain two inner vertices, and the last domino configuration (in line 3 of Fig. 6.13) which contain three inner vertices.

In Fig. 6.13, we get the first and second domino configurations (in line 3) with three inner vertices by conducting τ_1 and τ_2 to the first graph in line 2. In addition, we can get the second, third, fourth, fifth and sixth domino configurations (in line 3) with 3 inner vertices by implementing operations $\tau_1, \tau_1', \tau_1', \tau_2$ and τ_2 on the second graph in line 2, respectively. Note that in the process of these operations,

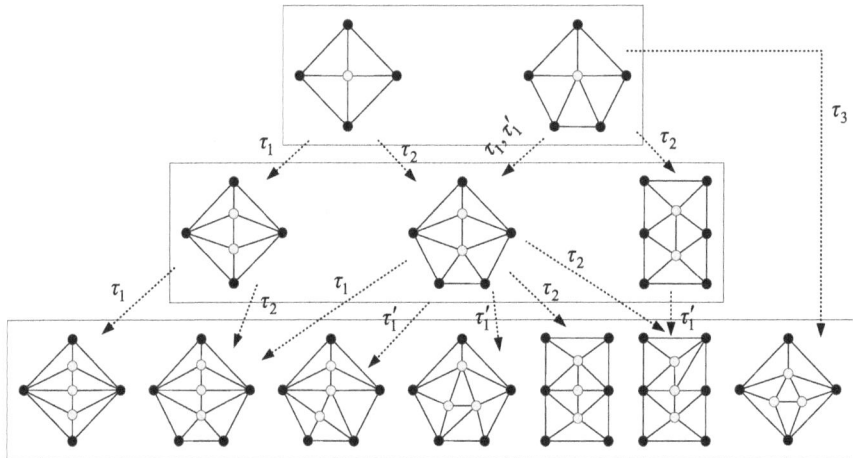

Fig. 6.13 All the domino configurations with 1 3 inner vertices

the involved contracted vertices are different. If we conduct τ_1' on the third graph in line 2, then we can also obtain the sixth graph in line 3.

Hence, the result holds for $t = 2, 3$.

Suppose that the result holds for $t = n (\geq 3)$. We now consider the case of $t = n + 1$. Let u, v be the contracted vertices of G^C. According to Lemma 6.1, we need to consider the following three cases.

Case 1 $|V(C)| = 4$

Let $C = uz_1vz_2u$. Then $d_{G^C}(z_1) \leq 4$, $d_{G^C}(z_2) \leq 4$, and there is at least one vertex among z_1, z_2 that is not adjacent to the initial contracted wheel-center x. Without loss of generality, assume z_1 is not adjacent to x. If $d_{G^C}(z_1) = 3$, then $G^C - z_1$ is a domino configuration according to Theorem 6.4. Thus, by the induction hypothesis, $G^C - z_1$ can be generated by $\langle \{W_4, W_5\}; \Gamma \rangle$. Notice that $G^C = \tau_1(G^C - z_1)$, that is, G^C can be generated by $\langle \{W_4, W_5\}; \Gamma \rangle$.

If $d_{G^C}(z_1) \leq 4$, then $G^C - Z_1$ is a domino configuration, which can be generated by $\langle \{W_4, W_5\}; \Gamma \rangle$. Notice that $\tau_3(G^C - z_1)$. So G^C can be generated by $\langle \{W_4, W_5\}; \Gamma \rangle$.

Case 2 $|V(G)| = 5$

Let $C = uz_1vz_2z_3u$. Then $d_{G^C}(z_1) \leq 4$, $d_{G^C}(z_2) = 3$ or $d_{G^C}(z_3) = 3$. Without loss of generality, assume that $d_{G^C}(z_2) = 3$. Similar to case 1, we can prove that $G^C - z_2$ is a domino configuration, which can be generated by $\langle \{W_4, W_5\}; \Gamma \rangle$. Note that $G^C = \tau_1'(G^C - z_1)$. So G^C can be generated by $\langle \{W_4, W_5\}; \Gamma \rangle$.

Case 3 $|V(C)| = 6$

Let $C = uz_1z_2vz_3z_4u$. Then $d_{G^C}(z_1) = 3$ or $d_{G^C}(z_2) = 3$, and $d_{G^C}(z_3) = 3$ or $d_{G^C}(z_4) = 3$. Without loss of generality, we assume that z_1 is not adjacent to the initial contracted wheel-center, and $d_{G^C}(z_1) = 3$. Similar to case 1, we can see that $G^C - z_1$ is a domino configuration, which can be generated by $\langle \{W_4, W_5\}; \Gamma \rangle$. Therefore, G^C can be generated by $\langle \{W_4, W_5\}; \Gamma \rangle$, since $G^C = \tau_1'(G^C - z_1)$.

Hence, the conclusion holds. ∎

Theorem 6.4 provides a method of generating domino configurations, by which any given domino configuration can be generated from W_4, W_5. The domino configuration is the core of extending-contracting operational system of maximal planar graphs.

6.3 Ancestor-Graphs and Descendent-Graphs

Regarding the construction of maximal planar graphs, we need to consider two basic problems:

(1) Where is a maximal planar graph from? More specifically, given a maximal planar graph G, what are the characteristics of the maximal planar graphs generating G by using extending wheel operations?

(2) How many non-isomorphic maximal planar graphs can be generated from a given one?

Theorem 6.4 plays a significant role in solving the above two problems. For this, we introduce the concepts of **ancestor-graphs** and **descendent-graphs**.

Suppose that G is a maximal planar graph with $\delta_G \geq 4$. If it can be obtained from another maximal planar graph $\zeta^-(G)$ with $\delta_{\zeta^-(G)} \geq 4$ and lower order, then we call $\zeta^-(G)$ an **ancestor-graph** of G, while G is referred to as a **descendent-graph** of $\zeta^-(G)$. Accordingly, for a maximal planar graph G with $\delta_G \geq 4$, if $\zeta^+(G)$ is a maximal planar graph with $\delta_{\zeta^-(G)} \geq 4$ which is obtained from G by implementing extending wheel operations, then G is an **ancestor-graph** of $\zeta^+(G)$, and $\zeta^+(G)$ is the **descendent-graph** of G. Now we give their definitions in details.

6.3.1 Descendent-Graphs

For a domino configuration G^C, we use $G_{v_2v_2'}^{C_4}$, $G_{v_2v_2'}^{C_5}$ and $G_{v_2v_2'}^{C_6}$ to denote the domino configurations with outer cycles' length 4, 5 and 6, respectively. We also denote by $\Im_{v_2v_2'}^{C_4}$, $\Im_{v_2v_2'}^{C_5}$, and $\Im_{v_2v_2'}^{C_6}$, the set of all domino configurations with outer cycles' length 4, 5 and 6, respectively, where v_2, v_2' are the contracted vertices of G^C. Similarly, descendent-graphs of G are classified into the following three types.

(1) Path-Type Descendent-Graphs

Let $P_3 = v_1 v_2 v_3$ be a 2-path of G. The extending-4-cycle-type semi-maximal planar graph of G based on P_3, denoted by $G_{P_3}^{C_4}$, is the resulting graph obtained by the following actions: replace P_3 by a 4-cycle $C_4 = v_1 v_2' v_3 v_2$; that is, split the vertex v_2 into two vertices v_2 and v_2', split $v_1 v_2$ into two edges $v_1 v_2$ and $v_1 v_2'$, and split $v_2 v_3$ into $v_2 v_3$ and $v_2' v_3$ respectively. All edges (incident with v_2) on the left of P_3 in G are incident with v_2, and all edges (incident with v_2) on the right of P_3 in G are incident with v_2', such that the resulting graph is still planar. This process is shown in Fig. 6.14, where v_2 and v_2' are called extended vertices of $G_{P_3}^{C_4}$.

Suppose that $G_{v_2v_2'}^{C_4} \in \Im_{v_2v_2'}^{C_4}$, $C_4 = v_1 v_2' v_3 v_2$, and v_2, v_2' are contracted vertices of $G_{v_2v_2'}^{C_4}$; see the last graph in Fig. 6.14. If $G_{P_3}^{C_4} \cap G_{v_2v_2'}^{C_4} = C_4 = v_1 v_2' v_3 v_2 v_1$, then we refer to $G_{P_3}^{C_4} \cup G_{v_2v_2'}^{C_4}$ as a **path-type descendent-graph** of G, or a **descendent-graph** of G based on $\{P_3, G_{v_2v_2'}^{C_4}\}$ specifically.

6.3 Ancestor-Graphs and Descendent-Graphs

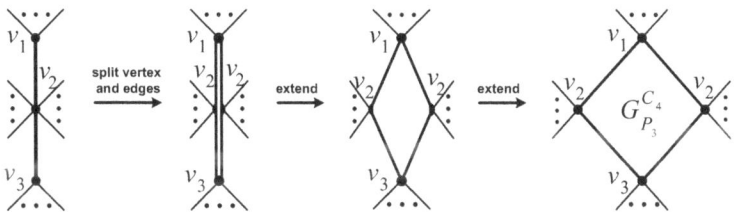

Fig. 6.14 The process of constructing an extending-4-cycle-type semi-maximal planar graph

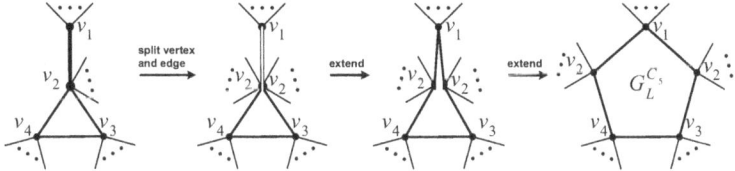

Fig. 6.15 The process of constructing an extending-5-cycle-type semi-maximal planar graph

(2) Funnel-Type Descendent-Graphs

Let $L = v_1 - \Delta v_2 v_3 v_4$ be a funnel of G. The **extending-5-cycle-type semi-maximal planar graph** of G based on L, denoted by $G_L^{C_5}$, is the resulting graph obtained by conducting the following procedures: replace L by a 5-cycle $v_1 v_2 v_3 v_4 v_2'$; that is, spilt the vertex v_2 into two vertices v_2 and v_2', and split the edge $v_1 v_2$ into two edges $v_1 v_2$ and $v_1 v_2'$. All edges (incident with v_2) on the left of L in G are incident with v_2, and all edges (incident with v_2) on the right of L in G are incident with v_2', satisfying that the resulting graph is still planar. This process is shown in Fig. 6.15, where v_2 and v_2' are called **extended vertices** of $G_L^{C_5}$.

Suppose that $G_{v_2 v_2'}^{C_5} \in \mathfrak{N}_{v_2 v_2'}^{C_5}$, $C_5 = v_1 v_2' v_3 v_4 v_2$ and v_2, v_2' are contracted vertices of $G_{v_2 v_2'}^{C_5}$. If $G_L^{C_5} \cap G_{v_2 v_2'}^{C_5} = C_5 = v_1 v_2' v_3 v_4 v_2 v_1$, then we refer to $G_L^{C_5} \cup G_{v_2 v_2'}^{C_5}$ as a **funnel-type descendent-graph** of G, or a **descendent-graph** of G based on $\{L, G_{v_2 v_2'}^{C_5}\}$ (Fig. 6.15).

(3) Dumbbell-Type Descendent-Graphs

Let $Y = \Delta v_1 v_3 v_2 - \Delta v_4 v_5 v_2$ be a dumbbell of G. The **extending-6-cycle-type semi-maximal planar graph** of G based on Y, denoted by $G_Y^{C_5}$, is the resulting graph obtained by the following actions: replace Y by a 6-cycle $v_1 v_3 v_2' v_5 v_4 v_2$; that is, spilt the vertex v_2 into two vertices v_2 and v_2'. All the edges (incident with v_2) on the left of Y in G are incident with v_2, and all edges (incident with v_2) on the right of Y in G are incident with v_2', such that the resulting graph is still planar. This process is shown in Fig. 6.16, where v_2 and v_2' are called **extended vertices** of $G_Y^{C_5}$.

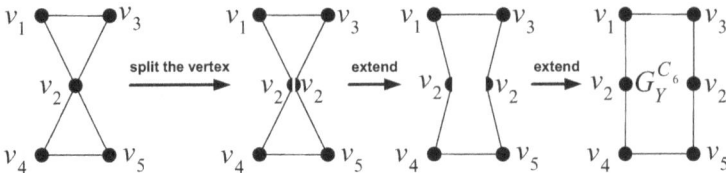

Fig. 6.16 The process of constructing an extending-6-cycle-type semi-maximal planar graph

Suppose that $G_{v_2v_2'}^{C_6} \in \mathfrak{Z}_{v_2v_2'}^{C_6}$, $C_6 = v_1v_3v_2'v_5v_4v_2$ and v_2, v_2' are contracted vertices of $G_{v_2v_2'}^{C_6}$. If $G_Y^{C_6} \cap G_{v_2v_2'}^{C_6} = C_6 = v_1v_3v_2'v_5v_4v_2v_1$, then we refer to $G_Y^{C_6} \cup G_{v_2v_2'}^{C_6}$ as a **dumbbell-type descendent-graph** of G, or a **descendent-graph** of G based on $\{Y, G_{v_2v_2'}^{C_6}\}$ (Fig. 6.16).

We collectively refer to the three types of descendent-graphs as **descendent-graphs**. Without taking the length of outer cycle into account, we also call the process of deriving a descendent-graph from a graph as **embedding a domino configuration in an extending-cycle-type semi-maximal planar graph**. By the foregoing discussion, we have that

$$|\mathfrak{Z}_{v_2v_2'}^{C_4}| \to \infty, |\mathfrak{Z}_{v_2v_2'}^{C_5}| \to \infty, |\mathfrak{Z}_{v_2v_2'}^{C_6}| \to \infty, \tag{6.3}$$

The above formula means that every maximal planar graph G with $\delta(G) \geq 4$ has infinite amount of descendent-graphs. So the descendent-graphs of G can be classified by the number of **inner vertices** of domino configurations. Generally, if there are $t(\geq 1)$ inner vertices in the domino configuration, then we call the corresponding descendent-graph H a t-**th descendent-graph** of G, and use $\zeta^{+t}(G)$ to denote the set of all t-th descendent-graphs of G. Particularly, the 1-th, 2-th and 3-th descendent-graphs are also called the **son-graph**, **grandson-graph** and **great-grandson-graph**, respectively.

Let $\Upsilon^+(G)$ denote the set of all descendent-graphs of G, then

$$\Upsilon^+(G) = \bigcup_{t=1}^{\infty} \zeta^{+t}(G) \tag{6.4}$$

In Formula (6.4), $\zeta^{+t}(G)$ only presents all the generic tth descendent-graphs of G, while the specific types of the involved domino configuration are not given. To address this issue, we introduce the concept of **identical subgraph**. Suppose that G is a maximal planar graph, and H, H' are two isomorphic subgraphs of G. Let $Aut(G)$ be the automorphism group of G. We say that H is **identical** to H' if $\exists \sigma \in Aut(G)$ satisfies $\sigma(H) = H'$; Otherwise, H is **non-identical** to H'.

6.3 Ancestor-Graphs and Descendent-Graphs

Throughout this paper, we denote by $\Im_G^H$ the set of all non-identical subgraphs of G. In particular, we use $\Im_G^{P_3}, \Im_G^L, \Im_G^{L^*}, \Im_G^Y, \Im_G^{Y^*}$ and $\Im_G^{Y_*^*}$ to denote the sets of all non-identical 2-path P_3, funnel subgraph L, semi-funnel subgraph L^*, dumbbell subgraph Y, semi-closed dumbbell subgraph Y^* and closed dumbbell subgraph Y_*^* of G, respectively.

With these conventions, $\zeta^{+t}(G)$ in Formula (6.4) can be written as

$$\zeta^{+t}(G) = \bigcup_{P_3 \in \Im_G^{P_3}} H_t^{P_3} \bigcup_{L \in \Im_G^L} H_t^L \bigcup_{L^* \in \Im_G^{L^*}} H_t^{L^*} \bigcup_{Y \in \Im_G^Y} H_t^Y \bigcup_{Y^* \in \Im_G^{Y^*}} H_t^{Y^*} \bigcup_{Y_*^* \in \Im_G^{Y_*^*}} H_t^{Y_*^*}$$
(6.5)

where $H_t^{P_3}, H_t^L, H_t^{L^*}, H_t^Y, H_t^{Y^*}$ and $H_t^{Y_*^*}$ denote the sets of all the t-th descendent-graphs of G based on 2-path P_3, funnel subgraph L, semi-funnel subgraph L^*, dumbbell subgraph Y, semi-closed dumbbell subgraph Y^* and closed dumbbell subgraph Y_*^*, respectively.

6.3.2 Ancestor-Graphs

Let G be a maximal planar graph with $\delta(G) \geq 4$. Suppose that $C_4 = v_1 v_2' v_3 v_2$ is a 4-cycle of G. If the subgraph of G induced by C_4 and its interior, denoted by $G_{v_2 v_2'}^{C_4}$, is a domino configuration with contracted vertices v_2, v_2'; and the subgraph of G induced by C_4 and its exterior, denoted by $G_{P_3}^{C_4}$, satisfies that $d_{G_{P_3}^{C_4}}(v_1) \geq 5$, $d_{G_{P_3}^{C_4}}(v_3) \geq 5$, then we call $G_{P_3}^{C_4} \circ \{v_2, v_2'\} = \zeta_{G_{v_2 v_2'}^{C_4}}^{-}(G)$ the **ancestor-graph** of G based on $G_{v_2 v_2'}^{C_4}$, or **the path-type ancestor-graph** of G.

Similarly, suppose that $C_5 = v_1 v_2' v_3 v_4 v_2$ is a 5-cycle of G. If the semi-maximal planar graph induced by C_5 and its interior is a domino configuration $G_{v_2 v_2'}^{C_5}$ with contracted vertices v_2, v_2', and $d_{G_L^{C_5}}(v_1) \geq 5, d_{G_L^{C_5}}(v_3), d_{G_L^{C_5}}(v_4) \geq 4$ where $G_L^{C_5}$ is the semi-maximal planar graph induced by C_5 and its exterior, then we call $G_L^{C_5} \circ \{v_2, v_2'\} = \zeta_{G_{v_2 v_2'}^{C_5}}^{-}(G)$ the **ancestor-graph** of G based on $G_{v_2 v_2'}^{C_5}$, or the **funnel-type ancestor-graph** of G.

Let $C_6 = v_1 v_3 v_2' v_5 v_4 v_2$ be a 6-cycle of G. If the semi-maximal planar graph consisting of C_6 and its interior is a domino configuration $G_{v_2 v_2'}^{C_6}$ with contracted vertices v_2, v_2', and $d_{G_Y^{C_6}}(v_1), d_{G_Y^{C_6}}(v_3), d_{G_Y^{C_6}}(v_4), d_{G_Y^{C_6}}(v_5) \geq 4$ in which $G_Y^{C_6}$ is the semi-maximal planar graph consisting of G and its exterior, then we refer to $G_Y^{C_6} \circ \{v_2, v_2'\} = \zeta_{G_{v_2 v_2'}^{C_6}}^{-}(G)$ as the **ancestor-graph** of G based on $G_{v_2 v_2'}^{C_6}$, or the **dumbbell-type ancestor-graph** of G.

When ignoring the length of outer cycle of domino configurations, the above three types of ancestor-graphs are collectively called **ancestor-graphs**.

Remark For a maximal planar graph G with $\delta(G) \geq 4$, different from its descendent-graphs, there is only one **ancestor-graph based on a given domino configuration**.

For a maximal planar graph G, similar to its descendent-graphs, the ancestor-graphs can also be classified according to the **number of inner vertices** of domino configurations $G_{v_2 v_2'}^{C_i}$ $(i = 4, 5, 6)$. Generally, we call $\zeta_{G_{v_2 v_2'}^{C_i}}^{-}(G)$ the t-th **ancestor-graph** of G (also denoted by $\zeta^{+t}(G)$ simply), if $\zeta_{G_{v_2 v_2'}^{C_i}}^{-}(G)$ has $t (\geq 1)$ inner vertices.

In particular, the 1-th, 2-th and 3-th ancestor-graphs are also called the **father-graph**, **grandfather-graph** and **great-grandfather-graph**, respectively.

Obviously, $\Im_G^H$ is closely related to $Aut(G)$. The more likely G has a symmetric structure, the smaller the size of $|\Im_G^H|$ is. For instance, let G be the icosahedron graph. Then

$$|\Im_G^{P_3}| = |\Im_G^L| = 1, \quad |\Im_G^Y| = 0 \tag{6.6}$$

In contrast, when $Aut(G)$ is a unit group, the size of $|\Im_G^H|$ may be sufficiently large.

Let $\Upsilon^-(G)$ denote the set of all ancestor-graphs of G. Then we have the following results.

Theorem 6.5 *Suppose that G is a maximal planar graph with $\delta(G) \geq 4$. Then $|\Upsilon^-(G)|$ is equal to the number of all non-identical domino configurations of G.*

As an illustration, we take the icosahedron for instance. Since icosahedron contains only one non-identical domino configuration, the 5-wheel, it follows that icosahedron has only one ancestor-graph according to Theorem 6.5; see Fig. 6.17a.

In addition, by Formula 6.6, we can see that icosahedron contains one non-identical 2-path, one non-identical funnel subgraph and no dumbbell subgraph. Therefore, according to Fig. 6.13 and discussions in Sect. 6.3.1, the number of the 1–3th descendent-graphs of icosahedron is 9; see Fig. 6.8b $\sim$j.

6.4 Construction of Maximal Planar Graphs

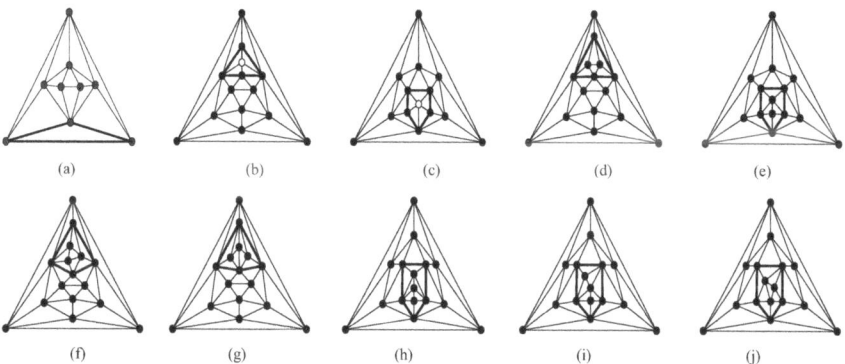

Fig. 6.17 The icosahedron together with its ancestor-graph and the 1 3th descendent-graphs. (**a**) the unqiue ancestor-graph. (**b**) son-graph. (**c**) son-graph. (**d**) grandson-graph. (**e**) grandson-graph. (**f**) great-grandson-graph. (**g**) great-grandson-graph. (**h**) great-grandson-graph. (**i**) great-grandson-graph. (**j**) great-grands- on-graph

6.4 Construction of Maximal Planar Graphs

The previous two sections give methods to construct ancestor-graphs and descendent-graphs of a maximal planar graph G with $\delta(G) \geq 4$. This section is devoted to considering how to construct a maximal planar graph of order n. First, we prove that every maximal planar graph can be generated from another one by a sequence of extending wheel operations, in other words, by some domino extending wheel operations. Then we describe how to construct a separating maximal planar graph. Finally, we show that **any maximal planar graph with order $n(\geq 11)$ and minimum degree ≥ 4 has an ancestor-graph of order $(n - 2)$ or $(n - 3)$**.

6.4.1 General Theory on Constructing Graphs

Theorem 6.6 *Suppose that G is a maximal planar graph of order n. Then, G can be contracted to K_3 by implementing a series of contracting i-wheel operations for $i = 2, 3, 4, 5$.*

Proof The proof proceeds by induction on the number n. When $n = 4$, there is only one maximal planar graph K_4. So the conclusion is true. Suppose that the conclusion holds for $n \leq p$ ($p \geq 4$), which means that any maximal planar graph with order at most p can be contracted to K_3 by implementing contracting 2-wheel, 3-wheel, 4-wheel and 5-wheel operations, repeatedly.

Now we consider the case when $n = p + 1$. For any maximal planar graph G of order $p+1$, if G has a 2-degree or 3-degree vertex, then we will get a maximal planar graph with order p, $\zeta_2^-(G)$ or $\zeta_3^-(G)$, by deleting a 2-degree or a 3-degree vertex and its incident edges. According to the induction hypothesis, the conclusion holds. If $\delta(G) = 4$ or 5, then properly implementing a contracting 4-wheel operation or a contracting 5-wheel operation for some 4-degree or 5-degree vertex, we will get a graph $\zeta_4^-(G)$ or $\zeta_5^-(G)$, which is a maximal planar graph of order $p - 1$. On the basis of the induction hypothesis, they can be contracted to K_3 by a series of contracting i-wheel operations for $i = 2, 3, 4, 5$. Hence, the conclusion holds. ∎

According to theorem 6.6, we can see that every maximal planar graph of order n can be contracted to K_3 by implementing four basic contracting wheel operations repeatedly. Accordingly, if we trace back to the reverses of contracting i-wheel operations of graph G, then by starting with K_3 and conducting the corresponding extending i-wheel operations, we can get the original graph G. So, the following corollary holds.

Corollary 6.1 *Any two maximal planar graphs can be transformed into each other by implementing the four pairs of contracting and extending operations.*

6.4.2 Construction of Separating Maximal Planar Graphs

Let H_1 and H_2 be maximal planar graphs, $H_1 \cap H_2 = \Delta v_1 v_2 v_3$. If $G = H_1 \cup H_2$ has minimum degree at least 4, then G is called **separating maximal planar graph**, or **separating graph** for short. Since every triangle face of a maximal planar graph can be regarded as ∞-**face** of the graph, without loss of generality we may assume that $\Delta v_1 v_2 v_3$ is the ∞-face of H_1; see Fig. 6.18a, while assume that $\Delta v_1 v_2 v_3$ is always the interior face of H_2; see Fig. 6.18b. Thus, $G = H_1 \cup H_2$ can be considered to be the resulting maximal planar graph by embedding H_1 in the interior face $\Delta v_1 v_2 v_3$ of H_2, where the process of embedding a graph in one face of another graph is referred to as an **embedding operation**.

Suppose that H_1 and H_2 are two maximal planar graphs, $\Delta v_1 v_2 v_3 \triangleq \Delta_1$ and $\Delta v_1 v_2 v_3 \triangleq \Delta_2$ are triangle faces of H_1 and H_2, respectively. The **embedding operation** of H_1 and H_2 based on $\{\Delta_1, \Delta_2\}$ is to relabel Δ_2 first; that is, define u_i as v_i for $i = 1, 2, 3$, and all the other vertices in H_1 and H_2 are labeled differently;

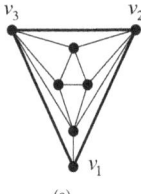 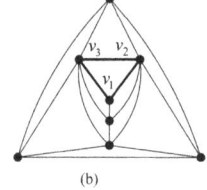 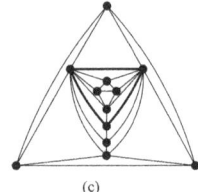

(a) (b) (c)

Fig. 6.18 The process of an embedding operation to generate a separable graph. (**a**) H_1. (**b**) H_2. (**c**) G

6.4 Construction of Maximal Planar Graphs

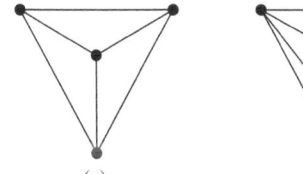
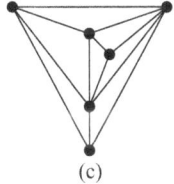

(a)　　　　　　　　(b)　　　　　　　　(c)

Fig. 6.19 Three recursive maximal planar graphs

Then, implement an union operation of H_1 and H_2, by which the resulting graph $G = H_1 \cup H_2$ is a separating maximal planar graph.

Remark In the process of relabeling Δ_2, u_i can also be defined in other ways. For example, u_1, u_2 and u_3 can be relabeled by v_2, v_3 and v_1, respectively. Of course, we will obtain different separating graphs by relabeling Δ_2 in different ways.

Obviously, when $\delta(H_i) \geq 4$, $i = 1, 2$, it has that $\delta(G) \geq 4$. However, when $\delta(H_i) = 3$, it may exist that $\delta(G) \geq 4$. For example, H_1, H_2 are maximal planar graphs with minimum degree 3, $H_1 \cup H_2 = \Delta v_1 v_2 v_3$, while $G = H_1 \cup H_2$ has minimum degree ≥ 4; see Fig. 6.18.

Let G be a maximal planar graph. We call G a **recursive maximal planar graph**, if it can be obtained from K_4 by embedding a 3-degree vertex in some triangular face continuously. We write Λ_n as the set consisting of all non-isomorphic recursive maximal planar graphs of order n. Let $\lambda_n = |\Lambda_n|$. Obviously, $\Lambda_4 = \Lambda_5 = \Lambda_6 = 1$. The corresponding recursive maximal planar graphs are shown in Fig. 6.19.

It is easy to prove that every recursive maximal planar graph has at least two vertices of degree 3. A recursive maximal planar graph is called a **(2,2)-type recursive maximal planar graph** if it contains only two vertices of 3-degree. For example, graphs shown in Fig. 6.19b, c are (2,2)-type recursive maximal planar graphs. More and more discussions on recursive maximal planar graphs are discussed in Chap. 8.

Suppose that H^* is K_4 or a (2,2)-type recursive maximal planar graph with a triangle face $\Delta v_1 v_2 v_3 \triangleq \Delta_1$ which is incident with a 3-vertex. Let H_2 be a maximal planar graph of minimum degree ≥ 4. **Embedding** H^* in the triangle face Δ_2 of H_2 means that an embedding operation of H^* and H_2 based on $\{\Delta_1, \Delta_2\}$, denoted by $H^* \cup H_2 \triangleq H_2^*$.

The following result can be easily proved.

Theorem 6.7 *Suppose that H_1 and H_2 are two maximal planar graphs, $H_1 \cap H_2 = \Delta v_1 v_2 v_3$. Then, $G = H_1 \cup H_2$ is a maximal planar graph with minimum degree ≥ 4 iff for any H_i, $i = 1, 2$, there is at most one 3-degree vertex in $\Delta v_1 v_2 v_3$ and all the other vertices in H_i have degree ≥ 4.*

The smallest maximal planar graph with minimum degree ≥ 4 has six vertices. The smallest maximal planar graph with exactly one 3-vertex is the graph shown in Fig. 6.18a. Thus, by Theorem 6.7, the smallest separating maximal planar graph has order 9 ($6 + 6 - 3 = 9$). Furthermore, according to Theorem 6.7, we give a method to generate any separating graph with order $n \geq 9$ as follows.

Let H_i be a maximal planar graph of order $n_i (\geq 6)$, $i = 1, 2$. We need to consider the following two cases for constructing separating maximal planar graphs.

Case 1: $n = n_1 + n_2 - 3$

In this case, we can construct a separating graph of order n using H_1 and H_2, two maximal planar graphs with minimum degree at least 4, by the following steps, where H_i has order n_i (≥ 6), $i = 1, 2$.

- **Step 1**: Find out all the non-identical triangle faces of H_1 and H_2, respectively;
- **Step 2**: For every non-identical triangle face of H_1, embed it in every non-identical triangle face of H_2, and the resulting graphs are our desired ones.

Case 2: $n < n_1 + n_2 - 3$

Let $m = n - n_1 - n_2 + 3$, $m = m_1 + m_2$, $m_1, m_2 \geq 0$, $t_i = m_i + n_i$, $i = 1, 2$. So, $n = t_1 + t_2 - 3$. We need to further consider two subcases:

Subcase 2.1

$t_1 = n_1$. Then $m_1 = 0$

- **Step 1**: Find out all the non-identical triangle faces of H_1 and H_2;
- **Step 2**: If $M_2 = 1$, then embed K_4 in every non-identical triangle face of H_2; if $M_2 \neq 1$, then embed the (2,2)-type recursive maximal planar graph H^* of order $(M_2 + 3)$ in every non-identical triangle face of H_2. Denote the resulting graph by H_2^*, and let Δ_2 be a triangle face of H_2^* with a 3-degree vertex;
- **Step 3**: For any triangle face of H_1, denoted by Δ_1, implement an embedding operation of H_1 and H_2^* based on $\{\Delta_1, \Delta_2\}$ respectively. Then, the resulting graphs are the desired ones.

Subcase 2.2: $m_i > 0$, $i = 1, 2$

- **Step 1**: Find out all the non-identical triangle faces of H_1 and H_2;
- **Step 2**: For $i = 1, 2$, embed the (2,2)-type recursive maximal planar graph H^* of order $(m_i + 3)$ in every non-identical triangle face of H_i. Denote the resulted graph by H_i^*. When $m_i = 1$, we have $H^* = K_4$. Let Δ_i be a triangle face of H_i^* with a 3-degree vertex.
- **Step 3**: For each H_1^* and H_2^*, implement an embedding operation based on $\{\Delta_1, \Delta_2\}$ respectively. The resulting graphs are the ones we desired.

By the above method, we construct all of the two separating maximal planar graphs of order 10 as follows.

Note that $10 = (6 + 7 - 3)$, and there is only one maximal planar graph of order i for $i = 6, 7$. In addition, one can readily confirm that each of the two maximal planar graphs of order 6 or 7 has only one non-identical triangle. Therefore, according to case 1, we can construct a separating maximal planar graph of order 10; see Fig. 6.20a. Additionally, since $10 = ((6 + 4) - 3) + 6 - 3$, by using the steps given in case 2, we can construct another separating maximal planar graph of order 10;

6.4 Construction of Maximal Planar Graphs

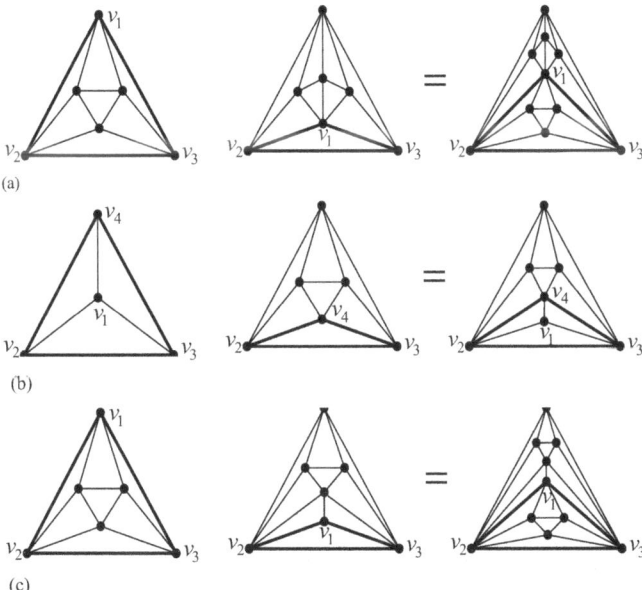

Fig. 6.20 Processes of constructing two separable maximal planar graphs of order 10. (a) an embedding operation of two maximal planar graphs with order 6, 7 and minimum degree. (b) embed in a maximal planar graph with order 6 and minimum degree at least 4. (c) an embedding operation of two maximal planar graphs with order 6, 7 and minimum degree at least 4

See Fig. 6.20b, c. It is easy to prove that there are only two separating maximal planar graphs of order 10.

By using this method, we can construct all of the nine separating maximal planar graphs of order 11 and all of the forty-three separating maximal planar graphs of order 12 [2].

6.4.3 Basic Theorem on Non-separating Maximal Planar Graphs Construction

Theorem 6.8 *Suppose that G is a non-separable maximal planar graph with order n (≥ 9) and minimum degree ≥ 4. Then G has an ancestor-graph of order $(n-2)$ or $(n-3)$.*

Proof Let G be an arbitrary non-separable maximal planar graph with order $n (\geq 9)$ and minimum degree ≥ 4. Denote by (i, j, t), $i \leq j \leq t$, a triangle $\triangle v_1 v_2 v_3$ of G, such that the degrees of v_1, v_2 and v_3 are i, j, and t, respectively.

When $\delta(G) = 4$, let $\triangle v_1 v_2 v_3$ be a $(4, j, t)$ triangle, where $4 \leq j \leq t$. We distinguish three types in terms of the values of j and t.

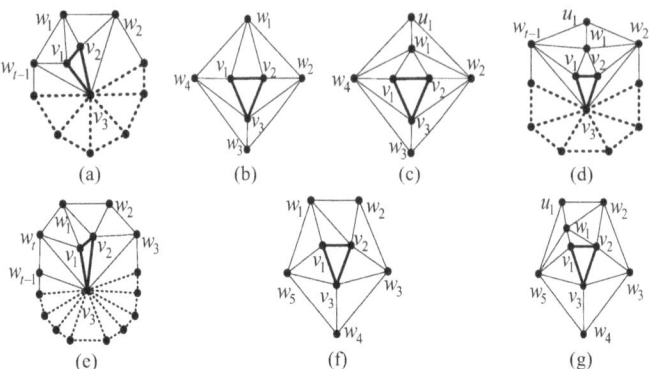

Fig. 6.21 Illustration of Theorem 6.8

Type 1: $\triangle v_1 v_2 v_3$ is $(4, 4, t)$, $t \geq 4$

The neighbors of v_1, v_2, and v_3 are denoted by $w_1, w_2, \ldots, w_{t-1}$ in clockwise, as shown in Fig. 6.21a. We then further deal with three cases as follows.

Case 1: $t = 4$. Then, G is a graph of order 6 or separable, and a contradiction.

Case 2: $t = 5$; see Fig. 6.21b. Then $d(w_1) \geq 5$ and $w_1 w_3 \notin E(G)$; otherwise, G is separable or a graph with order 7. If $d(w_1) = 5$, let u_1 be the neighbor of w_1 different from w_2, v_2, v_1, w_4; see Fig. 6.21c. Obviously, $d(w_2), d(w_4) \geq 6$, and G has a basic domino configuration with outer cycle $w_1 w_2 v_3 w_4$ and inner vertices v_1, v_2 (w_1, v_3 are contracted vertices). If $d(w_1) \geq 6$ and $d(w_3) \geq 5$, then we have $d(w_2), d(w_4) \geq 5$, and G has a basic domino configuration with outer cycle $w_1 w_2 w_3 w_4 w_1$ and inner vertices v_2, v_3 (v_1, w_2 are contracted vertices). If $d(w_1) \geq 5$ and $d(w_3) = 4$, then $d(w_2), d(w_4) \geq 6$, and G has a basic domino configuration with outer cycle $w_1 w_2 v_3 w_4$ and inner vertices v_1, v_2 (v_3, w_1 are contracted vertices).

Case 3: $t \geq 6$. If $d(w_1) \geq 6$, then the 4-wheel with wheel-center v_1 is a domino configuration (v_2, w_{t-1} are contracted vertices). If $d(w_1) = 5$, then w_1 has a neighbor, denoted by u_1 not in $\{v_1, v_2, v_3, w_1, w_2, w_3, \ldots, w_{t-1}\}$, and clearly $d(w_{t-1}), d(w_2) \geq 5$; see Fig. 6.21d. If $d(u_1) \geq 5$, then G has a basic domino configuration with outer cycle $v_3 v_1 w_{t-1} u_1 w_2$ and inner vertices v_2, w_1 (v_1, w_2 are contracted vertices); if $d(u_1) = 4$, then $d(w_{t-1}), d(w_2) \geq 6$. Therefore, G has a basic domino configuration with outer cycle $w_2 v_2 v_3 w_{t-1} u_1$ and inner vertices v_1, w_1 (u_1, v_2 are contracted vertices). If $d(w_1) = 4$, then G is separable, and a contradiction.

Type 2: $\triangle v_1 v_2 v_3$ is $(4, 5, t)$, $t \geq 5$ The neighbors of v_1, v_2, and v_3 in this situation are shown in Fig. 6.21e.

Case 1: $t = 5$; see Fig. 6.21f. If $d(w_1) = 4$, then $\triangle v_1 w_1 v_2$ is $(4, 4, 5)$, and by Type 1 the result holds.

If $d(w_1) = 5$, then w_1 has a neighbor u_1 not in $\{v_1, v_2, v_3, w_1, w_2, w_3, w_4\}$; see Fig. 6.21g. Obviously, $d(w_5) \geq 5$. If $d(w_3) = 4$, then $d(w_4), d(w_2) \geq 5$, and

G has a basic domino configuration with outer cycle $w_3w_4w_5v_1w_1w_2$ and inner vertices v_2, v_3 (v_1, w_3 are contracted vertices). If $d(u_1), d(w_3) \geq 5$, then G has a basic domino configuration with outer cycle $v_3v_1w_5u_1w_2w_3$ and inner vertices w_1, v_2 (v_1, w_2 are contracted vertices). If $d(w_3) \geq 5$ and $d(u_1) = 4$, then we have $d(w_5) \geq 6$ and $d(w_2) \geq 5$. Therefore, the 5-wheel with wheel-center w_1 is a domino configuration (v_1, u_1 are contracted vertices).

If $d(w_1) \geq 6$ and $d(w_5) = 4$, then $\Delta v_1 w_5 v_1$ is of the Type 1. Therefore, we only need to consider the case that $d(w_1) \geq 6$ and $d(w_5) \geq 5$. Then, when $d(w_3) \geq 5$, the 5-wheel with wheel-center v_2 is a domino configuration (v_1, w_2 are contracted vertices); when $d(w_3) = 4$, we have $d(w_4), d(w_2) \geq 5$, and there is a basic domino configuration in G with outer cycle $w_3w_4w_5v_1w_1w_2$ and inner vertices v_2, v_3 (v_1, w_3 are contracted vertices).

Case 2: $t \geq 6$. In this case, if $d(w_1) \geq 6$, then the 4-wheel with wheel-center v_1 is a domino configuration (v_2, w_t are contracted vertices); if $d(w_1) = 5$, then $\Delta v_1 w_1 v_2$ is (4,5,5) and the result holds; if $d(w_1) = 4$, then $\Delta v_1 w_1 v_2$ is (4,4,5), which belongs to Type 1.

Type 3: $\Delta v_1 v_2 v_3$ is $(4, j, t)$, $6 \leq j \leq t$. Let w_1 be a common neighbor of v_1 and v_2 different from v_3. If $d(w_1) \geq 4$ or 5, then $\Delta v_1 w_1 v_2$ is a $(4, 4, j)$ or $(4, 5, j)$ triangle, which belongs to Type 1 or Type 2. If $d(w_1) \geq 6$, then the 4-wheel with wheel-center v_1 is a domino configuration.

When $\delta(G) = 5$, the triangles with a 5-degree vertex in G can be distinguished into two types: $(5, 5, t_1)$ and $(5, j, t_2)$, where $t_1 \geq 5, 6 \leq j \leq t_2$. Analogously to the proof of $\delta(G) = 4$, we can also show that there is a basic domino configuration in G.

Hence, the theorem holds. ∎

6.4.4 A Recursive Method of Generating Non-separating Maximal Planar Graphs

Based on the Theorem 6.8, an approach to construct non-separable maximal planar graphs recursively will be described. Suppose that $G(n)$ is the set of all non-identical and non-separable maximal planar graphs with order n and minimum degree ≥ 4. Now, we generate all of graphs in $G(n)$ by the following.

Step 1 For every $H \in G(n-2)$, construct all of its 1**-th descendent-graphs**; that is, implement an extending 4-wheel or 5-wheel operation in H. The specific procedures are as follows.

Step 1.1 For every H in $G(n-2)$, find out $\Im_H^{P_3}$ and $\Im_H^L$, the set of non-identical 2-paths and the set of funnels.

Step 1.2 For every H in $G(n-2)$, implement once extending wheel operation on every 2-path in $\Im_H^{P_3}$ and funnel in $\Im_H^L$, respectively. We can obtain all the 1-th descendent-graphs of H.

Step 2 For every H in $G(n-3)$, construct all of its 2-**th descendent-graphs** by the methods given in Sect. 6.3.1. The specific procedures are as follows.

Step 2.1 For every H in $G(n-3)$, find out the sets of non-identical 2-paths, funnels, semi-funnels, dumbbells, semi-closed dumbbells and closed dumbbells, denoted by $\Im_H^{P_3}, \Im_H^L, \Im_H^{L^*}, \Im_H^Y, \Im_H^{Y^*}$ and $\Im_H^{Y^*_*}$, respectively.

Step 2.2 For every H in $G(n-3)$, we conduct the following operations.

Based on $\Im_H^{P_3}$ and the first domino configuration that contains two inner vertices (in Fig. 6.7), we construct all the path-type descendent-graphs of H with order n.

Based on $\Im_H^L$ and the second domino configuration that contains two inner vertices (in Fig. 6.7), we construct all the funnel-type descendent-graphs of H with order n.

Based on $\Im_H^{L^*}$ and the second domino configuration that contains two inner vertices (in Fig. 6.7), we construct all the funnel-type descendent-graphs of H with order n.

Based on $\Im_H^Y$ and the third domino configuration that contains two inner vertices (in Fig. 6.7), we construct all the dumbbell-type descendent-graphs of H with order n.

Based on $\Im_H^{Y^*}$ and the third domino configuration that contains two inner vertices (in Fig. 6.7), we construct all the dumbbell-type descendent-graphs of H with order n.

Based on $\Im_H^{Y^*_*}$ and the third domino configuration that contains two inner vertices (in Fig. 6.7), we construct all the dumbbell-type descendent-graphs of H with order n.

We illustrate the process of constructing $G(9)$ as follows.

Notice that there is only one non-separable maximal planar graph of minimum degree ≥ 4 and order 7, denoted by G; see Fig. 6.22a. It is easy to see that $|\Im_G^{P_3}| = 3$ and $\Im_G^Y = 1$ (the bold lines in Fig. 6.22a–d). Thus, if we implement an extending wheel operation on every 2-path in $\Im_G^{P_3}$ and funnel in $\Im_G^L$, respectively, then we can obtain four maximal planar graphs with order 9 and minimum degree ≥ 4; see Fig. 6.22a'–d', in which two graphs shown in Fig. 6.22a', c' are isomorphic.

In addition, one can readily confirm that $G(6)$ contains only one graph, denoted also by G, see Fig. 6.22e. This graph has strongly symmetrical characteristics, that is, $|\Im_G^{P_3}| = |\Im_G^L| = |\Im_G^{Y^*}| = 1$, $|\Im_G^{L^*}| = |\Im_G^L| = |\Im_G^{Y^*_*}| = 0$. Based on the elements (paths and funnels) in $\Im_G^{P_3}$ and $\Im_G^L$, we can construct three descendent-graphs of G with order 9. These three graphs are isomorphic to the graphs shown in Fig. 6.22 (a')-(c'), respectively. Moreover, if we try to construct descendent-graphs of G with order 9 based on the unique closed dumbbell in $\Im_G^{Y^*_*}$, then we will get the graph shown in Fig. 6.22g.

Above all, we construct all of the four non-isomorphism and non-separable maximal planar graphs with minimum degree ≥ 4 and order 9; see Fig. 6.22.

6.5 Conclusion

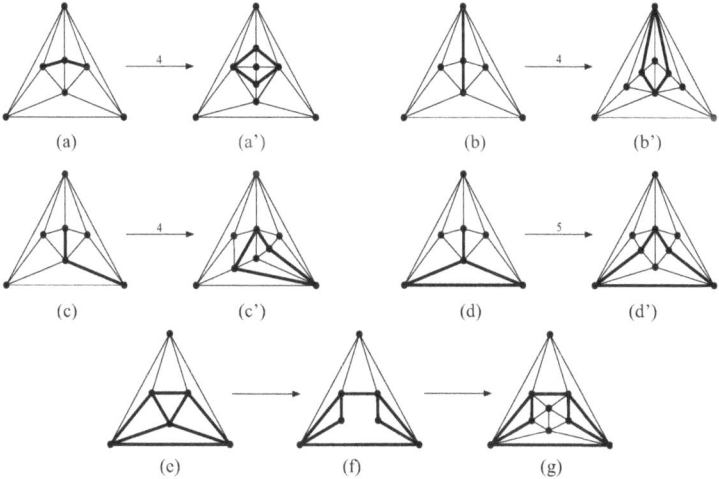

Fig. 6.22 Procedures of constructing $G(9)$. (**a**) 4444455. (**a'**) 444445566. (**b**) 4444455. (**b'**) 444444477. (**c**) 4444455. (**c'**) 444445566. (**d**) 4444455. (**d'**) 444455556

By using the methods on how to generate separable and non-separable maximal planar graphs, prescribed in Sects. 6.4.2 and 6.4.3, all of the maximal planar graphs with order 6-12 and minimum degree ≥ 4 can be generated [2].

6.5 Conclusion

This chapter describes some useful techniques and tools for constructing maximal planar graphs:

(1) A new method, called **extending-contracting operation**, is established to generate maximal planar graphs, which can connect the structure and coloring of an arbitrary maximal planar graph closely.
(2) A class of subgraphs in maximal planar graphs of minimum degree ≥ 4 is observed and studied. We characterize the structures of these graphs in depth and propose an approach to construct them. This work is the foundation to construct maximal planar graphs recursively.
(3) We introduce the definitions of ancestor-graphs and descendent-graphs of a maximal planar graph of minimum degree at least 4, and propose a method to construct them.
(4) It is proved that every maximal planar graph with order $n(\geq 11)$ and minimum degree ≥ 4 has an ancestor-graph of order $(n-2)$ or $(n-3)$ (Theorem 6.8), based on which a recursive method is given to construct maximal planar graphs of order $n(\geq 8)$. As examples, all maximal planar graphs with order 6-12 and minimum degree ≥ 4 are constructed.

Table 6.1 Enumeration of maximal planar graph of minimum degree at least 4 and of order from 6 to 23

Order	6	7	8	9	10	11	12
Numbers	1	1	2	5	12	34	130
Order	13	14	15	16	17	18	19
Numbers	525	2472	12400	65619	357504	1992985	11284042
Order	20	21	22	23			
Numbers	64719885	375126827	2194439398	12941995397			

Note that Theorem 6.8 is the foundation for our subsequent study.

Based on the content in this Chapter, we will argue how to establish a connection between structures and colorings of maximal planar graphs, in Chaps. 8 and 9.

To illustrate the main result in this chapter, we need to known the enumeration of maximal planar graphs of order $6 \sim 12$ with minimum degree at least 4. In 2007, Brinkmann and Mckay studied this problem and established a generating algorithm [1]. We here depict the numbers of maximal planar graphs of minimum degree at least 4 and of orders from 6 to 23 (Table 6.1).

References

1. G Birnkmann and B Mckay. Fast generation of planar graphs. *MATCH Communications in Mathematical and in Computer Chemistry*, 58(58):323–356, 2007.
2. J Xu. Theory on the structure and coloring of maximal plnaar graphs (2) domino configurations and extending-contracting operations. *Journal of Electronics and Information Thchnology*, 38(6):1271–1327, 2016.
3. J Xu, Z Li, and E Zhu. On purely tree-colorable planar graphs. *Information Processing Letters*, 116(8):532–536, 2016.

Open Access This chapter is licensed under the terms of the Creative Commons Attribution 4.0 International License (http://creativecommons.org/licenses/by/4.0/), which permits use, sharing, adaptation, distribution and reproduction in any medium or format, as long as you give appropriate credit to the original author(s) and the source, provide a link to the Creative Commons license and indicate if changes were made.

The images or other third party material in this chapter are included in the chapter's Creative Commons license, unless indicated otherwise in a credit line to the material. If material is not included in the chapter's Creative Commons license and your intended use is not permitted by statutory regulation or exceeds the permitted use, you will need to obtain permission directly from the copyright holder.

Chapter 7
Recursion Formulae of Chromatic Polynomial and Four-Color Conjecture

Abstract This chapter describes a recursion formula of the chromatic polynomial of a maximal planar graph, which is different from that of edge contraction. Based on this, two ideas for proving the Four Color Conjecture are proposed (Xu, J. Electron. Inf. Technol. **38**(4), 33–40 (2016)).

7.1 Recursion Formulae of Chromatic Polynomial by Contracting Wheels

In this chapter, we use $f(G, t)$ to denote the number of colorings for the vertices of a labeled graph with t colors. Here we follow the notations and terminology of Ref. [9]. Obviously, if $t < \chi(G)$, G can not be properly colored, so $f(G, t) = 0$. But if $t \geq \chi(G)$, then G admits a t-coloring and hence $f(G, t) > 0$. For every planar graph G, if we can prove $f(G, t) > 0$, then the Four-Color Conjecture is confirmed. This is the method that Birkhoff [1, 2] proposed for attacking the Four-Color Problem in 1912. Later on, it was found that $f(G, t)$ is a polynomial in the number t, called the **chromatic polynomial** of graphs, which has become a fascinating branch in the field of graph theory at present [3]. But it was a pity that Birkhoff's aim had not been reached. The research on chromatic polynomials of graphs has attracted much interest [1–7], in which the best result, due to Tutte [5], was that when $t = \tau(\sqrt{5}) = 3.618\ldots$ (where $\tau = \frac{\sqrt{5}+1}{2}$), $f(G, \tau\sqrt{5}) > 0$. It seems a pity that this result brushed past the Four-Color Conjecture since the Four-Color Conjecture holds if $f(G, 4) > 0$.

In order to calculate the chromatic polynomial of a given graph, the basic tool is the **Edge Deletion & Contraction Formula**. Recall that for an edge e of a graph G, $G - e$ and $G \circ e$ are the graph obtained from G by deleting e and contracting e, respectively. Throughout this section, we assume that in the process of contracting operation, all graphs (except W_2) have no loops and parallel edges.

The Edge Deletion-Contract Formula [1] Let G be a simple graph. For any edge, we have

$$f(G, t) = f(G - e, t) - f(G \circ e, t)$$

Moreover, in [8, 10], the author obtained a recursion formula of a chromatic polynomial by vertex deletion formula and a chromatic polynomial between a graph and its complement. Perhaps because of Tutte's perfect work and his high status in academia, once upon a time, it was thought that attacking the Four-Color Problem by chromatic polynomial was impossible. Nevertheless, our works below give new hope for solving the Four-Color Conjecture by chromatic polynomial.

We first give two useful lemmas as follows.

Lemma 7.1 *Every planar graph without loops is 4-colorable if and only if*

$$f(G, 4) > 0 \tag{7.1}$$

Lemma 7.2 *Let $G = G_1 \cup G_2$ be the union of G_1 and G_2. If $G_1 \cap G_2$ is a complete graph of order k, then*

$$f(G, t) = \frac{f(G_1, t) \times f(G_2, t)}{t(t-1) \cdots (t-k+1)} \tag{7.2}$$

Theorem 7.1 *Let G be a maximal planar graph, v a vertex of degree four, and $N_G(v) = \{v_1, v_2, v_3, v_4\}$ (see Fig. 7.1). Then*

$$f(G, 4) = f(G_1, 4) + f(G_2, 4) \tag{7.3}$$

where $G_1 = (G - v) \circ \{v_1, v_3\}$, $G_2 = (G - v) \circ \{v_2, v_4\}$.

Proof In the following derivation, we use the notation $G[\overline{N(v)}]$ to denote the graph G. We first compute the graph G chromatic polynomial using the Edge Deletion-Contraction Formula. For the sake of understanding clearly, we adopt the method introduced by Zykov [11] here, where the chromatic polynomials are represented by

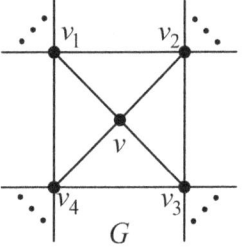

Fig. 7.1 A maximal planar graph with a vertex of degree 4

7.1 Recursion Formulae of Chromatic Polynomial by Contracting Wheels

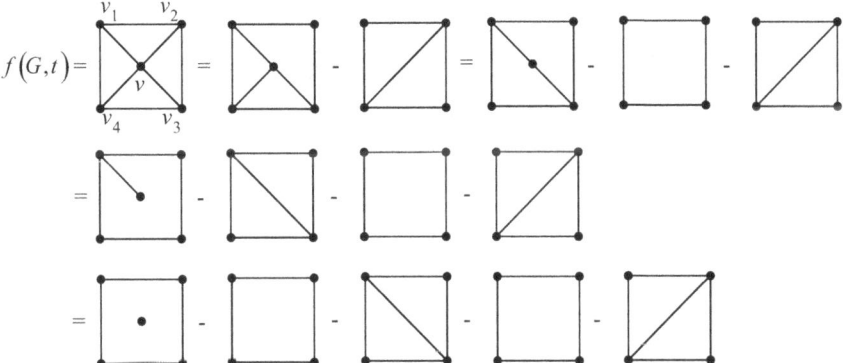

Fig. 7.2 The derivative process of the chromatic polynomial based on a vertex with degree four

Fig. 7.3 The result of the derivation presented in Fig. 7.2

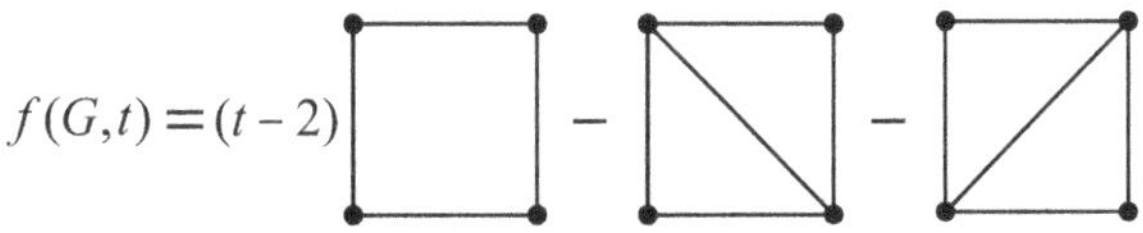

$$f(G,t) = (t-2)\left[\;\square\;-\;\boxtimes\;-\;\boxslash\;\right]$$

the corresponding graphical graphs without t. Notice that if at least two edges are between two vertices, only one edge remains, and others are deleted, except W_2.

By Lemma 7.2, the chromatic polynomial of the first subgraph in Fig. 7.2 is $t \cdot f(G - v, t)$. Therefore, one gets (Fig. 7.3)

When $t = 4$,

Notice that the two graphs in Fig. 7.4 denote $(G - v) \circ \{v_1, v_3\}$ and $(G - v) \circ \{v_2, v_4\}$, respectively. It is easy to prove that they are both maximal planar graphs of order $n - 2$. Thus, we have

$$f(G, 4) = f((G - v) \circ \{v_1, v_3\}) + f((G - v) \circ \{v_2, v_4\}) = f(G_1, 4) + f(G_2, 4)$$

∎

Theorem 7.2 *Let G be a maximal planar graph, v a vertex of degree five, and $N_G(v) = \{v_1, v_2, v_3, v_4, v_5\}$ (see Fig. 7.5). Then*

$$\begin{aligned}f(G, 4) = & (f(G_1, 4) - f(G_1 \cup \{v_1v_4, v_1v_3\}, 4)) \\ & + (f(G_2, 4) - f(G_2 \cup \{v_3v_1, v_3v_5\}, 4)) \\ & + (f(G_3, 4) - f(G_3 \cup \{v_1v_4\}, 4))\end{aligned} \quad (7.4)$$

where $G_1 = (G - v) \circ \{v_2, v_5\}$, $G_2 = (G - v) \circ \{v_2, v_4\}$, $G_3 = (G - v) \circ \{v_3, v_5\}$.

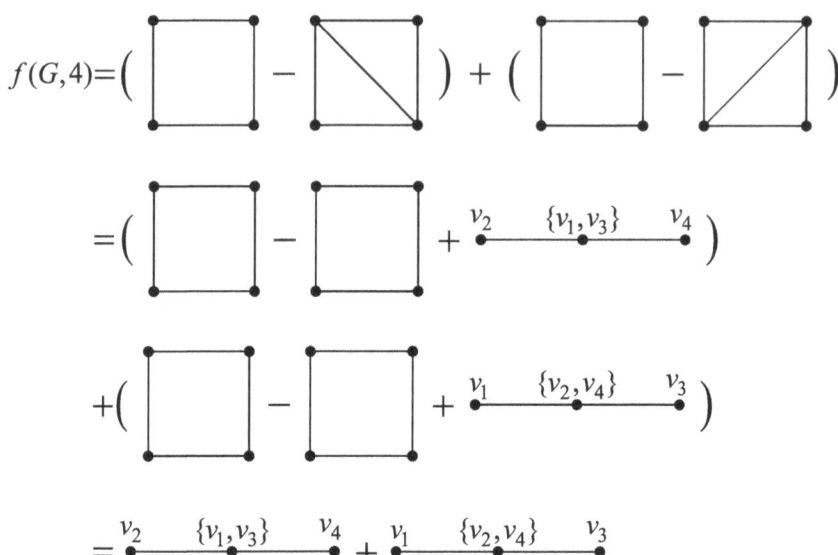

Fig. 7.4 The derivation of $f(G, 4)$ based on a vertex of degree four

Fig. 7.5 A maximal planar graph with a vertex of degree 5

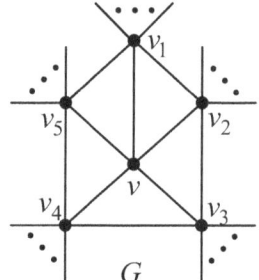

Proof The graph G is represented by $G[\overline{N(v)}]$. The chromatic polynomial of G can be calculated by repeatedly applying the Edge Deletion-Contraction Formula. If parallel edges appear in the process, reserve only one edge excluding W_2. We use W_5 to represent the chromatic polynomial of G. In this way, we can obtain that

By Lemma 7.2, the chromatic polynomial of the first graph in Fig. 7.6 is $t \cdot f(G - v, t)$. Therefore, we have (Fig. 7.7)

7.1 Recursion Formulae of Chromatic Polynomial by Contracting Wheels 183

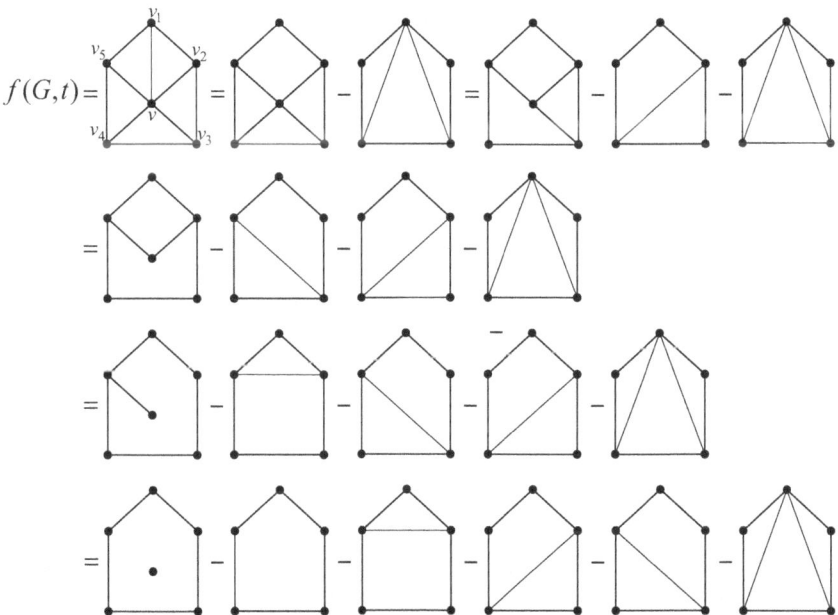

Fig. 7.6 The derivative process of the chromatic polynomial based on a vertex with degree five

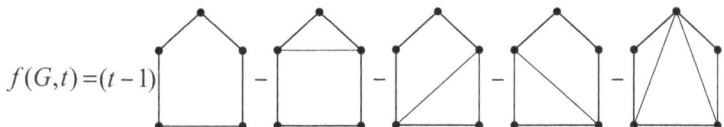

Fig. 7.7 The result of the derivation presented in Fig. 7.6

When $t = 4$, it has that

Notice that the fourth graph in Fig. 7.8, denoted by G', contains a subgraph isomorphic to K_5, and so $f(G', 4) = 0$. Thus, we can obtain that

Actually, the first graph in the first bracket of Fig. 7.9 is $G_1 = (G - v) \circ \{v_2, v_5\}$; the first graph in the second bracket is $G_2 = (G - v) \circ \{v_2, v_4\}$; and the first graph in the third bracket is $G_3 = (G - v) \circ \{v_3, v_5\}$. This completes the proof. ∎

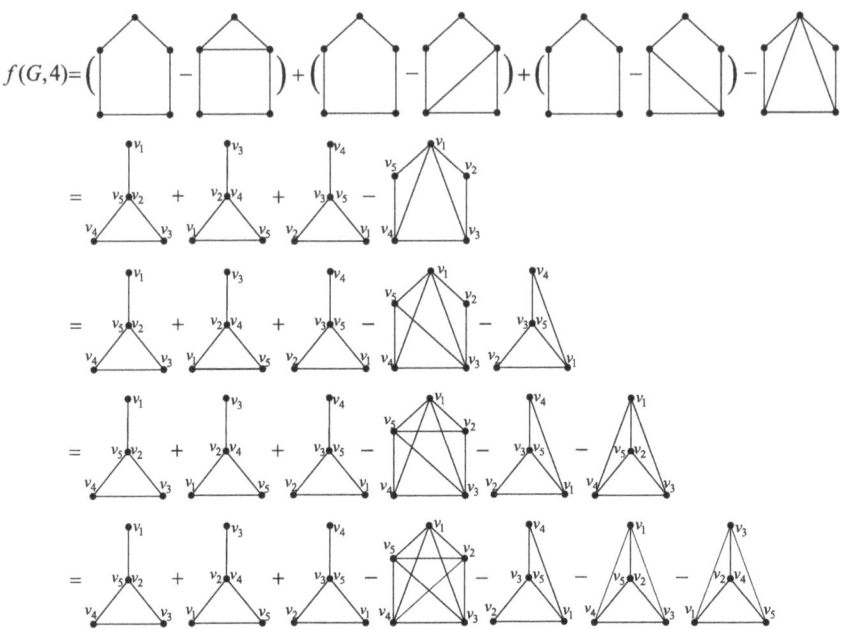

Fig. 7.8 The derivation of $f(G, 4)$ based on a vertex of degree five

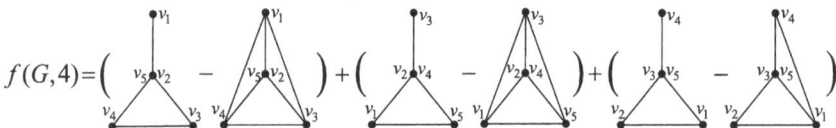

Fig. 7.9 The result of the derivation of $f(G, 4)$ based on a vertex of degree five

7.2 Two Mathematical Ideas for Attacking Four-Color Conjecture Based on Theorem 7.2

It is well known that mathematical induction is an effective method to prove the Four-Color Conjecture, in which maximal planar graphs are classified into three cases in terms of their minimum degrees. The case of minimum degree 3 or 4 is easy to prove by induction, but no mathematical method has been found for the case of minimum degree 5. Based on Theorems 7.1 and 7.2, a new method to prove the Four-Color Conjecture is presented as follows.

In order to prove $f(G, 4) > 0$ for a maximal planar graph G, we use a mathematical induction on the number $|V(G)| = n$. When $n = 3, 4, 5$, the result is obviously true. Assume that $n \geq 5$ and the result is true for any maximal planar graph of order at most $n - 1$. We consider the case that the order of graphs is n. We

7.2 Two Mathematical Ideas for Attacking Four-Color Conjecture Based on...

only consider simple maximal planar graphs. Notice that for any maximal planar graph G, it follows that $3 \leq \delta(G) \leq 5$. So we consider the following three cases.

Case 1. $\delta(G) = 3$

Let $v \in V(G)$, $d_G(v) = 4$, $G_1 = G[\overline{N(v)}]$ and $G_2 = G - v$. Then, we have $G_1 \cap G_2 = G[N(v)] \cong K_3$. Observe that $G_1 = G[\overline{N(v)}] \cong K_4$; we can obtain the following result by Lemma 7.2.

$$f(G, t) = f(G_1 \cup G_2, t) = \frac{f(G_1, t) \times f(G_2, t)}{f(K_3, t)} = (t - 3)f(G_2, t)$$

By the induction hypothesis, $f(G_2, 4) > 0$. Thus, $f(G, 4) = f(G_2, 4) > 0$ and the result is true when $\delta(G) = 3$.

Case 2. $\delta(G) = 4$

Let $v \in V(G)$, $d_G(v) = 4$, $N_G(v) = \{v_1, v_2, v_3, v_4\}$; see Fig. 7.1 in which G is denoted by $G[\overline{N(v)}]$. By Theorem 7.1, we have $f(G, 4) = f(G_1, 4) + f(G_2, 4)$, where $G_1 = (G - v) \circ \{v_1, v_3\}$, $G_2 = (G - v) \circ \{v_2, v_4\}$. It is easy to prove that both G_1 and G_2 are maximal planar graphs of order $n - 2$. By the induction hypothesis, we have that $f(G_1, 4) > 0$ and $f(G_2, 4) > 0$, and hence $f(G, 4) = f(G_1, 4) + f(G_2, 4) > 0$ and the result holds for $\delta(G) = 4$.

The key ingredient of the proof for the Four-Color Conjecture is the following Case.

Case 3. $\delta(G) = 5$

The icosahedron is the maximal planar graph of minimum degree 5 with minimum order, as shown in Fig. 7.10a, which has 12 vertices. Obviously, the icosahedron is 4-colorable. There is no maximal planar graph of minimum degree 5 with 13 vertices. Notice that for any maximal planar graph of order at least 14 and minimum degree 5, there exists a vertex v such that $d_G(v) = 5$ and $d_G(v_1) \geq 6$, where $N_G(v) = \{v_1, v_2, v_3, v_4, v_5\}$ (see Fig. 7.5). Hence, the graph G_1 in Theorem 7.2 is a 4-colorable maximal planar graph of minimum degree at least 4. Based on this observation, we present two mathematical ideas to prove $f(G, 4) > 0$ for the case $\delta(G) = 5$ as follows.

The **first idea** is based on the fact that the value of each square bracket in Formula (7.4) is no less than zero. Hence, the Four-Color Conjecture can be proved if the value in some square bracket is greater than zero. Conversely, the value of

Fig. 7.10 Three graphs in Case 3. (**a**) The icosahedron. (**b**) A funnel subgragh

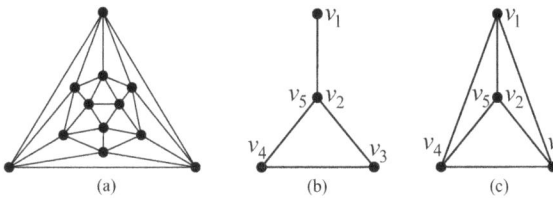

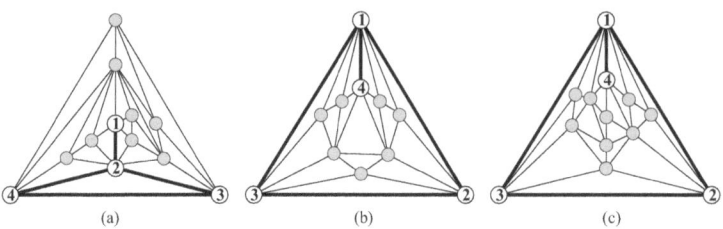

Fig. 7.11 Three 4-chromatic-funnel pseudo uniquely-4-colorable maximal planar graphs. (**a**) A 4-chromatic-funnel type graph of order 12. (**b**) A 4-chromatic-funnel type graph of order 11. (**c**) A 4-chromatic-funnel type graph of order 13

the Formula (7.4) is zero if and only if each square bracket in Formula (7.4) is equal to zero. Observe that the value of the first square bracket is greater than zero if and only if there exists $f_1 \in C_4^0(G_1)$ such that $f_1(v_1) = f_1(v_3)$ or $f_1(v_1) = f_1(v_4)$, i.e., the value of the first square bracket is equal to zero if and only if for any $f_1 \in C_4^0(G_1)$, $f_1(v_1) \neq f_1(v_3)$ and $f_1(v_1) \neq f_1(v_4)$. That is, for any $f_1 \in C_4^0(G_1)$, the colors of vertices of the funnel shown in Fig. 7.10b are pairwise different. Such maximal planar graphs are called **4-chromatic-funnel pseudo uniquely-4-colorable maximal planar graphs**. For instance, each graph in Fig. 7.11 is a 4-chromatic-funnel pseudo-uniquely 4-colorable maximal planar graph.

A k-chromatic graph G is called a k-**colorable coordinated graph** if there are k vertices $v_1, v_2, \ldots, v_k$ such that $f(v_1), f(v_2), \ldots, f(v_k)$ are pairwise different for any k-coloring f of G. All 4-colorable coordinated maximal planar graphs can be divided into three classes: (1) uniquely 4-colorable maximal planar graphs, namely these graphs have only one k-partition of color classes; (2) quasi uniquely-4-colorable maximal planar graphs, namely these graphs contain a subgraph that is uniquely 4-colorable; (3) pseudo uniquely-4-colorable maximal planar graphs, that is, these graphs are neither uniquely 4-colorable nor quasi uniquely-4-colorable.

Now we give the second idea to prove $f(G, 4) > 0$. The maximal planar graphs G_1, G_2 and G_3 in Theorem 7.2 can be regarded as the graphs obtained from G by deleting a vertex v of degree 5 and contracting $\{v_2, v_5\}$, $\{v_2, v_4\}$ and $\{v_3, v_5\}$, respectively. Moreover, the 5-cycle consisting of the neighbors of v in G is contracted to a funnel subgraph $L_1 = v_1 - \triangle v_2^5 v_3 v_4$, $L_2 = v_3 - \triangle v_2^4 v_1 v_5$ and $L_3 = v_4 - \triangle v_3^5 v_1 v_2$, where v_2^5, v_2^4 and v_3^5 are the new vertices obtained by contracting $\{v_2, v_5\}$, $\{v_2, v_4\}$ and $\{v_3, v_5\}$, respectively (see Fig. 7.12).

By the induction hypothesis, G_1, G_2 and G_3 are 4-colorable. In order to prove $f(G, 4) > 0$, it is sufficient to prove that at least one of the funnel subgraphs L_1, L_2 and L_3 is not a 4-chromatic funnel subgraph.

Therefore, the **second idea** is to prove that for any maximal planar graph G of minimum degree 5, there exists a 5-wheel W_5^v in G such that at least one of the funnel subgraphs L_1, L_2 and L_3 corresponding to G_1, G_2 and G_3 is not a 4-chromatic-funnel. For instance, the graph in Fig. 7.11a can be regarded as the

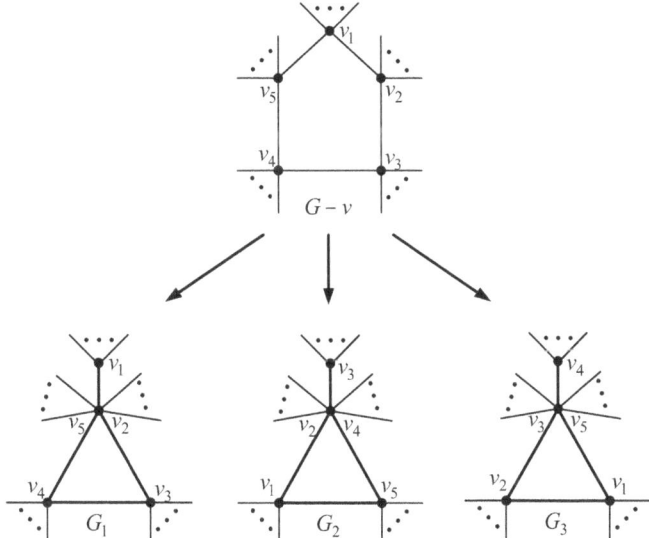

Fig. 7.12 The processes of generating the three funnel subgraphs

Fig. 7.13 A maximal planar graph that can be contracted to the graph of Fig. 7.11a.

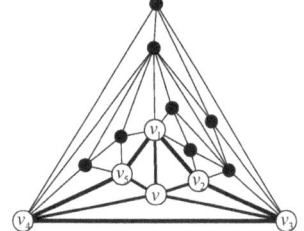

maximal planar graph obtained from the graph of Fig. 7.13 by conducting the operation (as shown in Fig. 7.12) on the 5-wheel $W_5^v = v - v_1v_2v_3v_4v_5$. It is not difficult to prove that the other two graphs obtained from Fig. 7.13 by conducting the operation (as shown in Fig. 7.12) are not a 4-chromatic funnel.

References

1. G D Birkhoff. A determinantal formula for the number of ways of coloring a map. *Annals of Mathmatics*, 14 (1/4):42–46, 1912.
2. G D Birkhoff and D Lewis. Chromatic polynomials. *Transactions of the American Mathematical Society*, 60 (3):355–451, 1946.
3. K M Koh, F M Dong, and K L Teo. Chromatic polynomials and chromaticity of graphs. *World Scientific, Singapore*, 23–215, 2005.
4. R C Read. An introduction to chromatic polynomials. *Combin. Theory.*, 4 (1):52–71, 1968.

5. W T Tutte. on chromatic polynomials and the golden ratio. *Journal of Combinatorial Theory*, 9 (3):289–296, 1970.
6. W T Tutte. Chromatic sums for planar triangulations. *Canadian Journal of Mathematics*, 26 (4):893–907, 1974.
7. H Whitney. on the coloring of graphs. *Annals of Mathematics*, 33 (4):688–717, 1932.
8. J Xu. Recursive formula for calculating the chromatic polynomial of a graph by vertex deletion. *Acta Mathematica Scientia.*, 24 (4):577–582, 2004.
9. J Xu. Theory on the structure and coloring of maximal planar graphs(1): Recursion formulae of chromatic polynomial and four-color conjecture. *Journal of Electronics and Information Technology*, 38 (4):33–40, 2016.
10. J Xu and Z Liu. The chromatic polynomial between graph and its complement. *Graph and Combinatorics.*, 11 (4):337–345, 1995.
11. A A Zykov. on some properties of linear complexes. *Matematicheskii Sbornik*, 24 (66): 163–168, 1949.

Open Access This chapter is licensed under the terms of the Creative Commons Attribution 4.0 International License (http://creativecommons.org/licenses/by/4.0/), which permits use, sharing, adaptation, distribution and reproduction in any medium or format, as long as you give appropriate credit to the original author(s) and the source, provide a link to the Creative Commons license and indicate if changes were made.

The images or other third party material in this chapter are included in the chapter's Creative Commons license, unless indicated otherwise in a credit line to the material. If material is not included in the chapter's Creative Commons license and your intended use is not permitted by statutory regulation or exceeds the permitted use, you will need to obtain permission directly from the copyright holder.

Chapter 8
Purely Tree-Colorable and Uniquely 4-Colorable Maximal Planar Graph Conjectures

Abstract A maximal planar graph is called the recursive maximal planar graph if it can be obtained from K_4 by embedding a 3-degree vertex in some triangular face continuously. The uniquely 4-colorable maximal planar graph conjecture states that a planar graph is uniquely 4-colorable if and only if it is a recursive maximal planar graph. This conjecture, which has 46 years of history, is a very influential conjecture in graph coloring theory after the Four-Color Conjecture. In this chapter, the structures and properties of dumbbell maximal planar graphs and recursive maximal planar graphs are studied, and an idea of proving the uniquely 4-colorable maximal planar graph conjecture is proposed based on the extending-contracting operation proposed in Chap. 6 (Xu, J. Electron. Inf. Technol. 38(6), 1328–1353 (2016)).

8.1 Introduction

Graph theory originated from the Königsberg seven bridges problem studied by Euler in 1736, and the electric network problem studied by Kirchhoff in 1847. In the last 70 years, graph theory was rapidly developed. To its reason, one is influenced by the development of the electronic computer; the other more important is the Four-Color Conjecture. Specifically, due to the Four-Color Conjecture, many areas of graph theory were created, such as topological graph theory, maximum independent set and maximum clique theory, vertex and edge covering theory, chromatic polynomial theory, Tutte-polynomial theory, factor theory and integer flow theory, especially the graph coloring theory and so on.

In the field of graph coloring, apart from the famous Four-Color Conjecture, researchers have proposed many conjectures, including the **uniquely 4-colorable maximal planar graph conjecture** discussed In this chapter. This conjecture was proposed by Greenwell and Kronk [18] in 1973, which is closely related to the Four-Color Conjecture, and has not been resolved yet.

The concept of uniquely colorable graphs was proposed by Gleason and Cartwright [15], and Cartwright and Harary [6] successively. Cartwright and Harary obtained some sufficient conditions for determining whether a labeled graph is uniquely colorable or not. Since then, many researches have been done in this field. For example, Harary, et al. [20] studied the connectivity and the number of edges of uniquely k-colorable graphs. Furthermore, many scholars studied on the problem that whether there exists a uniquely k-colorable graph without K_3 for $k \geq 3$. Nešetil [29, 30] studied the properties of critical-uniquely colorable graphs and proved that there exist uniquely k-colorable graphs without triangles. In 1974, Greenwell and Lovász [19] proved that there exist uniquely k-colorable graphs without short odd cycles; and in 1975, Müller [27] solved the general case of this problem by the method of construction (also see [28]), that is, for any integer $k \geq 3$ and t, there exists a uniquely k-colorable graph with girth greater than t. Müller [27, 28], Aksionov [2], Melnikov and Steinberg [25] investigated the edge-critical uniquely colorable graphs. Wang and Artzy [36] showed that for $k \geq 3$, if there exists a uniquely k-colorable graph without K_3, then the number of edges of the graph is greater than $k^2 + k - 1$. Osterweil [32] constructed a kind of uniquely 3-colorable graphs by the so-called 6-cliquerings. Moreover, he demonstrated how to use this technique to construct uniquely k-colorable graphs, $k > 3$. Bollobás and Sauer [4] proved that for all $k \geq 2$ and $g \geq 3$, there exists a uniquely k-colorable graph with girth at least g. Also, they proved that for any $k \geq 3$ and n, there always exists a critical-uniquely k-colorable graph with at least n vertices. Dmitriev [10] generalized the result of BollobáS [3]. Xu [41] proved that if G is a uniquely k-colorable graph with order n and size m, then $m \geq (k-1)n - (1/2)k(k-1)$, and showed this bound is the best possible. Furthermore, he conjecture that if G is a uniquely k-colorable graph with order n and size $(k-1)n - (1/2)k(k-1)$, then G contains K_k. At the same time, Chao and Chen [7] showed that for any integer $n \geq 12$, there exists a uniquely 3-colorable graph of order n without triangles. Akbari, et al. [26] proved that there exists a K_3-free uniquely 3-colorable graph G with 24 vertices and $SH(G) = 45$ edges, where $SH(G) = (k-1)n - (1/2)k(k-1)$. This result disproved Xu's conjecture [41].

In terms of the uniquely edge-colorable graphs, Greenwell and Kronk [18] studied this problem first in 1973. They proposed a conjecture as follows.

Conjecture 8.1 If G is a uniquely 3-edge-colorable cubic graph, then G is a planar graph that contains a triangle.

In 1975, Fiorini [11] independently studied the problem of uniquely edge-colorable graphs, and obtained some similar results to that of Greenwell and Kronk [18]. After that, many scholars involved in this field, such as Thomason [34, 35], Fiorini and Wilson [12], Zhang [42], Goldwasser and Zhang [16, 17], and Kriessell [21].

In 1977, Fiorini and Wilson [12], and Fisk [13] independently proposed the following conjecture, respectively.

Conjecture 8.2 Any uniquely 3-edge-colorable cubic planar graph with at least 4 vertices contains a triangle.

This conjecture was proposed based on Conjecture 8.1. Fowler [14] also investigated this conjecture in detail. However, it is still open.

8.2 Tree-Colorings and Cycle-Colorings

As for uniquely colorable planar graphs, Chartrand and Geller [8] completed many important works in 1969. They proved that any uniquely 3-colorable planar graph of order $n \geq 4$ contains at least two triangles, **any uniquely 4-colorable planar graph is a maximal planar graph**, and there is no uniquely 5-colorable planar graph.

What is the necessary and sufficient condition for a planar graph to be uniquely 3-colorable? This problem is still open. Many scholars studied the properties of uniquely 3-colorable planar graphs. In 1977, Aksionov [1] proved that uniquely 3-colorable planar graphs with order ≥ 6 contain at least 3 triangles, also described the structure of those graphs contain exactly 3 triangles. In the same year, Melnikov and Steinberg [25] investigated the edge-critical uniquely 3-colorable planar graphs and proposed the following problem: find the exact upper bound $size(n)$ of edges in edge-critical uniquely 3-colorable planar graphs with order n; in 2013, Matsumoto [24] proved $size(n) \leq 8/3n - 17/3$ which was improved in [22, 23] by showing that $size(n) \leq 5/2n - 6$, $n \geq 6$, and there exist adjacent triangles in uniquely 3-colorable planar graphs containing at most 4 triangles.

Naturally, a problem will be raised that which maximal planar graphs are uniquely 4-colorable? In other words, what is the characteristic of uniquely 4-colorable planar graphs? Obviously, this problem is the key to study uniquely 4-colorable planar graphs. So far, many scholars have been investigating this problem [9, 33, 40, 42].

Indeed, Fisk [13] proposed a conjecture equivalent to Conjecture 8.2.

Conjecture 8.3 A planar graph G is uniquely 4-colorable if and only if G is a recursive maximal planar graph.

It can be checked that Conjectures 8.2 and 8.3 are equivalent, and both of them are the special case of Conjecture 8.1. In 1998, Bohme, et al. [33] proved that the minimum counterexample of this conjecture is 5-connected. We call Conjecture 8.3 the **uniquely 4-colorable maximal planar graph conjecture**. This conjecture was also called **GK**-conjecture, due to the fact that it was indicated in Conjecture 8.1 (proposed by Greenwell and Kronk) [18]. GK-conjecture turn out to be very important in graph coloring theory. Clearly, studying properties and structures will help to resolve the GK-conjecture.

In our study of GK-conjecture, we observe a class of maximal planar graphs, called (2,2)-recursive maximal planar graphs, which plays an important role in proving the GK-conjecture [38]. In Sect. 8.4, the properties of recursive maximal planar graphs will be argued explicitly, especially for the (2,2)-recursive maximal planar graphs.

8.2 Tree-Colorings and Cycle-Colorings

Let G be a 4-colorable maximal planar graph, $C(4) = \{1, 2, 3, 4\}$ be the color set, and $f \in C_4^0(G)$. If there exists a cycle $C_{2m} = v_1 v_2 \ldots v_{2m}$ in G such that

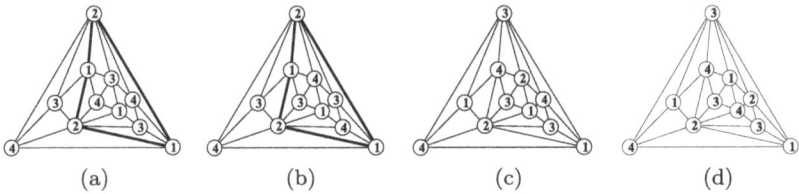

Fig. 8.1 All 4-colorings of a maximal planar graph with order 11. (**a**) f_1: 12-cycle. (**b**) f_2: 12-cycle. (**c**) f_3: tree-coloring. (**d**) f_4: tree-coloring

$|\{f(v_1), f(v_2), \ldots, f(v_{2m})\}| = 2$, then we refer to C_{2m} as a **bicolored cycle** of f, or say f contains a **bicolored cycle**, and we call f a **cycle-coloring** of G and G a **cycle-colorable** graph. If the colors on C_{2m} are i and t, then we call C_{2m} an it-**cycle**. On the other hand, if $f \in C_4^0(G)$ contains no bicolored cycle, then f is called a **tree-coloring** of G and G is called **tree-colorable**. For the 4-colorings of the graph shown in Fig. 8.1, f_1, f_2 are cycle-colorings and f_3, f_4 are tree-colorings. All maximal planar graphs can be divided into three categories according to the cycle-colorings and tree-colorings: **pure tree-coloring graphs**, namely such graphs have only tree-colorings; **pure cycle-coloring graphs**, namely these graphs have only cycle-colorings; and **impure coloring graphs** that have both cycle-colorings and tree-colorings. For example, the graph shown in Fig. 8.1 belongs to impure coloring graphs.

A maximal planar graph G is cycle-colorable if there exists a $f \in C_4^0(G)$ such that f is a cycle- coloring, and tree-colorable if there exists a $f \in C_4^0(G)$ such that f is a tree coloring. A statistics on the number of 4-colorings of non-separable maximal planar graphs with order $n(7 \leq n \leq 11)$ and minimum degree ≥ 4 shows that the proportion of tree-colorings is about 2%, that is to say the proportion of cycle-colorings is about 98%. At present, there are few studies on the structure and properties of the tree-colorable maximal planar graphs. In [43], Zhu, et al. proved that every tree-colorable maximal planar graph G with minimum degree ≥ 4 contains at least 4 vertices of odd degree, and when G contains exactly 4 vertices of odd degree, the induced subgraph of the 4 vertices contains no triangles and is not the claw.

There are totally 54 maximal planar graphs with order $n(7 \leq n \leq 11)$ and minimum degree ≥ 4, in which only one is purely tree-colorable graph (see Fig. 8.4a), called the **9-dumbbell maximal planar graph** (or **basic dumbbell maximal planar graph**) [39], denoted by J^9. Notation and terminology not defined here follow [5, 37].

8.3 Purely Tree-Colorable Maximal Planar

In Sect. 8.2, maximal planar graphs are classified into three categories: purely tree-colorable graphs, purely cycle-colorable graphs, and impure colorable graphs. It is difficult to give a necessary and sufficient condition to determine which class a maximal planar graph belongs to, even to describe the structure of these three kinds of maximal planar graphs. In fact, if we can characterize the purely tree-colorable graphs, then the uniquely 4-colorable maximal planar graph conjecture is proved naturally. So, we will study these three kinds of maximal planar graphs in the following series of papers, and mainly consider the purely tree-colorable graphs in this section.

8.3.1 Purely Tree-Colorable Maximal Planar Graph Conjecture with Minimum Degree 5

In [39], it has been found that the icosahedron is a purely tree-colorable maximal planar graph with minimum degree 5, which has ten different tree-colorings shown in Fig. 8.2.

Let G be a planar graph. If there exists a $\sigma \in Aut(G)$ such that $\sigma(u) = v$ for any two vertices $u, v \in V(G)$, then G is said to be **vertex transitive**. Obviously, the icosahedron is **vertex transitive**. Therefore, the domino configuration contained in the icosahedron with 2 inner vertices must be unique. We can choose the bold domino configuration of the first graph in Fig. 8.2 as a representative.

Conjecture 8.4 Let G be a maximal planar graph with minimal degree 5. Then G is purely tree-colorable if and only if G is the icosahedron.

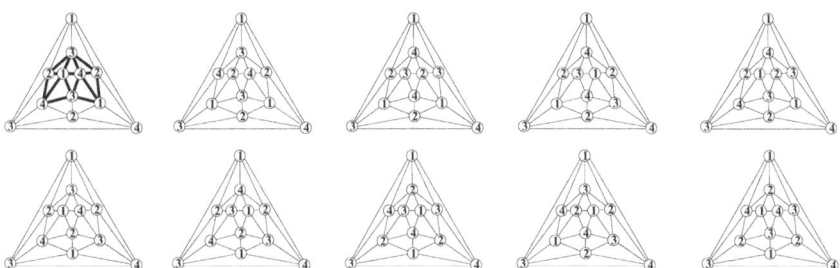

Fig. 8.2 The icosahedron and its all ten 4-colorings

8.3.2 Dumbbell-Maximal Planar Graphs

8.3.2.1 Dumbbell Transformation

The object graph of dumbbell transformation is a closed dumbbell, namely a 4-wheel, shown in Fig. 8.3. The so called **dumbbell transformation** is to replace the closed dumbbell by the fourth graph shown in Fig. 8.3a or b. The specific steps are as follows:

Step 1 Split the wheel center v_2 into two vertices v_2 and v'_2, vertically or horizontally, shown in the second graph of Fig. 8.3a or b, respectively.

Step 2 Extend to the third graph of Fig. 8.3a or b.

Step 3 Add a 2-length path in the 6-cycle $v_1 v_3 v'_2 v_5 v_4 v_2 v_1$, vertically or horizontally, and then join edges between the 2-length path and 6-cycle to form the configuration shown in the fourth graph of Fig. 8.3a or b.

Moreover, the inverse operation of dumbbell transformation is called **dumbbell contracting-transformation**, and the fourth graph in Fig. 8.3a is called the **object graph of dumbbell contracting-transformation**. In Fact, the dumbbell transformation is equivalent to the extending 334-wheel operation, as shown in Fig. 8.3c. For more information on dumbbell transformation, see Chap. 6.

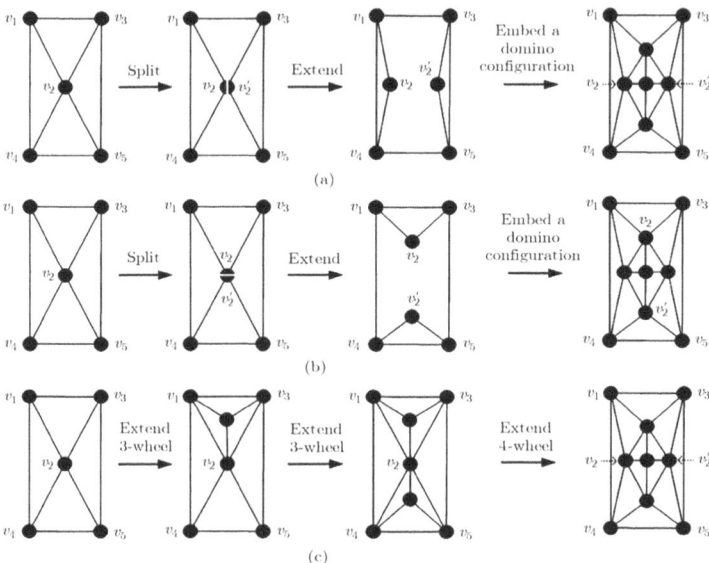

Fig. 8.3 The object graph and the process of dumbbell transformation. (**a**) Split vertically. (**b**) Split horizontally. (**c**) Extending 334-wheel operation

8.3.2.2 Construction of Dumbbell-Maximal Planar Graphs

Let J^{4k+1} be a maximal planar graph with order $4k + 1$ and minimum degree 4, and contain a dumbbell contracting-transformation object subgraph. If the graph obtained by implementing the dumbbell contracting-transformation still contains such an object subgraph, then implement the dumbbell contracting-transformation again. Continue in this way, we call J^{4k+1} a **dumbbell-maximal planar graph** if the finally obtained graph is J^9. According to this definition, the graph obtained by implementing the dumbbell transformation from a dumbbell-maximal planar graph is also a dumbbell-maximal planar graph.

In the following, we describe the process of constructing a dumbbell-maximal planar graph of order $4k + 5$ from $J^{4k+1} (k \geq 2)$.

Step 1 Find all unidentical closed dumbbells in J^{4k+1} (that is, find all unidentical 4-wheels). Figure 8.4a–d are the dumbbell-maximal planar graphs with orders 9, 13, 17, and 17, respectively, which contain 1, 2, 2, and 2 unidentical 4-wheels, respectively and each of which contains three 4-wheels.

Step 2 Implement the dumbbell transformation on each unidentical 4-wheel in J^{4k+1}, by which one can obtain dumbbell-maximal planar graphs with order $4k + 5$. For example, J^{13} (as shown in Fig. 8.4b) is obtained by implementing the dumbbell transformation on the 4-wheel bolded in J^9 (as shown in Fig. 8.4a). It is easy to prove that there are two closed dumbbells in J^{13} which are identical. So, we obtain two dumbbell-maximal planar graphs with order 17 by implementing the dumbbell transformation, as shown in Fig. 8.4c, d, respectively.

8.3.2.3 Properties of Dumbbell-Maximal Planar Graphs

We further argue some properties of dumbbell maximal planar graphs in the following.

Theorem 8.1

(1) *Every dumbbell-maximal planar graph contains exactly* 3 *vertices of degree* 4;
(2) *every dumbbell-maximal planar graph has* $4k + 1$ *vertices, where* $k \geq 2$;

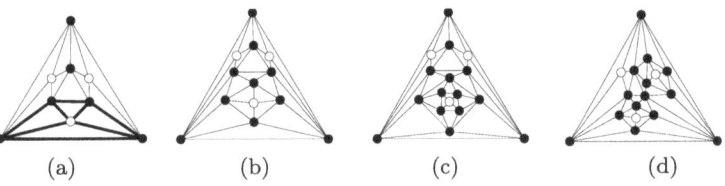

Fig. 8.4 Four dumbbell-maximal planar graphs with lower orders. (**a**) Order 9. (**b**) Order 13. (**c**) Order 17. (**d**) Order 17

(3) *every dumbbell-maximal planar graph is purely tree-colorable, and each dumbbell maximal planar graph with order $4k + 1$ has exactly 2^{k-1} different colorings.*

Proof (1) and (2) Note that J^9 has 3 identical vertices of degree 4. According to the definition of dumbbell transformation, there exist exactly 3 vertices of degree 4 in the dumbbell-maximal planar graph J^{13}, which is obtained from J^9 by a dumbbell transformation. Continue in this way, it is known that for any $k \geq 2$, J^{4k+1} contains exactly 3 vertices of degree 4 and each dumbbell-maximal planar graph has $4k + 1$ vertices.

(3) By induction. Obviously, the result holds if $k = 2$. The dumbbell-maximal planar graph of order 13 has totally 4 different colorings and each of these colorings is tree-coloring, shown in Fig. 8.5. So, the theorem holds.

Suppose that the result holds for $k \geq 3$, that is, J^{4k+1} is purely tree-colorable and has exactly 2^{k-1} different colorings. Now, we discuss the case of $k + 1$. Let $W_4 = v_2 - v_1 v_4 v_5 v_3$ be a 4-wheel of J^{4k+1} and v_2 be the center of the wheel, as shown in Fig. 8.6b. Implement the dumbbell transformation on dumbbell $X_1 = \Delta v_1 v_2 v_3 \cup \Delta v_2 v_4 v_5$ of W_4 (shown in Fig. 8.6a, c). Suppose that the obtained graph $\zeta_{334}^+(J^{4k+1})$ contains a bicolored cycle, then there must exist a $f \in C_4^0(\zeta_{334}^+(J^{4k+1}))$ such that f contains a bicolored cycle. So, there are two cases: one is $f(v_2') = f(v_2)$, shown in Fig. 8.6a; the other is $f(x_1) = f(x_2)$, as shown in Fig. 8.6c. For both of the two cases, we can obtain J^{4k+1} by implementing the dumbbell contracting-transformation. Since the dumbbell contracting-transformation is indeed implementing contract 4-wheel operation one time and then contract 3-wheel two times, the natural coloring (based on f) of the obtained graph contain bicolored cycles. This contradicts the fact that J^{4k+1} is purely tree-colorable. So, $\zeta_{334}^+(J^{4k+1})$ is purely tree-colorable.

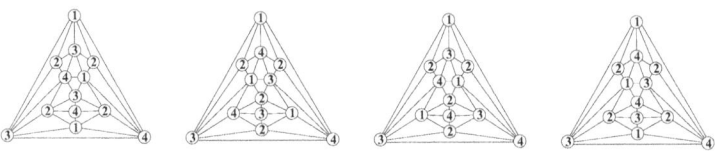

Fig. 8.5 All 4-colorings of the dumbbell maximal planar graph with order 13

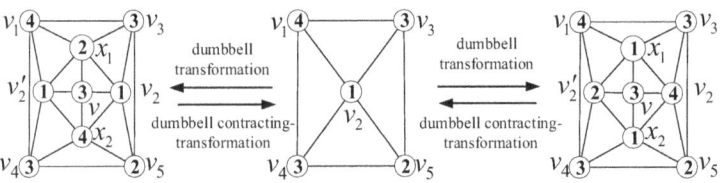

Fig. 8.6 Dumbbell transformation and dumbbell contracting-transformation based on colorings

8.4 Recursive Maximal Planar Graphs

Without loss of generality, we may suppose that each 4-wheel of J^{4k+1} is colored as Fig. 8.6b. Then, subject to the coloring of the external cycle, the dumbbell contracting-transformation object subgraph of $\zeta_{334}^{+}(J^{4k+1})$ has exactly 2 colorings, as shown in Fig. 8.6a, c, respectively. So, $\zeta_{334}^{+}(J^{4k+1})$ has exactly $2^{k-1} \times 2 = 2^k$ different colorings. The proof is completed. ∎

8.3.2.4 Enumeration

J^9 is the unique dumbbell maximal planar graph with order 9. Since the three 4-wheels in J^9 are identical, the dumbbell maximal planar graph with order 13 is also unique. Recall that two closed dumbbells in J^{13} are identical. So, there are two distinct dumbbell-maximal planar graphs with order 17, as shown in Fig. 8.4c, d. More generally, we have:

Theorem 8.2 *Let t_k denote the number of dumbbell maximal planar graphs with order $4k + 9$, where $k \geq 0$. Then*

$$t_k = \frac{(k+3)^2}{12} - \frac{7}{72} + \frac{(-1)^k}{8} + \frac{2}{9} \cos \frac{2k\pi}{3}$$

The proof of Theorem 8.2 can be found in [39].

8.4 Recursive Maximal Planar Graphs

The so called **recursive maximal planar graph** (abbreviated RMPG) is obtained from K_4 by embedding a 3-degree vertex in some triangular face repeatedly, where embedding a 3-degree vertex in a triangular is to add a vertex on the face of this triangular, and then connect this vertex to the three vertices of the triangular. In this chapter, Λ denotes the set consisting of all RMPGs and Λ_n the set of graphs in Λ with order n. Let $\gamma_n = |\Lambda_n|$. Obviously, $\gamma_n = 1$ for $n = 4, 5, 6$, and the corresponding RMPGs are shown in Fig. 8.7.

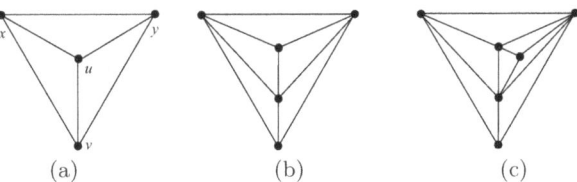

Fig. 8.7 RMPGs with order 4, 5, and 6

8.4.1 Basic Properties

Theorem 8.3 *Let G be an RMPG with order n. Then G has at least two vertices of degree 3. When $n \geq 5$, any two vertices of degree 3 are not adjacent to each other.*

Proof By induction on the number n of vertices. When $n = 4, 5, 6$, $\gamma_4 = \gamma_5 = \gamma_6 = 1$, and the corresponding graphs are shown in Fig. 8.7. So the result is true obviously.

Assume that the theorem holds when $n \geq 6$. That is, every RMPG G of order n contains at least two 3-vertices and all of the 3-vertices are not adjacent to each other.

A graph $G \in \Lambda_{n+1}$ is constructed by embedding a 3-vertex v in any triangular face of an RMPG with n vertices, assuming $N_G(v) = \{v_1, v_2, v_3\}$. By induction, there are at least two 3-degree vertices, and all the 3-vertices are not adjacent to each other in $G - v$. For $G - v$, if 3-vertices are included in $\{v_1, v_2, v_3\}$, then one exists at most, saying v_1. Obviously, there is at least another 3-vertex except for v_1 in $G - v$, and all those 3-vertices are not adjacent to each other. Since v is a 3-vertex of G and it is not adjacent to any other vertices except for $\{v_1, v_2, v_3\}$, there are also at least two 3-vertices in G and all of those 3-vertices are not adjacent to each other. Thus, the conclusion holds. If $\{v_1, v_2, v_3\}$ contains no 3-vertices in $G - v$, then the conclusion holds by the same way above. The theorem follows by the principle of induction. ∎

Theorem 8.4

(1) *There exists no maximal planar graph having exactly two adjacent 3-vertices;*
(2) *there exists no maximal planar graph with exactly three 3-vertices adjacent to each other.*

Proof

(1) By way of contradiction. Assume that G is a maximal planar graph with two adjacent vertices $u, v \in V(G)$, satisfying $d(u) = d(v) = 3$. Let $N(u) = \{v, x, y\}$. Notice that G is a maximal planar graph and u must be in a triangular face which is incident with vertices $v, x,$ and y. In other words, v is adjacent to x and y. These four vertices can form a subgraph K_4, as shown in Fig. 8.7a. Since G is a maximal planar graph, if there exists another vertex of G, then it can form a triangle with u or v. It contradicts $d(u) = d(v) = 3$; otherwise, if there exists no other vertices, then G is isomorphism to K_4, which has four 3-vertices. Therefore, there exists no maximal planar graph with two adjacent vertices of 3-degree exactly.
(2) can be proved with a similar line of thought.

∎

Theorem 8.5 *If G is a maximal planar graph with only one 3-vertex, then a graph without any 3-vertex can be obtained from G by deleting 3-vertices, repeatedly.*

8.4 Recursive Maximal Planar Graphs

Proof Let v be the unique 3-vertex in G, and $N_G(v) = \{u_1, u_2, u_3\}$. Thus, these three vertices can form a triangle. Let $G_1 = G - v$. Obviously, G_1 is a maximal planar graph. There exist four possible cases in G_1 as follows:

(1) $\delta(G_1) \geq 4$;
(2) There exists only one 3-vertex;
(3) There exactly exist two 3-vertices;
(4) There exactly exist three 3-vertices.

Case (1) is obvious, and by Theorem 8.4 Cases (3) and (4) do not exist. So, we sufficiently consider the Case (2). In this case, there exists only one 3-vertex in subgraph G_1, denoted by u_1. Let $G_2 = G_1 - u_1$. Analogous to the method mentioned above, if $\delta(G_2) \geq 4$, then the result holds; otherwise, G_2 must contain a 3-vertex. In this way, we infer that $\delta(G_m) \geq 4$ within finite m steps; if not, $G_m \cong K_4$ when G_m contains only four vertices. This means that the graph G is an RMPG. But there is only one 3-vertex in G, which contradicts Theorem 8.3. ∎

Theorem 8.6 *Let G be an RMPG with order ≥ 5 and v be a 3-vertex in G. Then $G - v$ is still an RMPG.*

Proof Let G be the RMPG obtained from $K_3 = v_1 v_2 v_3$ by adding 3-degree vertices $v_4, v_5, \ldots, v_n$ successively. If $v \in \{v_4, v_5, \ldots, v_n\}$, then $G - v$ is an RMPG when $v = v_n$; when $v = v_i$, $4 \leq i \leq n - 1$, delete 3-degree vertices $v_n, v_{n-1}, \ldots, v_{i+1}$ successively in $G - v$, the resulting graph denoted by G'. It is easy to prove that G' can be obtained from G by deleting 3-vertices $v_n, v_{n-1}, \ldots, v_{i+1}, v_i$ successively, and G' is an RMPG. So, $G - v$ is still an RMPG. If $v \in \{v_1, v_2, v_3\}$, say $v = v_1$, then $G - v$ is an RMPG obtained from the triangle $\triangle v_2 v_3 v_4$ by adding 3-vertices $v_5, v_6, \ldots, v_n$ successively. ∎

8.4.2 (2,2)-Recursive Maximal Planar Graphs

In this subsection, we describe a special class of RMPGs, called (2, 2)-RMPGs. An RMPG is called a (2, 2)-**RMPG** if it contains only two 3-vertices, and the distance between them is 2. It is easy to check that there exists only one (2,2)-RMPG with orders 5 and 6, as shown in Fig. 8.8a, b, respectively.

Fig. 8.8 (2,2)-RMPGs with orders 5 and 6. (**a**) A (2,2)-RMPG of order 5. (**b**) A (2,2)-RMPG of order 6

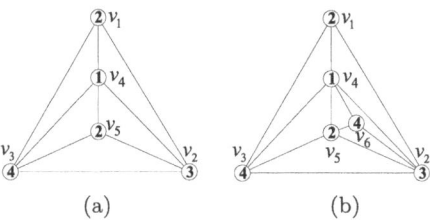

Fig. 8.9 The basic frame diagram of the color-coordinate system

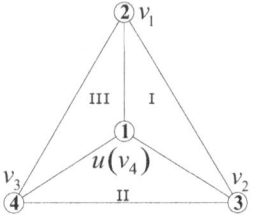

To study the structure of (2, 2)-RMPGs explicitly, we divide the three inner faces of the complete graph K_4 into three regions, and label its vertices correspondingly. In Fig. 8.9, the triangle incident with v_1, v_2, v_3 is called the **outside triangle**, and the vertex u is called the **central vertex**. Here, the vertices v_1, v_2, v_3, v_4 are colored with color 2, color 3, color 4, and color 1, respectively. The four vertices and their corresponding colorings are called the **basic axes** in the **color-coordinate system** of a (2, 2)-RMPG. Four color axes are u(color 1), v_1(color 2), v_2(color 3), v_3(color 4). Obviously, there exists no (2, 2)-RMPG with order 4; and there is only one (2, 2)-RMPG with 5 vertices up to isomorphism, which can be obtained by embedding a 3-degree vertex in the region I, II or III of the graph K_4 (as shown in Fig. 8.9). Without loss of generality, we suppose that new vertices are only added in the region II. Thus, the vertex is colored by color 2 (Fig. 8.8a); the non-isomorphic (2, 2)-RMPGs with order 6 can be obtained by embedding a 3-vertex in any region of the (2, 2)-RMPG with order 5. It is easy to prove that any pair of graphs of order 6, obtained by embedding a new vertex in any face of the (2, 2)-RMPG of order 5, are isomorphic to each other. Thus, there is only one (2, 2)-RMPGs with order 6. In general, we make an **agreement** that the 6th vertex is embedded in the face composed of the vertices v_2, v_4, v_5 (i.e. the sub-region I of the region II), which is colored by color 4 (Fig. 8.8b). Furthermore, for (2, 2)-RMPGs with higher orders, we restrict that new vertices are only added in the regions I and II, but not in the region III.

Based on the above agreement, we classify (2, 2)-RMPGs according to the following two methods.

The **first** is based on the region where the 3-vertices are embedded: (1) (2, 2)-RMPGs which are obtained by successively embedding 3-degree vertices only in the region II, such graphs are shown in Fig. 8.10; (2) (2, 2)-RMPGs are obtained by successively and randomly embedding 3-vertices in the regions I and II, as shown in Fig. 8.11. For maximal planar graphs, we have a straightforward fact as follows.

Proposition 8.1 ([31]) *Any face in a maximal planar graph can become the infinite outside face.*

By Proposition 8.1, for the (2, 2)-RMPGs which are obtained by embedding 3-vertices randomly in the regions I and II, we can transform any 3-vertex in the regions I or II to the outside triangular face and then the (2, 2)-RMPGs belong also to first classification, i.e., the class of (2, 2)-RMPGs obtained by successively

8.4 Recursive Maximal Planar Graphs

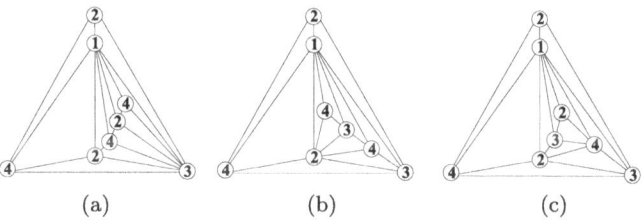

Fig. 8.10 The (2,2)-RMPGs obtained by embedding 3-degree vertices only in the region II. (**a**) The adjacent type. (**b**) The non-adjacent type. (**c**) The non-adjacent type

Fig. 8.11 The (2,2)-RMPGs obtained by embedding 3-vertices in the regions I and II, randomly

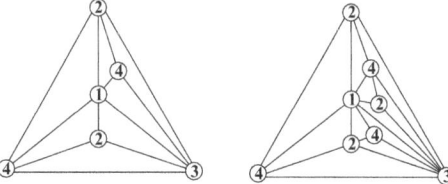

embedding 3-degree vertices only in the regionII. Therefore, we only consider this kind of graphs in the following.

The **second** method is based on whether or not there exists a common edge between the two triangular faces of two 3-vertices. It is called the **adjacent type** if there is a common edge; otherwise, the **non-adjacent type**. As shown in Fig. 8.10, the first graph belongs to the adjacent type, while the last two graphs belong to the non-adjacent type.

In Fig. 8.8a, the (2, 2)-RMPG with order 5 is a **double-center wheel**, and the degree of vertices in the neighbor of each center is 4, where a **double-center wheel** is a specific maximal planar graph constructed by the join of a cycle and two single vertices. When the order of a (2, 2)-RMPG is not less than 6, we have the following results.

Theorem 8.7

(1) *Let G be a $(2, 2)$-RMPG with order $n(\geq 6)$. Then for each 3-vertex v in G, there only exists one vertex with order 4 in $N(v)$.*

(2) *Every $(2, 2)$-RMPG G of non-adjacent type with order $n(\geq 7)$ has only one $(n-1)$-vertex, and it is called the **central vertex** of the graph G, denoted by u. Furthermore, in any partitions of color class in G, only the central vertex is colored with 1.*

(3) *For the $(2, 2)$-RMPGs of adjacent type obtained by embedding the 3-vertices only in the region II, only its central vertex is colored with color 1 and also only its color axis v_2 is colored with color 3.*

Proof (1) By induction. There is only one maximal planar graph of order 5 (shown in Fig. 8.8a), which is a double-center wheel, so all triangular faces of the this graph are equivalent. Therefore, up to isomorphism, there exists only one RMPG with order 6, also a (2, 2)-RMPG (shown in Fig. 8.8b). Thus, the theorem holds when $n = 6$.

Assume that the theorem holds when $n \geq 6$. Consider a (2, 2)-RMPG G of order $n + 1$. Suppose that v is a 3-vertex in G. Then there are two cases as follows:

Case 1 two or three vertices of 4-degree are included in $N(v)$. Then, $G - v$ is also an RMPG with order at least 6 which contains two or three 3-vertices adjacent to each other, which contradicts with Theorem 8.3.

Case 2 There exists no 4-vertex in $N(v)$. Then, $G - v$ is also an RMPG with order at least 6 which contains only one 3-vertex, which contradicts with Theorem 8.3.

In conclusion, we have proved that only one 4-vertex is contained in $N(v)$.

(2) and (3) can be proved by the process of gradually constructing (2, 2)-RMPGs, and the proof is completed. ∎

Corollary 8.1 *Let G be a (2, 2)-RMPG with order at least 6. Then for any 3-vertex v in G, $G - v$ is a (2, 2)-RMPG.*

Theorem 8.8 *Let η_n denote the number of the non-isomorphic(2, 2)-RMPG with order $n(\geq 6)$. Then, $\eta_n \leq 2^{n-6}$. In particular, $\eta_6 = 1$, $\eta_7 = 2$, $\eta_8 = 3$, $\eta_9 = 6$.*

Proof Any (2, 2)-RMPG can be obtained by embedding 3-vertices in the region II from the (2, 2)-RMPG with order 6. When embedding the $(i + 1)$-th vertex in (2, 2)-RMPG with order i, $6 \leq i \leq n - 1$, there are only 2 triangles which can be chosen for the non-adjacent type and 3 triangles for the adjacent type. It is easy to prove that the graphs obtained by embedding 3-vertices in the two faces incident with the 4-vertex are isomorphic. Therefore, $\eta_n \leq 2^{n-6}$. The (2, 2)-RMPGs with orders 7, 8, and 9 are shown in Fig. 8.12, respectively. This completes the proof. ∎

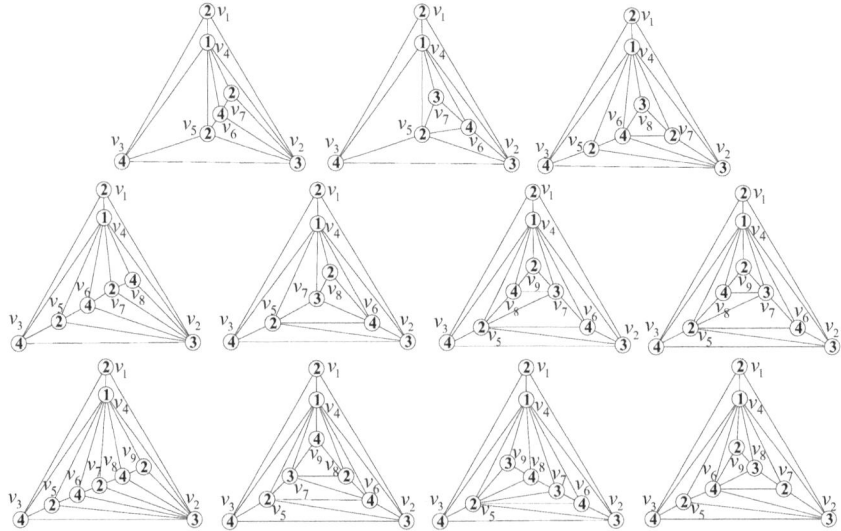

Fig. 8.12 All of the (2,2)-RMPGs with orders 7, 8, 9

8.4.3 The Colorings of Extending 4-Wheel Operation Graphs

Without loss of generality, we may assume that the (2, 2)-RMPGs are obtained by embedding 3-vertices only in the region II in the following. Thus, a (2, 2)-RMPG G can be uniquely represented by its color sequence.

Let $V(G) = \{v_1, v_2, v_3, v_4 = u, v_5, \ldots, v_n\}$, where vertex $v_1 = x$ indicates the first fixed 3-vertex, vertex $v_n = y$ indicates the second 3-vertex; the vertices $v_1 = x, v_2, v_3$ and $v_4 = u$ indicate the 1st, 2nd, 3rd, 4th color axis, respectively; the vertex $v_4 = u$ is the central vertex; the vertex v_{n-1} denotes the 3-vertex of the subgraph $G_{n-1} = G - v_n$; the vertex v_{n-2} denotes the 3-degree vertex of the subgraph $G_{n-2} = G_{n-1} - v_{n-1}$; and the rest can be deduced in the same way. The sequence $c_1 c_2 \ldots c_n$ is used to indicate the corresponding color sequence of the vertex sequence $v_1, v_2, \ldots, v_n$, where c_i is the color of v_i in the (2, 2)-RMPG G and $c_i \in \{1, 2, 3, 4\}$.

According to the definition of (2, 2)-RMPGs, this representation also determines the structure of a graph. This structure starts from K_4 (shown in Fig. 8.9), and selects a triangular face to embed vertices according to the color of each vertex.

For example, for the color sequence $c_1 c_2 c_3 c_4 c_5 c_6 c_7 c_8 c_9 = 234124323$, its corresponding (2, 2)-RMPG is the third graph of row 3 in Fig. 8.12.

Regarding the color sequence of a (2, 2)-RMPG, we have the following theorem.

Theorem 8.9 *Let $c_1 c_2 \ldots c_n$ be the color sequence of a (2, 2)-RMPG G. With the agreement "embedding 3-degree vertices only in the region II", the colors of the first six vertices in this sequence are determined, namely $c_1 = 2$, $c_2 = 3, c_3 = 4$, $c_4 = 1$, $c_5 = 2$, $c_6 = 4$; if G belongs to the adjacent type, then $c_7 = 2$; otherwise, $c_7 = 3$ or 2.*

Proof It follows from Fig. 8.9 that $c_1 = 2$, $c_2 = 3$, $c_3 = 4$ and $c_4 = 1$. Then, we have $c_5 = 2$ by Fig. 8.8a and $c_6 = 4$ by Fig. 8.8b. Again by Fig. 8.8b, $c_7 = 3$ or 2. The proof is completed. ∎

Now, we turn to the discussion of the vertex coloring problem of the induced graph from a (2, 2)-RMPG by extending 4-wheel operation. We know that any given (2, 2)-RMPG is uniquely 4-colorable and every vertex can also be colored determinately.

Let G be a (2, 2)-RMPG, f the unique 4-coloring of G, and xuy be a 3-path in G. Obviously, there exists a coloring f^* of the graph $\zeta_4^+(G)$ which is induced from G by extending 4-wheel operation on the path xuy, and

$$f^*(z) = \begin{cases} f(u), & z = u', \text{ or } u \\ \{1, 2, 3, 4\} \setminus \{f(x), f(u), f(y)\}, & z = v \\ f(z), & otherwize \end{cases}$$

where v is the new added vertex of the 4-wheel. Namely, f^* is a 4-coloring of graph $\zeta_4^+(G)$. Vertices u and u' are assigned the same color under f^*, and the new added vertex v is assigned the color different from vertices x, u, y, while the colors of the rest vertices remain unchanged. We refer to f^* as the **natural 4-coloring** of $\zeta_4^+(G)$.

Naturally, one question is proposed that whether or not the graph $\zeta_4^+(G)$ obtained by extending 4-wheel operation is uniquely 4-colorable. Indeed, the answer is negative, that is, $|C_4^0(\zeta_4^+(G))| \geq 2$.

Theorem 8.10 *Let G be a $(2, 2)$-RMPG with order n, f be the unique 4-coloring of G, x, y be two 3-vertices and u be the central vertex of G. Then the graph $\zeta_4^+(G)$, obtained from G by extending 4-wheel operation on the path xuy, is not uniquely 4-colorable.*

Proof Obviously, the conclusion holds when $f(x) = f(y)$. So we only need to consider the case that $f(x) \neq f(y)$. Let $N(x) = \{u, x_1, x_2\}$, $f(u) = 1$, $f(x) = 2$, $f(x_1) = 3$, $f(x_2) = 4$. According to Theorem 8.7, only vertex u in G can be colored with coloring 1, so the vertex y should be colored with coloring 3 or 4. Without loss of generality, we may assume that $f(y) = f(x_1) = 3$. Since G is a $(2, 2)$-RMPG, it can be obtained from $K_4 = G[\{x, u, x_1, x_2\}]$ by adding $n - 4$ 3-vertices in turn, namely $v_1, v_2, \ldots, v_{n-4}$. Let w be the vertex adjacent to x_1 and with the largest subscript in $v_1, v_2, \ldots, v_{n-4}$, then $f(w) = 2$ or 4.

In $\zeta_4^+(G)$, let v and u' be the new added vertices, where v is the center of the 4-wheel obtained. $N(v) = \{x, y, u, u'\}$, where u is adjacent to x_1 and u' is adjacent to x_2. By the definition of natural coloring, $f^*(w) = f(w) = 2$ or 4.

If $f^*(w) = 2$, then remove the color of vertices x, x_1, v and exchange the colors of the 14-component (namely, some component of the graph induced by all vertices colored 1 and 4) containing u. Then, color the vertices x, x_1, and v with 3,1, and 2, respectively. Obviously, we obtain a 4-coloring of $\zeta_4^+(G)$ which is different from f^*. If $f^*(w) = 4$, then remove the color of vertices x, x_1 and exchange the colors of the 12-component containing u. Then, color the vertices x and x_1 with colors 3 and 1, respectively. Also, the obtained coloring is a 4-coloring of $\zeta_4^+(G)$ different from f^*. The proof is completed. ∎

Remark In Theorem 8.10, we showed that the graph $\zeta_4^+(G)$, obtained from a $(2, 2)$-RMPG G by extending a 4-wheel operation on the path xuy, is not uniquely 4-colorable, where x, y must be 3-vertices of G. When x, y are not 3-vertices, the graph $\zeta_4^+(G)$ may be uniquely 4-colorable.

8.5 An Idea to Prove the Uniquely 4-Colorable Maximal Planar Graph Conjecture

The uniquely 4-colorable maximal planar graph conjecture is still open. The object of this conjecture is the RMPG, so such kind of graphs should be studied extensively. In [20], we proposed the purely tree-colorable maximal planar graph conjecture, the verification of which can imply the uniquely 4-colorable maximal planar graph conjecture. For this, a class of maximal planar graphs, called dumbbell maximal planar graphs (see Sect. 8.3), was studied. Here we present an idea to prove the uniquely 4-colorable maximal planar graph conjecture, which in fact is an idea to prove the purely tree-colorable maximal planar graph conjecture.

Let G be a purely tree-colorable maximal planar graph with a 4-wheel W_4 and a 5-wheel W_5. We use τ_i, $i = 1, 2, 3$ and τ_1' to denote the four generating operators of the domino configuration(in [37]), and use $\tau_i(W_4)$ to denote the graph obtained by implementing τ_i operation on a 4-wheel W_4 of G. Other symbols can be defined similarly.

We now give an idea to prove the purely tree-colorable maximal planar graph conjecture. Specifically, we need to consider the following nine statements.

Case 1 If G is a purely tree-colorable maximal planar graph, then $\tau_1(W_4)$ is cycle-colorable.

Case 2 If G is a purely tree-colorable maximal planar graph, then $\tau_1(W_5)$ and $\tau_2(W_5)$ are cycle-colorable.

Case 3 If G is a purely tree-colorable maximal planar graph, then $\tau_2(W_5)$ is cycle-colorable.

Case 4 If G is a purely tree-colorable maximal planar graph, then $\tau_3(W_5)$ is cycle-colorable.

Case 5 If G is a purely tree-colorable maximal planar graph, then $\tau_1(\tau_1(W_4))$ is cycle-colorable.

Case 6 If G is a purely tree-colorable maximal planar graph, then $\tau_2(\tau_1(W_4))$ and $\tau_1(\tau_2(W_4))$ are cycle-colorable.

Case 7 If G is a purely tree-colorable maximal planar graph, then $\tau_1'(\tau_2(W_4))$ is cycle-colorable.

Case 8 If G is a purely tree-colorable maximal planar graph, then $\tau_1'(\tau_2(W_5))$ is cycle- colorable.

Case 9 If G is a purely tree-colorable maximal planar graph, then $\tau_2(\tau_2(W_4))$ is purely tree-colorable.

For more information, we refer the reader to Xu [37] (or Sect. 6.2.4, especially the Fig. 6.13). In addition, studies on this conjecture will be given in the later books of this series.

8.6 Conclusion and Prospection

In this chapter, we mainly introduced a famous conjecture in graph coloring theory, the uniquely 4-colorable maximal planar graph conjecture. Since any uniquely 4-colorable maximal planar graph is conjectured to be an RMPG, we fucus on the study of this kind of graphs.

In [39], we proposed the purely tree-colorable graphs conjecture, which states that a maximal planar graph is purely tree-colorable if and only if it is the icosahedron or a dumbbell maximal planar graph. Moreover, we proved that if this conjecture holds, then the uniquely 4-colorable maximal planar graph conjecture holds. So, we further studied the structures and properties of dumbbell maximal planar graphs.

Finally, we give an idea to prove the purely tree-colorable graphs conjecture. Specifically, suppose that G is purely tree-colorable. There are nine cases to prove the conjecture based on the extending-contracting operation and the result that any maximal planar graph with order ≥ 9 and minimum degree ≥ 4 has a father-graph or a grandfather-graph. Among the nine cases, eight cases are negative and only one is positive.

The work of this chapter lays a foundation for proving the purely tree-colorable graphs conjecture. In the later books of this series, we will give the extending-contracting operational system of 4-colored maximal planar graphs, simply as the colored extending-contracting operational system. On this basis, the purely tree-colorable graphs conjecture is expected to be solved.

References

1. V A Aksionov. On uniquely 3-colorable planar graphs. *Discrete Mathematics*, 20(3):209–216, 1977.
2. V A Aksionov. Chromatically connected vertices in planar graphs. *Diskret Analiz, Russian*, 31(31):5–16, 1977.
3. B Bollobas. Uniquely colorable graphs. *Journal of Combinatorial Theory, Series B*, 25(1):54–61, 1978.
4. B Bollobas and N W Sauer. Uniquely colourable graphs with large girth. *Canadian Journal of Mathematics*, 28(6):1340–1344, 1976.
5. J A Bond and U S R Murty. *Graph Theory*. Springer, 2008.
6. F D Cartwright and F Harary. On the coloring of signed graphs. *Elemente Der Mathematik*, 23(4):85–89, 1968.
7. C Chao and Z Chen. On uniquely 3-colorable graphs. *Discrete Mathmatics*, 112(1):21–27, 1993.
8. G Chartrand and D Geller. On uniquely colorable planar graphs. *Journal of Combinatorial Theory*, 6(3):271–278, 1969.
9. D P Dailey. Uniqueness of colorability and colorability of planar 4-regular graphs are np-complete. *Discrete Mathematics*, 30(3):289–293, 1980.
10. I G Dmitriev. Weakly cyclic graphs with integral chromatic spectra. *Metody Diskret Analiz*, 34(34):3–7, 1980.
11. S Fiorini. On the chromatic index of a graph, iii: Uniquely edge-colorable graphs. *Quarterly Journal Mathmatics*, 26(3):129–140, 1975.
12. S Fiorini and R J Wilson. Edge colouring of graphs. *Research Notes in Mathmatics*, 23(1):237–239, 1977.
13. S Fisk. Geometric coloring theory. *Advances in Mathematics*, 24(3):298–340, 1977.
14. T Fowler. *Unique coloring of planar graphs*. PhD thesis, Georgia Institute of Technology, 1998.
15. T C Gleason and F D Cartwright. A note on a matrix criterion for unique colorability of assigned graph. *Psychometrika*, 32(3):291–296, 1967.
16. J L Goldwasser and C Q Zhang. On the minimal counterexamples to a conjecture about unique edge-3-coloring. *Congressus Numerantium*, 113:143–152, 1996.
17. J L Goldwasser and C Q Zhang. Uniquely edge-colorable graphs and snarks. *Graphs and Combinatorics*, 16(3):257–267, 2000.

18. D Greenwell and H V Kronk. Uniquely line colorable graphs. *Canadian Mathematical Bulletin*, 16(4):525–529, 1973.
19. D Greenwell and L Lovasz. Applications of product coloring. *Acta Mathematica Academiae Scientiarum Hungaricae*, 25(3):335–340, 1974.
20. F Harary, S T Hedetniemi, and R W Robinson. Uniquely colorable graphs. *Journal of Combinatorial Theory*, 6(3):264–270, 1969.
21. M Kriesell. Contractible non-edges in 3-connected graphs. *Journal of Combinatorial Theory, Series B*, 74(2):192–201, 1988.
22. Z P Li, E Q Zhu, Z H Shao, and Jin Xu. A note on uniquely 3-colorable planar graphs. *International Journal of Computer Mathematics*, pages 1–8, 2016.
23. Z P Li, E Q Zhu, Z H Shao, and J Xu. Size of edge-critical uniquely 3-colorable planar graphs. *Discrete Mathematics*, 339(4):1242–1250, 2016.
24. N Matsumoto. The size of edge-critical uniquely 3-colorable planar graphs. *The Electronic Journal of Combinatorics*, 20(4):1823–1831, 2013.
25. L S Melnikov and R Steinberg. One counterexample for two conjectures on three coloring. *Discrete Mathematics*, 20(77):203–206, 1977.
26. V S Mirrokni S Akbari and B S Sadjad. k_r-free uniquely vertex colorable graphs with minimum possible edges. *Journal of Combinatorial Theory, Series B*, 82(2):316–318, 2001.
27. V Muller. On colorable critical and uniquely colorable critical graphs. *Recent Advances in Graph Theory*, pages 385–386, 1974.
28. V Muller. On coloring of graphs without short cycles. *Discrete Mathematics*, 26(2):165–176, 1979.
29. J Nešetřil. On critical uniquely colorable graphs. *Archiv Der Mathematik*, 23(1):210–213, 1972.
30. J Nešetřil. On uniquely colorable graphs without short cycles. *Casopis pro pěstování matematiky*, 98(2):122–125, 1973.
31. O Ore. *The four color problem*. Academic Press, New York, 1967.
32. L J Osterweil. Some classes of uniquely 3-colorable graphs. *Discrete Mathmatics*, 8(1):59–69, 1974.
33. M Stiebitz T Bohme and M Voigt. On uniquely 4-colorable planar graphs[ol], 1998.
34. A G Thomason. Hamiltonian cycles and uniquely edge colourable graphs. *Annals of Discrete Mathematics*, 3:259–268, 1978.
35. A G Thomason. Cubic graphs with three hamiltonian cycles are not always uniquely edge colorable. *Journal of Graph Theory*, 6(2):219–221, 1982.
36. C C Wang and E Artzy. Note on the uniquely colorable graphs. *Journal of Combinatorial Theory, Series B*, 15(2):204–206, 1973.
37. J Xu. Theory on the structure and coloring of maximal plnaar graphs (2) domino configurations and extending-contracting operations. *Journal of Electronics and Information Thchnology*, 38(6):1271–1327, 2016.
38. J Xu Theory on the structure and coloring of maximal planar graphs(3): Purely tree-colorable and uniquely 4-colorable maximal planar graph conjectures. *Journal of Electronics and Information Technology*, 38(6):1328–1353, 2016.
39. J Xu, Z P Li, and E Q Zhu. On purely tree-colorable planar graphs. *Information Processing Letters*, 116(8):532–536, 2016.
40. J Xu and X S Wei. Theorems of uniquely k-colorable graphs. *Journal of Shaanxi Normal University (Natural Science Edition)*, 23:59–62, 1995.
41. S J Xu. The size of uniquely colorable graphs. *Journal of Combinatorial Theory, Series B*, 50(2):319–320, 1990.
42. C Q Zhang. Hamiltonian weights and unique edge-3-colorings of cubic graphs. *Journal of Graph Theory*, 20(1):91–99, 1995.
43. E Q Zhu, Z P Li, Z H Shao, and Jin Xu. Acyclically 4-colorable triangulations. *Information Processing Letters*, 116(6):401–408, 2016.

Open Access This chapter is licensed under the terms of the Creative Commons Attribution 4.0 International License (http://creativecommons.org/licenses/by/4.0/), which permits use, sharing, adaptation, distribution and reproduction in any medium or format, as long as you give appropriate credit to the original author(s) and the source, provide a link to the Creative Commons license and indicate if changes were made.

The images or other third party material in this chapter are included in the chapter's Creative Commons license, unless indicated otherwise in a credit line to the material. If material is not included in the chapter's Creative Commons license and your intended use is not permitted by statutory regulation or exceeds the permitted use, you will need to obtain permission directly from the copyright holder.

Chapter 9
Kempe Change

Abstract The Kempe change is the essence of the Kempe's "proof" of the Four Color Conjecture (Kempe, Am. J. Math. **2**(3), 193–200 (1879)), by which a new 4-coloring of a maximal planar graph can be generated from a given 4-coloring. The fundamental reason why it fails to prove the Four Color Conjecture by using this technique is that there exist many maximal planar graphs G such that the set of all 4-colorings of G can not be generated by applying Kempe change from any given 4-colorings of G. Nevertheless, due to the NP-completeness of the vertex coloring of graphs, Kempe change has been a fundamental and most powerful tool in the study of theory, algorithm, and application of graph colorings since 1879. This chapter is devoted to the introduction of related theory on Kempe change, including Kempe equivalence of colorings, σ-characteristic graphs (which depicts the relation of all colorings), and non-Kempe graphs.

9.1 Definitions and Fundamental Properties

Here we follow the notations and terminology of Ref. [14]. Let G be a k-colorable graph, and f be a k-coloring of G. Recall that a **bichromatic induced subgraph** G_{ij}^f is subgraph of G induced by vertices with color i or j under f; each component of G_{ij}^f is called a ij-**component under f of G** or **bichromatic component under f of G** uniformity. A **Kempe change with respect to vertex coloring**, or **K-change** for short, is the operation of interchanging the colors of some bichromatic component of G. Given two coloring f, f', we say that they are **Kempe equivalent** (or **K-equivalent** for short) if each can be obtained from the other by a sequence of **K**-changes; otherwise, **non-K-equivalent**. The equivalence classes $F^f(G)$, consisting of colorings that are **K**-equivalent to f, is called the **Kempe classes on** f (or just **K-classes**). We use $\kappa(G, k)$ to denote the number of **K**-classes of G.

K-change, in essence, is an induced coloring operation. Under a k-coloring f of a graph G, a new k-coloring in $C_k^0 \setminus \{f\}$ may be derived by once or more **K**-changes.

For example, consider the graph in Fig. 9.1. Starting with the 4-colorings f_1 (Fig. 9.1a), one can obtain the 4-colorings f_2 (Fig. 9.1b) and f_3 (Fig. 9.1c), by

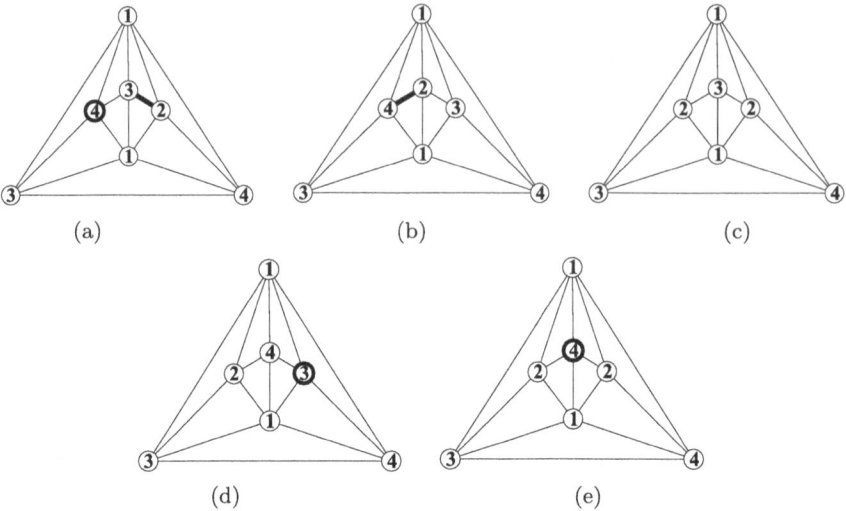

Fig. 9.1 All of the 4-colorings of the smallest maximal planar graph of minimum degree at least 4. (**a**) f_1. (**b**) f_2. (**c**) f_3. (**d**) f_4. (**e**) f_5

the **K**-change on 23-component (the bold edge in Fig. 9.1a) and on 24-component (the bold vertex in Fig. 9.1a), respectively; moreover, one can obtain the 4-coloring f_4 (Fig. 9.1d) by the **K**-change on 24-component (the bold edge in Fig. 9.1b), the 4-coloring f_5 (Fig. 9.1e) by the **K**-change on 23-component (the bold vertex in Fig. 9.1d), and the 4-coloring f_3 (Fig. 9.1c) by the **K**-change on 34-component (the bold vertex in Fig. 9.1e). Thus, all of the 4-colorings of G are induced from f_1.

Notice that **K**-change can not always produce a new coloring, up to color isomorphism. For example, there are 4-colorable graphs containing a 4-coloring f under which the six bichromatic induced subgraphs are connected, i.e., exactly six bichromatic components. Thus, the coloring obtained from f by **K**-change on each bichromatic component is still the coloring f.

Let G be a k-colorable graph and f a k-coloring of G. If there exists a **K**-change on some bichromatic component by which a new k-coloring of G in C_k^0, different from f, can be generated, then we call G is **K-changeable under** f.

Theorem 9.1 *Let G be a k-colorable graph and $f \in C_k^0(G)$. Then, G is not **K**-changeable under f if and only if G has $\frac{k(k-1)}{2}$ bichromatic component under f.*

Proof Suppose that G has $\frac{k(k-1)}{2}$ bichromatic component under f. Since f uses k colors, G has in total $\frac{k(k-1)}{2}$ bichromatic induced subgraphs. Therefore, each bichromatic induced subgraph is connected, which implies that the coloring obtained by **K**-change on some bichromatic component is still the f itself. Consequently, f is not **K**-changeable under f.

Conversely, if G is **K-changeable under** f, then it must be the case that each bichromatic induced subgraph under f is connected, and hence the result holds. ∎

9.1 Definitions and Fundamental Properties

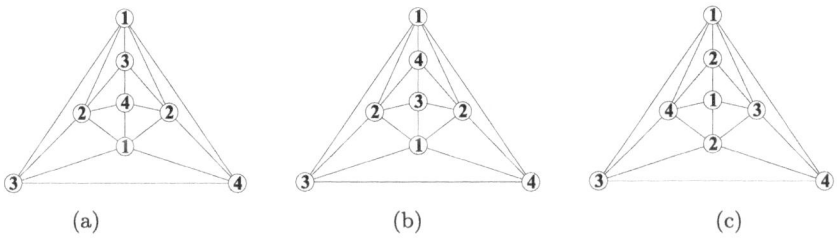

(a)   (b)   (c)

Fig. 9.2 All of the 4-colorings of a 4-colorable maximal planar graph of order 8. (**a**) f_1. (**b**) f_2. (**c**) f_3

Fig. 9.3 A 6-regular graph of order 8

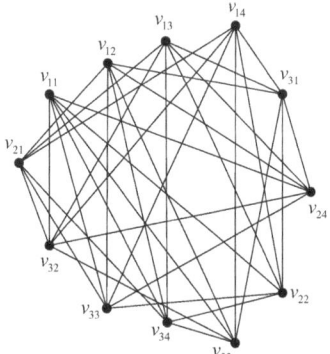

Although a graph G is **K**-changeable under some k-coloring f of G, it is also not necessary to generate all k-colorings of G by **K**-change, starting with f. Let G be a k-colorable graph. If any pair of distinct k-colorings of G is **K**-equivalent, then we call G a k-**Kempe graph**. For example, the graph shown in Fig. 9.2 is not 4-Kempe, since it has in total three 4-colorings f_1, f_2, and f_3 (Fig. 9.2a $\sim$ c) where f_1 and f_2 are **K**-equivalent but f_1 and f_3 are not **K**-equivalent. The set of 4-colorings of this graph consists of two **K**-classes, i.e., $\kappa(G, 4) = 2$.

Observe that for any k-colorable graph G, $\kappa(G, k)=1$ is not a sufficient condition for $\kappa(G, k+1)=1$. The following theorem show this, due to Mohar [17].

Theorem 9.2 *For any two integers ℓ, k such that $\ell \geq 3$ and $k > \ell$, there exists a k-chromatic graph G for which $\kappa(G, \ell) = 1$ and $\kappa(G, k) > 1$.*

Consider the graph G shown in Fig. 9.3; it is 6-regular and contains only one 3-coloring, say f, such that $f(v_{ij}) = i$ for $i = 1, 2, 3, j = 1, 2, 3, 4$. So, $\kappa(G, 3) = 1$. Meanwhile, G has a 4-coloring f' such that $f'(v_{ij}) = j$. Since each bichromatic induced subgraph under f' is connected, it follows from Theorem 9.1 that G is not **K**-changeable under f'. In addition, one can readily get another 4-coloring of G distinct from f'. Therefore, $\kappa(G, 4) > 1$.

The purpose of study **K**-change is to determine the number of **K**-classes, or determine the value of k such that $\kappa(G, k) = 1$. However, the problem of finding a necessary and sufficient condition for a k-chromatic graph to be k-Kempe is extremely hard, even when one restricts attention to determining the number of **K**-classes of special classes of graphs.

We also attempt to use **K**-change to generate other colorings from a given one. This associates closely with Four Color Conjecture. It has been known that any two 5-colorings of a planar graph are **K**-equivalent [16]. Thus, if a planar G is 4-colorable, then we would like to determine whether or not there exists a sequence of **K**-changes by which a 5-coloring of G can be transformed into a 4-coloring of G. In the following sections, we first present some known results on **K**-classes, and then introduce an operation for maximal planar graph, called σ-operation (see Sect. 9.3)

9.2 Kempe Classes

This section depicts the development of **K**-classes of G with respect to vertex coloring, edge coloring and the reconfiguration graph of the vertex colorings.

9.2.1 K-Classes with Respect to Vertex Coloring

Literature on this topic mainly focus on special classes of graphs, including planar graphs, perfect graphs, and regular graphs, just to name a few. Fisk [11] was the first one who studied **K**-change after Kempe. He proved, in 1997, that

Theorem 9.3 ([11]) *Let G be a 3-colorable maximal planar graph. Then, $\kappa(G, 4) = 1$.*

According to Theorem 9.3, for a 3-colorable maximal planar graph G, one can deduce all 4-coloring, starting with a 3-coloring or a 4-coloring, by **K**-changes. This is not the case for 4-colorable planar graphs, although it has been proved that $\kappa(G, 5) = 1$. This result was first obtained by Meyniel [16] (written in French). We here present a proof, which is given in [25].

Theorem 9.4 ([16]) *Every planar graph G satisfies $\kappa(G, 5) = 1$.*

In [17] and [19], the authors extended the result in Theorem 9.4.

Theorem 9.5 ([17]) *All k-colorings of a planar graph G with $\chi(G) < k$ are **K**-equivalent.*

Theorem 9.6 ([19]) *All 5-colorings of a K_5-minor free graph are **K**-equivalent.*

Observe that every planar graph is 5-colorable; the following corollary follows from Theorems 9.4 and 9.5 directly.

Corollary 9.1 *Let G be a planar graph and k an integer. If $k \geq 5$, then $\kappa(G, k) = 1$.*

9.2 Kempe Classes

Let G be a graph and $S \subseteq V(G)$. If $G[S]$ is a complete, then S is called a **clique** of G. If G contains no clique with more vertices than $|S|$, then we all S a **maximum clique**. We use $\omega(G)$ to denote the cardinality of a maximum clique of G. If every induced subgraph H of G satisfies that $\chi(H) = \omega(H)$, then G is called a **perfect graph**.

Let u, v be two distinct vertices of a graph G. If every path between u and v has even number of edge, then they are called an **even pair**. If there is a sequence of graphs, $G_0, G_1, \ldots, G_s$ such that $G_0 = G$, G_s is a complete graph, and G_i can be obtained from G_{i-1} by identifying one even pair for $i = 1, 2, \ldots, s$, then G is called **even contractile**. If every induced subgraph of G is even contractile, then G is called **perfectly contractile**.

Theorem 9.7 ([2]) *Let G be a perfectly contractile graph. Then, G is perfect and $\kappa(G, k) = 1$ if $k \geq \chi(G)$.*

As for the Kempe equivalence on k-regular graph, there is a conjecture proposed by Mohar [17], which has been studied extensively.

Conjecture 9.1 ([17]) If $k \geq 3$ is an integer, then every connected k-regular graph G that is not K_{k+1} satisfies $\kappa(G, k) = 1$.

In [10], the author disproved Conjecture 9.1 for the case $k = 3$. They prove that if G is a connected cubic graph that is neither K_4 nor the 3-prism, then all 3-colorings of G are **K**-equivalent. Moreover, Conjecture 9.1 was settled for the case $k \geq 4$ in [9].

9.2.2 K-Classes with Respect to Edge Coloring

Let G be a k-edge-colorable graph and f be a k-edge-coloring of G, where the color set is $\{1, 2, \ldots, k\}$. We refer to the subgraph of G induced by the edges assigned colors i and j under f, $i \neq j, i, j \in \{1, 2, \ldots, k\}$ as a **bichromatic edge induced subgraph**, denoted by $G_{ij}^{'f}$. The components of $G_{ij}^{'f}$ is called a ij-**edge-component under f of G** (or just **bichromatic edge-component of G**).

A **Kempe change with respect to edge coloring**, or **K-edge-change** for short, is the operation of interchanging the colors of some bichromatic edge-component of G. Given two k-edge-coloring f, f', we say that they are **edge-Kempe equivalent** (or **edge-K-equivalent** for short) if each can be obtained from the other by a sequence of **K**-edge-changes. The equivalence classes $F_E^f(G)$, consisting of colorings that are **K**-equivalent to f, are called the **edge-Kempe classes with respect to f** (or just **edge-K-classes**). We use $\kappa_E(G, k)$ to denote the number of edge-**K**-classes of G.

An natural question on this topic is: what are the sufficient conditions for a graph G satisfying $\kappa_E(G, k) = 1$?

Theorem 9.8 ([17]) *Let G be a graph, and k a positive integer. If $k \geq \chi'(G) + 2$, then $\kappa_E(G, k) = 1$.*

Moreover, it is observed that the number of edge-**K**-classes of a graph is related to the maximum degree of the graph.

Theorem 9.9 ([17]) *Let G be a graph. If $\Delta(G) \leq 3$, then $\kappa_E(G, 4) = 1$; if G is bipartite graph such that $\Delta(G) \leq k - 1$ for an integer k, then $\kappa_E(G, 4) = 1$.*

In 2012, Mcdonald, et al. [15] extend the above results.

Theorem 9.10 ([15]) *Let G be a graph. If $\Delta(G) \leq 3$, then $\kappa_E(G, \Delta(G) + 1) = 1$; If $\Delta(G) \leq 4$, then $\kappa_E(G, \Delta(G) + 2) = 1$.*

By Theorem 9.10, one see that all $(\Delta(G) + 1)$-edge-colorings of a graph G such that $\Delta(G) \leq 3$ are edge-**K**-equivalent. Indeed, the inverse also holds.

Theorem 9.11 ([15]) *Let G be a graph. If $\kappa_E(G, \Delta(G) + 1) = 1$, then $\Delta(G) \leq 3$.*

In [1], the authors discussed the edge-**K**-equivalence classes of 3-edge-colorable cubic graphs.

Theorem 9.12 ([1]) *Let G be a 3-edge-chromatic cubic planar bipartite graph. Then $\kappa_E(G, 3) = 1$.*

9.2.3 Reconfiguration Graph of the k-Colorings

The **reconfiguration graph of the** k**-colorings** of a graph G, denoted by $P_k(G)$, is a graph whose vertex set consists of all the k-colorings of G for which two coloring are adjacent if and only if they differ in color on just one vertex of G. If $P_k(G)$ is connected, then we call G k-**mixing**. Regarding the study on the reconfiguration graph of the k-colorings, we mainly fucus on how to determine a graph to be k-mixing or not [12]. The following first presents a fact observed by Cereceda, et al. [7].

Theorem 9.13 ([7]) *Let G be a k-chromatic graph. If $k \in \{2, 3\}$, then $P_k(G)$ is disconnected; if $k \geq 4$, then there are graphs G_1 and G_2 such that $P_k(G_1)$ is connected and $P_k(G_2)$ is not connected.*

The complexity of determining whether a k-colorable graph is k-mixing has been studied. When $k=3$, this problem was shown to be solvable in time $O(n^2)$ [8], but when $k \geq 4$, it is **PSPACE**-complete [5].

The **mixing number** of graph G, denoted $m(G)$, is the minimum value such that for any $k \geq m(G)$ G is k-mixing. There is a upper bound on this parameter.

Theorem 9.14 ([13]) *Let G be a graph. Then, $m(G) \leq \Delta(G) + 2$.*

9.2 Kempe Classes

Although the mixing number has a upper bound, there exists a graph G such that $\frac{m(G)}{t}$ can become arbitrary large, where t is minimum value k for which G is k-mixing [6].

We call a graph d-**degenerate** if every subgraph of G has a d^--vertex. The k-**recoloring diameter** of a k-mixing graph G is defined as the diameter of $P_k(G)$. The treewidth of a graph G is denoted by $tw(G)$.

Let G be a k-degenerate graph. If $tw(G) = k$, then G is $(k+2)$-mixing [6]; if $k \geq tw(G) + 2$, then the k-recoloring diameter of G is at most $2n^2 + n$ [3].

Recall that a **separator** of a graph $G = (V, E)$ is a set $S \subseteq V$ such that $G - S$ has more connected components than G; if two vertices u and v that belong to the same connected component in G are in two different connected components of $G - S$, then we say that S **separates** u and v.

In [4] the concept of k-**color-dense graphs** is introduced. Given a positive integer k, a k-colorable graph of order n is called k-color-dense if one of the following condition holds:

(1) G is the disjoint union of cliques, each of which has at most k vertices;
(2) G has a separator S, and $G - S$ has components D and D' with vertices $u \in D$ and $v \in D'$ such that $|D| = 1$ or $|D \cup S| \leq k$, $S \subseteq N_G(v)$, and identifying u and v in G results in a k-color-dense graph G'.

For example, chordal bipartite graphs and $k(\geq 1)$-colorable chordal graphs are k-color-dense graphs [4].

Theorem 9.15 ([4]) *(1) Let G be a k-color-dense graph of order n and $\ell \geq k + 1$ an integer. Then, $P_\ell(G)$ is connected and the ℓ-recoloring diameter of G is $O(n^2)$; (2) for any integer $k \geq 2$, there exist a k-colorable chordal graph G such that $(k+1)$-recoloring diameter of G is $\Theta(n^2)$.*

For a graph G, the following theorem shows that the connectedness of $P_k(G)$ is related to the value of $k - \Delta(G)$.

Theorem 9.16 ([10]) *Let G be a graph with maximum degree Δ. For any integer k,*

(1) *when $k \leq \Delta$, $P_k(G)$ might be disconnected and it is possible that its connected components have super polynomial diameter;*
(2) *when $k = \Delta + 1$, $P_k(G)$ consists of isolated vertices and at most one component with diameter $O(n^2)$;*
(3) *when $k \geq \Delta + 2$, $P_k(G)$ is connected and has diameter $O(n^2)$;*
(4) *if G is not isomorphic to a complete graph or a cycle with an odd number of vertices, or a $(\Delta = k - 1)$-regular, then a Δ-colouring of G can be obtained from a given k-coloring by a sequence of $O(n^2)$ **K**-change such that each **K**-change only changes the color of one color (using only the original k colors).*

For any graph G, the computational complexity of the problem of determining whether two k-colorings of G belong to the same component of $P_k(G)$ is associated with its maximum degree. The following results is due to Feghali, et al. [10].

Let G be a n-order graph with maximum degree Δ. The computational complexity of the problem of deciding whether two k-colourings of G belong to the same component of $P_k(G)$ is

(1) $O(n^2)$ time solvable for $k = 3$;
(2) PSPACE-complete for $4 \leq k \leq \Delta$;
(3) $O(n)$ time solvable for $k = \Delta + 1$;
(4) $O(1)$ time solvable for $k \geq \Delta + 2$ (the answer is always yes).

The **K**-change is a powerful tool for solving the Four Color Conjecture. Although the attempt at proving the Four Color Conjecture through **K**-change, introduced by Kempe, had failed, its method has proved to be a powerful tool with applications to several areas such as timetables [18], theoretical physics [21, 22], and Markov chains [20], etc. Moreover, the problem of frequency redistribution in wireless communication networks can be modeled as a recoloring problem of graphs, which can be studied via **K**-change. Whether or not there is an approach for which two k-colorings of a graph, belonging to distinct **K**-classes, can be transformed into each other? To this end, we have to break through the restriction of **K**-change. This is the main concern in our following study on **K**-change.

9.3 σ-Operation

All graphs considered in this section are planar graphs. For maximal planar graph, we introduce an operation, called σ-operation, which was first studied in [23]. By this operation, one can characterize clearly the relation among all colorings of a maximal planar graph, and classify **K**-classes of maximal planar graphs into certain types accordingly.

9.3.1 2-Chromatic Ears

In this section, we first give the definition and classification of 2-chromatic cycles, and then we introduce the 2-chromatic ears, which is the root of implementing σ-operations continuously.

Let G be a 4-colorable maximal planar graph, H a subgraph of G, and f a 4-coloring of G. We use $f(H)$ to denote the set of colors assigned to $V(H)$ under f. The sets of vertices in the interior and exterior of a given cycle C of G are denoted by V_C^{in} and V_C^{out}, respectively. Suppose that C is an even-cycle of G. If $|f(C)| = 2$, then we call C a **2-chromatic cycle** of f; we also say that f **contains the 2-chromatic cycle** C. The two colors in $f(C)$ are called **cycle-colors** and the other two colors are **non-cycle-colors**. For a 2-chromatic cycle C of f, let u, v be two different vertices of C. If $uv \notin E(C)$, $uv \in E(G)$ and uv is in the interior of C, then C is called a **2-chromatic chord-cycle of** f, and the edge uv is called a

9.3 σ-Operation

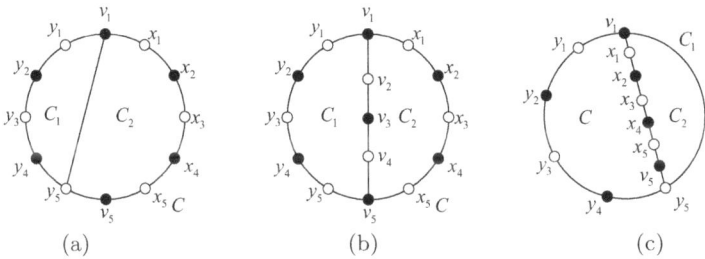

Fig. 9.4 (a) 2-chromatic chord-cycle, (b) 2-chromatic chord-path cycle, (c) 2-chromatic basic cycle

chord of C; if there is a path $P(\neq uv)$ colored with $f(C)$ in the interior of C that connects u and v, then C is referred to as a **2-chromatic chord-path cycle of** f, and P is called a **chord-path** of C; If C is neither a 2- chromatic chord-cycle nor a 2-chromatic chord-path cycle, then we call C a **2-chromatic basic cycle**.

For example, the cycle C shown in Fig. 9.4a is a 2-chromatic chord-cycle with a chord $v_1 y_5$; the cycle C shown in Fig. 9.4b is a 2-chromatic chord-path cycle with a chord-path $v_1 v_2 v_3 v_4 v_5$; the cycles C_1 and C_2 shown in both Fig. 9.4a, b are 2-chromatic basic cycles.

Notice that a 2-chromatic cycle of a 4-colorable maximal planar graph may belong to different types in different planar embeddings of the graph. Consider the graph shown in Fig. 9.4a, c is one of its planar embeddings, in which C_1 is a 2-chromatic chord-path cycle with a chord-path $v_1 x_1 x_2 x_3 x_4 x_5 v_5 y_5$ while C and C_2 are the 2-chromatic basic cycles. Unless special declaration, all 2-chromatic cycles in the following argument are 2-chromatic basic cycles. Given a maximal planar graph G and a coloring $f \in C_4^0(G)$, we denote by $C^2(f)$ the set of all 2-chromatic cycles under f. A cycle C of G is **2-colorable** if there exists a coloring $f \in C_4^0(G)$ such that $|f(C)| = 2$. We use the notation $C^2(G)$ to denote the set of all 2-colorable cycles of G. Obviously,

$$C^2(G) = \bigcup_{f \in C_4^0(G)} C^2(f) \tag{9.1}$$

Let G be a 4-chromatic maximal planar graph with $\delta(G) \geq 4$, f is a 4-coloring of G, and C_1 and C_2 be two 2-chromatic cycles of f. We say that C_1 and C_2 are **intersected under** f if the following two conditions hold: $|f(C_1) \cap f(C_2)| = 1$; and $V_{C_1}^{in} \cap V(C_2) \neq \emptyset$ and $V_{C_1}^{out} \cap V(C_2) \neq \emptyset$. Otherwise, C_1 and C_2 are **disintersected under** f.

Suppose $C^2(G) = \{C_1, C_2, \cdots, C_m\}$ with $m \geq 2$. For any pair of $C_{t_1}, C_{t_\ell} \in C^2(G)$, $t_1, t_\ell \in \{1, 2, \ldots, m\}$, if there exists a sequence of 2-colorable cycles $C_{t_1}, C_{t_2}, \cdots, C_{t_\ell}$ of the corresponding 4-colorings $f_1, f_2, \cdots, f_t$, respectively, such that C_{t_i} and $C_{t_{i+1}}$ $(1 \leq i \leq \ell - 1)$ are intersected under f_i, then we say that C_{t_1} and C_{t_ℓ} are **relevant**; otherwise, they are **irrelevant**.

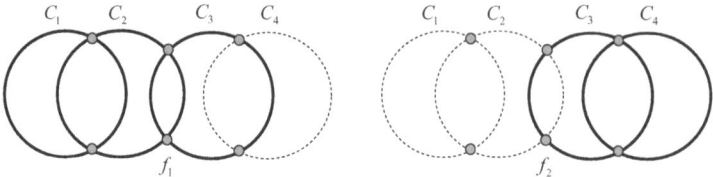

Fig. 9.5 Two relevant 2-chromatic cycle C_1 and C_4

In Fig. 9.5, let G be the underlying maximal planar graph. Suppose that $C^2(G)=\{C_1, C_2, C_3, C_4\}$, and f_1 and f_2 are two colorings of G, where C_1, C_2, C_3 are three successively intersected 2-chromatic cycles of f_1 and C_3, C_4 are two intersected 2-chromatic cycles of f_2. Then, C_1 and C_4 are relevant.

Suppose that G is a 4-chromatic maximal planar graph and $f \in C_4^0(G)$. Let $C \in C^2(f)$ with cycle-colors c_1 and c_2 under f, and x, y be two different vertices in C with the same color under f. We use $P(x, y)$ to denote a path between x and y such that $|V(P(x, y|))| \geq 3$. If $f(P(x, y)) \neq \{c_1, c_2\}$ and $|f(P(x, y))| = 2$, then we call $P(x, y)$ a **2-chromatic ear under** f of C (or simply an **ear** of C), and call x, y the **ear-roots** of $P(x, y)$. We use $Ed(C)$ to denote the set of all ears of C. We classify the ears of a cycle into two types in terms of the position where they lie in the cycle: **inner ear** and **outer ear**, which are ears in the interior and the exterior of the cycle, respectively. Moreover, if $f(P(x, y)) = \{c_1, c_3\}$, then $P(x, y)$ is called c_1c_3-**ear**. Analogously, we have c_1c_4-**ear**, c_2c_3-**ear**, and c_2c_4-**ear**, where $\{c_1, c_2, c_3, c_4\} = \{1, 2, 3, 4\}$. We call the color in $f(P(x, y))\setminus f(C)$ **ear-edge color**. Obviously, the ear-edge color is neither c_1 nor c_2.

For a 4-chromatic maximal planar graph, let C be a 2-chromatic cycle of a 4-coloring, and $P(x, y)$ and $P(x', y')$ be two ears of C. If $f(x) = f(x')$, then we say $P(x, y)$ and $P(x', y')$ to be **homologous**; if $x = x'$ and $y = y'$, then we say $P(x, y)$ and $P(x', y')$ to be **co-rooted**. Obviously, if two ears are **co-rooted**, then they must be **homologous**, but the converse may not be true. Furthermore, we say $P(x, y)$ and $P(x', y')$ to be **homochromatic** if one of the following conditions hold:

(1) Both $P(x, y)$ and $P(x', y')$ are inner ears (or outer ears), and $f(P(x, y)) = f(P(x', y'))$.
(2) $P(x, y)$ and $P(x', y')$ are inner ear and outer ear, respectively, and they are a pair of homologous ears with different ear-edge colors.

If $P(x, y)$ and $P(x', y')$ are not homochromatic, then they are called **heterochromous** ears.

Suppose that $P_1, P_2, \cdots, P_m (m \geq 3)$ are a sequence of ears of a 2-chromatic cycle C, under a 4-coloring of a 4-chromatic maximal planar graph G. We refer to them as **path-connected** if $P_1 \cup P_2 \cup \cdots \cup P_m$ is a path of G, and to be **cycle-connected** if $P_1 \cup P_2 \cup \cdots \cup P_m$ is an even-cycle of G. Let $Q(C)$ be the set of cycles formed by the union of ears of C. A cycle in $Q(C)$ is called an **inner ear-cycle on** C (resp. **outer ear-cycle on** C) if it contains only inner (resp. outer) ears of C;

9.3 σ-Operation

Fig. 9.6 Illustration for ears, co-rooted ears and homologous ears

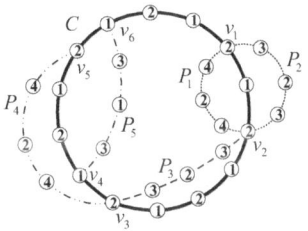

moreover, if it contains both inner ear-cycles and outer ear-cycles, then we call it a **mixing ear-cycle on** C. The sets of inner ear-cycles on C, outer ear-cycles on C and mixed ear-cycles on C are written $Q^i(C)$, $Q^e(C)$, and $Q^m(C)$, respectively. It is clear from the definition that

$$Q(C) = Q^i(C) \cup Q^e(C) \cup Q^m(C) \tag{9.2}$$

Figure 9.6 contains 5 ears P_1, P_2, P_3, P_4 and P_5 of a 2-chromatic cycle C. P_1, P_2, P_3, P_4 are homologous; P_1 and P_2 are co-rooted; P_1, P_3, P_5 are inner ears; P_2 and P_4 are outer ears. P_1, P_3, P_4 (resp. P_2, P_3, P_4) are path-connected; P_1, P_2 are cycle-connected.

Theorem 9.17 *Suppose that G is a 4-chromatic maximal planar graph with $\delta(G) \geq 4$ and $f \in C_4^0(G)$, where the color set is $\{1, 2, 3, 4\}$. If f contains only one 2-chromatic cycle C with cycle-colors 1 and 2, then*

(1) *Every cycle in $Q^i(C) \cup Q^e(C)$ contains a pair of heterochromous ears of C;*
(2) *let f^c be the 4-coloring of G, obtained from f by interchanging the colors of vertices of all 34-components in the interior of C. Then, f^c contains a 2-chromatic cycle C' which is different from C if and only if*

$$c' \in Q^m(C) \quad under \quad f^c \tag{9.3}$$

and any two ears of C that are contained in C' are homochromatic under f.

Proof

(1) Suppose, to the contrary, that $Q^i(C) \cup Q^e(C) \neq \emptyset$ contains a cycle C_1 consisting of only homochromatic ears (under f). Then, it follows from the definition of homochromatic ears that C_1 is a 2-chromatic cycle of f. This contradicts the assumption of C, since $c \neq C_1$.
(2) Necessity. Since C is the unique 2-chromatic cycle of f, $C' \in Q^m(C)$ (under f^c). Observe that any two ears of C that are contained in C' are homologous. Suppose that C' contains two heterochromous ears P and P' of C (under f). Then, P and P' are inner ears, or outer ears, or one is an inner ear and the other is an outer ear of C. However, in either case C' is by no means a 2-chromatic cycle of f^c, a contradiction.

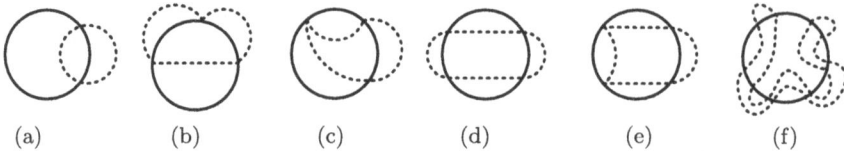

Fig. 9.7 The possible structures formed by homochromatic ears of a 2-chromatic cycle C, where C is remarked by full lines. (**a**) Two ears. (**b**) Three ears. (**c**) Three ears. (**d**) Four ears. (**e**) Four ears. (**f**) Multiple ear

Sufficiency. Since $C' \in Q^m(C)$ (under f^c), C' is a cycle and any pair of ears of C that are contained in C' are homologous. Let P and P' be two ears of C (under f) that are contained in C'. By the assumption, P and P' are homochromatic (under f). Thus, when P and P' are inner ears (or outer ears), $f(P) = f(P')$; when one is an inner ear and the other is an outer ear, $|f(P) \cup f(P')| = 3$ and $\{1, 2\} \nsubseteq f(P) \cup f(P')$. Therefore, $P \cup P'$ are colored using exactly two colors under f^c, i.e. C' is a 2-chromatic cycle of f^c. This completes the proof of the theorem. ∎

Let G is a 4-chromatic maximal planar graph. Suppose that $f \in C_4^0(G)$ contains exactly one 2-chromatic cycle, say C, and $f(C) = \{1, 2\}$. Let f^c be a new coloring obtained from f by interchanging the colors of vertices of all 34-components in the interior of C. If f^c contains at least two 2-chromatic cycles, then by Theorem 9.17 any 2-chromatic cycle $C'(\neq C)$ of f^c consists of only homochromatic ears of C (under f); the following give a specific description.

(1) If C has exactly two homochromatic ears, then one is an inner ear, and the other is an outer ear; see Fig. 9.7a;
(2) if C has three homochromatic ears, then the possible structures are illustrated in Fig. 9.7b, c;
(3) if C has four homochromatic ears, then the structures are illustrated in Fig. 9.7d, e;
(4) if C' contains five or more homochromatic ears, then its structure is shown in Fig. 9.7f.

9.3.2 The σ-Operation

Let G be a 4-colorable maximal planar graph with color set $\{1, 2, 3, 4\}$, $f \in C_4^0(G)$. If $\exists i, j \in \{1, 2, 3, 4\}$ such that G_{ij}^f has a cycle, then f is referred to as a **cycle-coloring** of G, and we call G is **cycle-colorable**. Conversely, if $\forall i, j \in \{1, 2, 3, 4\}$, G_{ij}^f are forest, then f is a **tree-coloring** of G, and G is **tree-colorable**. If G is tree-colorable (or cycle-colorable) but not cycle-colorable (or tree-colorable), the G is

9.3 σ-Operation

called **purely tree-colorable** (or **purely cycle-colorable**). Furthermore, if G is both tree-colorable and cycle-colorable, then G is also called mixed colorable.

Suppose that f is a cycle-coloring and C is a 2-chromatic cycle of f such that $f(C) = \{1, 2\}$. A σ-**operation respect to** C **under** f (or σ-operation for short), denoted by $\sigma(f, C)$, is the operation of interchanging the colors of vertices of all 34-components (with respect to f) inside C. Obviously, a σ-operation is a kind of **coloring-derived** operations, by which a new cycle-coloring (denoted by f^c) can be obtained from a given cycle-coloring f, namely

$$\sigma(f, C) = f^c \tag{9.4}$$

We say that f^c and f are **complementary respect to** C. Formula (9.4) can also be represented as $\sigma(f) = f^c$ if there is no confusion. It is easy to see that if there is only one 34-component (with respect to f) inside C, then the σ-operation is equal to the **K**-change; otherwise, a σ-operation is a sequence of **K**-changes. Therefore, f^c and f are **K**-equivalent.

An 11-order maximal planar graph has eight 4-colorings, denoted by $f_1 \sim f_8$, respectively, is shown in Fig. 9.8. One can see that $\sigma(f_1, C_1) = f_2, \sigma(f_2, C_2) = f_3$, and $\sigma(f_3, C_3) = f_4$. Moreover, G has in total seven 2-colorable cycles $C_1 \sim C_7$, i.e., $|C^2(G)| = 7$.

The following is a straight forward result by the definition of σ-operations.

Theorem 9.18 *Suppose f is a 4-coloring of a 4-colorable maximal planar graph G, and C is a 2-chromatic cycle of f. Then*

$$\sigma(\sigma(f, C), C) = f \tag{9.5}$$

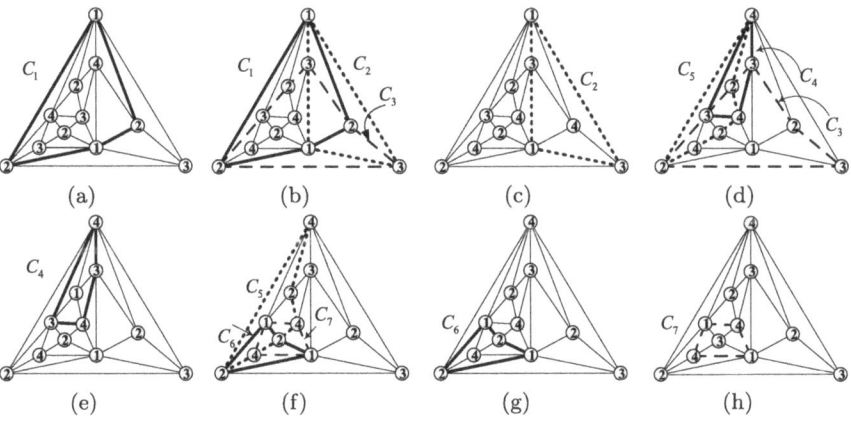

Fig. 9.8 σ-operation. (**a**) f_1. (**b**) f_2. (**c**) f_3. (**d**) f_4. (**e**) f_5. (**f**) f_6. (**g**) f_7. (**h**) f_8

The aim of the σ-operations is to derive the **K**-class $F^f(G)$, starting with a 4-coloring f in $C_4^0(G)$, by a sequence of σ-operations. It has been known that all 5-colorings of a planar graph are **K**-equivalent. But the situation will become more complex for 4-colorings. This will be discussed in the subsequent sections.

9.4 σ-Characteristic Graphs

In this section, we introduce reconfiguration graph of the 4-colorings of a maximal planar graph G based on σ-operation, called σ-characteristic graphs, by which one can clearly characterize the relations of all 4-colorings of G.

9.4.1 Definition

Let G be a 4-colorable maximal planar graph, and $C_4^0(G) = \{f_1, f_2, \cdots, f_n\}$. The σ-**characteristic graph** of G, denoted G_4^σ, is a graph with the vertex set $\{f_1, f_2, \cdots, f_n\}$ such that two vertices f_i and f_t are adjacent in G_4^σ if and only if they are complementary respect to some 2-chromatic cycle C in G for $i \neq t, i, t = 1, 2, \cdots, n, i \neq t$. By this definition, we can view a σ-characteristic graph as an edge-labelled graph, in which the label appearing on an edge is a 2-chromatic cycle that results in two complementary colorings (the two ends of the edge). When we only concern the topological structure of a σ-characteristic graph, the labels in G_4^σ can be deleted.

The graph G shown in Fig. 9.8 has totally eight 4-colorings. Its σ-characteristic graph and corresponding topological structure are shown in Fig. 9.9a,b. It is evident that G_4^σ is connected and is a tree. Therefore, we can obtain all 4-colorings of G by σ-operations based on any given 4-coloring. In addition, consider the icosahedron; it has totally ten 4-colorings, each of which is a tree-coloring. So its σ-characteristic graph is an empty graph of order 10.

Fig. 9.9 The σ-characteristic graph of the graph in Fig. 9.8. (**a**) σ-characteristic graph. (**b**) Topological structure

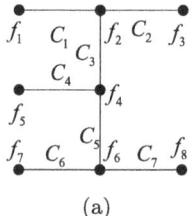
(a)

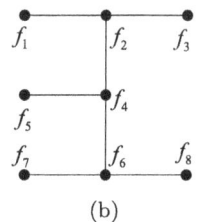
(b)

9.4.2 Basic Properties

Let G be a 4-colorable maximal planar graph. If $|C_4^0(G)| = 1$, then we call G a **uniquely 4-colorable maximal planar graph**. The following theorem follows from the definition of σ-characteristic graph.

Theorem 9.19 *For a 4-colorable maximal planer graph G, let G_4^σ be the σ-characteristic graph of G. We have*

(1) *G is uniquely 4-colorable if and only if $G_4^\sigma \cong K_1$;*
(2) *For any vertex $f \in V(G_4^\sigma)$, $d_{G_4^\sigma}(f) = k$ if and only if f contains k 2-chromatic cycles;*
(3) *If there exists a $f \in C_4^0(G)$, which contains $k (\geq 1)$ 2-chromatic cycles, i.e. $d_{G_4^\sigma}(f) = k$, then*

$$|C_4^0(G)| \geq k + 1 \qquad (9.6)$$

Among all maximal planar graphs with order at most 11, the number of tree-colorings accounts for about 2 percent of the total number of 4-colorings [24]. We conjecture that the number of tree-colorings is much less than that of cycle-colorings of maximal planar graphs with $\delta \geq 4$. Hence, for a given cycle-coloring f of a 4-colorable maximal planar graph G it is possible to derive almost all 4-colorings of $C_4^0(G)$ from f by means of the σ-operations. The following theorem is obvious.

Theorem 9.20 *Let G be a 4-colorable maximal planar graph. If G_4^σ is connected, then the running time of algorithms generating all 4-colorings is greater than that of algorithms generating one 4-coloring by only $|V(G_4^\sigma)| - 1$.*

According to Theorem 9.20, if G is a maximal planar graph such that $\kappa(G, 4) = 1$, then the algorithm finding all 4-colorings is polynomial time equivalent to the algorithm finding one 4-coloring.

Obviously, G_4^0 and $C_4^0(G)$ are tightly related with each other. Thus, exploring the structure of G_4^0 is an essential work for the study of $C_4^0(G)$.

Theorem 9.21 *Let G be a 4-colorable maximal planar graph with $\delta(G) \geq 4$ and $f \in C_4^0(G)$. Then, G_4^σ contains no triangles.*

Proof By way of contradiction. Suppose that G_4^σ contains a triangle $f_1 f_2 f_3 f_1$. Without loss of generality, we assume

$$\sigma(f_1, C_1) = f_2, \sigma(f_1, C_2) = f_3, \sigma(f_2, C_3) = f_3 \qquad (9.7)$$

Then, $C_1, C_2 \in C^2(f_1)$, $C_1, C_3 \in C^2(f_2)$, $C_2, C_3 \in C^2(f_3)$; see Fig. 9.10a. Let $C(4) = \{1, 2, 3, 4\}$ be the color set. Denote by $V_{C_i}^{*in}$ the set of vertices in the interior of C_i which are colored without cycle-colors, for $i = 1, 2$. We consider two cases as follows.

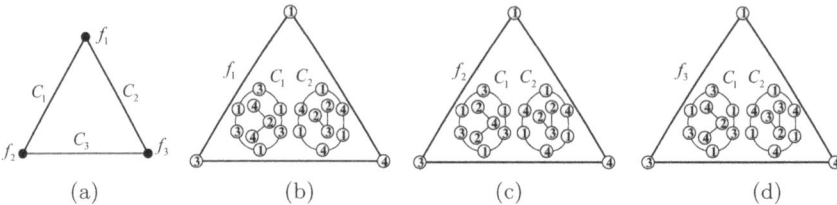

Fig. 9.10 Illustration for the case that C_1 and C_2 are disintersected

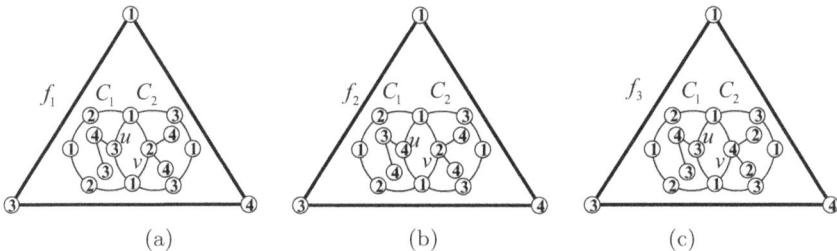

Fig. 9.11 Illustration for the case that C_1 and C_2 are intersected

Case 1 C_1, C_2 are intersected under f_1; see Fig. 9.10b.

Obviously, $f_1(u) \neq f_2(u)$ for any $u \in V_{C_1}^{*in}$ and $f_1(v) = f_2(v)$ for any $v \in V(G) \setminus V_{C_1}^{*in}$ (see Figs. 9.10b, c). Similarly, $f_1(u) \neq f_3(u)$ for $\forall u \in V_{C_2}^{*in}$ and $f_1(v) = f_3(v)$ for $\forall v \in V(G) \setminus V_{C_2}^{*in}$ (see Fig. 9.10b, d). Therefore, for any $u \in V_{C_1}^{*in} \cup V_{C_2}^{*in}$, we have $f_2(u) \neq f_3(u)$, and for $\forall v \in V(G) \setminus V_{C_1}^{*in} \cup V_{C_2}^{*in}$ we have $f_2(v) = f_3(v)$. Thus, there does not exist a 2-chromatic cycle C_3 satisfying the condition $V_{C_3}^{*in} = V_{C_1}^{*in} \cup V_{C_2}^{*in}$ for f_2, f_3, a contradiction.

Case 2 C_1, C_2 are intersected under f_1. Then $f_1(C_1) \neq f_1(C_2)$. Without loss of generality, we assume $f_1(C_1) = \{1, 2\}$ and $f_1(C_2) = \{1, 3\}$ (see Fig. 9.11a). Let $u \in V_{C_1}^{*in} \cap V(C_2)$ and $V_{C_2}^{*in} \cap V(C_1)$. Then, $f_1(u) = 3, f_1(v) = 2; f_2(u) = 4, f_2(v) = 2; f_3(u) = 3, f_3(v) = 4$ (see Fig. 9.11b, c). Clearly, f_2 does not contain any 2-chromatic cycle C_3, such that f_2 and f_3 are two complementary colorings respect to C_3, a contradiction.

This completes the proof of Theorem 5. ∎

By Theorem 9.21, the σ-characteristic graph G_4^σ of a 4-colorable maximal planar graph G with $\delta \geq 4$ is triangle-free, which means that the induced subgraph $G_4^\sigma[\overline{N^f(G)}]$ is a star, where $\overline{N^f(G)} = N_{G_4^\sigma}(f) \cup \{f\}$. So, we have,

Corollary 9.2 *Let G be a 4-colorable maximal planar graph with $\delta \geq 4$. Then, for any cycle-coloring of G, the induced subgraph $G_4^\sigma[\overline{N^f(G)}]$ is a star.*

9.4 σ-Characteristic Graphs

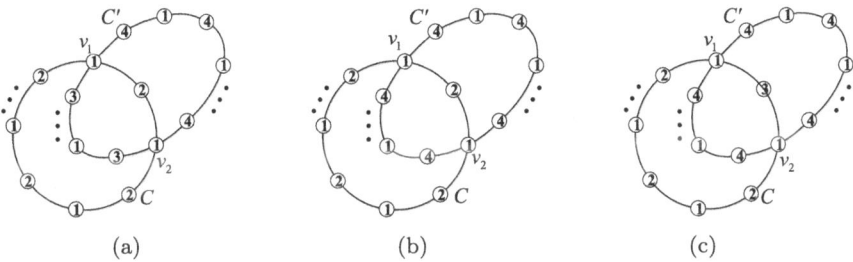

Fig. 9.12 Illustration for Theorem 9.22. (**a**) f. (**b**) f^c. (**c**) f'

Theorem 9.22 *Suppose that G is a 4-colorable maximal planar graph with a $f \in C_4^0(G)$ such that $d_{G_4^\sigma}(f) = 1$. Let C be the 2-chromatic cycle for which $\sigma(f, C) = f^c$. If f^c has degree at least 2 in G_4^σ, then G has a 4-coloring f' such that $|f'(C)| \geq 3$.*

Proof Without loss of generality, we assume that $f(C) = \{1, 2\}$ (see Fig. 9.12a). Because f^c contains at least two 2-chromatic cycles, there exist at least a pair of vertices of C assigned the same color under f, say v_1, v_2, at which there are a 14-ear outside C and a 13-ear inside C (see Fig. 9.12a), where we assume that $f(v_1) = f(v_2) = 1$. Now, we can obtain a 4-coloring f^c by implementing a σ-operation respect to C. Notice that f^c contains at least two 2-chromatic cycles C and C', as shown in Fig. 9.12b. Therefore, we can obtain a new 4-coloring f' by implementing a σ-operation respect to C', and $|f'(C)| = 3$ (see Fig. 9.12c). ∎

Theorem 9.23 *Suppose that G is a 4-colorable maximal planar graph with $\delta(G) \geq 4$. Then, G_4^σ does not contain any pair of adjacent vertices with degree 1 and 2, respectively.*

Proof To the contrary, suppose that f_1, f_2 are two adjacent vertices in G_4^σ such that $d_{G_4^\sigma}(f_1) = 1$ and $d_{G_4^\sigma}(f_2) = 2$. Let C_1 be the unique 2-chromatic cycle of f_1, and let f_2 contain two intersected 2-chromatic cycles C_1, C_2. Clearly, f_1 and f_2 are complementary respect to C_1. Without loss of generality, assume that $f_1(C_1) = \{1, 2\}$, $f_2(C_1) = \{1, 2\}$, $f_2(C_2) = \{1, 3\}$. We use $G_1^{C_1}$ and $G_2^{C_1}$ to denote the subgraphs of G induced by $C_1 \cup V_{C_1}^{in}$ and $C_1 \cup V_{C_1}^{out}$, respectively, and use r_{ij} to denote the number of ij-components in $G_1^{C_1}$, for $i, j \in \{1, 2, 3, 4\}$ and $i \neq j$.

Since the graph G, under the coloring f_1, has a unique 2-chromatic cycle C_1, we have that G_{34} consists of two connected components, and $G_{13}, G_{14}, G_{23}, G_{24}$ are connected. Now, we can see that the r_{14} 14-components of $G_1^{C_1}$ are connected by the $(r_{14} - 1)$ 14-paths of $G_2^{C_1}$ and the r_{13} 13-components of $G_1^{C_1}$ are connected by the $(r_{13} - 1)$ 13-paths of $G_2^{C_1}$.

Then, we can obtain a 4-coloring f_2 by interchanging the colors of vertices of 34-component inside C_1. Under the coloring f_2, it is easy to see that the number of

13-components in $G_1^{C_1}$ is r_{14}, and $G_2^{C_1}$ still contains $(r_{13} - 1)$ 13-paths with both the initial vertex and the terminus vertex on C_1. Because all of these 13-paths connect the r_{14} 13-components of $G_1^{C_1}$ into a component which contains a 13-cycle C_2, we have that $r_{13} > r_{14}$. In addition, the number of 14-components in $G_1^{C_1}$ is changed into r_{13}, and $G_2^{C_1}$ still contains $(r_{14} - 1)$ 14-paths with both the initial vertex and the terminus vertex on C_1. Since $r_{13} > r_{14}$, it follows that the r_{13} 14-components in $G_1^{C_1}$ can not be connected into a component by the $(r_{14} - 1)$ 14-paths. Hence, G_{14} is disconnected under the coloring f_2, i.e. G_{23} contains a 2-chromatic cycle, a contradiction. Hence, the result holds. ■

The case of G_4^σ being disconnected is the key point of our research, which will be studied deeply in the following section.

9.5 Kempe Classes of Maximal Planar Graphs

Let G be a 4-colorable maximal planar graph and $f, f' \in C_4^0(G)$. If f and f' are not K-equivalent, then f' can not be obtained by implementing a series of σ-operations starting with f. The reason can be summarized in the following three points in terms of 2-chromatic cycles of f: (1) $C^2(f) = \emptyset$, i.e. f is a tree-coloring; (2) $C^2(f)$ contains **2-chromatic unchanged-cycles**; (3) $C^2(f)$ contains the **circular 2-chromatic cycle** (these definitions will be defined later). Based on these three cases, we classify K-classes of graphs with more than one K-classes into three types: tree-type, cycle-type, and circular-cycle-type. In the following, we will introduce them, respectively. For convenience, we use the notation.

9.5.1 Tree-Type K-Class

If f is a tree-coloring of a 4-colorable maximal planar graph G, then $C^2(f) = \emptyset$, that is, all of the six bichromatic induced subgraphs are connected. Therefore, $F^f(G) = \{f\}$. We refer to this **K**-class as a **tree-type K-class** of G, and call G a **tree-type maximal planar graph**. Thus, for any $f' \in C_4^0(G)$ and $f' \neq f$, we have

$$f' \notin F^f(G) \tag{9.8}$$

It follows that

Theorem 9.24 *Suppose that G is a non-uniquely 4-colorable maximal planar graph. Then, $\kappa(G, 4) \geq 2$. Particularly, $\kappa(G, 4) = |C_4^0(G)|$ if G is purely tree-colorable; $\kappa(G, 4) \geq t + 1$ if G is mixed colorable and $C_4^0(G)$ contains t tree-colorings.*

9.5.2 Cycle-Type K-Class

Suppose that G is a 4-colorable maximal planar graph, $f \in C_4^0(G)$, and $C \in C^2(f)$. If $Q^m(C)$ contains no cycle consisting of homochromatic ears, then we call C a **2-chromatic unchanged-cycle** of f, f a **2-chromatic unchanged-cycle coloring** of G, and G a **cycle-type maximal planar graph based on** C. By this definition, if we denote by f^c the resulting coloring obtained by implementing σ-operations respect to C under f, then we have,

$$C^2(f) = C^2(f^c) \tag{9.9}$$

In Formula (9.9), we do not consider the colors on 2-chromatic cycles in $C^2(f)$ and $C^2(f^c)$. That is to say, for a 2-chromatic cycle C both in $C^2(f)$ and $C^2(f^c)$, $f(C)$ may be different from $f^c(C)$.

Obviously, the cycle-coloring f^c satisfying Formula (9.9) is also a 2-chromatic unchanged-cycle coloring of G. For example, the graph in Fig. 9.13 is a cycle-type maximal planar graph. It has in total four 4-colorings f_1, f_2, f_3 and f_4, where f_1 and f_2 are two complementary 2-chromatic unchanged-cycle colorings with respect to C, and the unique 2-chromatic unchanged-cycle of them is 12-cycle.

Figure 9.14 exhibits two cycle-type maximal planar graphs G_1 (the first graph) and G_2 (the last graph), each of which contains two 2-chromatic unchanged-cycles. The two 2-chromatic unchanged-cycles in G_1 have two common vertices. In the first ten graphs we give the totally ten 4-colorings of G_1 and in the eleventh graph its σ-characteristic graph is illustrated. The last graph has two disintersected 2-chromatic unchanged-cycles (marked by thick lines).

Let G be a 4-colorable maximal planar graph. Let $f \in C_4^0(G)$ be a cycle-coloring and $C \in C^2(f)$. If there exists a $f' \in C_4^0(G)$ such that

$$|f'(C)| \geq 3 \tag{9.10}$$

then we say C is **breakable**.

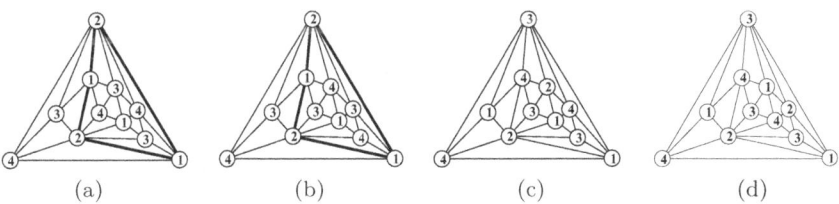

Fig. 9.13 A maximal planar graph with only one 2-chromatic unchanged-cycle. (**a**) f_1: cycle-coloring (12-cycle), (**b**) f_2: cycle-coloring (12-cycle), (**c**) f_3: tree-coloring (**d**) f_4: tree-coloring

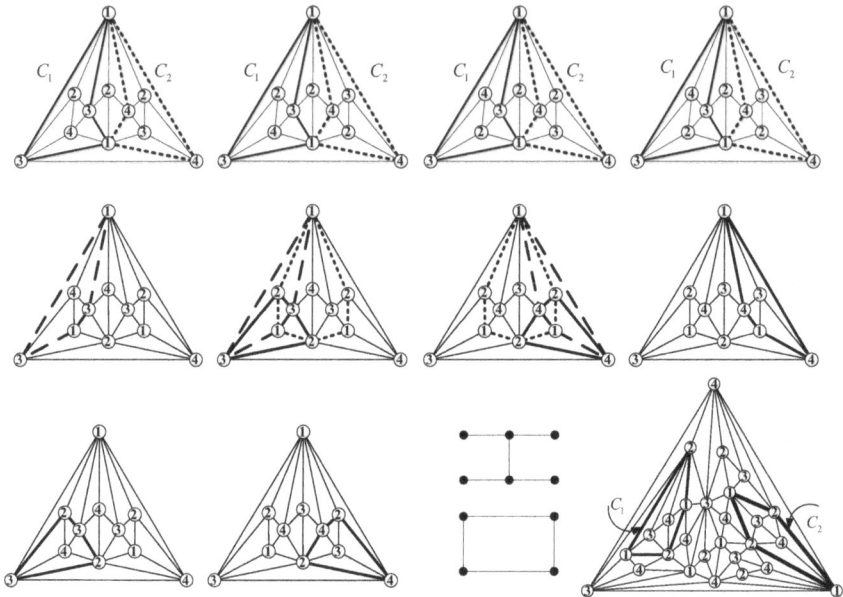

Fig. 9.14 Maximal planar graphs with two 2-chromatic unchanged-cycles

Theorem 9.25 *Let G be a 4-colorable maximal planar graph with $\delta(G) \geq 4$, C_1 and C_t be two relevant 2-colorable cycles of C. Then both C_1 and C_t are breakable.*

Proof The result follows from definitions of the 2-chromatic colorable-cycles and σ- operations. ∎

For two 2-chromatic cycles satisfying the condition of Theorem 9.25, one see that they are breakable. However, we can not break a 2-chromatic unchanged-cycle C of f by implementing σ-operations starting with f, i.e. we can not obtain a $f' \in C_4^0(G)$ satisfying Formula (9.10) through σ-operations and f. So, f and f' are non-**K**-equivalent. The underlying reason that f and f' are non-**K**-equivalent is due to the 2-chromatic unchanged-cycle. We refer to such an equivalent class $F^f(G)$ as a **cycle-type K-class**.

For a 4-colorable maximal planar graph G, let S be a set of 4-colorings of G containing exactly $k(\geq 2)$ 2-chromatic unchanged-cycles. Then, the induced subgraph $G_4^\sigma[S]$ is a k-hypercube.

Theorem 9.26 *Suppose G is a 4-colorable maximal planar graph with $\delta(G) \geq 4$ and f is a 4-coloring of G containing exactly k 2-chromatic cycles which are 2-chromatic unchanged-cycles. Then, $|F^f(G)| = 2^k$, and $G_4^\sigma[F^f(G)] = B^k$ where $B = \{0, 1\}$.*

9.5 Kempe Classes of Maximal Planar Graphs

Proof Suppose that $C_1, C_2, \cdots, C_k$ are the k 2-chromatic unchanged-cycles of f. For each $C_i (1 \leq i \leq k)$, we denote by 1 if we implement a σ-operation with respect to C_i; otherwise by 0. Then, we can establish a one-one correspondence between 2-chromatic unchanged-cycles $C_1, C_2, \cdots, C_k$ and a 0-1 sequence of k-length. Because implementing one σ-operation with respect to $C_i (1 \leq i \leq k)$ exactly corresponds to a 4-coloring of G. This implies that there is a 0-1 sequence $\{(x_1, x_2, \cdots, x_k) : x_i = 0, 1, i = 1, 2, \cdots, k\}$ corresponding to a coloring of $F^f(G)$. Hence, the connected component of G_4^σ containing f has at least 2^k colorings.

On the other hand, without loss of generality, we assume that the k-length 0-1 sequence corresponding to f is $(0, 0, \cdots, 0)$. Let $f_i' (1 \leq i \leq k)$ be the resulting coloring after implementing a σ-operation with respect to $C_i (1 \leq i \leq k)$. Then, f induces exactly k complementary colorings. Similarly, we can prove that each coloring $f_i' (1 \leq i \leq k)$ induces exactly k complementary colorings. Therefore, we can further prove that each 4-coloring of the 2^k colorings exactly induces k complementary colorings. Notice that each 4-coloring can induce its complementary coloring if and only if the Hamming distance between the two k-length 0–1 sequences corresponding to the two colorings is equal to 1. Hence, the graph formed by this 2^k 0–1 sequences corresponding to the 2^k 4-colorings is a hypercube.

Obviously, these 2^k 4-colorings are closed under σ-operations, i.e. they can not induce any other 4-coloring by σ-operation. This completes the proof of the theorem. ∎

Now, a question naturally arises. Is any 2-chromatic cycle of any 4-coloring breakable? For this, we propose a conjecture as follows.

Conjecture 9.2 Suppose that G is a 4-colorable maximal planar graph with $\delta \geq 4$. Then, any 2-chromatic cycle of any 4-coloring of G is breakable.

9.5.3 Circular-Cycle-Type K-Classes

Let G be a 4-colorable maximal planar graph with $\delta(G) \geq 4$, $\mathbb{C} \subseteq C^2(G)$. If the following three conditions hold: (1) $\forall C_1, C_2 \in \mathbb{C}$, C_1 and C_2 are relevant, (2) $|\mathbb{C}| \geq 2$, and (3) $\mathbb{C}$ is a set of maximal relevant cycles (i.e. $C^2(G) \setminus \mathbb{C}$ contains no 2-chromatic cycle C' relevant to any 2-chromatic cycle of $\mathbb{C}$), then we refer to each 2-chromatic cycle of $\mathbb{C}$ as a **circular 2-chromatic cycle** and every coloring of $F^f(G)$ as a **circular-cycle coloring**, where $f \in C_4^0(G)$ contains a 2-chromatic cycle $C \in \mathbb{C}$ relevant to some 2-chromatic cycle of $\mathbb{C} \setminus C$. Moreover, $\mathbb{C}$ is called **circular 2-chromatic cycles set** of $F^f(G)$. If $F_\mathbb{C}^f(G)$ contains no 2-chromatic unchanged-cycle coloring, then we refer to the equivalent class $F_\mathbb{C}^f(G)$ as the **circular-cycle-type K-class**. If G contains a circular-cycle-type K-class, then G is called a **circular-cycle-type maximal planar graph**.

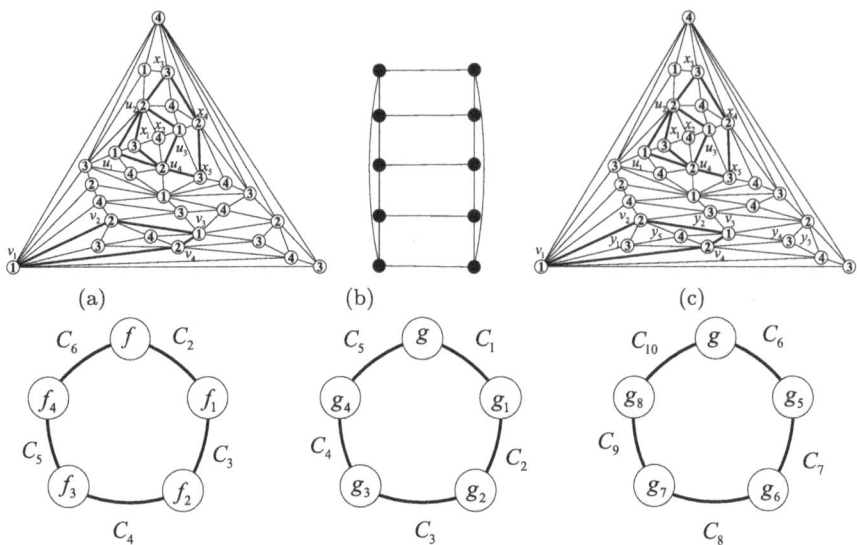

Fig. 9.15 Illustration for cycle-type and circular-cycle-type **K**-classes. (a) $G : f$. (b) $G_4^\sigma[F^f(G)]$. (c) $H : g$. (d) $G_4^\sigma[F_{\mathbb{C}}^f(G)]$. (e) $G_4^\sigma[F_{\mathbb{C}_1}^f(G)]$. (f) $G_4^\sigma[F_{\mathbb{C}_2}^f(G)]$

Figure 9.15 gives two graphs G and H with their 4-coloring f and g, respectively. It is not hard to verify that f is a both 2-chromatic unchanged-cycle coloring and circular-cycle coloring. Specifically,

(1) f is a 2-chromatic unchanged-cycle coloring based on the cycle $C_1 = v_1v_2v_3v_4v_1$;
(2) f is a circular-cycle coloring based on the circular 2-chromatic cycles set $\mathbb{C} = \{C_2, C_3, C_4, C_5, C_6\}$, where $C_2 = u_1u_2u_3u_4u_1$, $C_3 = x_2u_2x_3x_4x_5u_4x_2$, $C_4 = x_1u_2u_3u_4x_1$, $C_5 = u_1u_2x_2u_4u_1$, $C_6 = x_1u_2x_3x_4x_5u_4x_1$; the set of circular-cycle colorings respect to $\mathbb{C}$ $F_{\mathbb{C}}^f(G) = \{f, f_1, f_2, f_3, f_4\}$, where $f_1 = \sigma(f, C_2)$, $f_2 = \sigma(f_1, C_3)$, $f_3 = \sigma(f_2, C_4)$, $f_4 = \sigma(f_3, C_5)$, and $f = \sigma(f_4, C_6)$. The subgraph of G_4^σ induced by $F_{\mathbb{C}}^f(G)$ is shown in Fig. 9.15d.

The coloring g is a 4-coloring of H and contains two sets of circular 2-chromatic cycles, $\mathbb{C}_{\not\vdash}$ and $\mathbb{C}_{\not\vdash}$. $\mathbb{C}_{\not\vdash} = \{C_1, C_2, C_3, C_4, C_5\}$ and $\mathbb{C}_{\not\vdash} = \{C_6, C_7, C_8, C_9, C_{10}\}$, where $C_1 = v_1v_2v_3v_4v_1$, $C_2 = y_5v_2y_2y_3y_4v_4y_5$, $C_3 = y_1v_2v_3v_4y_1$, $C_4 = v_1v_2y_5v_4v_1$, $C_5 = y_1v_2y_2y_3y_4v_4y_1$, $C_6 = u_1u_2u_3u_4u_1$, $C_7 = x_2u_2x_3x_4x_5u_4x_2$, $C_8 = x_1u_2u_3u_4x_1$, $C_9 = u_1u_2x_2u_4u_1$, $C_{10} = x_1u_2x_3x_4x_5u_4x_1$. Two circular-cycle coloring sets with respect to $\mathbb{C}_1$ and $\mathbb{C}_2$ are $F_{\mathbb{C}_{\not\vdash}}^g(H) = \{g, g_1, g_2, g_3, g_4\}$ and $F_{\mathbb{C}_{\not\vdash}}^g(H) = \{g, g_5, g_6, g_7, g_8\}$, respectively, where $g_1 = \sigma(g, C_1)$, $g_2 = \sigma(g_1, C_2)$, $g_3 = \sigma(g_2, C_3)$, $g_4 = \sigma(g_3, C_4)$, $g = \sigma(g_4, C_5)$, $g_5 = \sigma(g, C_6)$, $g_6 = \sigma(g_5, C_7)$, $g_7 = \sigma(g_6, C_8)$, $g_8 = \sigma(g_7, C_9)$, $g = \sigma(g_8, C_{10})$. Figures 9.15e, f illustrate the subgraphs of H_4^σ induced by $F_{\mathbb{C}_{\not\vdash}}^g(H)$ and $F_{\mathbb{C}_{\not\vdash}}^g(H)$, respectively.

(3) $F^f(G)$ is a cycle-type **K**-class. The connected component of G_4^σ containing f is shown in Fig. 9.15b. $F^g(H)$ is a circular-cycle-type **K**-class.

Remark 9.1 *There exist a graph that has the same 2-chromatic cycle under different colorings of the graph, but these colorings belong to different **K**-classes.*

Remark 9.2 *Let G be a maximal planar graph with $\delta \geq 4$. It is possible that $C_4^0(G)$ contains all of the above three types of **K**-classes; also the number of the same type of **K**-class may be multiple. For instance, the icosahedron contains ten tree-type **K**-classes.*

References

1. S M Belcastro and R Haas. Counting edge-kempe- equivalence classes for 3-edge-colored cubic graphs. *Discrete Mathematics*, 325(13):77–84, 2014.
2. M E Bertschi. Perfectly contractile graphs. *Journal of Combinatorial Theory Series B*, 50(2):222–230, 1990.
3. M Bonamy and N Bousquet. Recoloring bounded treewidth graphs. *Electronic Notes in Discrete Mathematics*, 44(5):257–262, 2013.
4. M Bonamy, M Johnson, I M Lignos, V Patel, and D Paulusma. Reconfiguration graphs for vertex colourings of chordal and chordal bipartite graphs. *Journal of Combinatorial Optimization*, 27:132–143, 2014.
5. P Bonsma and L Cereceda. Finding paths between graph colourings: pspace-completeness and superpolynominall distances. *Theoretical Computer Science*, 410(50):738–749, 2007.
6. L Cereceda. Mixing graph colourings. *[PhD Thesis], London School of Economics and Political Science*, pages 1–121, 2007.
7. L Cereceda, J V D Heuvel, and M Johnson. Connectedness of the graph of vertex-colourings. *Discrete Mathematics*, 308(5/6):913–919, 2008.
8. L Cereceda, J V D Heuvel, and M Johnson. Johnson m. finding paths between 3-colorings. *Journal of Graph Theory*, 67(1):69–82, 2011.
9. C Feghali, M Johnson, M Bonamy, and N Bousquet. On a conjecture of mohar concerning kempe equivalence of regular graphs. *Computer Science*, 2015.
10. C Feghali, M Johnson, and D Paulusma. Kempe equivalence of colourings of cubic graphs. *Electronic Notes in Discrete Mathematics*, 49:243–249, 2015.
11. S Fisk. Geometric coloring theory. *Advances in Mathematics*, 24(3):298–340, 1977.
12. J V D Heuvel. The complexity of change. surveys in combinatorics. *arXiv: 1312.2816v1 [cs.DM] 10 Dec*, 2013.
13. M Jerrum. A very simple algorithm for estimating the number of k-colorings of a low-degree graph. *Random Structures and Algorithms*, 7(2):157–165, 1995.
14. A B Kempe. On the geographical problem of the four colors. *American Journal of Mathematics*, 2(3):193–200, 1879.
15. J Mcdonald, B Mohar, and D Scheide. Kempe equivalence of edge-colorings in subcubic and subquartic graphs. *Journal of Graph Theory*, 70(2):226–239, 2012.
16. H Meyniel. Les 5-colorations d'un graphe planaire forment une classe de commutation unique. *Journal of Combinatorial Theory Series B*, 24(3):251–257, 1978.
17. B Mohar. *Kempe equivalence of colorings*. Graph Theory in Paris, Birkhäuser Basel, 2006.
18. M Muhlenthaler and R Wanka. The connectedness of clash-free timetables. *10th International Conference of the Practice and Theory of Automated Timetabling PATAT 2014*, York, United Kindom:330–346, 2014.

19. M L Vergnas and H Meyniel. Kempe classes and the hadwiger conjecture. *Journal of Combinatorial Theory Series B*, 31(1):95–104, 1981.
20. E Vigoda. Improved bounds for sampling colorings. *Symposium on Foundations of Computer Science. IEEE Computer Society,*, 51, 1999.
21. J S Wang, R H Swendsen, and R Kotecky. Antiferromagnetic potts models. *Physical Review Letters*, 63(63):109–112, 1989.
22. J S Wang, R H Swendsen, and R Kotecky. Three-state antiferromagnetic potts models: a monte carlo study. *Physical Review B Condensed Matter*, 42(4):2465–2474, 1990.
23. J Xu. Theory on structure and coloring of maximal planar graphs (4): σ-operations and kempe equivalent classes. *Journal of Electronics and Information Technology*, 38(7):1557–1585, 2016.
24. J Xu. Theory on structure and coloring of maximal planar graphs (3): Purely tree-colorable and uniquely 4-colorable maximal planar graph conjectures. *ournal of Electronics and Information Technology*, 38(6).
25. J Xu and X Liu. Research progress on the theory of kempe changes. *Journal of Electronics and Information Technology*, 39(6).

Open Access This chapter is licensed under the terms of the Creative Commons Attribution 4.0 International License (http://creativecommons.org/licenses/by/4.0/), which permits use, sharing, adaptation, distribution and reproduction in any medium or format, as long as you give appropriate credit to the original author(s) and the source, provide a link to the Creative Commons license and indicate if changes were made.

The images or other third party material in this chapter are included in the chapter's Creative Commons license, unless indicated otherwise in a credit line to the material. If material is not included in the chapter's Creative Commons license and your intended use is not permitted by statutory regulation or exceeds the permitted use, you will need to obtain permission directly from the copyright holder.

The manufacturer's authorised representative in the EU is Springer Nature Customer Service Centre GmbH, Europaplatz 3, 69115 Heidelberg, Germany. If you have any concerns regarding our products, please contact ProductSafety@springernature.com

Printed and bound by CPI Group (UK) Ltd, Croydon, CR0 4YY

26/03/2026

02078939-0002